GOD THE REVEALED

Christology

Expanded Version of the Gunning Lectures

Edinburgh 2004

GOD THE REVEALED

Christology

Michael Welker

translated by

Douglas W. Stott

William B. Eerdmans Publishing Company
Grand Rapids, Michigan / Cambridge, U.K.

Wm. B. Eerdmans Publishing Co.
2140 Oak Industrial Drive N.E., Grand Rapids, Michigan 49505 /
P.O. Box 163, Cambridge CB3 9PU U.K.

Originally published 2012 in German under the title
Gottes Offenbarung: Christologie
by Neukirchener Verlagsgesellschaft, Neukirchen-Vluyn

19 18 17 16 15 14 13   7 6 5 4 3 2 1

ISBN 978-0-8028-7157-2

www.eerdmans.com

For Ulrike Welker

Contents

INTRODUCTION

"Who Is Jesus Christ for Us Today?"

"God revealed himself in Jesus Christ!" Christian faith has claimed this for nearly 2000 years. Christianity *proclaims* it as good news, as *gospel*, in cathedrals and chapels, monasteries and house churches. It *teaches* it as the core of belief, as *dogma*, in universities and colleges, in scholarly works, schoolbooks, and catechisms. And it *confesses* it over a broad spectrum, from personal testimonies to ecumenical world councils: God revealed himself in Jesus Christ!

This insight of faith is often accompanied by the joy and elation that God himself[1] in his glory and fullness has come intimately close and indeed become accessible to human beings in a human life—in Jesus of Nazareth. Rather than remaining in the obscurity of some distant transcendence, God makes himself known in the person and life of Jesus Christ. In Jesus Christ, God comes intimately close to human beings!

The formulation of this central statement of the Christian faith, however, is ambiguous. God *revealed* himself in Jesus Christ. Is this a reference to a past event, one that happened two millennia ago? If so, then this life, through its message and example, could and still can perhaps tell us something about God and God's will. Yet how could we then still say with the letter to the Colossians that "in him the whole fullness of deity dwells bodily!" (Col 2:9)? And how could we claim with Luther's *Large Catechism* that in Jesus Christ, God "has given himself completely to us, withholding nothing"?[2] If God's revelation in Jesus Christ has to be regarded as a past event, then statements such as those in the *Nicene Creed* similarly present enormous problems: "We believe in . . . Jesus

---

1. I use the masculine pronouns for God based on the grammar alone. In no way do I intend to support androcentric or patriarchal representations. I follow the biblical witness of Genesis 1:27 (NRSV), "in the image of God he created them, male and female he created them."

2. Martin Luther, "Large Catechism," in *The Book of Concord*, ed. Timothy Wengert and Robert Kolb, trans. Charles Arand (Minneapolis: Fortress, 2000), 434.

Christ, . . . God from God, Light from Light, true God from true God . . ."[3]
For how could the true God be a past one?

If it is then also claimed that God revealed himself in Jesus Christ
and in his life such that this person and this life, and God with him and
in him, are genuinely present even today in the power of the Spirit, how
could we continue to hold that this life is a real human life? But if this
revelation in a real human life becomes questionable, the joy and elation elicited by the realistic proximity and transparency of the revelation itself would also be called into question. How is one to counter the
objection that this "revelation" itself is more cryptic than all the talk
of a God who is incomprehensible, transcendent, and inaccessible to
human cognition?

Christology's task is to elucidate that the proclamation and confession "God revealed himself in Jesus Christ!" does genuinely offer a reliable *insight* of faith. Five problems, however, must be addressed if one is
to access and understand this insight.

1. For decades, theological research was of the opinion that we can
know next to nothing about the historical Jesus. We encounter him only
through "legendary glosses" in the New Testament. Those who can say
nothing about the historical Jesus, however, can also offer little more
than mental constructs and speculative fantasies about the exalted
Christ. At the end of the twentieth century, research using the catch
phrase "the third quest for the historical Jesus" began to forge a way out
of this theological impasse. The Christology presented here will retrace
the development of the "three quests" for the historical Jesus and propose to move on to the "fourth quest." It describes ways leading out of
the tension between excessive historical skepticism, which threatened to
empty Christology, and excessive optimism, which was virtually intent
on "excavating" the historical Jesus.

The agenda of the "fourth quest" facilitates discernment of continuities between the life of the historical Jesus of Nazareth and the living
presence of Jesus Christ in the power of the Spirit. Still, however, the
question of the historical Jesus is as unlikely to be answered definitively
as is that concerning any living person. We must open up experiential,
conceptual, and research spaces that permit us to approach more closely

---

3. "Creed of Nicea (325)," in *Creeds of the Church: A Reader in Christian Doctrine
from the Bible to the Present*, rev. ed., ed. John Leith (Richmond, VA: John Knox Press,
1973), 30-31. See also "Das Glaubensbekenntnis der allgemeinen I. Kirchenversammlung
zu Nizäa (325)," in Josef Neuner and Heinrich Roos, *Der Glaube der Kirche in den Urkun-
den der Lehrverkündigung*, ed. Karl Rahner and Karl-Heinz Weger (Regensburg: Pustet,
12th ed. 1986), 121.

to his life and personality in the search for truth, a search that also stands on solid scholarly ground (part 1).[4]

2. To discern the continuities between the pre-Easter Jesus and his post-Easter life despite radical discontinuity, a second challenge to perception must be addressed. This challenge consists in the *confusion between "resurrection" and "physical revivification."* This confusion is taken as the point of departure among both pious fundamentalists and aggressive critics of the idea of the resurrection. The former, full of religious certainty, claim that the resurrection is a revivification of the pre-Easter Jesus, and that those who do not accept this are denying the core of Christian faith. The latter scornfully argue that the Bible and Christians portray the resurrection as a revivification of the pre-Easter Jesus, and that those who accept this as true have abandoned honesty, reality, and truth.

Over many years, international dialogue between theology and the natural sciences has explored the question: If the resurrection is *not* a physical revivification of the pre-Easter Jesus as the biblical witnesses show, then what kind of reality can be attributed to it? The question of the reality of the resurrection of necessity raises the question of the reality of the Spirit and spiritual presence of the sort familiar to us in secular contexts, e.g., in music or mathematics. Beyond this, the question also demands that we articulate and understand the connections between spirit and body, body and spirit. A culture that thinks in naturalistic terms, however, has considerable difficulty accessing the reality of the resurrection and the Spirit, which is why it so easily remains mired in arguments for or against physical revivification that in the final analysis

---

4. See Martin Hengel, "Zur historischen Rückfrage nach Jesus von Nazareth," in *Gespräch über Jesus: Papst Benedikt XVI. im Dialog mit Martin Hengel, Peter Stuhlmacher und seinen Schülern in Castel Gandolfo 2008*, ed. Peter Kuhn (Tübingen: Mohr Siebeck, 2010), 4: "With the possible exception of the Passion narrative, the issue is not that of an internally contiguous account or even a consistent representation of Jesus' proclamation, but rather of the clearest possible elaboration of clear contours, we could also say *approaches*, whose results are admittedly astounding, indeed utterly singular." Disclosing and elaborating such clear contours and approaches, however, requires epistemological processes and a research program that can claim a measure of reliably demonstrated veracity without thereby eliminating the possibility of correctives and further progress. This approach is appropriate not only in research on the historical Jesus, but also in investigations concerning the reality of the resurrection and the presence of the exalted Christ in the power of the Spirit. Concerning the methodology of communities that seek such truth and the testing and demonstration of truth claims, see John Polkinghorne and Michael Welker, *Faith in the Living God: A Dialogue* (London: SPCK, 2001), 139ff. See also John Polkinghorne, *Science and Religion in Quest of Truth* (New Haven and London: Yale University Press, 2011).

offers no real comfort or consolation in any case. Christology must find new paths for mediating how the reality of the resurrection is to be comprehended (part 2).

3. The third challenge to the task of Christology is associated with the essentially good and important insight that God desires to be encountered not only in the poverty and humility of the earthly life of Jesus of Nazareth, but also, and radically, in his cross and suffering. The doctrine of the "crucified God" has been developed by Luther, Hegel, and Bonhoeffer on to Moltmann, Jüngel, and Kitamori. This focus on the suffering God, however, made it easy to overlook the fact that God already takes on the "rulers of the world" and the world under the "power of sin" on the cross itself, and not just in the resurrection. There has been insufficient recognition of the conspiracy of the collected world powers against God and his presence on the cross. The global power Rome as well as the religious leaders of Israel, the appeal to Jewish and Roman law, public opinion, and the intimate circle of Jesus's own disciples collaborate in a disastrous fashion in the crucifixion. Without the realization that God has *already* taken on sin and evil on the cross, talk of the "Crucified One" is downplayed and God's revelation in him obscured. Confession to the resurrected and exalted Christ is also deprived of its seriousness and depth. God's nearness to creation in its most unfathomable suffering and profound helplessness—on the cross—and God's faithfulness to creation in its preservation and elevation in the power of the resurrection and the Spirit must be neither blurred nor separated one from the other (introduction and part 3).

4. A fourth hurdle to the development of Christology is the tendency to shift the reality and efficacy of the Spirit and the reign of God and thus also the presence of the resurrected and exalted Christ to the numinous, to an inaccessible transcendence or some more or less distant future. Most philosophies and theologies as well as so-called "good common sense" use monistic, dual, dualistic, or, at best, triadic structures and conceptual figures. These, however, are insufficient for comprehending the "pouring out of the Holy Spirit," the community of the exalted Christ "with his own," the edification of Christ's body with its members, the "coming" reign of God, and other polyphonic realities—realities that challenge the insights of faith.

In this regard, we have received assistance from various conceptual developments in our postmodern cultures and pluralistic societies, in interdisciplinary scholarly endeavors and multicontextual investigations into social and contemporary history. Although we are indeed not yet able to move conceptually as easily within multicontextual, polyphonic, and emergent realities as within the good old, familiar two-sided figures, the conceptual constructs of "above" and "below," and the friend-foe models, nonetheless the progress of theological insight associated with these conceptual figures can already be discerned and more expected (part 4).

5. The fifth problem is found in the field of eschatology, the so-called "doctrine of the last things." In the collaboration between systematic theology and biblical exegesis, on the one hand, and between theology and the natural sciences, on the other, we have been able to alter one paradigm of eschatology that, although evident enough to common sense in the formula "present or future eschatology?" has only minimally aided the development of any realistic theology. As we are now aware, as a "coming reality" the reign of God is to be understood as being both already present and not yet fully realized, as both present and future. From this concept, however, one must distinguish "eternal" eschatological reality, which is admittedly extremely misleading with its reference to the "second coming of Christ" and the "end-times theophany." Logic supported by sacrament and liturgy (John Polkinghorne's "liturgy-assisted logic") along with a Trinitarian theology (albeit one requiring further development) can help us catch at least a distant glimpse of the "presence of Jesus Christ in eternal life" and of participation in this life.

This life of the new creation is neither "eternal stillness" nor an existence in mystical mist. Rather, it is a blessed, eternal life that "even now" acquires contours through the reality of the resurrection and reign of Jesus Christ both within and outside of churches. Blessed, eternal life is already anticipated here on earth in the experiences and acts of love and forgiveness, in the dignified celebration of worship and sacrament that seeks knowledge of God, in God-fearing prayer and in self-forgetting joy, but also in the persistent pursuit of liberating truth and justice (part 5).

0.1 Dietrich Bonhoeffer's First Legacy:
"Only the Suffering God Can Help!"

"What keeps gnawing at me is the question, what is Christianity, or who is Christ actually for us today?"[1] Bonhoeffer wrote this in a letter from prison one year before his murder. His answer: Jesus Christ reveals the God who is powerless and suffering in the world. "God consents to be pushed out of the world and onto the cross; God is weak and powerless in the world and in precisely this way, and only so, is at our side and helps us."[2] Bonhoeffer speaks of his deep trust in "the God of the Bible, who gains ground and power in the world by being powerless." This trust in the weak and suffering God has deeply moved many people. Bonhoeffer's words have been repeated again and again—almost devoutly: ". . . only the suffering God can help."[3] But can they remain genuinely persuasive in the long run?

In his prison cell, Bonhoeffer was defenselessly exposed to the bombing raids on Berlin. "The screams and frenzied struggles of the prisoners locked in their cells during a severe attack . . . is unforgettable for anyone who has heard it."[4] Bonhoeffer was living not only in a state of constant threat to his own life and the lives of his fellow prisoners, but also in a state of constant concern for his family in the burning city, for his friends on the frontlines, and for his relatives, who were daily in danger because they had joined the resistance against Hitler. He had to watch as the Second World War, the omnipresent terror of the Nazis, and even a corrupt church poisoned and ravaged people's lives. The future appeared dark: either the war would be lost and Germany would be ostracized the world over, or—but such was unfathomable—the world would come under Nazi

1. Dietrich Bonhoeffer, *Letters and Papers from Prison*, DBWE, vol. 8, ed. Eberhard Bethge (Minneapolis: Fortress Press, 2010), 362 (letter of April 30, 1944); *Widerstand und Ergebung: Briefe und Aufzeichnungen aus der Haft*, Dietrich Bonhoeffer Werke 8 (DBW), ed. Christian Gremmels, Eberhard Bethge, and Renate Bethge in collaboration with Ilse Tödt (Gütersloh: Kaiser, 1998), 402. For the contextualization of Bonhoeffer's christological orientation, see Hans-Jürgen Abromeit, *Das Geheimnis Christi: Dietrich Bonhoeffers erfahrungsbezogene Christologie*, Neukirchener Beiträge zur Systematischen Theologie 8 (Neukirchen-Vluyn: Neukirchener, 1991), esp. 12ff.

2. DBWE 8, 479; DBW 8, 534 (letter of July 16, 1944).

3. DBWE 8, 479–80; DBW 8, 535, 534 (letter of July 16, 1944).

4. DBWE 8, 346; DBW 8, 385 ("Report on Prison Life after One Year in Tegel," ca. April 1944). Bonhoeffer was arrested on April 5, 1943. The letters speak again and again of air-raids, firebombs, explosive bombs, and phosphorous bombs. For example, Bonhoeffer wrote to Eberhard Bethge on June 21, 1944: "This morning we had the nastiest of all the air raids so far. For several hours my room was so dark from the cloud of smoke that hung over the city that I would almost have switched on the light" (DBWE 8, 439; DBW 8, 491f).

rule. Was it this hopeless, desperate situation that made Bonhoeffer trust solely in the suffering God?

God is revealed on the cross and in suffering! Bonhoeffer's letters from prison are not the first place this scandalous assertion can be found. As early as 200 C.E., Tertullian spoke of the dead and crucified God.[5] During the early Reformation and at a certain high point of modern philosophy, this strange reference claimed to provide a central point of orientation. Bonhoeffer's ideas resonate in an anticipatory fashion in Luther's "Theology of the Cross" and Hegel's philosophical reference to the "death of God" (see parts 3.1 and 3.2). Martin Heidegger and Jürgen Moltmann will take up this legacy in their discussions of the "crucified God" in the second half of the twentieth century (see part 3.3).[6] And yet the assertion that God "gains ground and power in the world by being powerless" is met with fierce doubt. Why is God—whom, after all, we call "the Almighty"—not rather called into question precisely through suffering and death? Why does God's presence not become unrecognizable in suffering and death? Why and how should, of all things, the suffering and dying Jesus on the cross reveal God? If, however, Bonhoeffer's assertion that "only the suffering God can help" could be explained by his desperate situation, then the question arises how this obscure discourse about the "crucified God" is supposed to speak to and persuade people living in less oppressive or even peaceful and pleasant times?[7]

This quandary is intensified by a further problem in Bonhoeffer's question. The question, "Who is Jesus Christ *for us today* [emphasis mine]?" seems contextually modest and thus appeals to many people today. Who is Jesus Christ, who is God concretely "for us"? What, however, will the answer be if "for us" no longer means "Bonhoeffer's situation" or "a situation full of affliction and despair"? Do different contexts not in principle require very different answers to the question, "Who is Jesus Christ for us today?" Will the answers in what we call Christian and post-Christian societies in Europe and in large parts of North America today not be completely different than in societies shaped by non-Christian

5. See Tertullian, *Tertullianus Against Marcion*, ed. Rev. A. Roberts and J. Donaldson, trans. P. Holmes, Ante-Nicene Christian Library, vol. VII (Edinburgh: T & T Clark, 1868), II.16, 89ff; II.27, 113 & 111f.

6. Martin Heidegger, "Phenomenology and Theology," trans. James G. Hart and John C. Maraldo, in Martin Heidegger, *Pathmarks*, ed. William McNeill (Cambridge: Cambridge University Press, 1998), 44; Jürgen Moltmann, *The Crucified God: The Cross as Foundation and Criticism of Christian Theology*, trans. R. A. Wilson and John Boden (New York: Harper & Row, 1974).

7. Cf. Andreas Schüle, "Introduction," in *Who is Jesus Christ for Us Today? Pathways to Contemporary Christology*, ed. Andreas Schuele and Günter Thomas (Louisville, Kentucky: Westminster/John Knox Press, 2009), xiv.

religions, societies unfamiliar with Christianity, or in those that may even fear and loathe it? Will the religiously tired and theologically sleepy mainline churches of western industrialized nations and information societies not provide different answers than countries in Africa, Asia, and Latin America with currently extremely dynamic churches and rapidly growing movements of faith? Across all these different contexts, can we really claim that "God would have us know that we must live as those who manage their lives without God. The same God who is with us is the God who forsakes us. . . . Before God, and with God, we live without God"?[8]

---

8. DBWE 8, 478–79; DBW 8, 533, 534 (letter of July 16, 1944).

0.2 "At the Beginning: the Stable—At the End: the Gallows": The Iconic Presence of Jesus

Near is
And difficult to grasp, the God.[1]

Hölderlin's grand statement impressively marks a tension that all reference to the nearness of God must take into account. Does God remain
withdrawn from human beings even when he is near to them? Is God
thus absent even in his presence?[2] This tension confronts all who confess
the revelation of God in the human being Jesus Christ and speak of the
"crucified God." This tension continues to produce a peculiar fascination
arising particularly from the suggestive depictions of the beginning and
end of Jesus's earthly life: the baby in a manger in Bethlehem and the
dying Jesus on the cross at Golgotha—so close does God come to humanity! The most important holidays of the Christian faith—Christmas, Good
Friday, and Easter—are closely associated with these images: "At the beginning the stable, at the end the gallows."[3]

We encounter the striking *iconic presence* of Jesus Christ in pictures
of the beginning of his life starting with early catacomb paintings. Artists
combined elements of the birth narratives from Luke (the birth of Jesus
was revealed first to the poor shepherds in the field, Luke 2:8–20) and
Matthew (signs in the sky revealed the great event to three wise men,
who rushed to the manger bringing precious gifts, Matt 2:1-12). Painters
experimented with settings amid a stable and straw (or ruins or a cave)
and with the birth at dusk or at night, shedding light thus on the unity
of poverty, powerlessness, and magic at the beginning of Jesus's life (see
parts 0.4 and 0.6). Ever since European Romanticism, the manger has
maintained a firm place in Christmas piety.

The cross has been regarded as a sign of victory within the church at
least since Constantine's vision before the Battle of Milvian Bridge in the

---

1. Friedrich Hölderlin, "Patmos," in *Gedichte nach 1800*, ed. Friedrich Beißner, Stuttgarter Hölderlinausgabe (Stuttgart: Kohlhammer, 1953), 173; trans. Michael Hamburger,
in Friedrich Hölderlin, *Hyperion and Selected Poems*, ed. Eric L. Santner (New York: Continuum, 2002), 245.

2. Eberhard Jüngel, following Rudolf Bultmann, claimed this as a foundational characteristic of revelation in *God as Mystery of the World* (Grand Rapids, Mich.: Eerdmans,
1983), 349ff. Cf. Rudolf Bultmann, *The Gospel of John: A Commentary* (Philadelphia:
Westminster Press, 1971), 160f, 295ff.

3. Walter Jens and H. A. P. Grieshaber, *Am Anfang der Stall, am Ende der Galgen:
Das Evangelium nach Matthäus* (Freiburg: Herder, 1999).

year 312 C.E.[4] From the eleventh century onward, large so-called "triumphal crosses" have been erected in churches. From the thirteenth century onward, however, a piety focused on the cross has gained acceptance on the iconic level and is still dominant today. This expression of piety focuses on the suffering Christ on the cross at Golgotha and on the "man of sorrows" marked by the crucifixion, in whom God encounters humankind in powerlessness and weakness.

Can this emotionally moving and fascinating iconic aura of the "manger and cross" not everywhere respond to the question, "Who is Jesus Christ for us today?" In Jesus Christ, it is the proximate, poor, powerless, and suffering God who reveals himself. Though he may perhaps be "difficult to grasp" as God, he still touches human beings in a somehow consoling manner, strengthening them emotionally and even in their compassion. Thus does he come close to them in this fascinating way.

Many biblical witnesses, however, fundamentally call into question the touching aura of the near God cultivated in these pictures. The story of the cross is the story of the brutal execution of an innocent person. It is a story of lies and betrayal, of torture, mockery, and torment. The scandalous film *The Passion of the Christ*[5] depicts it perhaps more accurately, confronting the audience as it does with more excessive brutality and violence than does a piety focusing on the "Man of Sorrows," which celebrates in song and meditates on its "dear beloved Jesus."[6] The story of the cross is first of all a story of impotence over against the "powers of this world" (1 Cor 2:8). At Jesus's execution on the cross, the political world power Rome worked together with the religion of Israel, a religion oppressed by this same world power. Those who invoked Jewish or Roman law were one with public morality and

---

4. See Ulrich Köpf, "Cross/Crucifixion; IV. Church History," in *Religion Past and Present* (Leiden: Brill, 2006ff), vol. 3, 582-85; in the Orthodox church, the iconic presence of the "enthroned Christ," of "Christ Pantocrator," the "Lord of All," continues to be formative; in Roman Catholicism, the image of the baby Jesus in Mary's arms is still prevalent; cf. Gertrud Schiller, *Christ's Incarnation. Childhood. Baptism. Temptation. Transfiguration. Works and Miracles*, vol. 1, *The Iconography of Christian Art* (London: Lund Humphries, 1971); *The Passion of Jesus Christ*, vol. 2 (1972); Alex Stock, "Christ, Representations of," in *Religion Past and Present*, vol. 2, 549-58; D. Thomas, *Jesus Christus: Sein Bildnis in der Kunst* (Zollikon: Albatros, 1980); Horst Schwebel, *Das Christusbild in der bildenden Kunst der Gegenwart* (Giessen: Wilhelm Schmitz, 1980).

5. Mel Gibson, prod., *The Passion of the Christ* (Los Angeles: New Market Films, 2004).

6. One example among countless others is the moving Good Friday hymn, *Herzliebster Jesu, was hast du verbrochen* (Ah Holy Jesus, what was your offense) by Johann Heermann, 1630.

opinion: "Crucify him!"[7] Even Jesus's own disciples abandoned him (see parts 3.4 and 5.4).

Neither, however, should the birth of Jesus (following Luke) be seen as a camping adventure "with oxen and donkeys" in the stable. Rather, it is the Roman Empire that drives Mary and Joseph to Bethlehem for a census without any consideration that the young woman is nearly ready to give birth. Mary can expect no help during her delivery.[8] The shepherds, the poorest of the poor, are the first to witness the birth of the Messiah. According to Matthew, the birth of Jesus provoked a political persecution that led to a brutal child massacre "in and around Bethlehem" (cf. Matt 2:16–18). Matthew comments along with Jeremiah 31:15: "A voice was heard in Ramah, wailing and loud lamentation, Rachel weeping for her children; she refused to be consoled, because they were no more." The suggestion that Joseph even doubted whether he should marry the pregnant Mary (Matt 1:18–19) also reflects how much at risk she and her child were.[9] Hence according to the biblical witnesses, Jesus was endangered not only at the end, but already at the beginning of his life as well. Why and in what way should God reveal himself in this particular man, of all people? And how should God bring help and salvation through this particular man and this revelation?

Old Testament traditions make it trenchantly clear that the joy and elation prompted by the nearness of God cannot be reduced to being aesthetically moved. They view enthusiasm about God's nearness in conjunction with the acknowledged status of the Law and the dissemination of justice and mercy among all people: "For what other great nation has a god so near to it as the Lord our God is whenever we call to him? And what other great nation has statutes and ordinances as just as this entire law that I am setting before you today?" (Deut 4:7–8).[10] The Law's goal

---

7. Mark 15:13f; Matt 27:22f; Luke 23:18, 22f; cf. the discussion and amplification of my thoughts so far on a theology of the cross in Dirk Smit, ". . . 'Under Pontius Pilate': On Living Cultural Memory and Christian Confession," in *Who is Jesus Christ for Us Today?* ed. Schuele and Thomas, 19–49 (see part 0.1, note 7).

8. The phrase "because there was no place for them in the inn" (Luke 2:7) highlights perhaps the hard-heartedness in the face of the needs of a woman in labor; in any case, it reveals the helplessness of these strangers from Galilee.

9. Cf. Beverly Roberts Gaventa, *Mary: Glimpses of the Mother of Jesus* (Columbia: University of South Carolina Press, 1995), 46; and the sobering summary of Geza Vermes, *The Nativity: History and Legend* (London: Penguin, 2006), 166: "The merry Christmas that people wish to each other is purged from the spoiling effects of the Matthean drama with Joseph's psychological torture in the face of the dilemma of what to do with the pregnant Mary and the fear, panic and tears caused by Herod's edict threatening with untimely extinction the budding life of the Son of God."

10. See also Pss 34:19; 75:2; 85:10; 119:151; 145:18; Isa 50:8; concerning the nearness

is justice and mercy among people, and worship in accordance with the will of God. For Israel, the Law and its efficacy among God's people were and continue to be inseparably bound to the revelation of the near God.[11] In accordance with the Law, in piety, and following their fundamentally moral guiding beliefs, Israel lived and continues to live in community with God. According to the Old Testament, this is the community with God that is owed to revelation.

If ultimately, however, such practical life orientation should avouch the nearness of God, then how do the revelation of God in Jesus Christ and the gospel of God's community with human beings in Jesus Christ shape interpersonal relationships and the reality of life? One is inclined to think first of the power of the church, its institutions, worship services, seminaries, hospitals, homes, and worship in liturgy, confession, and proclamation. In extolling the enormous legal, political, educational-historical, and charitable impact of Christian religiosity and churches, can we thus speak of a genuine triumphal procession of the revelation of God in human history?

A brief consideration of the oppressive fact that countless pogroms, campaigns of repression and persecution, Crusades and witch-burnings, wars, colonialism, and general disrespect for human dignity have been committed in the name of the Christian religion and its churches is sufficient to warn against viewing the revelation of God in direct conjunction with religious and ecclesial displays of power. Human enterprise and machinations all too eagerly adorn themselves with the brilliance and aura of the sacred and the divine. The burning question then becomes how to differentiate a legitimate claim to a life with the immanent God in light of his revelation from self-righteous, even mendacious abuse of his alleged presence.

If talk of God's presence in Jesus Christ did not facilitate making precisely this distinction, were it merely to lull people aesthetically and thereby impede discernment of the distinction between true revelation and religious misuse, then a disastrous suspicion would arise—namely, that not only all this talk about God's presence and nearness, but also God's presence itself, his nearness to humankind, are nothing more than a dangerous illusion.

---

of God in the Law, see the contributions of *A God so Near: Essays on Old Testament Theology in Honor of Patrick D. Miller*, ed. Brent A. Strawn and Nancy R. Bowen (Winona Lake: Eisenbrauns, 2003), 183ff; concerning nearness perceived in cultic and temple theology, see Bernd Janowski, *Gottes Gegenwart in Israel: Beiträge zur Theologie des Alten Testaments* (Neukirchen-Vluyn: Neukirchener, 1993), 119ff.

11. Cf. Michael Fishbane, *Sacred Attunement: A Jewish Theology* (Chicago: University of Chicago Press, 2008), esp. 108ff.

Is common sense correct when it states that we speak either of an obviously powerful God or of a powerless human, but that the claim that God is revealed and present in this man Jesus is simply completely unbelievable? Are the other monotheistic religions justified in complaining that Christianity steps shockingly out of line with its assertion that God revealed himself in Jesus Christ? It abandons any sensible notion of and faith in God. Talk of the powerless and crucified God simply dissolves all talk of God.

Under the pressure of these questions and accusations attacking the fascination with the God who is near in powerlessness, Dietrich Bonhoeffer's second legacy offers a liberating perspective. Hitherto, however, this second legacy has hardly been discussed, not even among those whose intention has been to appropriate and pass on Bonhoeffer's insights and his confession of faith. It helps to recognize that Bonhoeffer is intent on speaking of the God who is near to us in the fullness of our lives. And this God is near to us even when the entire world attempts or seems to successfully shut itself off from his presence.[12] Bonhoeffer wants to speak about God *in the polyphony of life* and about how faith itself contributes to the acceptance of this polyphony and multidimensionality. Here Bonhoeffer in fact is referring to the presence of God in the Spirit of God. Although this Spirit sometimes operates openly, it also often does so in hidden ways in different situations, in different people and groups of people. It comes over them, stirs them, and fuses them together into a living unity. God's power in the agency of the Spirit and God's powerlessness on the cross and in suffering—both dimensions must be considered in comprehending God's revelation in Jesus Christ.

12. Cf. Michael Welker, "Bonhoeffers theologisches Vermächtnis in Widerstand und Ergebung," in Welker, *Theologische Profile. Schleiermacher-Barth-Bonhoeffer-Moltmann*, Edition Chrismon (Frankfurt: Hansisches Druck- und Verlagshaus, 2009), 103–19.

0.3 Dietrich Bonhoeffer's Second Legacy: God in the "Polyphony of Life"

In May 1944, an idea formed in Bonhoeffer's mind that would never let go of him. This idea was the "polyphony of life":

> I often notice hereabouts how few people there are who can harbor many different things at the same time. The bombers come, they are nothing but fear itself; when there's something good to eat, nothing but greed itself; when they fail to get what they want, they become desperate; if something succeeds, that's all they see. They are missing out on the fullness of life and on the wholeness of their own existence. . . . Christianity, on the other hand, puts us into many different dimensions of life at the same time; in a way we accommodate God and the whole world within us. We weep with those who weep at the same time as we rejoice with those who rejoice. We fear . . . for our lives, but at the same time we must think thoughts that are much more important to us than our lives. . . . Life isn't pushed back into a single dimension, but is kept multidimensional, polyphonic. What a liberation it is to be able to *think* and to hold on to these many dimensions of life in our thoughts. . . . One has to dislodge people from their one-track thinking—as it were, in "preparation for" or "enabling" faith, though in truth it is only faith itself that makes multidimensional life possible . . . [1]

It is from this realization that Bonhoeffer formulates his conviction that we must "recognize God not only where we reach the limits of our possibilities. God wants to be recognized in the midst of our lives."[2] Insofar as faith in God, who reveals himself in Jesus Christ, does indeed depend on the suffering and powerless God, it thereby also depends on the kingdom of this God that encompasses *all* of human life:

> A kingdom stronger than war and danger, a kingdom of power and might, a kingdom that is eternal terror and judgment for some and eternal joy and righteousness for others. It is not a kingdom of the heart but reigns over the earth and the whole world . . . a kingdom for which it is worth risking our lives.[3]

---

1. Bonhoeffer, DBWE 8, 404–5; DBW 8, 453f (letter of May 29, 1944; see part 0.1, footnote 1). Also see the letter of May 20 (DBWE 8, 393–94; DBW 8, 439ff) and May 21, 1944 (DBWE 8, 395–96; DBW 8, 442ff; "The image of polyphony is still following me around," DBWE 8, 397; DBW 8, 444). Also see Tomi Karttunen, *Die Polyphonie der Wirklichkeit: Erkenntnistheorie und Ontologie in der Theologie Dietrich Bonhoeffers*, University of Joensuu Publications in Theology 11 (Joensuu: University of Joensuu, 2004), 215ff.

2. DBWE 8, 406; DBW 8, 455 (letter of May 29, 1944).

3. DBWE 8, 395; DBW 8, 442f (letter of May 21, 1944).

In the vastness of this reign that yet hovers somewhat unclearly before Bonhoeffer's eyes, he conceives of a successful *multidimensional, polyphonic life* also capable of incorporating and accommodating the dark sides, hardships, and threats of human existence. This life corresponds to Christian faith and becomes viable through the power of faith. On the basis of the revelation of God in Jesus Christ who is "the center of life,"[4] we must, according to Bonhoeffer, counter a cultural and religious development that pushes God increasingly far away and turns him into an increasingly marginal figure, a God of boundary situations and at the boundaries of knowledge. We must take seriously that God wants to be encountered precisely in the multidimensionality of our lives.

But does Bonhoeffer not contradict this very idea with his first legacy, which takes as its point of departure the suffering and powerless God who was forced out of the world? Indeed, with his talk about the suffering and powerless God, did not he himself contribute toward moving God away from the fullness of life?

Only when we look at the correlation between Bonhoeffer's two messages can we participate in his search for convincing language about God and for a sustainable Christian faith.[5] Only then can we understand his "critique of religion," which has generated much speculation, and his talk of our "religionless age." It is perplexing that a man as devoutly religious as Dietrich Bonhoeffer could speak so passionately about a "postreligious age" and could call for a criticism of religion.[6] Did Bonhoeffer

---

4. DBWE 8, 406; DBW 8, 455 (letter of May 29, 1944).

5. Bonhoeffer combines both impulses with suggestive considerations to "being pulled along into the—messianic—suffering of God in Jesus Christ . . . in the NT" and to "participating in God's powerlessness in the world," cf. DBWE 8, 481–82; DBW 8, 536f (letter of July 18, 1944); cf. also similar sayings: "yet all the while, God is in charge," DBWE 8, 505; DBW 8, 563 (letter of August 10, 1944). Cf. the words of Karl Barth on the eve of his death in conversation with Eduard Thurneysen: "Yes, indeed, the world is dark. But there is no need to be so down in the mouth! Not ever! For things *are* being governed, not just in Moscow or in Washington or in Peking, but wholly from above, from heaven. God *does* reign. Hence I myself do not fear. Let us remain confident even at the darkest hour! And not allow our hope to fade for all human beings, for the entire world of nations! God will not let us fall, not a single one of us, nor all of us together! Things are indeed being governed!" in Karl Barth, "Gespräch mit E. Thurneysen, December 9, 1968," in Barth, *Gespräche 1964–1968, Gesamtausgabe*, vol. 4, ed. Eberhard Busch (Zurich: TVZ, 1996), 562. In his biography of Barth, Busch points out that the saying "Es wird regiert," associated with God and Jesus Christ, derives from Christoph Blumhardt, see Eberhard Busch, *Karl Barths Lebenslauf: Nach seinen Briefen und autobiographischen Texten*, 5th ed. (Gütersloh: Kaiser/Gütersloher, 1993), 515.

6. See also the qualification: "Even those who honestly describe themselves as 'religious'. . . presumably mean something quite different by 'religious'" (DBWE 8, 362; DBW 8, 403; letter of April 30, 1944).

simply deceive himself with his prognosis that we were about to enter a "religionless age"? How is this prognosis to be reconciled with the religious boom occurring in many parts of the world at the beginning of the third millennium?

We must closely examine what Bonhoeffer understands by "religion" and "religiouslessness":

> Human beings have learned to manage all important issues by themselves, without recourse to the working hypothesis "God." In questions of science or art, as well as in ethical questions, this has become a matter of course, so that hardly anyone dares rock the boat anymore. But in the last hundred years or so, this has also become increasingly true of religious questions; it's becoming evident that everything gets along without "God" and does so just as well as before. As in the scientific domain, so in human affairs generally, "God" is being pushed further and further out of our life, losing ground.[7]

Bonhoeffer speaks about the "Working hypothesis: God." Following Barth, he criticizes a religious strategy that attempts to "save some room for religion in the world or over against the world,"[8] thereby allowing God to become a merely marginal figure, a fringe phenomenon at the boundaries.

He sharply attacks the conceptions and ideas of God held in abstract theism and metaphysics with their assumption of an entity that from within "transcendence" determines everything. He likewise criticizes the concepts and ideas of God rooted in a person's "innermost subjectivity."[9] He is convinced that whoever attempts to defend these religious bastions exclusively "in an afterlife" or in the "most interior depths" can succeed only with "intellectually dishonest persons" or with "weak minds" who allow themselves to be religiously raped.[10] Here Bonhoeffer is also attacking a form of intellectual piety that, by referencing a religious core inhering in every person and preceding all experience, is appealing to each person's inwardness and conscience[11] (this complex is addressed in

7. DBWE 8, 425–26; DBW 8, 476f (letter of June 8, 1944).

8. DBWE 8, 429; DBW 8, 480 (letter of June 8, 1944); see also the letter of June 30, 1944 (DBWE 8, 448–52; DBW 8, 501ff).

9. See the warning to "not regard psychotherapy and existentialist philosophy as scouts preparing the way for God," DBWE 8, 457; DBW 8, 511 (letter of July 8, 1944).

10. He asserts this as early as April 30, 1944 (DBWE 8, 361–63; DBW 8, 401ff, 403, 404).

11. Concerning the appeal to a "religious a priori" see Ernst Troeltsch, *Zur religiösen Lage, Religionsphilosophie und Ethik: Gesammelte Schriften*, vol. 2, 2nd ed. (Tübingen: Mohr Siebeck, 1922), 494f. See also Richard Rothe, *Theologische Ethik*, vol. 1, rev. ed. (Wittenberg: Herman Koelling, 1869), 69ff. George Simmel already proposed an idea of the

detail in part 0.5). He sees a "historically conditioned and transitory form of human expression" in this religiosity, the "garb in which Christianity is clothed," but one that turns out to be something like the emperor's new clothes, namely, merely an empty theological construct.[12]

Bonhoeffer criticizes the "God" of abstract foundations just as he does the "God" of vague boundary situations. "Religious people speak of God at a point where human knowledge is at an end (or sometimes when they're too lazy to think further), or when human strength fails. . . ." Over against all attempts to "leave room for God only out of anxiety"—be it in a metaphysical beyond or in the deepest interiority preceding all experience—Bonhoeffer provocatively stresses his intention to speak of God "at the center" of life and in "human goodness": "God is beyond in the midst of our lives."[13] At the center of our lives, in the polyphony of life, we encounter the living, but at the same time powerless God who does not simply efface the power of the world and of people, but instead allows himself to be pushed out of their world—even onto the cross.

But how is Bonhoeffer's double legacy to be understood today? Has the world at the beginning of the third millennium really left behind the metaphysical supports and religious invocation of inwardness as religious foundations and supports of Christian faith? How does God encounter us in multidimensional, polyphonic reality—in the suffering Christ and in the inconspicuousness of the coming reign? We will examine Bonhoeffer's theological impulses by reiterating the question, "Who is Jesus Christ for us today?" Do Bonhoeffer's insights remain true in contexts other than his own?

---

religious a priori in "Rembrandts religiöse Kunst," *Frankfurter Zeitung*, vol. 58 (1914), nos. 179, 1–3 and 180, 1–2.

12. DBWE 8, 362–63; DBW 8, 403 and 404 (letter of April 30, 1944).

13. DBWE 8, 366–67; DBW 8, 407 and 408 (letter of April 30, 1944). Concerning Bonhoeffer's concept of believing cognition, refer to Christiane Tietz-Steiding, "Verkrümmte Vernunft und intellektuelle Redlichkeit: Dietrich Bonhoeffers Erkenntnistheorie," in *Religion im Erbe: Dietrich Bonhoeffer und die Zukunftsfähigkeit des Christentums*, ed. Christian Gremmels and Wolfgang Huber (Gütersloh: Kaiser, 2002), 293ff, esp. 301ff.

0.4 Jesus Christ as Cultural Icon, "Christophobia in Europe," and Contextual Christologies Across the World

"Last fall, God prepared my mother for redemption. She came to faith in Jesus Christ." A young Asian scholar, far removed from western pietism or certainly fundamentalism, surprised me one day by making this casual remark with beaming eyes. At the beginning of the third millennium, how many people in Europe could sincerely share such profound joy and elation in Jesus Christ as "the Redeemer"? If in soberly considering "Who is Jesus Christ for us today?" we conceive the qualifier "today" as expansively as possible and survey those parts of the West in which the vast majority of people consider themselves Christians, then we likely cannot but respond that for most of "us today," Jesus Christ is first of all—a cultural icon.

Jesus Christ is present in manifold ways in western culture, so present, in fact, that his presence is desensitizing. Very few give any thought to the fact that the calendar year and the most important holidays are determined by the life of Jesus Christ. Each year, the manger with Mary, Joseph, and the baby Jesus, the shepherds, the angels, and the so-called three kings ritualistically and iconically make their ways into shops and under Christmas trees. Each year, Good Friday, Easter, and Ascension—secularized to whatever degree—dictate the course of the year. In nearly every church, in museums and art books, in cemeteries and obituaries, in the silver jewelry of communion and confirmation gifts, we encounter the image of the cross and occasionally even Jesus on the cross with his crown of thorns and outspread arms. Jesus Christ is a cultural icon of the first order. Were there a vote in Euro-American parts of the world not only for a "man of the year," but for a "man of the millennium" as well, Jesus Christ would easily have received this title twice over.

Both inside the church itself and outside the Christian community at large, public enthusiasm for Jesus Christ as "superstar" repeatedly emerges. *Jesus Christ Superstar*, Andrew Lloyd Webber's rock musical, was the longest-running musical in London's West End between 1972 and 1980.[1] Georg Friedrich Händel's *Messiah*, Johann Sebastian Bach's *Christmas Oratorio*, and other enduring megahits of spiritual music could also bear this title: "Jesus Christ Superstar!" Far beyond the Christian church, there is a market for Jesus in our culture that has repeatedly revived, exploited, and otherwise animated interest in this superstar and cultural icon. Articles or even entire issues dealing with Christ in promi-

---

1. Norman Jewison, dir., *Jesus Christ Superstar* (Los Angeles: Universal Studies, 1973).

nent newspapers and magazines similarly illustrate, year after year, our culture's persistent sense of being challenged by this man, his life, and the significance of his impact: "You Can't Beat Jesus Christ!"[2]

None of this, however, means that particularly many people in this part of the world are animated by any persistently authentic or even regularly anticipated, genuine enthusiasm for Jesus Christ, or that they are interested in carrying on their culture's more profound shaping according to his example and ministry. To the contrary, it is precisely in a latent fashion that Jesus Christ's powerful cultural influence functions in rehearsed traditions and patterns of life that people are disinclined to link to his living, spiritual charisma. "An interesting person from 2000 years ago—absolutely. But please, do not combine that with religious propaganda!" The aversion to the perpetual and living vibrancy of this person and this life emerges especially when people are confronted with the topic of the "revelation of God in Jesus Christ" or, certainly, the "deity of Christ." The massive defense is generally, "Just don't tread too near with your Jesus!"

This "christophobic" attitude has assumed clearer contours in Europe than in other parts of the world, though it extends to all of Christianity in general.[3] In the U.S.A., there was considerable surprise and even annoyance that the final draft of the constitution of the European Union[4] did not include a single word about God, Christ, or Christianity: ". . . a treaty of some 70,000 words (ten times longer than the U.S. Constitution!) could not find room for one word, 'Christianity.'"[5]

In his book, *The Cube and the Cathedral: Europe, America, and Politics without God*,[6] George Weigel, senior fellow at the Ethics and Public Policy Center in Washington, D.C., speculated on the connections be-

---

2. Billy Joe Shaver, *You Can't Beat Jesus Christ, Johnny Cash* (Nashville, TN, May 21, 1980).

3. Joseph H. H. Weiler, South Africa–born orthodox Jew, professor of law and European Union at New York University's famous School of Law and College of Europe in Bruges, identified this cultural and historical amnesia as "Christophobia" in *Ein christliches Europa: Erkundungsgänge*, with a foreword by Ernst-Wolfgang Böckenförde (Salzburg and Munich: Anton Pustet, 2004), esp. 75ff. Here Weiler suggests that Europe is controlled by a Christophobia that blocks engagement with its cultural and spiritual foundations as well as with its cultivation and further creative development.

4. In 2004 this constitution was launched on the difficult path to ratification through the Treaty of Rome.

5. George Weigel, "Is Europe Dying? Notes on a Crisis of Civilizational Morale," in *New Atlantic Initiative*, ed. American Enterprise Institute for Public Policy Research (March/April 2005), 2.

6. George Weigel, *The Cube and the Cathedral: Europe, America, and Politics without God* (Cambridge: Basic Books, 2005).

tween the marginalization of the Christian faith by Europe's leading intellectuals and in public life in the twentieth century, the decline of religious education, moral disorientation, and the radical population decline
in Europe—the largest since the plague in the fourteenth century. With
reference to Henri de Lubac[7] and other culturally pessimistic theological
and philosophical thinkers, he discerned at the foundation of this development a spiritual crisis that was already present in the atheistic humanism of the nineteenth century, which in its own turn declared faith in God
to be irreconcilable with human freedom. Weigel refers to, among other
things, a bleak vision by Helmuth von Moltke, who in July 1914 predicted
that the imminent First World War would destroy the civilization of most
of Europe for decades.[8] The recognition of this profound crisis of European civilization was allegedly merely obscured by the world wars and
their difficult aftermath, by the brief, illusory peace between the wars,
by the Great Depression, then further by the euphoria that initially accompanied totalitarianism, by the jolting experiences of the horrors
and terrors triggered by totalitarianism, and, finally, by the enduring
Cold War.

The majority of such seemingly pro-Christian cultural diagnoses
are, to be sure, christologically empty, being barely stirred by any interest in—not to speak of passion for—Jesus Christ, the charismatic
power of his Spirit, and the efficacious power of his coming reign. They
developed instead out of concern for the potential erosion of Europe's
democratic societies and the possibility that—political correctness quite
aside and following the conspiracy theories formulated by the British
historian Gisèle Littman (pseudonym: Bat Ye'or)—Europe could become
"Eurabia."[9] Such detached and exaggerated ideas should draw attention
to the fact that many defenders of "Christian Europe" and "Christian values" operate within a not inconsiderable christological void, one which,
ironically, they nonetheless appear to lament. At most they may invoke
Jesus Christ as a cultural icon when the need arises, though in an open
or concealed fashion they are actually harboring culturally chauvinistic
ideas only externally associated with Jesus Christ and Christianity.

Such manipulative use of Jesus as a cultural icon, however, does not
come strictly from outside the church. At the end of Pope John Paul II's

7. Henri de Lubac, *The Drama of Atheist Humanism* (San Francisco: Ignatius Press,
1995).

8. Cf. David Fromkin, *Europe's Last Summer: Who Started the Great War in 1914?*
(New York: Alfred Knopf, 2004), 224.

9. Bat Ye'or, *Eurabia: The Euro-Arab Axis* (Cranbury: Associated University Presses,
2005); see also the title of *Time Magazine*, August 30, 2010: "Is America Islamophobic?"
12ff.

papacy, the Vatican made several attempts to identify the Pope with Jesus Christ in a media-friendly fashion. In 2005, it even attracted the attention of the magazine *Der Spiegel*, which is typically not particularly
subtle with respect to theological and religious discourse. The magazine
noticed that the Vatican staged the hospital stays of Pope John Paul II, at
the time suffering badly from Parkinson's disease, as well as his various
returns home from the hospital as stations of the cross and resurrection.
This effort to stage the papacy christomorphically continued seamlessly
when Benedict XVI associated his election as Pope with the affliction
of Jesus Christ in Gethsemane (Matt 26:39, 42, 44; Mark 14:36; Luke
22:42). At his first large audience of German pilgrims, he said, "When I
saw the ax [of his new ministry] descending on me, I prayed to God, but
he did not answer my voice." Soon after the Pope's accession to office and
during his visit to World Youth Day in 2005 in Cologne—and quite along
the same lines—Cardinal Meisner felt compelled to associate the Pope's
trip on the Rhine with Jesus's discourse on the Sea of Galilee. The Cardinal announced that Benedict would preach from the ship on the Rhine
"like the Savior on the Sea of Galilee."[10]

Are these merely incidental embarrassments? Or do they signal an
alarm from within the church as well that cannot but make clear to us
that there are simply too many problematic practices with regard to the
question, "Who is Jesus Christ for us today?" each of which requires a
discernment of spirits. For example, do references to and invocations of
the presence of Jesus Christ and of what is "Christian," or allusions to
such, then necessarily express all the possible needs, hardships, wishes,
longings, and attendant issues of status and dominion? Can we discern
the interests, wishes, and longings that distract us from his person, life,
ministry, message, and call to discipleship, or that, indeed, run quite
contrary to all the latter? Conversely, is there perhaps also evidence that
in specific concerns and contexts he himself, his life, his word, and his
Spirit, and therefore also the revelation of God among human beings is
efficaciously present and alive?

It is precisely these queries that some academic and church theologians have directed to various christologically oriented contextual, feminist, and liberation theologies that emerged globally in the final decades
of the twentieth century. While the tranquil influence of the cultural icon

---

10. "Das Kreuz mit den Deutschen," *Der Spiegel* 33 (2005), 136–51, 141. Cf also
Joachim Frank, "Traum von einem Wunder: Papst Benedikt XVI. besucht Deutschland.
Und was bringt er mit?" *Zeitzeichen* 12 (September 2011), 8: "Before the grand event, the
host, Cardinal Joachim Meisner, asserted in all seriousness that following the event the
seminaries would fill up again with young men. As we all know, this boom failed to mate-
rialize. On the contrary . . ."

Jesus Christ extending from its incorporation into political culture and media to the papacy is patiently tolerated, any appeal to Jesus Christ that invokes his spiritual and moral vibrancy in contemporary situations of crisis and conflict elicits nervousness and concern. Is such evocation perhaps functionalizing Jesus Christ in relation to worldview and ideology? We must take several steps in order to differentiate theological and christological seriousness from theologically embellished and ideologically defensive gestures.

1. It must be demonstrated that *theology devoid of context does not exist*; nor did contextualized theology and Christology first emerge only within the twentieth century.

2. It must be self-critically acknowledged that countless "purely academic" theologies and Christologies, or those claiming abstract proofs of purity of whatever sort, have not only failed miserably in contexts and situations that are aggressively ideologically driven and contemptuous toward human dignity, but in many ways also, at least unconsciously, reinforced regnant injustice through their ideas and teachings. Taking into consideration this critique, which is also to be extended to classical Christologies, and for the reasons explicated in what follows (cf. parts 4.1–4.3), a broad nexus of christological orientation must be disclosed. Christologies must not be played off against one another that:

- accentuate primarily a theology of discipleship in spiritual education and service,

- orient themselves primarily toward pastoral, spiritual, and liturgical concerns,

- consider the development of a prophetic theology in political, moral, economic, and ideological situations of crisis to be urgent (see parts 4.4, 5.3, 5.5).

3. Theology must not only subject itself to extra-theological critiques of religion, but also itself actively engage in a christologically oriented critique of religion.

Concerning 1): In his book *Jesus through the Centuries*,[11] Jaroslav Pelikan traced portrayals of Christ from various theological perspectives across two millennia. In the New Testament witnesses, he finds Jesus the rabbi, teacher, and prophet, a justifiable if one-sided observation that fails to discern the breadth of Jesus's ministry (see part 1) and similarly does not take seriously how soon after the resurrection Jesus was being

11. *Jesus Through the Centuries: His Place in the History of Culture* (New Haven: Yale University Press, 1985).

worshiped as heavenly kyrios, as Lord and "God of God" (see parts 1.3, 2.5, 4, and 5). Pelikan finds the proclamation of Jesus Christ as the "turning point of history" in the church father Tertullian at the end of the second century[12] and later in Augustine's grand historical-theological work, *The City of God*.[13] Pelikan similarly encounters the identification of Jesus as the "light of the world" as early as the middle of the second century with Justin Martyr,[14] and even more conspicuously at the end of the century in Clement of Alexandria.[15] Most church fathers, Pelikan finds, concur with what the "Father of Church History," Eusebius of Caesarea, repeatedly emphasizes in his *Church History* and *Life of Constantine*, namely, that Jesus Christ is the "King of Kings" (see part 4.4).[16] References to the "cosmic Christ" reflect the efforts of the three Cappadocians, Basil of Caesarea (the Great),[17] Gregory of Nazianzus, and Gregory of Nyssa,[18] to grasp and articulate the creative *logos* in Christ, while in the fifth century, Augustine provides a christological orientation for the later triumph of Christian anthropology and psychology with the phrase, "the Son of Man."[19]

"The crucified God" in Luther (see part 3.1), "the monk who rules the world" among the Benedictines, "the bridegroom of the soul" among the mystics, "the teacher of healthy human understanding" among moderns, "the poet of the soul" among the Romantics, "the liberator" in many twentieth-century theologies (see below and part 5.5)—the more contexts and contextualizations of Jesus Christ that come into view, the more urgent the need becomes to develop criteria for distinguishing between appropriate and inappropriate characterizations of his person and

12. See, for example, *Against Praxeas* 2.1 (*Adversus Praxean liber: Tertullian's treatise against Praxeas*, trans. Ernest Evans [Eugene, Ore.: Wipf & Stock, 2011]).

13. Sancti Aurelii Augustini, *De Civitate Dei* (CChrSL 48) (Turnholt: Brepols, 1955), esp. books 16 and 17.

14. *Iustini Martyris apologiae pro christianis*, ed. Miroslav Marcovich (Berlin and New York: de Gruyter, 1994), apologies I and II.

15. Clement of Alexandria, *The Stromata, or Miscellanies*, in *Fathers of the Second Century*, vol. 10 of the *Ante-Nicene Fathers*, ed. A. Cleveland Coxe (Peabody, MA: Hendrickson, 1995), 299-568, esp. V, 444-79.

16. Eusebius, *Life of Constantine* (Clarendon Ancient History Series), trans. Averil Cameron and Stuart Hall (Oxford: Oxford University Press, 1999).

17. Basil of Caesarea, *The Nine Homilies of the Hexameron*, trans. Blomfield Jackson, in *Nicene and Post-Nicene Fathers*, vol. 8 (Peabody, MA: Hendrickson Publishers, 1994), Homilies 1 (52-58) and 6 (81-89).

18. Gregory of Nyssa, *On the Making of Man*, trans. H. A. Wilson, in *Nicene and Post-Nicene Fathers*, vol. 5 (Edinburgh: T & T Clark, 1988), 387-427.

19. See Sancti Aurelii Augustini, *Confessiones*, CChr.SL 50 (New York: Johnson, 1962), esp. book 7; *De Trinitate*, libri 1–12 and 13–15, CChr.SL50 and 50a, ed. W. J. Mountain (Turnholt: Brepols, 1968), 2 and 16; just as in a multitude of other writings.

ministry. Although this task is indispensable, it must not degenerate into a religio-political-moral offensive or defensive strategy that exhausts itself in theologies and Christologies within contemporary political, moral, and cultural debates.

Concerning 2): The shocking failure of large parts of German and Italian theology during the period of Fascism, of large parts of Dutch-South African theology during the period of Apartheid, and the initially only haltingly engaged attempts to come to terms with colonialism in both history and the present along with the active and passive roles of theologians and churches in precisely this history have increased our awareness of the indispensability of self-criticism on the part of all theology in the light of revelation. A powerful impetus for such increasingly enlightened awareness has come and indeed continues to come from the biblical and christological reflections of feminist theology.[20] Elisabeth Schüssler Fiorenza has coined the term "kyriarchal"[21] in drawing attention to the fact that from the biblical traditions themselves on to allegedly modern, "gender-neutral" cultural developments, Christologies have carried forward androcentric, patriarchal, and monarchic-hierarchical patterns of orientation, even such that have emerged out of resistance to oppression and the struggle for liberation.[22] She has proposed developing Christology more strongly in light of wisdom traditions and the Jesuanic proclamation of the reign of God.[23] Despite the perpetually weak institutional position of feminist theology in ecclesial and academic contexts, she has

20. See *Vom Verlangen nach Heilwerden: Christologie in feministisch-theologischer Sicht*, ed. Doris Strahm and Regula Strobel, 2nd ed. (Luzern: Edition Exodus, 1993); Elisabeth Moltmann-Wendel, "Frauen sehen Christus: Ansätze einer feministischen Christologie," in *Jesus von Nazaret. Neue Zugänge zu Person und Bedeutung*, ed. J. Thomassen (Würzburg: Echter, 1993) 23–37; Julie Hopkins, *Towards a Feminist Christology: Jesus of Nazareth, European Women, and the Christological Crisis* (Grand Rapids: Eerdmans, 1995).

21. *But She Said: Feminist Practices of Biblical Interpretation* (Boston: Beacon 1992), 8 et passim.

22. The justifiably respected Barmen Declaration (1934) offers a trenchant example. Against the ideology of the German Christians, this declaration propagated a "christocratic brotherhood" and the problematic concept of a dominion-Christology based on a distorted exegesis of Ephesians 4:16; see Michael Welker, "Barmen III: Woran orientieren? Die Gestalt der Kirche in gesellschaftlichen Umbrüchen," in *Begründete Freiheit—Die Aktualität der Barmer Theologischen Erklärung: Vortragsreihe zum 75. Jahrestag im Berliner Dom*, Evangelische Impulse 1, ed. Martin Heimbucher (Neukirchen-Vluyn: Neukirchener, 2009), 59ff.

23. See Elisabeth Schüssler Fiorenza, *Jesus. Miriam's Child, Sophia's Prophet: Critical Issues in Feminist Christology* (New York: Continuum, 1995), and *In Memory of Her: A Feminist Theological Reconstruction of Christian Origins* (New York: Crossroad, 1984), esp. chap. 4.

demanded the critical and self-critical combination and collaboration of feminist theologies with other theologies of emancipation (political theologies, liberation theologies, post-colonial theologies).[24]

Alongside and in connection with feminist theologies and trends shaped by liberation, political, and "post-colonial" theological perspectives, numerous contextual theologies and Christologies have developed today through encounters with Buddhism, Hinduism, tribal religions, and other religious traditions. These Christologies shape both processes of cultural and social demarcation and adaptation in relation to other religions. Contextual liberation theologies and Christologies can serve the critical confrontation with Christian colonialism[25] or ac-

---

24. See Elisabeth Schüssler Fiorenza, *The Power of the Word: Scripture and the Rhetoric of Empire* (Minneapolis: Fortress, 2007); idem, "Die kritisch-feministische The*logie der Befreiung: Eine entkolonisierend-politische The*logie," in *Politische Theologie: Neuere Geschichte und Potenziale*, Theologische Anstöße 1, ed. Francis Schüssler Fiorenza, Klaus Tanner, and Michael Welker (Neukirchen-Vluyn: Neukirchener, 2011), 23–39. Concerning efforts to integrate multicontextual liberation theologies, see also Jürgen Moltmann, *Experiences in Theology: Ways and Forms of Christian Theology*, trans. Margaret Kohl (Minneapolis: Fortress, 2000). Concerning the difficulties Moltmann has experienced in developing a polycontextual liberation theology, see esp. 293-302; and idem, *Weiter Raum: Eine Lebensgeschichte* (Gütersloh: Gütersloher, 2006), 219ff. The strongest impulses for the liberation and political theologies developing in many parts of the world can be traced back to Moltmann's major works, viz., from his christologically and eschatologically oriented *Theology of Hope: On the Ground and the Implications of a Christian Eschatology*, trans. James W. Leitch (New York: Harper and Row, 1967), and from his theology of the cross, *The Crucified God* (see part 0.1, note 6); see also part 3.3.

25. See the anthology documenting the classic positions of Latin-American liberation theology and their most important themes, *Systematic Theology: Perspectives from Liberation Theology* (Readings from Mysterium Liberationis), ed. Jon Sobrino and Ignacio Ellacuria (Maryknoll, New York: Orbis, 1996); liberation and feminist theological perspectives are combined in Pietro Selvatico and Doris Strahm, *Jesus Christus*, Studiengang Theologie VI, 2 (Zürich: Edition NZN bei TVZ, n.d.); for a treatment of the christological discourse during the time of Latin and South American colonialism and the influence of Leonardo Boff in Brazil and Jon Sobrino in El Salvador, see Volker Küster, *The Many Faces of Jesus Christ: Intercultural Christology* (London: SCM Press, 2001), 41ff, 47ff; and Leonardo Boff, *Jesus Christ Liberator: A Critical Christology of Our Time* (Maryknoll, NY: Orbis, 1978). See also Hugo Assmann, "The Power of Christ in History: Conflicting Christologies and Discernment," in *Frontiers of Theology in Latin America*, ed. Rosino Gibellini, 3rd ed. (Maryknoll: Orbis, 1983), 133ff; Jon Sobrino, *Jesus the Liberator: A Historical-Theological Reading of Jesus of Nazareth*, trans. Paul Burns and Francis McDonagh (Maryknoll: Orbis, 1999), esp. section II; Jon Sobrino, "Zurück zu Jesus von Nazareth," in *Der Preis der Gerechtigkeit: Briefe an einen ermordeten Freund*, Ignatianische Impulse 25 (Würzburg: Echter, 2007), 95-104; idem, *Christ the Liberator: A View from the Victims* (Maryknoll: Orbis 2001). Concerning feminist Christology in Latin America, see Doris Strahm, *Vom Rand in die Mitte: Christologie aus der Sicht von Frauen in Asien, Afrika, und Lateinamerika* (Luzern: Edition Exodus, 1997), 271ff; Nelly Ritchie, "Women and Christology,"

company what are sooner appeasement efforts with respect to the so-called "fusion of traditions."[26] Struggles against racist repression[27] or efforts at racial reconciliation[28] variously take their orientation from the power of Christ's example and Christology. In India, there is a similar call for a reconciling "Christ-centered humanism"[29] and to a liberation of the repressed untouchables[30] in the name of discipleship in Christ. The search for an ecumenically and globally integrated theology as well as for the affirmation of regional and contextual identities[31]

in *Through Her Eyes: Women's Theology from Latin America*, ed. Elsa Tamez (Maryknoll: Orbis, 1989), 81ff; and Maria Clara Bingemer, "Jesus Christ and the Salvation of the Woman," in *Voices from the Third World*, 11/2 (1988), 125ff.

26. See models of African Christology in Küster, *The Many Faces of Jesus Christ*, 57ff (see part 0.4, note 25); of African feminist Christology in Strahm, *Vom Rand*, 151ff (see part 0.4, note 25); Teresa M. Hinga, "Between Colonialism and Inculturation," in *The Power of Naming: A Concilium Reader in Feminist Liberation Theology*, ed. Elisabeth Schüssler Fiorenza (Maryknoll: Orbis, 1996), 36ff; Charles Nyamiti, *Christ as Our Ancestor: Christology from an African Perspective* (Gweu: Mambo Press, 1984), esp. 69ff; Mercy Amba Oduyoye, *Hearing and Knowing: Theological Reflections on Christianity in Africa* (Maryknoll: Orbis, 1986); Elizabeth Amoah and Mercy A. Oduyoye, "The Christ for African Women," in *With Passion and Compassion: Third World Women Doing Theology* (Maryknoll: Orbis, 1988), 35-46; François Kabasèlè, "Christ as Chief, " in *Faces of Jesus in Africa*, ed. Robert J. Schreiter (Maryknoll: Orbis 1991), 103ff; Theo Sundermeier, *Konvivenz und Differenz: Studien zu einer verstehenden Missionswissenschaft*, ed. Volker Küster (Erlangen: Verlag Evang. Luth. Mission, 1995), 126ff.

27. See James Cone, *Black Theology and Black Power* (Maryknoll: Orbis, 1997), esp. chapter 2: "The Gospel of Jesus, Black People, and Black Power," 31ff.

28. Allan Boesak, *Walking on Thorns: The Call to Christian Obedience* (Geneva: World Council of Churches Publications, 1984).

29. See M.M. Thomas, *Risking Christ for Christ's Sake: Towards an Ecumenical Theology of Pluralism* (Geneva: World Council of Churches Publications, 1987), with strong impetus from Raimundo Panikkar, *The Unknown Christ of Hinduism: Towards an Ecumenical Christophany* (Maryknoll: Orbis, 1981); see also Küster, *The Many Faces of Jesus Christ*, 83ff, 77ff (see part 0.4, note 25); Monica Melanchthon, "Christology and Women," in *We Dare to Dream: Doing Theology as Asian Women*, ed. Virginia Fabella and Sun Ai Lee-Park (Hong Kong: Asian Women's Resource Centre for Culture and Theology, 1989), 15ff.

30. See *A Reader in Dalit Theology*, ed. Arvind P. Nirmal (Madras: Gurukul Lutheran Theological College & Research Institute, n.d.); Virginia Fabella, "Christology from an Asian Christian Woman's Perspective," in Fabella/Lee-Park, *We Dare to Dream*, 3ff (see part 0.4, note 29).

31. More recent drafts of Chinese-Christian theologies seek to combine both perspectives; see, for example, Liu Xiaofeng, "Sino-Christian Theology in the Modern Context," in *Sino-Christian Studies in China*, ed. Huilin Yang and Daniel H. N. Yeung (Newcastle: Cambridge Scholars Press, 2006), 52ff; these are joined by an interest in "Contemporary Faces and Images of Jesus Christ," see *The Chinese Face of Jesus Christ*, Monumenta Serica Monograph Series L/3b, ed. Roman Malek (Nettetal: Steyler Verlag, 2007), esp. 1638ff.

and for liberating practices in the face of repression are shaped by christological impulses.[32]

If one examines the vast array of contextually motivated christological concepts and contextually shaped Christologies only from the outside, without participation in the contextual seriousness and without any clear perspectives on Jesus's life and ministry and the diverse capabilities of his Spirit and kingdom, one can quickly sense, albeit perhaps vaguely, the presence of ideology. Is Jesus Christ being functionalized here merely for moral and political conflict engagement and goals? Is Christology merely an alibi for imposing religious emphasis on human needs and goals? On the one hand, these facile external observations must yield to an encounter with and critical examination of the seriousness attaching to specific contexts. On the other, they themselves must be examined within a theologically informed view of the christological and pneumatological abundance of the self-presentation of Jesus Christ. The following chapters seek to provide encouragement for precisely this undertaking.

Concerning 3): The classic philosophical religious critiques of Ludwig Feuerbach,[33] Karl Marx,[34] and Friedrich Nietzsche[35] attacked the appeal to religious content en bloc as a projection, as an appeal to illusory reality, as the dissemination of the "opiate of the people," and as "priestly deception." Dietrich Bonhoeffer, however, as well as other highly respected theologians of his time such as Karl Barth[36] and Paul Tillich,[37] saw an indispensable and unending theological task in the critique of

32. See Byung-Mu Ahn, "Die Träger der Überlieferung des Jesusereignisses," in *Draußen vor dem Tor: Kirche und Minjung in Korea: Theologische Beiträge und Reflexionen*, ThÖ 20 (Göttingen: Vandenhoeck, 1986), 99ff; a vigorous international discussion was generated by the proposal from Hyun Kyung Chung for developing a syncretistic theology and to view Jesus in various female roles, for instance, as a female shaman: idem, "Who is Jesus for Asian Women?" in *Liberation Theology: An Introductory Reader*, ed. Curt Casorette et al. (Maryknoll: Orbis, 1992), 123ff; see also Man Ja Choi, "Feminist Theology," in *Asian Women Doing Theology: Report from Singapore Conference*, November 20–29, 1987 (Hong Kong: Asian Women's Resource Center for Culture and Theology, 1989), 174ff.

33. Ludwig Feuerbach, *The Essence of Christianity*, trans. George Eliot (New York: Harper, 1957).

34. Concerning his critique of Hegel's philosophy of law, cf. Karl Marx, *Early Texts*, trans. and ed. David McLellan (New York: Harper and Row, 1972), 115ff.

35. Friedrich Nietzsche, *Twilight of the Idols*, and *The Anti-Christ*, in *The Anti-Christ, Ecce Homo, Twilight of the Idols, and Other Writings*, ed. Aaron Ridley and Judith Norman (Cambridge: Cambridge University Press, 2010), 153-230 and 1-68.

36. *Church Dogmatics I/2, The Doctrine of the Word of God, Prolegomena to Church Dogmatics*, § 17, 280ff.

37. *Systematic Theology*, vol. III: *Life and the Spirit: History and the Kingdom of God* (Chicago: University of Chicago Press, 1963), 245ff.

religion. On their view, theology should constantly try to learn from even the most severe philosophical critiques of religion. For Christian religiosity—even a theology and piety appealing to Jesus Christ in subjectively sincere engagement on behalf of justice and truth—is continually and repeatedly prompted to engage in self-criticism in the light of revelation.[38] Its critique, however, must not concentrate solely on current or certainly only on particularly vibrant developments, nor also exclude the voices and classic writers of tradition. Finally, it must not single out for criticism those contextual theologies whose striving toward pastoral and prophetic-practical imitation of Christ give political (or other) offense.

Bourgeois and petit-bourgeois religiosity in the West has found a form of expression that appears to uphold and value the "nearness of God" without exposing itself to virtually any of the previously described irritations that accompany the revelation of God and faith in Jesus Christ. The concentrated uneasiness toward a God who is near in the cross and in suffering, and toward God's presence "in the fullness of life," along with the apprehension that contextual theologies invoke Jesus Christ exclusively for moral and political goals and those that stabilize group identity—all these have been and continue to be circumvented by a form of piety that can be called "subjectivist faith." In the name of a "pure" piety and also in the name of academic and philosophical earnestness, this "faith" leaves Christology and all its theological challenges and confusing and conflict-laden contextualizations behind. Why should the "near God" not be sought and indeed found in a way that *in principle* is capable of addressing *any context* and that strives to keep itself wholly detached from the questions and problems that God's revelation in Jesus Christ presents?

---

38. This challenge for the Christian religion to engage in self-criticism, or, more exactly, in "critical self-examination" in view of the content and form of revelation, is frequently overlooked precisely with regard to what is known as "Barth's critique of religion"; see *CD* I/2, 297ff.

0.5 Excursus – Subjectivist Faith: The Christophobic Search for the Nearness of God

A strange, almost eerie relationship obtains in western society today under the guise of "faith."[1] On the one hand, the believing individual is allegedly related to a "wholly other," a "transcendent power," or an otherworldly, vaguely conceived personal entity. On the other hand, this same entity is tremendously near to the believer, profoundly intimate, more intimate in fact—to use Augustine's phrase—than one can be to oneself.[2] A profound inner certainty, called "faith," sustains this relational tension between a "transcendent entity" and the experience of its extreme nearness.

The discovery of each person's relationship to the self in thought, of which human beings are typically unaware even though this relationship can always be activated within *conscious* life, was not just a product of European modernity.[3] That notwithstanding, great modern European philosophers such as René Descartes and Immanuel Kant initiated what has been called a *Copernican shift* in the knowledge of self and world that has come to be associated with the "essence of modernity." This shift came about through illuminating explorations of the human cognitive capacity and especially through striking programmatic formulations such as "I think, therefore I am"[4] or "It must be possible for the 'I think' to accompany all my representations."[5] On this view, modern human beings disclose reality by concentrating *first* on their own consciousness and self-consciousness. With this shift—thus the whole-hearted asser-

1. The following sections draw from Michael Welker, "Subjektivistischer Glaube als religiöse Falle," *Evangelische Theologie* 64 (2004), 239–48.

2. *The Confessions of St. Augustin*, trans. J. G. Pilkington, in *Nicene and Post-Nicene Fathers*, Series 1, Vol. 1, ed. Philip Schaff (Peabody, Mass.: Hendrickson Publishers, 1995), 45–207; Book III, chapter 6, 11: "Thou wert more inward to me than my most inward part; and higher than my highest" (63).

3. See *Die autonome Person—eine europäische Erfindung?* ed. K. P. Köpping, R. Wiehl, and M. Welker (Munich: Fink, 2002).

4. Cf. René Descartes, "Second Meditation," in *Meditations on First Philosophy. With Selections from the Objections and Replies*, trans. and ed. John Cottingham (Cambridge: Cambridge University Press, 2002), 16-23; in an astute examination, Andreas Kemmerling, *Ideen des Ichs: Studien zu Descartes' Philosophie*, 2nd ed. (Frankfurt: Klosterman, 2005), 93ff, has critically illuminated this "self-circular idea" (121) that is in fact found at most only "between the lines" in the Cartesian Meditations (93).

5. Immanuel Kant, *Critique of Pure Reason*, trans. Norman Kemp Smith (New York: Modern Library, Random House), 1958, B 132; cf. Dieter Henrich, *Selbstverhältnisse: Gedanken und Auslegungen zu den Grundlagen der klassischen deutschen Philosophie* (Stuttgart: Reclam, 1982), 176ff; Henrich, "Das Selbstbewusstsein und seine Selbstdeutungen," in *Fluchtlinien: Philosophische Essays* (Frankfurt: Suhrkamp, 1982), 99ff.

tion—theocentric and cosmocentric worldviews were replaced by an-thropocentric ones. More precisely, the analysis of the experiential forms of human cognition through what is known as "transcendental philoso-phy" was elevated to the preferred methodology of science and of human disclosure of the world generally.

Many conceptual developments of the nineteenth and twentieth cen-turies have challenged this monopoly of transcendental philosophy and posited alongside it various other modes for examining human beings as such and cognitive theory specifically. In popular philosophy and over a broad spectrum of European academic theology, however, one particular development—one that might be called "transcendental Philistinism"—declared as problematical or even as invalid all religious content that could not be classified under the rubric of "final certainty" within the more or less acute, clear-cut reflection of human consciousness and self-consciousness. Karl Barth quite correctly labeled the remnants of Chris-tian faith within this theory as "indirect Cartesianism."[6] That is to say, "I feel somehow dependent, therefore I am," or "I feel somehow dependent, therefore I believe."

When religious communication and especially Christian theol-ogy accepted this subjectivist "faith," they emphasized—surprisingly, perhaps—that this subjectivist "faith" was the exact opposite of the human relationship to the self. To precisely the same extent that this "inner certainty" is extoled as "faith," any and all variations of the human relationship to the *self* become stigmatized from the religious perspective, since any attempt to distinguish innocent, trivial, and healthy relationships with the self from problematic fixations and ob-sessive forms could not but appear risky. A paradoxical and neuroti-cally inclined mentality accompanies this religious-secular form called "faith." For how was a pure, inner certainty of the (religious) "wholly other" to be distinguished from a quite simple, foundational form of the human relationship with the self, which in its own turn had come to terms with its own inner structure and realized that any relation-ship with the self must include an element of difference if it is to be experienced as "certainty" that is focused or simply capable of being such? And how is this form still to understand itself as "religious" if the "inner other" is also arbitrarily accessible *without* any accompany-ing religious tinge?

One advantage of this religiously *and* secularly interpretable struc-ture of inner certainty from a religious perspective was the impossibility of anyone escaping this type of "faith"—at least not within cultures and

6. Karl Barth, *Church Dogmatics, I/1, The Doctrine of the Word of God,* 243.

mindsets for which the conscious self-relationship of the individual is central, that is, cultures that view themselves as part of the typically modern "world community."[7] This popular form, which is presented both as a religious phenomenon and as a phenomenon of the secular, dialectic self-relation, has been confused with theologically and philosophically more sophisticated fundamental forms of religious, moral, and metaphysical orientation. The popular form could be viewed approximately as follows:

- as a popularized variation of the religious "feeling of absolute dependence" (à la Schleiermacher);[8] or

- as a popularized variation of the simultaneity—asserted by moral philosophy—of self-certainty and self-challenge within the coincidence of moral consciousness and the inner voice of moral law that says "you ought!" (à la Kant);[9] or

- as a trivialized variation of metaphysical unity and tension between "existence and essence" (à la Tillich).[10]

Søren Kierkegaard in particular can be adduced as a pioneer of this religious-secular form of faith. In *The Sickness unto Death*, his central later work, he repeatedly emphasizes that the formula for "faith" is "relating itself to its own self, and by willing to be itself, the self is grounded transparently in the Power which constituted it," or: "Faith is: that the self in being itself and in will to be itself is grounded transparently in God." For him, this formula was nothing less than the "sure mariners' mark" "by which I steer my course in the whole of this work."[11]

---

7. It is worth pointing out that such reference to the "typically modern world community" sooner corresponds to the spirit of the early nineteenth century and to that of early twentieth-century existentialism than to the complex multicontextual and structured pluralistic forms we today associate with "globalization." Cf. Michael Welker, "Globalisierung. In wissenschaftlich-theologischer Sicht," *EvTh* 68 (2008), 365–82; William Schweiker, *Theological Ethics and Global Dynamics in the Time of Many Worlds* (Oxford: Blackwell, 2004), 5ff; Boike Rehbein and Hermann Schwengel, *Theorien der Globalisierung*, UTB (Constance: UVK, 2008).

8. Friedrich Schleiermacher, *The Christian Faith in Outline*, trans. D.M. Baillie (Edinburgh: Henderson, 1922).

9. Cf. Immanuel Kant, *Groundwork for the Metaphysics of Morals*, trans. Arnulf Zweig, ed. Thomas E. Hill, Jr. and Arnulf Zweig (Oxford and New York: Oxford University Press, 2002); idem, *Critique of Practical Reason*, ed. Mary J. Gregor (Cambridge, UK, and New York: Cambridge University Press, 1997).

10. Paul Tillich, *Systematic Theology I: Reason and Revelation, Being and God* (Chicago: University of Chicago Press, 1973).

11. Søren Kierkegaard, *Sickness unto Death* (Radford, VA: Wilder Publishing, 2008), 40, 67; see also, *Fear and Trembling*, in *Kierkegaard's Writings*, vol. 6, ed. Howard V. Hong and Edna H. Hong (Princeton: Princeton University Press, 1983), 69: "On the one

Beginning with the adoption of Schleiermacher's and Kierkegaard's fundamental premises (often in forms simplified by popular philosophy) and extending to the appropriation of existentialist positions such as that of Rudolf Bultmann,[12] a not inconsiderable number of academically influential attempts have been made over the past two centuries to capture, describe, and propagate this type of empty "faith." Most concur in trying to demonstrate that this ultimate certainty, on the one hand, is a clear anthropological phenomenon, while, on the other, it is to be seen as God given, as grounded in divine grace—and not as a trivial, weakly reflected self-relationship or the result of a quotidian attempt to gain certainty.

The relationship described here, presented as an experience of religious certainty and called "faith," can appear extraordinarily valuable. To wit, it makes it possible to introduce an element of allegedly religious communication at potentially every point of individual experience and interpersonal communication. For as soon as I as an individual try to view my "inner self" thematically, I come upon the experience—one accompanied by a sense of certainty—of the fundamentally "other within

---

hand [faith] contains the expression of extreme egoism . . . and on the other the expression of the most absolute devotion (doing it for God's sake)." This position is accompanied by a particular emphasis on inwardness or interiority. More precisely, the pure inwardness of faith is polemically and radically opposed to any alleged objectivity of the knowledge of faith: cf., for example, Kierkegaard, *Einübung im Christentum, Gesammelte Werke*, 26, Abteilung (Düsseldorf/Köln: Diederichs, 1955), 216 (*Practice in Christianity*, vol. 20 [1991]): "The first condition for becoming a Christian is that a person be absolutely turned inward"; and Kierkegaard, *Concluding Unscientific Postscript to Philosophical Fragments*, vol. 12 (1992): ". . . an objective knowledge about the truth or the truths of Christianity is precisely untruth. To know a creed by rote is paganism, because Christianity is inwardness." This concept of faith could not but ultimately become self-referential: "Faith itself is, as it were, the object of faith" (Kierkegaard, *Erbauliche Reden 1843/44, Gesammelte Werke*, 7., 8., 9. Abteilung [1956], 85).

12. Rudolf Bultmann offers a particularly compelling version of this figure. See, for example, "What Does it Mean to Speak of God?" in *Faith and Understanding*, ed. Robert Funk, trans. Louise Pettibone Smith (Philadelphia: Fortress, 1987), 53-65, 63: "For if the realization of our own existence is involved in faith and if our existence is grounded in God and is non-existent outside God, then to apprehend our existence means to apprehend God"; and "The Problem of 'Natural Theology,'" in ibid., 313-331, 316: "Existence in faith comes to be in a new understanding of existence." The most radical formulation can likely be found in a text from 1929 that was not published until 1984: "Wahrheit und Gewißheit," in *Theologische Enzyklopädie*, ed. Eberhard Jüngel and K.W. Müller (Tübingen: Mohr Siebeck, 1984), 183ff, 202: "I understand God by understanding myself anew." For a more thorough appraisal of Bultmann's position, see Konrad Stock, *Die Theorie der christlichen Gewißheit: Eine enzyklopädische Orientierung* (Tübingen: Mohr Siebeck, 2005), esp. 162ff; idem, *Die Gegenwart des Guten: Schriften zur Theologie*, Marburger theologische Studien 96 (Marburg: Elwert, 2006), 42ff.

myself." What is this element of the "other" that I encounter when I reach the utmost depth of my inner self? Is it not perhaps God?

What we seem to have before us here is what Calvin called "an awareness of divinity . . . by natural instinct," but in a form that accommodates modern concepts and sensibilities.[13] This, however, is actually a culturally domesticated natural certainty. Where Calvin saw a vague, ambivalent sense of reverence in the face of profoundly moving aesthetic powers, cosmic laws, and comprehensive social structures, the modern religious variant refers merely to the meager dialectic of empty self-consciousness.

Considerable portions of the theology, doctrine, and proclamation of the traditional mainline denominations in western industrialized nations have greatly extolled this form of abstract and empty "faith" and done much to disguise the religious banality and arbitrary accessibility of this sense of inner certainty. They adopted the assurance of philosophical idealism that precisely this sense of certainty constitutes the "ground" of self-consciousness, the key to all epistemological and moral value, and the true foundation of human personality, then surrounded this paltry form with all sorts of variations of the rhetoric of "wholeness" and "irreducibility." What we have before us here is not merely a more or less interesting function of consciousness, but the "core of the person," the final and irreducible "unity of the self," the fundamental unity of subjectivity itself! Theologically the assurance is generally that this innermost certainty derives "from the outside" and is received "by grace." But as the vehement disputes concerning the various reflective theories of self-consciousness show,[14] this fundamental dialectical relationship permits only an essentially unfounded, arbitrary choice between the predominance of the "active" or the "passive" side of the relation insofar as the two modes occur simultaneously in self-referential certainty. The frequently contentious debates over what allegedly is and ought to be the true and "correct" priority between giving and receiving, activity and passivity in this supposed relationship between God and the human individual resemble debates over whether the emperor's new clothes are black or white.

This analysis of the inner constitution of a distorted, typically modern

---

13. Cf. John Calvin, *Institutes of the Christian Religion: In Two Volumes*, ed. John T. McNeill, trans. Ford Lewis Battles, The Library of Christian Classics 20 (Louisville: Westminster John Knox Press, 1960), I. 3.1; Michael Welker, *Creation and Reality* (Fortress: Minneapolis, 1999), chap. 2.

14. Cf. Dieter Henrich, *Fichtes ursprüngliche Einsicht*, Wissenschaft und Gegenwart 34 (Frankfurt, 1967); idem, *Selbstverhältnisse* (see part 0.5, note 5); Michael Welker, *Der Vorgang Autonomie: Philosophische Beiträge zur Einsicht in theologischer Rezeption und Kritik* (Neukirchen-Vluyn: Neukirchener, 1975).

understanding of "faith" and its disappointing results should not, how-ever, mislead one to underestimate the power of this form of religious ex-perience, since it permits the unproblematic integration of religious and secular views of consciousness. It facilitates the instantaneous transition from religious to moral communication, from religious to epistemologi-cal or metaphysical speculation, and vice versa.[15] It endlessly engages the tension between fulfillment and alienation, between intimacy with one-self and the encounter with the wholly other, between utmost certainty and dialectical experience of difference. At the same time, it seems to bless the religious mentality as such with a universalistic aura by signal-ing the ongoing message that "in a concealed manner, a rational person cannot but be religious!" This assertion seems to secure the existence of an "incurably religious" and irrefutably "believing" nature within human beings.

Just as Calvin appreciated the power of the "natural instinct" of the divine—despite its vagueness and ambivalence—so also should the cul-tural power of the subjective "faith" described above be taken seriously. That said, one should also clearly point out that it systematically thwarts any genuinely substantive piety and both structurally and methodically drives such a believer into a position of religious speechlessness and an incapacity for communication. At least five mutually supportive factors allow this neo-Protestant, subjectivist "faith" to acquire the strength not only to distort the Christian faith, but also to systematically undermine and destroy it. The seemingly inexorable self-secularization of tradi-tional mainline churches in western industrialized nations, which in its own turn is generally followed by the self-banalization of religion,[16] is not least an ill-bred fruit of this neo-Protestant concept of "faith."

1. This neo-Protestant faith appears in the form of a mere **transcen-dental principle**. It does not present itself—as faith ought to do—as a form of experience that directly stimulates and invigorates the commu-nication of faith. This neo-Protestant faith individuates[17] and is sterile, though such is disguised by its universal accessibility.

---

15. Karl Rahner's mature work offers rich conceptual material for this complex of ideas. See *Foundations of Christian Faith: An Introduction to the Idea of Christianity* (New York: Crossroad, 1990), 24ff; see also Eilert Herms, *Offenbarung und Glaube: Zur Bildung des christlichen Lebens* (Tübingen: Mohr Siebeck, 1992), esp. 457ff.

16. See Michael Welker, "Selbst-Säkularisierung und Selbst-Banalisierung," *Brenn-punkt Gemeinde* 1/2001: *Gott-Ferne in und außerhalb der Gemeinde*, 15–21; Ingolf U. Dal-ferth, "'Was Gott ist, bestimme ich!' Reden von Gott im Zeitalter der 'Cafeteria-Religion,'" in *Heute von Gott reden*, ed. J. Beutler and E. Kunz (Würzburg: Echter, 1998), 57–77.

17. That is to say, precisely by separating individuals out, it does *not* strengthen them. The young Dietrich Bonhoeffer spoke of an "individualistic social atomism" (*Sanctorum*

2. Neo-Protestant faith appears as a necessarily **empty** religious form. It does not appear—as faith should—as a form of experience shaped by its content that *also* discloses that same content, a form that attains and promotes knowledge of God and in the light of that very knowledge then renders possible substantive knowledge of the self and of the communities, environments, and world that shape the self.

3. Neo-Protestant faith appears as unconditional, ultimate **certainty**. It is a self-sufficient secular-religious form. Although this "faith" can and must be repeatedly activated, it provides no regulative principle—as faith should—for advancing from mere certainty to the individual and communal search for truth and to the progressive disclosure of truth content.[18] It appears as if caught in the proverbial hamster wheel—moving ever forward without ever getting anywhere.

4. Neo-Protestant faith appears as a paradoxical, perpetually self-irritating, obstructing, and **neuroticizing** form in its combination of immediacy and negation (the wholly other is immediately, directly accessible, but is nonetheless still withdrawn). It does not promote—as faith should—the self-critical search for truth and the profound joy in the truth claims attaching to the knowledge of God, nor does it promote the glorification of God or the elation of those who are moved by faith and testify to it.

5. Neo-Protestant faith has an **escapist** quality to it. It fosters an inclination to withdraw from expressive, celebratory communicative forms of religious life or even works contrary to such forms—something faith neither should nor needs to do.

It has been both accurately and uneasily observed that the form of this faith's existence resembles what one experiences in a "house of mirrors."[19] A more sober description might perhaps speak of being captive in a quasi-religious state of consciousness that, as Hegel put it, confines a person "to its own self and its own petty actions, a personality brooding over itself, as wretched as it is impoverished."[20] The paltry,

---

Communio: A Theological Study of the Sociology of the Church, DBWE 1, 33; cf. also the note on 26f (DBW 1, 18, cf. 205ff).

18. See Michael Welker, "Bezwingende Gewissheit—Befreiende Wahrheit: Selbstgewissheit—Wahrheitsgewissheit—Glaubensgewissheit," in *Leben und Kirche: Festschrift Wilfried Härle*, ed. Uta Andrée, et al. (Marburg: Elwert, 2001), 107ff; Polkinghorne/Welker, *Faith in the Living God*, final chapter (see introduction, note 4).

19. Falk Wagner, "Religion der Moderne—Moderne der Religion," in *Religion als Thema der Theologie: Geschichte, Standpunkte und Perspektiven theologischer Religionskritik und Religionsbegründung*, ed. Wilhelm Gräb (Gütersloh: Gütersloher Verlag, 1999), 12–44, 26, 29.

20. Georg Wilhelm Friedrich Hegel, *Phenomenology of Spirit*, trans. A. V. Miller (Oxford: Clarendon, 1977), 136.

endless search for meaning associated with this religiosity is concealed with pompous rhetoric, its purpose allegedly being to leave "the wound of meaning open."[21] Jesus himself is represented as a transcendental petit-bourgeois whose life up until his death on the cross was allegedly a "search for his true self and thus for the absolute ground from whose perspective he could then know himself as this particular, specifically shaped individual."[22]

The theological instability and disorientation associated with this insinuation cannot be attributed simply to the initially Enlightenment, then ideological power with which transcendental "subjectivity" established itself as the characteristic feature of modernity.[23] We must examine a multifaceted blockade of theological knowledge if we are to understand why subjectivist faith was and is the form in which many Christians and not a few theologians have sought to take seriously and experience the christologically promised nearness of God. Although subjectivist faith can be criticized as a conceptually amorphous and theologically irresponsible accommodation of religiosity to modern popular philosophy, one must also recognize that a christologically confused situation made it extremely difficult to make comprehensible theological sense of the message of the imminent God in Jesus Christ.

- A general scholarly consensus arose during the second half of the twentieth century that was already being formulated in the nineteenth century, namely, that in reality we know next to nothing about the historical Jesus. The biblical texts largely offer "legendary glosses." As such, piety that takes its orientation from Jesus of Nazareth is naive and childish (see in this regard part 1).

- Resurrection is a theme for fundamentalists who, though knowing better, claim to be focusing on a numinous "counterreality": *credo quia absurdum*—I believe because it is nonsensical.[24] This assertion, however, is unacceptable for even moderately educated or cultivated people who are sincere in their search for truth (see in this regard part 2).

21. Wilhelm Gräb, *Sinn fürs Unendliche: Religion in der Mediengesellschaft* (Gütersloh: Gütersloher, 2002), 74f.

22. Wilhelm Gräb, "Kirche als Ort religiöser Deutungskultur: Erwägungen zum Zusammenhang von Kirche, Religion und individueller Lebensgeschichte," in *Gott im Selbstbewußtsein der Moderne: Zum neuzeitlichen Begriff der Religion*, ed. U. Barth/W. Gräb (Gütersloh: Gütersloher, 1993), 222–39, 233, 237.

23. Gunther Wenz, *Offenbarung: Problemhorizonte moderner evangelischer Theologie* (Göttingen: Vandenhoek, 2005), 7.

24. Although this statement is attributed to Tertullian, for him it refers only to Christ's death on the cross rather than to faith as such; cf. MPL 2, 806.

- The cross of Christ reveals to us the merciful God who shares human powerlessness and suffering. We are confronted with the obscure assertion that precisely in this self-abasement, God seeks not only to be near, but also to help us (see in this regard part 3).

- In its references to Jesus Christ's ascension and second coming in judgment, faith seems to lose contact with reality once and for all and with any notion of the nearness of God promised in the humanity of Jesus. Whoever continues to speak of "revelation" in this context has suspended all standards of honesty. Not only scholarly theology, but also educated common sense simply cannot follow along this path (see in this regard parts 4 and 5).

If we but consider this difficult christological situation, we can easily enough see how subjectivist faith has offered a ready and cogent solution for religiously inclined people who are yet intent on holding on to the notion of the immanent God.[25]

25. In connection with the papal conclave and the general discourse about the "return of religion," the magazine *Der Spiegel* questioned public figures about their "faith" (no. 33, 15 August 2005). It consistently encountered the notion of subjectivist faith, e.g., with the author Alexa Hennig von Lange: "I listen to my inner voice, pray, and clearly discern, comprehend, and consider myself" (141); and the movie director Caroline Link: "My faith in God or in a 'higher authority' has a great deal to do with my conscience, with values that I have probably internalized, and thus—naively—with the fact that it does matter to me that some authority or entity 'registers' when I act contrary to my own values" (144); and the musician and comedian, Helge Schneider: "I see myself as a rather small part of the universe and have God as a friend. He is a part of my life, and I have no need to fear him. I believe in fate, coincidence, and the unforeseeable. For me, all that is God" (146).

0.6 God Revealed: From the Subjectivist and Iconic Turns toward Multicontextual and Pneumatological Turns – The Presence of God in the History of Jesus, in the Spirit of the Resurrection of Christ, and in the Coming of His Reign

Large parts of the world, sometimes bewildered, sometimes taken aback, stand before the assertion "God revealed himself in Jesus Christ!" How can one actually believe that God can be encountered in a human being?! One might search for such a self-revelation of God in transcendence, in the numinous, in the fullness of meaning, in the highest being, in absolute omnipotence, perhaps even in substance, in being, in nature and history. God may well become tangible and accessible in all that can stand for the One, for the whole, for the first and the last or the highest. But God in Jesus Christ? Is this not an absurd notion?

For many, the disconcertment increases when it becomes clear that the statement "God revealed himself in Jesus Christ" is a *confession* expressing the central content and indeed the very foundation of Christian faith. With this confession of the revealed God, Christians clearly distinguish themselves from other religious convictions and traditions. Here they are articulating what is typical of and characterizes the Christian faith, to which at the beginning of the third millennium more than two billion people belong—a third of the world's population.

"God revealed himself in Jesus Christ." This statement is also a *proclamation* and "gospel" for the Christian faith, that is to say, a joyful, liberating, uplifting message. It speaks of a momentous event that seeks to touch the hearts of human beings, to strengthen their consciences, to invigorate their spirits, indeed to animate, secure, and elevate their entire lives. With this self-revelation of God in Jesus Christ, God is intent on approaching intimately close to humans, on awakening their faith and trust and giving orientation, shape, and grounding to both their individual and communal lives, and on bringing them into eternal community with God. But are these anything more than grandiose words, mere assurances, at best pious wishes and at worst an "opiate for the people"? Does this foundational expression of Christian faith, its confession and proclamation, lend itself to critical examination and conceptual articulation and understanding?

To answer these questions, one must engage in *theology*, in the self-examination of Christian faith. Such theological self-examination comes about by way of reflection that is accountable not only within the realm of the church, but also that of scholarly and public discourses,

48

or, to put it in a modern way, before the tribunal of universal human reason.[1] In focusing on this one sentence, "God revealed himself in Jesus Christ!" we enter the theological discipline of *Christology*, the doctrine of Jesus Christ, and closely related disciplines such as ecclesiology, the doctrine of the church, and pneumatology, the doctrine of the Holy Spirit.

Theologically reflective faith in the living God seeks understanding. In the faith awakened by revelation, people can and should become *familiar with and close to the living God* in the same, open way they become familiar with another person or a story. An expansive province of memory, experience, and expectation is disclosed to those who focus on God in faith, for they realize that God is not simply an "ultimate thought," a mere idea, or a metaphysical entity that can be appropriated in any conceptually definitive fashion.

Archimedes, the great mathematician of antiquity, is attributed with saying, "Give me a fixed point where I can stand, and I will move the earth!" Philosophy and religiosity have time and again sought precisely such an unshakable "Archimedean point." The revelation that discloses God's affection and faithfulness to humans, however, cannot be adequately articulated by the notion of a "fixed point," an "ultimate thought," or an innermost or ultimate counterpart conceived as a point of reference.

"Subjectivist faith" (see part 0.5) seems to overcome this problem in a splendid fashion by associating its seemingly divine inner counterpart with the entire breadth of its own consciousness. On the one hand, subjectivist faith thus appears as highly concentrated, focusing as it does on its innermost self-consciousness, the core of the "I." On the other hand, this concentration is accompanied by a "consciousness of the *infinity of the consciousness*," as Ludwig Feuerbach clearly saw.[2] Nor is this consciousness simply a chimera, for we do, after all, consistently experience that our consciousness can be expanded and extended insofar as memory and imagination can present ever new content to our mind's eye. At the same time, we believe that the contents of consciousness that we connect with "reality" and "truth" can potentially be "shared" with us by all other people. This is why—thus Feuerbach's explanation—we feel connected with the entire human race via our self-consciousness and consciousness.[3]

These observations can be interpreted from either a believing or an

---

1. Cf. Barth, *CD I/1*, 1ff (see part 0.5, note 6).
2. Feuerbach, *Essence of Christianity*, 2f (see part 0.4, note 33).
3. Cf. ibid., 2.

atheistic perspective. Feuerbach followed the latter. For him, the infinitude of religion is nothing more than the infinitude of consciousness, a position, however, that ultimately declares that very consciousness to be a transcendent counterpart:

> And so far as *thy nature* reaches, so far reaches thy *unlimited self-consciousness*, so far *art thou God* . . . It follows that if thou *thinkest* the infinite, thou perceivest and affirmest the *infinitude of the power of thought*; if thou feelest the infinite, thou feelest and affirmest the *infinitude of the power of feeling.*[4]

By contrast, a believing interpretation is able to associate the experience of the astonishing breadth of consciousness and the feeling of being simultaneously inwardly focused with the proximity of the divine. This "proximity of God" seems to many people to be considerably more persuasive than the revelation of God in Jesus Christ. Over and against this, serious Christian faith sooner seems lacking, for after all, when it speaks of revelation, it is referring to a

> reality which is very insignificant-looking and outwardly most unpromising; it speaks quite simply of a single concrete fact in the midst of the numberless host of facts and the vast stream of historical events, it speaks of a single human person living in the age of the Roman empire: it speaks of *Jesus Christ*. When the Christian language speaks of God it does so not on the basis of some speculation or other, but looking at this fact, this story, this person.[5]

From the perspective of this fact, this story, and this person, Christian faith takes the liberty of regarding the entire, truly impressive depth and breadth of human consciousness—taken in and for itself—as being *not* particularly illuminating or informative with respect to knowledge of God, i.e., theologically. Although our seemingly infinite consciousness is indeed capable of producing astonishing feats of memory and imagination, it can also turn into a veritable rubbish dump of the spirit or even a psychological torture chamber, and its well-being, moreover, is largely dependent on a steadfast heart, on an at least somewhat pacified conscience and clear mind, and on other intellectual parameters.

Feuerbach's bold claim that the "consciousness of God is [human] self-consciousness, knowledge of God is self-knowledge,"[6] corresponds

---

4. Ibid, 8f, emphasis mine.

5. Karl Barth, "The Christian Understanding of Revelation," in *Against the Stream: Shorter Post-War Writings 1946–52*, trans. Stanley Godman (London: SCM Press, Ltd, 1954), 211, emphasis in German text.

6. Feuerbach, *Essence of Christianity*, 12 (see part 0.4, note 33).

to the abstract-existential "God" of subjectivist faith. When one prays to this God, one is actually speaking only with oneself. This God is nothing but a moderately impressive idol. Karl Barth accurately reiterated insights from Hans Ehrenberg's edition of Feuerbach's *Grundsätze der Philosophie der Zukunft*:[7]

> [Feuerbach,] "as a true child of his century" . . . was a man who "did not know (*Nichtkenner*) death" and who "misunderstood (*Verkenner*) evil." Truly any man who knew that we human beings are evil from head to foot, and who bore in mind that we all die, would know that the illusion of all illusions is the notion that the being of God is the being of man. Even if he held the good God to be a dream he would certainly leave him free of any identification with such as we.[8]

Feuerbach fails to recognize the personal loneliness of the human being who suffers under the power of sin and death, fails to see our inability to definitively address this personal loneliness in our fellow human beings, and fails to see that we perpetually force one another, intentionally or not, precisely into the isolation of such personal loneliness rather than mutually liberating one another from it. In short, Feuerbach's conviction that human beings could become God to one another and that this is the mystery of religion is clearly an illusion.

Still, this criticism of the subjective or subjectivist turn in religiosity does not yet alleviate the discomfiture accompanying the focus on revelation in the form of "a single human person living in the age of the Roman Empire."[9] Christology must clarify how the creative God has revealed himself in the power of the divine Spirit in Jesus Christ, in this person and this story. How does God, from within this life whose earthly dimension is long past, continue to reveal himself in the power of the divine Spirit and in the coming of the divine reign and thereby to seize, keep, save, and elevate human life? This is why it is imperative to replace the "subjectivist turn" with a "pneumatological turn." It has to be shown how the *human* spirit becomes capable of knowledge of God precisely through God's Spirit, revelation, and Word even though according to the apostle Paul it can but groan or speak in incomprehensible tongues before God[10] (see part 2.5 concerning the crucial distinction between the Spirit of God

---

7. Ludwig Feuerbach, *Grundsätze der Philosophie der Zukunft*, 1843, ed. Hans Ehrenberg, Frommanns philosophische Taschenbücher (Stuttgart: Frommann, 1922); cf. Welker, *Theologische Profile*, 157–81 (see part 0.2, note 12).

8. Karl Barth, "Ludwig Feuerbach," in *Theology and the Church: Shorter Writings 1920–1928*, trans. Louise Pettibone Smith (New York: Harper & Row, 1962), 235.

9. Barth, "Revelation," 211 (see part 0.6, note 5).

10. Cf. Rom 8:26; 1 Cor 14:2.

and the human spirit, not to mention the reduction to consciousness and self-consciousness).

In this context, a certain skepticism must also be adopted toward the still considerably admired "iconic turn" that has been proposed as the grand replacement for the "subjectivist turn" and for other cultural fashions. The evocation of the "return of imagery"[11] and the "omnipresence of imagery" affirms a contextual aestheticization that reinforces the individual's position as a reactive spectator in a culture dominated by visual media. Similarly, one should not simply accept uncritically the demands that an excessively intellectualized theology and joyless piety, as popular clichés have it, ought to better utilize the "iconic turn" and its visually aesthetic treasures. It is certainly true that for two thousand years, the "iconic presence" of Jesus Christ has lost none of its emotional appeal, particularly in images of the manger and the cross. When this iconic presence is combined with the message of the "suffering God" who entered into the poverty and wretchedness of human existence, it is surrounded by a theological aura that resonates considerably with God's revelation. Yet it constricts the view, referring as it does *only* to the life of the pre-Easter Jesus, where the manger and the cross mark *only* its beginning and end. Even in this, its most powerful form, the regnant iconic presence of Jesus obstructs both one's attention and sensibility for the enormous richness of his presence in the power of the Spirit (see parts 4 and 5).

The writings, sermons, and catechisms of the reformers positioned the believing individual quite firmly in the center. "*I* believe . . . that God has created *me* . . . ," "*I* believe that by my own understanding or strength *I* cannot believe in Jesus Christ *my* LORD or come to him;"[12] "What is your only comfort, in life and in death? . . . That *I* belong—body and soul, in life and in death—not to *myself* but to *my* faithful Savior, Jesus Christ."[13] This Reformation focus on the believing individual provided many followers of subjectivist faith with a point of departure for their religious options. It is, however, not merely this close affiliation of the believer with his/her "Lord and Savior Jesus Christ" that is striking in these and countless other Reformation-era confessional texts. It also becomes quite clear that God creatively preserves, saves, and elevates the

---

11. Gottfried Boehm, "Die Wiederkehr der Bilder," in *Was ist ein Bild?* ed. Gottfried Boehm (Munich: Fink, 1994), 11ff; cf. *Iconic Turn: Die neue Macht der Bilder*, ed. Christa Maar and Hubert Burda (Cologne: DuMont, 2004), esp. 15ff, 216ff, 323ff.

12. Luther, Small Catechism, *Book of Concord*, 355 (see the introduction, note 2).

13. Question 1, *The Heidelberg Catechism* (Boston: United Church Press), 9 (emphasis mine).

believing individual "together with all that exists," and that through the Holy Spirit, God "calls, gathers, enlightens, and makes holy [me . . . and] the whole Christian church."[14] It is confessed that "not only to others, but to me also God has given the forgiveness of sins, everlasting righteousness and salvation."[15]

This indispensable connection with the polyphony of the life of creation and the multicontextuality of "the whole Christian church" has to be explicitly taken into consideration if "the believing self" is to perceive revelation in an undistorted way and to grasp his/her "own self" in both its real and religious dimensions in a fashion that does justice to both. As Bonhoeffer clearly observed (cf. part 0.3), faith in the resurrected and exalted Jesus Christ both enables and compels us to engage in consistently multiperspectival and multicontextual perception. The life of the historical Jesus already requires a multicontextual perception (see part 1.4). Indeed, the life of the resurrected one, who constitutes his post-Easter body through the various gifts of the Spirit and in the creative interplay of its members in order to make his presence known in this world, simply cannot be grasped without a multicontextual approach. Similarly, the Spirit of God, which embraces men and women, young and old, servants and maids, but explicitly also people of different nations, cultures, and languages through its "outpouring," can be discerned in a theologically appropriate way only within a "multicontextual turn."[16] Such is not to be confused with the currently popular discourse concerning how we live in "pluralistic societies," how "plurality" is increasing, how we are involved in "processes of pluralization," and how these vague pluralizations do not spare even religion or the church.

In order to engage the "multicontextual" and "pneumatological" turns theologically, we will have to counter "soft postmodernism," diffuse enthusiasm for vague "plurality," and an "anything goes" mentality. Although the power of the divine Spirit and the reign of the resurrected Christ are indeed enormously expansive and far-reaching, they do nonetheless have clear contours. Because for Christian faith and Christian theology these contours become clear as soon as the Spirit of God and God's reign are perceived as the Spirit and reign of Jesus Christ, we may spare no efforts in seeking and articulating knowledge of revelation (see parts 4 and 5). The statement in the Gospel of John, "In my father's house are many rooms" (John 14:2), is an expression of God's far-reaching in-

---

14. Luther, Small Catechism, *Book of Concord*, 354, 355 (see the introduction, note 2).

15. Question 21, *The Heidelberg Catechism*, 27.

16. Cf. Michael Welker, *God the Spirit*, trans. John F. Hoffmeyer (Minneapolis: Fortress Press, 1992), 222ff, 228ff concerning the outpouring of the Spirit.

vitation. This invitation does not necessarily have its boundaries where some churches—to wit, those inclined to administer salvation monopolistically—draw them (see parts 4.4 and 5.5). Just as little, however, does it mean that every self-made religious home has already been erected in the reign of God.

PART 1

The Historical Jesus

1.1 "Excavating Jesus!"? – Approaches to the "Third Quest" for the Historical Jesus: Archaeology, Textual Archaeology, Archaeologism (Charlesworth, Crossan, Reed)

Serious academics do not doubt that Jesus actually lived. Klaus Berger summarizes why skepticism is largely unwarranted:

> For the following reasons, it is highly probable that Jesus lived: there are four fully preserved biographies of his life (the Gospels) along with an array of biographical fragments. . . . No other figure from antiquity is as well represented in this regard. Moreover, not only do ten other theological authors in the New Testament refer to Jesus quite apart from the Gospels, most independently from one another . . . [he is] also mentioned by outside sources.[1]

Berger cites the Roman historians Suetonius[2] and Tacitus,[3] the Syrian Mara bar Serapion,[4] the Jewish historian Flavius Josephus,[5] and other early sources. We have references to Jesus in a variety of languag-

---

1. Klaus Berger, *Wer war Jesus wirklich?* (Stuttgart: Quell, 1995), 21f; cf. 21ff.

2. Caius Suetonius, *Lives of the Caesars*, trans. Catherine Edwards (Oxford: Oxford University Press, 2000), 25. The biographies appeared ca. 121 C.E.

3. Claudius Tacitus, "The Annals 15:38–45," in *The Annals & the Histories*, ed. Moses Hadas, trans. Alfred John Church and William Jackson Brodribb (New York: The Modern Library, 2003), 324–28 (concerning the burning of Rome during Nero's reign in the year 64).

4. William Cureton, *Spicilegium Syriacum: Containing Remains of Bardesan, Meliton, Ambrose, and Mara Bar Serapion* (London: F. and J. Rivington, 1855), 70–77. Cf. also F. Schulhess, *Der Brief des Mara bar Serapion*, ZDMG 51 (1897), 365–91.

5. *Judean antiquities*, vols. I-III, trans. and commentary Louis H. Feldman, Paul Spilsbury, and Christopher Begg (Leiden; Boston; Köln: Brill, 2000-2005) [*Antiquitates Judaicae*, from the year 93, section 18, 63f (though with disputed authenticity), and section 20, 200]. See in this regard Gerd Theissen and Annette Merz, *The Historical Jesus: A Comprehensive Guide*, trans. John Bowden (London: SCM Press, 1998), 64ff.

es, from non-Jewish and non-Christian authors as well, at least one of whom—Thallos[6]—was almost contemporaneous to Jesus. Robert Van Voorst draws attention to the wide spectrum of attitudes toward Jesus among the earliest of extrabiblical witnesses: "These writers have a range of opinion: from those perhaps sympathetic to Christ (Mara); through those moderately hostile (Pliny) and those fully hostile, but descriptive (Tacitus, Suetonius); to those not interested in description but who vigorously attack Christianity and in the process attack Christ (Lucian and Celsus)."[7] This broad distribution of witnesses offers a good basis for concluding that we are indeed dealing with historical objectivity.

And yet despite the evidence that Jesus did indeed live,[8] theological research in the twentieth century long operated on the assumption that we are unable to approach the historical Jesus because—as was argued—in the biblical texts we encounter him only in so-called "legendary glosses." He is allegedly embedded in such a variety of hopes for salvation and redemption that we are no longer capable—thus the conclusion—of discerning the historical Jesus. This situation changed dramatically in the last quarter of the twentieth century, when the Jesus quest underwent a complete paradigm shift,[9] one that within the history of theological and scientific scholarship went by the name "'third quest' for the historical Jesus."[10] What had happened?

Irrefutable archaeological findings initiated this reversal in the Jesus quest's skepticism. This "archaeological turn" was accompanied by broad interest in witnesses to Jesus outside the canonical biblical tradition.[11]

6. See Theissen/Merz, *The Historical Jesus*, 84f.

7. Robert E. Van Voorst, *Jesus Outside the New Testament: An Introduction to the Ancient Evidence* (Grand Rapids: Eerdmans, 2000), 68.

8. Rudolf Bultmann: "Das Entscheidende ist schlechthin das 'Daß'" ("What is decisive is simply the 'that'"), in "Das Verhältnis der urchristlichen Christusbotschaft zum historischen Jesus," *Sitzungsberichte der Heidelberger Akademie der Wissenschaften, Philosophische Klasse, 1960*, 3rd paper, 9f.

9. See Thomas S. Kuhn, *The Structure of Scientific Revolutions*, 2nd ed. (Chicago: University of Chicago Press, 1970), esp. 92ff. Paradigm shifts follow the realization that the current epistemological level is insufficient and must be replaced, even if previously stabilized by a broad consensus. The Copernican revolution, the success of Kant's transcendental philosophy, and the replacement of the Newtonian conception of the universe by Einstein's theory of relativity are all textbook examples of paradigm shifts.

10. See scholarship as early as Stephen Neill and Tom Wright, *The Interpretation of the New Testament 1861–1986*, 2nd ed. (New York: Oxford University Press, 1988), 379ff; only seven years later, a broad typology for the new direction of the "third quest" was laid out in Ben Witherington III, *The Jesus Quest: The Third Search for the Jew of Nazareth*, 2nd ed. (Downers Grove: Intervarsity Press, 1997).

11. Such includes various newly discovered Old Testament pseudepigraphies, reassessed Qumran texts, Nag-Hammadi codices, and Arabic translations of Josephus that

Its theological breakthrough was facilitated when scholars recognized that the confession of Jesus's divinity spread very soon after his death ("Jesus Christ is lord, he is *kyrios!*"), as well as by a "socio-historical turn" and various other factors (see part 1.3). The following discussion will examine the archaeological turn separately first in order to illuminate its indisputable relevance, its strengths, and its limitations.

Over the past several years, James Charlesworth, Jonathan Reed, and others have been documenting the findings with relevance for the Jesus quest.[12] I will mention but a few of the archaeological discoveries that allegedly have brought the Palestine of Jesus's day considerably nearer to us and, along with it, the Jesus of history.

1. Archaeological excavations have shown that first-century Jerusalem was quite cosmopolitan. The widespread impression that Israel was relatively isolated is false. Excavations have unearthed a hippodrome, sports complexes, and theaters. Most importantly, countless inscriptions in Greek, Aramaic, Latin, and Hebrew have been discovered in and around Jerusalem, a diversity of languages that helps explain the speech event at Pentecost (Acts 2:9–11). Inscriptions also, however, offer evidence for various political figures mentioned in the biblical texts, e.g., Pilate and Quirinius—who was very likely the governor mentioned in Luke's birth narrative (Luke 2:2).[13]

2. Somewhat more risky, but not irrelevant or entirely implausible, is the suspicion that what was possibly the house of Simon Peter and his mother-in-law has been excavated next to the Capernaum synagogue and directly on the shore—a house that Jesus himself may have visited: "As soon as he left the synagogue, he entered the house of Simon," where he healed "Simon's mother-in-law" (Mark 1:29; cf. Luke 4:38f).[14]

3. Archaeological excavations at the Temple Mount make it possible to understand how Jesus's opposition to commerce in the Temple and what is known as the cleansing of the Temple might have transpired.

---

facilitate a more nuanced understanding of Jesus's cultural, ideological, and religious environment.

12. James Charlesworth, *Jesus Within Judaism: New Light from Exciting Archaeological Discoveries* (New York: Doubleday, 1988); Jonathan L. Reed, *Archaeology and the Galilean Jesus: A Re-examination of the Evidence* (Harrisburg: Trinity, 2000); James Charlesworth, "Hat die Archäologie Bedeutung für die Jesus-Forschung?" *EvTh* 68 (2008), 246–65.

13. Cf. Charlesworth, *Jesus Within Judaism*, 104ff; concerning the following, see ibid., 109ff.

14. Reed, *Archaeology*, 157ff (see part 1.1, note 12).

Formerly, we thought that Jesus may have "cleansed" the Temple, but that the mention of "oxen" and "sheep" by the author of John (John 2:14) was simply another clue that the Fourth Evangelist was ignorant of Jerusalem. This impression and evaluation may now be disproved. . . . a passageway . . . from the Double Gates, to the so-called Solomonic Stables has now apparently been discovered. Formerly, we knew that the latter held stalls for large animals in Herodian times, but no connection with the Temple could be found. It is now clear that large animals could easily have been led from these stalls (which still reveal niches in which large animals were tethered) to the halls of money changers.

From the straw bedding or tethers accompanying such large animals, Jesus could easily have fashioned a whip, as the evangelist John states . . . (John 2:15).[15]

Charlesworth evaluates the evidence cautiously, not taking the spatial precision of John's description as a guarantee for his temporal precision in the positioning of this story within Jesus's ministry, viewing the Synoptic dating of the so-called Temple cleansing in the time *preceding* Jesus's condemnation as more probable than John, who placed it at the beginning of Jesus's ministry. Still, these archaeological findings do close a gap in our understanding.

4. The archaeological discoveries of two pools with five porticoes behind the Sheep or Lion's Gate are similarly relevant to the Jesus quest. Prior to these finds, John's references to the Bethesda pools near the Sheep's Gate (John 5:2–9) were dismissed as "allegorical theology." Now it appears that the Gospel of John's spatial details, previously contested, are observably consistent with the conditions of his day.[16]

5. According to Charlesworth, further excavations can selectively, but still strikingly improve our understanding of the Passion story. The course of the original Via Dolorosa, which differs from today's route, can be retraced. We can open up meaningful discussions about the location of the crucifixion, and similarly for the location of Herodium and various synagogues where Jesus may have taught.

6. Ongoing excavations not only in Jerusalem, but also in Nazareth, Cana, Bethsaida, and other locations, improve—albeit often only in extremely small increments—our understanding of the setting of Jesus's ministry. Above all, it becomes trenchantly clear that Jesus's Galilee was not characterized exclusively by villages and agriculture, a fact that challenges us to review some of the prevalent images of Jesus. The depiction in earlier European bedroom pictures of the "Good Shepherd" roaming

15. Charlesworth, *Jesus Within Judaism*, 117, cf. 117ff (see part 1.1, note 12).
16. Charlesworth, *Jesus Within Judaism*, 119f.

from village to village is at the very least an extremely one-sided representation.

The success of archaeology in the physical realm has prompted what may be called an archaeology of texts—or textual archaeology—that in its own turn has yielded striking results. First and foremost, John Dominic Crossan has rigorously engaged in textual archaeology in two successful books.[17]

Crossan begins with the confusing fact that in the two decades preceding his own publications on Jesus, six respected New Testament scholars presented seven different versions of Jesus:[18] Samuel George Frederick Brandon—Jesus, the political revolutionary;[19] Morton Smith—Jesus, the magician;[20] Geza Vermes—Jesus, the Galilean charismatic;[21] Bruce Chilton—Jesus, the Galilean rabbi;[22] Harvey Falk—Jesus, the proto-Pharisee, or Jesus, the Essene;[23] and Ed Parish Sanders—Jesus, the eschatological prophet.[24] In response, Crossan seeks an objective entry point into Jesus's life capable of overcoming the uncertainty implied in these diverse roles. He describes his approach as a "triple triadic process"[25] that engages three levels of observation: socio-anthropological, historical, and literary.

First, a culturally and temporally comprehensive social anthropology should offer orientation on a *macrocosmic level*. A social and cultural anthropology focused on the Mediterranean region should identify characteristic features of ancient Mediterranean society, paying particular attention to the *Pax Romana* and the related unrest and conflict in the

---

17. John Dominic Crossan, *The Historical Jesus: The Life of a Mediterranean Jewish Peasant* (San Francisco: Harper, 1992); idem, *Jesus: A Revolutionary Biography* (San Francisco: Harper, 1995).

18. Cf. Crossan, *The Historical Jesus*, xxvii. For German research in this area, cf. Martin Karrer, *Jesus Christus im Neuen Testament*, NTD Ergänzungsreihe 11 (Göttingen: Vandenhoeck, 1998), 176ff.

19. S.G.F. Brandon, *Jesus and the Zealots: Study of the Political Factor in Primitive Christianity* (New York: Scribner's, 1967).

20. Morton Smith, *Jesus the Magician* (New York: Harper, 1978).

21. Geza Vermes, *Jesus the Jew: A Historian's Reading of the Gospels* (London: SCM Press, 1983); idem, *Jesus and the World of Judaism* (Philadelphia: Fortress, 1984).

22. Bruce Chilton, *A Galilean Rabbi and His Bible: Jesus' Use of the Interpreted Scripture of His Time* (Wilmington: Glazier, 1984).

23. Harvey Falk, *Jesus the Pharisee: A New Look at the Jewishness of Jesus* (New York: Paulist, 1985).

24. E.P. Sanders, *Jesus and Judaism*, 3rd ed. (London: SCM Press, 1991).

25. Crossan, *The Historical Jesus*, xxviii (see part 1.1, note 17); concerning the following, cf. Cilliers Breytenbach, "Jesusforschung: 1990-1995. Neuere Gesamtdarstellungen in deutscher Sprache," *Berliner Theologische Zeitschrift* 12 (1995), no. 2: Neutestamentliche Forschung, 232ff.

provinces under Roman rule. As far as Jesus and his environment are concerned, Crossan is particularly interested in the implications of the social stratification between the upper classes and the slaves in the agrarian society at the time. Second, the *mesocosmic level* draws on historical traditions—particularly Hellenistic and Greco-Roman history around the beginning of the common era. The third, or *microcosmic level*, examines the literary traditions directly relevant to Jesus.

Crossan similarly engages the microcosmic level in an extremely broad and differentiated fashion. Attempts to get closer to the historical Jesus should not rely exclusively on the four canonical Gospels, which are the accumulated result of lengthy transmission traditions. Crossan instead distinguishes four temporal strata divided according to the following periods: between 30 and 60, between 60 and 80, between 80 and 120, and between 120 and 150 C.E.[26]

The first stratum includes Jesus's words in the authentic Pauline letters and in several apocryphal (biblically proximate but not canonical) gospels, among which are reckoned the oldest stratum of the Coptic Gospel of Thomas, the Gospel of the Hebrews (not to be confused with the Letter to the Hebrews), the Egerton Gospel, and other fragmentary and reconstructed texts.[27] The second level includes the Gospel of Mark, the Letter to the Colossians, and again several apocryphal gospels: the Gospel of the Egyptians, fragments of the secret Gospel of Mark, the Dialogue of the Savior from Nag Hammadi, and others. It is only to the third stratum that Matthew, Luke, John, and several of the remaining New Testament writings are assigned, though also some of the earlier writings of the apostolic fathers. The fourth stratum includes the Acts of the Apostles, the letters of Timothy and Peter, and yet another group of apocryphal texts.[28]

Following this arrangement of texts, Crossan examines which accounts and references to Jesus in mutually *independent* versions are attested in *multiple* instances. He finds that of 522 analyzed textual elements, 33 occur more than three times, 42 exactly three times, and 105 at least twice. The 342 pericopes appearing but once are thus initially disregarded even though the group includes texts as theologically significant and influential as the Sermon on the Mount and the parable of the Good Samaritan. For the reconstruction of the life and ministry of the

26. Cf. Crossan, *The Historical Jesus*, esp. 427–50.

27. See Wilhelm Schneemelcher, *New Testament Apocrypha*, ed. R. McL. Wilson, trans. A. J. B. Higgins et al., 2 vols. (Philadelphia: Westminster Press, 1965). One might mention in passing that Crossan's selection and dating has prompted some critical scholarly debate.

28. Cf. Crossan, *The Historical Jesus*, xxxi-xxxiv and 427–50 (see part 1.1, note 17).

historical Jesus, Crossan assigns greatest significance to texts attested in multiple witnesses within the earliest stratum. Interestingly, this group includes the invitation, "Let the little children come to me; do not stop them; for it is to such as these that the kingdom of God belongs."[29]

Working from this approach, Crossan depicts a Jesus who comes from a relatively uneducated stratum of society but not from the lowest class of slaves or the needy poor. He also shows a Jesus who persistently supports changing the two basic structures of ancient society—familial and political relationships. By taking on social outcasts in healing the sick and communal dining, Jesus prompts a subtle, incremental reform of society. Old and young, women and men, pure and impure, slaveholders and slaves coalesce into a new community. The Jesus movement, which issues in a dynamic rural community development, Crossan views as a rural analogy to the urban phenomenon of itinerant Cynic philosophers.[30] In the combination of his astonishing healings among his fellow human beings, his communal meals, and even his symbolic mass "feedings," Jesus practiced "a religious and economic egalitarianism that negated alike and at once the hierarchical and patronal normalcies of Jewish religion and Roman power." He was not simply the "new broker of a new God"; instead, his parables, healings, and communal meals were to "force individuals into unmediated physical and spiritual contact with God and unmediated physical and spiritual contact with one another," functioning thus as a power that slowly and unremittingly transformed the Jewish and even Greco-Roman culture with all their military strength and imperial ambitions.[31]

Just as with archaeological excavations, such textual archaeology unequivocally yields interesting and wholly plausible conclusions. The historical Jesus understands, embraces, and concretely satisfies basic human needs—food, health, and social acceptance. At the same time, however, he questions contemporary iterations of the basic familial and political structures of ancient society, critically examining power relationships within the family by siding with women and children, on the

---

29. Mark 10:13–16; Matt 19:13–15; Luke 18:15–17; see also Mark 9:36f par.; cf. Crossan, *The Historical Jesus*, 266–69.

30. Crossan, *The Historical Jesus*, 421f; idem, *A Revolutionary Biography*, 114–22 (see part 1.1, note 17); Burton L. Mack pointedly represents the theory of Jesus the Cynic in *The Lost Gospel: The Book of Q and Christian Origins* (San Franscisco: Harper, 1993); idem, *Who Wrote the New Testament? The Making of the Christian Myth* (San Francisco: Harper, 1995). The Cynics were followers of a philosophical school that can be traced back to Antisthenes, a student of Socrates, and Diogenes of Sinope. They reacted with open criticism and derision to traditional customs and laws.

31. Crossan, *A Revolutionary Biography*, 198.

one hand, and questioning political dynamics, on the other. His preaching and ministry address social outcasts, simultaneously liberating and elevating them. He contrasts existing domestic and political authority structures with open table fellowship that accepts sinners and tax collectors alike and yet simultaneously questions regnant authority dynamics at such meals and in conversation. Jesus's preaching speaks of the coming kingdom of God, but *not* as an otherworldly reality. By addressing wholly basic human needs such as health, nutrition, and coexistence in freedom, this proclamation articulates an "emerging practice of divine authority from below" that both undermines and transforms regnant authority structures. Thus the image of the preaching and activity of the earthly Jesus that John Dominic Crossan reconstructs.

Crossan has indisputably identified several foundational features of Jesus's life and ministry, vividly evoking a neighbor-focused ethos characterized by concrete person-to-person encounters and convivial forms of communication. Although he also impressively connects this conceptual world with biblical and extrabiblical witnesses (see in this regard esp. parts 4.3 and 4.4), more complex social, political, historical, religious, and eschatological constellations in the life and ministry of Jesus and the resurrected Christ are only vaguely articulated and sooner recede within the larger picture (by contrast, see parts 1.3, 2.4 and parts 4 and 5).

The sensational but problematic *reductionism* of this approach becomes especially obvious in the title and goals of the book, *Excavating Jesus: Beneath the Stones, Behind the Texts.*[32] The authors, Crossan and Reed, are fascinated by the excavation and restoration of a boat from the first century C.E. discovered in the Sea of Galilee in 1986,[33] a boat allegedly allowing for the reconstruction of "the world of fishers and craftsmen at the time of Jesus." They repeatedly stress that archaeology can "excavate Jesus"—especially with the help of the insights conveyed by this boat, and that archaeology must now fill out "as completely as possible" the social world in which Jesus ministered.[34] This orientation

---

32. John Dominic Crossan and Jonathan L. Reed, *Excavating Jesus: Beneath the Stones, Behind the Texts* (San Francisco: Harper, 2001).

33. On display in the Yigal Allon Museum (3.5 miles north of Tiberias on the Sea of Galilee).

34. "Yes, you can excavate Jesus from that boat, but very, very carefully and only within the realities of antiquity's elite-controlled economies rather than in modernity's conceptions of entrepreneurial possibilities.... Archaeology excavates and can excavate Jesus not just by digging up where he lived and traveled, but by filling out as completely as possible the social world in which he operated," in Crossan/Reed, *Excavating Jesus*, xvii (see part 1.1, note 32).

signals a simultaneous turn toward both enthusiasm and naïveté. Here archaeological and what we have been calling "textual-archaeological" enthusiasm turns particularly clearly into an "archaeologism" that reduces Jesus's ministry to dietary, healing, and community-focused contributions and a commensurately organized movement. This archaeologism is just as problematic as the other extreme of historical skepticism, which the "*third quest* for the historical Jesus" tried to overcome, skepticism found in the phase of New Testament research that has come to be called the "*second quest* for the historical Jesus" (previously also known as "the new quest"). Let us look first, however, to the "*first quest* for the historical Jesus" in order to understand the source of the Jesus quest's enduring scholarly paralysis.

1.2 Jesus "Only in Legends!"? The "First" and "Second Quest" for the Historical Jesus (Schweitzer, Käsemann, Bornkamm)

"No one is any longer in the position to write a life of Jesus." The Heidelberg New Testament scholar Günther Bornkamm, a representative of the "second quest for the historical Jesus," began his successful 1956 book with this sentence articulating an enduring consensus in New Testament scholarship.[1] Bornkamm spoke of a "completely hopeless position" arising from the fact that no "mathematical certainty" could be attained "in the exposition of a bare history of Jesus, unembellished by faith." The extent to which scholarship during this period was permeated by excessively positivistic conceptions of historical objectivity and even "mathematical certainty" in historical matters is evident in the following excerpt:

> We possess no single word of Jesus and no single story of Jesus, no matter how incontestably genuine they may be, which do not contain at the same time the confession of the believing congregation or at least are embedded therein. This makes the search after the bare facts of history difficult and to a large extent futile.[2]

Albert Schweitzer's classic work, *The Quest of the Historical Jesus*,[3] marked the end of the lengthy "first quest" for the historical Jesus and paved the way for this scholarly consensus. According to Bornkamm, Schweitzer's work "has erected its memorial [to research on the life of Jesus], but at the same time has delivered its funeral oration."[4] His eulogy can be heard in his almost resigned "Conclusion," which remarks that the Jesus quest "set out in quest of the historical Jesus, believing that when it had found him it could bring him straight into our time as a teacher and saviour. . . . But he did not stay; he passed by our time

---

1. Günther Bornkamm, *Jesus of Nazareth*, trans. Irene McLuskey, Fraser McLuskey, and James M. Robinson (New York: Harper & Brothers, 1960), 13. Cf. Rudolf Bultmann, *Jesus and the Word*, trans. Louise Pettibone Smith and Erminie Huntress Lantero (New York: Scribner & Sons, 1958), 8: "I do indeed think that we can now know almost nothing concerning the life and personality of Jesus, since the early Christian sources show no interest in either, are moreover fragmentary and often legendary; and other sources about Jesus do not exist."

2. Bornkamm, *Jesus of Nazareth*, 14.

3. Albert Schweitzer, *The Quest of the Historical Jesus*, first published 1906, 1st Fortress Press ed., ed. John Bowden, trans. W. Montgomery and J.R. Coates (Minneapolis: Fortress Press, 2001).

4. Bornkamm, *Jesus of Nazareth*, 13 (see part 1.2, note 1).

and returned to his own."[5] Instead of engaging in the futile endeavor of reconstructing a life of Jesus, Schweitzer held that "the entire quest into the life of Jesus has ultimately only one purpose, to safeguard the natural and unaffected picture which is contained in the Gospel reports,"[6] albeit while remaining ever mindful that in Jesus's hopes and desires, he was completely oriented toward the kingdom of God. Schweitzer stresses that "it is the strength and vehemence of belief in the kingdom of God which governs the level of understanding of the historical Jesus in a religion. . . . How much we possess of him depends on how much we let him tell us of the kingdom of God."[7]

If our intention is to allow the real Jesus to speak, we must earnestly embrace his challenge to "seek first the kingdom of God and his righteousness!" (Matt 6:33; Luke 12:31). In true nineteenth-century style, Schweitzer links this proclamation of the kingdom to that of a "universal morality." Even more, he envisions a "Jesus mysticism" in which "Jesus's will" and our will should align. These highly questionable systematic intrusions exercised almost no influence on the "second quest's" research—quite in contrast to two of Schweitzer's findings that did indeed profoundly inform the direction of the "second quest," namely, that

1. the historical Jesus cannot be comprehended apart from his proclamation of the kingdom of God, and

2. a life of Jesus cannot be written in any case.

Schweitzer's work is characterized by self-awareness: "the greatest achievement of German theology is the critical investigation of the life of Jesus. . . . it has to describe the most tremendous thing which the religious consciousness has ever dared and done."[8] He assesses this grand achievement in a survey of nearly two hundred years of life-of-Jesus scholarship ranging from Hermann Samuel Reimarus to William Wrede.[9]

Apart from a Persian-language text written by a sixteenth-century Jesuit, Hermann Samuel Reimarus's 1778 publication, *Von dem Zwecke Jesu und seiner Jünger*, was the first attempt to historically grasp the life of Jesus.[10] Reimarus distinguishes between the disciples' faith and

---

5. Schweitzer, *Quest of the Historical Jesus*, 478 (see part 1.2, note 3).

6. Schweitzer, *Quest of the Historical Jesus*, 480.

7. Schweitzer, *Quest of the Historical Jesus*, 484.

8. Schweitzer, *Quest of the Historical Jesus*, 3f.

9. The first German edition of 1906 was titled *Von Reimarus zu Wrede. Eine Geschichte der Leben-Jesu-Forschung*. It was not until the second, significantly expanded edition of 1913 referred to here that the book was given the current title.

10. Hermann Samuel Reimarus, *Von dem Zwecke Jesu und seiner Jünger. Noch ein*

Jesus's own proclamation, which Reimarus views as being shaped by its Jewish context. Moreover, Reimarus is already suspicious that the resurrection hope was in fact a fabrication of Jesus's disciples prompted by the unavailing anticipation of Jesus's second coming (the so-called delay of the Parousia). He further distinguishes between a historically contingent message of political liberation from the Romans and a universal eschatological message for all people.

The historical life-of-Jesus quest commences with the allegation that Jesus's views diverged from those of the disciples. Although research during what is known as the "first quest for the historical Jesus" was shaped by additional perspectival variances as well, various counter proposals continued to be made for discovering synthesis and harmony between the biblical authors and traditions. In addition to historical distinctions and systematic syntheses, aesthetic and moral approaches were proposed as well, though also several clearly fantastical representations.

In his own publications,[11] Johann Gottfried Herder already separates the Synoptics from the Gospel of John, stressing that the biblical authors offer us differently nuanced works of art that should be read "with taste." Several waves of novelistic representations of Jesus's life followed characterized in part by adventurous notions about his life—such as his membership in secret organizations—or something akin to the international bestseller of our time, *The Da Vinci Code*.[12] The grandly conceived work of the rationalist Heinrich Eberhard Gottlob Paulus, *Das Leben Jesu, als Grundlage einer reinen Geschichte des Urchristentums*, marked a systematic-historical breakthrough to what may be called more strictly scholarly or scientific research by developing comprehensive Synoptic

---

Fragment des Wolfenbüttelschen Ungenannten, ed. Gotthold Ephraim Lessing (Braunschweig: Waisenhausbuchhandlung, 1778). Gerd Theissen acknowledges Reimarus's exemplary, still striking historical sensibility in *Jesus als historische Gestalt. Beiträge zur Jesusforschung*, ed. Annette Merz, Forschungen zur Religion und Literatur des Alten und Neuen Testaments 202 (Göttingen: Vandenhoeck, 2003), esp. 3ff.

11. Johann Gottfried Herder, *Vom Erlöser der Menschen. Nach unsern drei ersten Evangelien* (Riga: Hartknoch, 1796); idem, *Von Gottes Sohn, der Welt Heiland. Nach Johannes Evangelium* (Riga: Hartknoch, 1797).

12. Dan Brown, *The Da Vinci Code* (London: Bantam, 2003). In only a few years, this book was translated into more than forty languages and sold more than fifty million copies, which sheds light on Jesus's "cultural force" (cf. part 0.4). The novel insinuates that Jesus had a relationship with Mary Magdalene and speculates concerning physical descendants he may have produced with her. In so doing, it follows the apocryphal Gospel of Philip, which arose ca. two hundred years after the death of Jesus; see Peter Lampe, *Küsste Jesus Magdalenen mitten auf den Mund? Provokationen—Einsprüche—Klarstellungen* (Neukirchen-Vluyn: Neukirchener, 2007).

comparisons and rigorously striving to reconstruct Jesus's life in an objective fashion.[13]

Schweitzer saw David Friedrich Strauss as the "prophet of a coming advance in knowledge" (90). His scandalous work *The Life of Jesus, Critically Examined*[14] critically exposed the problems attaching equally to the belief in miracles and the resurrection, but also attempted to explain them in terms of "myth formation" in the context of Jesus's time.[15] Another important scholarly distinction emerged in Christian Hermann Weisse's discovery that Mark was the "original evangelist."[16] This "Markan hypothesis" brought a consolidation of historical reconstructions. A two-source theory (Mark and a reconstructed source "Q") was developed, with Mark becoming the foundational text for further attempts at reconstructing Jesus's life commensurate with historically valid standards.[17] That notwithstanding, historical skepticism also increased within life-of-Jesus research. Beginning in 1840, the critical Hegelian Bruno Bauer—in the spirit of David Friedrich Strauss—published one biblical "critique" after another,[18] though it did take him nearly a decade to come to a de-

13. Heinrich E.G. Paulus, *Das Leben Jesu, als Grundlage einer reinen Geschichte des Urchristentums*, 2 vols. (Heidelberg: C.F. Winter, 1828); cf. Schweitzer, *Quest of the Historical Jesus*, 47-55 (see part 1.2, note 3).

14. David Friedrich Strauss, *The Life of Jesus, Critically Examined*, trans. George Eliot (Bristol, England: Thoemmes Press, 1998) (original German publication 1835, 1836) (for a detailed analysis, see part 2.1). Both the positive and critical reception have been exhaustively discussed: see especially *Dr. Neanders auf höhere Veranlassung abgefaßtes Gutachten über das Buch des Dr. Strauß' "Leben-Jesu" und das in Beziehung auf die Verbreitung desselben zu beachtende Verfahren* (Berlin: Haude & Spener, 1836); Christoph Friedrich Ammon, *Die Geschichte des Lebens Jesu mit steter Rücksicht auf die Quellen*, 3 vols. (Leipzig, 1842–47); cf. Schweitzer, *Quest of the Historical Jesus*, 116ff.

15. Schleiermacher's tiered assessment of miracles in his lectures on the subject in 1832 are similar, though they were not published until 1864, see Friedrich Schleiermacher, *The Life of Jesus*, ed. Jack C. Verheyden, trans. S. Maclean Gilmour (Philadelphia: Sigler Press, 1997); cf. Schweitzer, *Quest of the Historical Jesus*, 59.

16. Christian Hermann Weisse, *Die Evangelische Geschichte kritisch und philosophisch bearbeitet*, 2 vols. (Leipzig: Breitkopf und Härtel, 1838). See also Christian Gottlob Wilke, *Der Urevangelist oder exegetisch kritische Untersuchung über das Verwandtschaftsverhältnis der drei ersten Evangelien* (Dresden and Leipzig: Gerhard Fleischer, 1838).

17. The most significant representative of this approach is Heinrich Julius Holtzmann, *Die synoptischen Evangelien: Ihr Ursprung und geschichtlicher Charakter* (Leipzig: Wilhelm Engelmann, 1863).

18. Bruno Bauer, *Kritik der evangelischen Geschichte des Johannes* (Bremen: Schünemann, 1840); idem, *Kritik der evangelischen Geschichte der Synoptiker*, 3 vols. (Leipzig, 1841–42); idem, *Kritik der Evangelien und Geschichte ihres Ursprungs*, 2 vols. (Berlin: Hempel, 1850–51); idem, *Kritik der paulinischen Briefe* (Berlin: Hempel, 1850–52).

finitively negative conclusion concerning Jesus's historicity, doing so in his critique of the Pauline letters.

Life-of-Jesus publications then began moving once more toward moralistic and increasingly psychological frameworks, the most successful representative being Ernest Renan's *Life of Jesus*—with eight editions in three months.[19] Even at the very beginnings of life-of-Jesus scholarship, this moralistic approach, being interested primarily in Jesus's ethical example, was considerably influenced by Kant's ethical and theoretical writings on religion.[20] Such was the case with Georg Wilhelm Friedrich Hegel, who as a tutor in Bern in 1795 wrote a life of Jesus in the spirit of Kant, albeit one Schweitzer could not have assessed insofar as it was not published until 1907, that is, basically contemporaneously with Schweitzer's own work.[21]

A series of studies on "Jesus's self-consciousness" and his proclamation of the kingdom of God changed the direction of scholarship once more, triggered this time by a short piece by Johannes Weiss, *Jesus' Proclamation of the Kingdom of God.*[22] Weiss suggested that the Jesus quest understand Jesus's person and ministry entirely in light of his proclamation of the kingdom of God. The foundations of life-of-Jesus scholarship collapsed, however, after William Wrede, in his book *The Messianic Secret,*[23] argued that Mark, influenced by the faith of the post-Easter community, had projected the notion of a "messianic secret" into his presentation of Jesus's life. Because Schweitzer himself recognized the problem of the projectional nature of depictions of the "historical" Jesus, he opted instead for a vague "eschatological," moral, and mysti-

19. Ernest Renan, *La vie de Jésus* (Paris, 1863); English: *Life of Jesus*, trans. Joseph H. Allen (Boston: Little, Brown, & Co., 1917).

20. Immanuel Kant, *Foundations of the Metaphysics of Morals, and What is Enlightenment?* trans. Lewis White Beck (Indianapolis: Bobbs-Merrill Co., 1959); idem, *Critique of Practical Reason*, ed. and trans. Mary Grego, Cambridge Texts in the History of Philosophy (Cambridge: Cambridge University Press, 1997); idem, *Religion within the Boundaries of Mere Reason: and Other Writings*, ed. and trans. Allen Wood and George Di Giovanni, Cambridge Texts in the History of Philosophy (Cambridge: Cambridge University Press, 1998).

21. Georg Wilhelm Friedrich Hegel, "Das Leben Jesu," in *Hegels Theologische Jugendschriften*, ed. Herman Nohl (Tübingen, 1907; repr., Frankfurt: Minerva, 1966), 73–136; also in idem, *Gesammelte Werke*, vol. 1, *Frühe Schriften I*, ed. Friedhelm Nicolin and Gisela Schüler (Hamburg: Meiner, 1989), 205–78. Concerning diverse liberal life-of-Jesus representations, see Schweitzer, *Quest of the Historical Jesus*, 168ff (see part 1.2, note 3).

22. Johannes Weiss, *Jesus' Proclamation of the Kingdom of God*, ed. and trans. Richard Hyde Hiers and David Larrimore Holland (Philadelphia: Fortress Press, 1971).

23. William Wrede, *The Messianic Secret*, trans. J.C.G. Greig, Library of Theological Translations (Greenwood, S.C.: Attic Press, 1971).

cal interpretation of Jesus's ministry and against any continuation of the Jesus quest.[24]

The "second quest for the historical Jesus" (known as the "new quest" prior to the inauguration of the "third quest") takes as its point of departure the skepticism expressed by Bultmann and Bornkamm vis-à-vis any attempts at historical reconstruction; its goal was instead to make do with securing a minimum of sustainable elements of the Jesus tradition that might allow for the establishment of concurrence between the Jesus of history and the Christ of faith.[25] This initiative was accompanied by a reductionist mode that sought to eliminate all content derived from Jewish and early Christian tradition[26] to arrive at what amounts to a "primal stratum" in the sense of a primal core of tradition. This *historical minimalism* was combined with a *kerygmatic minimalism* that sought to derive from the New Testament accounts a *single* "message" that remained constant in Jesus's life and ministry. This message admittedly varies according to the interpreter. For Rudolf Bultmann, it is Jesus's "call to decision," one that sounds somewhat overwrought by today's standards, the "will of God, as calling man in the present to decision."[27] For Ernst Käsemann and Günther Bornkamm, it is Jesus's certainty that "the will of God is present in such an immediate fashion," combined with his critique of the Law.[28] According to Ernst Fuchs, it is the "proclamation of God's love to sinners,"[29] and for Gerhard Ebeling, "Jesus's faith."[30]

The influence of Martin Kähler's essay "The So-called Historical Jesus and the Historic Biblical Christ"[31] on the development of the "sec-

---

24. See Albert Schweitzer, *The Mystery of the Kingdom of God: The Secret of Jesus's Messiahship and Passion*, trans. Walter Lowrie (London: A.&C. Black, 1925).

25. Cf. David Fergusson, "The Doctrine of the Incarnation Today," *Expository Times* 113 (2001), 76; Josef L. Hromádka, "Zur Frage des historischen Jesus und des kerygmatischen Christus (1961)," in *Sprung über die Mauer: Ein Hromádka-Lesebuch*, ed. Milan Opočenský (Wuppertal: Peter Hammer, 1991), 75–80. A helpful and nuanced outside perspective on German New Testament exegesis can be found in Neill/Wright, *The Interpretation of the New Testament, 1861–1986*, esp. 205ff (see part 1.1, note 10).

26. On the following, cf. Theissen/Merz, *The Historical Jesus*, 7 (see part 1.1, note 5): "Methodologically the place of the literary-critical reconstruction of the earliest sources in the 'old' quest of liberal theology is replaced by a comparison which makes use of the history of religions and the history of tradition: the 'criterion of difference.'"

27. Bultmann, *Jesus and the Word*, 131 (see part 1.2, note 1).

28. Ernst Käsemann, *Jesus Means Freedom: A Polemical Survey of the New Testament*, trans. Frank Clarke (London: SCM Press, 1969); Bornkamm, *Jesus of Nazareth*, 100 (see part 1.2, note 1).

29. Ernst Fuchs, *Studies of the Historical Jesus*, trans. Andrew Scobie (Naperville, IL: A.R. Allenson, 1964), esp. 48ff.

30. Gerhard Ebeling, "Jesus und der Glaube," *ZThK* 55 (1958), 64ff.

31. Originally published as a book in 1892 and expanded in 1896: *Der sogenannte*

ond quest" should not be underestimated. Kähler proposes distinguishing between nuances of "historical" (Germ. *historisch*: a past presence) and "historic" (Germ. *geschichtlich*: a continuing past). It is the "historic Christ" who "originates and bequeaths a permanent influence. He is one of those dynamic individuals [as is also the biblical Christ; M.W.] who intervene in the course of events."[32] In his classic essay "Das Problem des historischen Jesus,"[33] Ernst Käsemann adopted the basic intent of this idea in emphasizing that history (Germ. *Historie*) is transmitted in kerygma, in the message, act, and content of the proclamation, not in an empty reconstruction of wholly bygone events. Put differently, it is through the proclamation that history, *Historie*, in the sense of historical material—these individual messages, acts, and content—becomes historic, *geschichtlich*.

Käsemann questions "whether the formula 'the historical Jesus' can be called at all appropriate or legitimate, because it is almost bound to awaken and nourish the illusion of a possible and satisfying reproduction of his 'life story'" (194). By contrast, the dimension of the historic (*geschichtlich*) inherently and always includes elements of subsequent personal and historical impact. The consumption of a lentil dish is an event that can be historically located. When, however, it alters the succession and dynamic relations in influential families, for example, it becomes a historically pregnant event (that we then mistakenly call a "historical [*historisch*] event!").[34] The living memory of Jesus as a person of impact, and not just as a person who appears at a given point in history (*Historie*), is provoked by the distinctive perspectives on his life emphasized in the Gospels. As is evident today, a perception blockage arose here among representatives of the "second quest." On one hand, they sought "the single message"; on the other, they followed Schweitzer's challenge "to safeguard the natural and unaffected picture which is contained in the Gospel reports." Their reductionism allowed them to see only "chaos" and "bewildering confusion" in the diverse perspectives of witnesses.

Referring to Matthew, Käsemann draws striking parallels between the life of Jesus and Moses's Haggadah, "the sense of which is: as with

---

historische Jesus und der geschichtliche, biblische Christus. Translated by Carl E. Braaten as *The So-called Historical Jesus and the Historic Biblical Christ* (Philadelphia: Fortress Press, 1988).

32. Kähler, *The So-Called Historical Jesus*, 63.

33. Ernst Käsemann, "The Problem of the Historical Jesus," in *Essays on New Testament Themes*, trans. W.J. Montague, Studies in Biblical Theology 41 (Naperville, IL: Alec R. Allenson, Inc., 1964), 15–47 (the following page numbers in the text refer to this essay).

34. Cf. in this regard the illuminating essay by Will Herberg, "Five Meanings of the Word 'Historical,'" *Christian Scholar* 47 (1964), 327–30.

the first Deliverer, so with the second. In both cases the birth of the child produces unrest on the part of the rulers, followed by consultation with wise men and the murder of children; in both cases there follows a wonderful deliverance in which Egypt becomes the land of refuge" (23). The depiction of Jesus as the future savior of the people of God, as the second and final Moses, combined historical and mythic elements in identifying Jesus as "the founder of an eschatologically oriented community life" (27), as "the bringer of the Messianic Torah" (27). An analogous configuration can be seen in Mark, combining historical and mythic elements insofar as, according to Käsemann, during "the earthly life of Jesus" "the glory of the risen Son of God" already bursts "victoriously into the demon-controlled world," revealing "to the earth and to the principalities and powers their eternal Lord" (28). By contrast, the Lukan writings sooner offer a history of salvation and position Luke as the first Christian historian, who tries "to sketch out the great stages of the plan of salvation and to work consistently on that basis. His Gospel is indeed the first 'life of Jesus'" (29). Käsemann's assessment is consciously succinct: "if, in the other Gospels, the problem of history is a special form of the problem of eschatology, in Luke eschatology has become a special form of the problem of history" (29).

As is typical for the "second quest," Käsemann speaks of a "bewildering confusion of allegedly trustworthy portraits of Jesus: now he appears as a rabbi, now as a teacher of wisdom, now as a prophet; or again, as the man who thought of himself as the Son of Man or the Suffering Servant, who stood for an apocalyptic or a realized eschatology: or finally, as some sort of a mixture of all these" (35). The "certain minimum" that Käsemann emphasizes is that Jesus truly perceived "this immediate assurance of knowing and proclaiming the will of God, which in him is combined with the direct and unsophisticated outlook of the teacher of wisdom. . . . he must have regarded himself as an instrument of the living Spirit of God, which Judaism expected to be the gift of the End" (42).

Scholarship within the framework of the "third quest for the historical Jesus" has dealt with considerably more caution with the numerous efforts to psychologically approach Jesus, to comprehend his "self-understanding," his "personal faith," or his "inner life" and "certainty of God." Scholars have developed a more even-tempered relationship with the multiplicity of biblical perspectives toward Jesus and have tried to discern and articulate coherence within the seemingly "disturbing confusion" of the biblical witnesses. They have overcome the fundamental disposition of notorious skepticism and the orientation to the ideal of a "certain minimum" of historical knowledge and have freed themselves from the need to reduce Jesus's life and proclamation to but "a single message." The success of archaeological excavations and a fresh, if occasionally naïve archaeological approach to the abundance of canonical and extra-canonical texts[35] have acted as a liberating force (see part 1.1). Nevertheless, it has only been in combination with additional research impulses that archaeology in the traditional sense along with broadly engaged textual archaeology has led to the "third quest's" paradigm shift.

35. See Robert W. Funk and the Jesus Seminar, *The Acts of Jesus: The Search for the Authentic Deeds of Jesus* (San Francisco: Harper, 1998).

1.3 A Paradigm Shift via the "Third Quest": High Christology, Social History, and an Analysis of the Politics of Symbol (Hengel, Dunn, Hurtado, Vermes, Theissen, and Merz)

Ninety years after Albert Schweitzer's classic work about the successes and failures of the Jesus quest, two books appeared: in Germany, the grandly conceived *Der historische Jesus* by Gerd Theissen and Annette Merz [Engl.: *The Historical Jesus*]; and in the United States, *The Acts of Jesus: The Search for the Authentic Deeds of Jesus* by Robert Funk and a group of scholars calling themselves the "Jesus Seminar." The volumes respectively end with a "Retrospect: A Short Life of Jesus" and a compendium to the question, "What do we really know about Jesus?"[1] Briefly, even though scholars saw more clearly than ever that precise dates concerning Jesus's life are indeed uncertain, they boldly undertook precisely what Schweitzer, Bornkamm, and the majority of New Testament scholars had already declared to be impossible.[2] The distinct profiles of the biblical authors themselves along with the striking differences between their depictions of Jesus were also more clearly delineated than previously—all of which sooner underscored the skepticism that emerged during the "second quest," since:

- for **Mark**, are Jesus's confrontations with demons not of particular importance for showing that the Son of God's actions are victorious *already* in this world?

- for **Matthew**, is Jesus not seen as the new and greater Moses who replaces the Law with new teaching?

- for **Luke**, does Jesus not wish to win people for the kingdom of God through the Spirit, which had filled him since birth?

- for **John**, does Jesus not wish to bring people into his eternal communion with the Father—through new birth in the power of the Spirit?

---

1. Theissen and Merz, *The Historical Jesus*, 569–72 (see part 1.1, note 5); Funk and the Jesus Seminar, *The Acts of Jesus*, 527–34 (see part 1.2, note 35).

2. Although Jesus was likely born during the final years of Herod's life and reign, and thus before 4 B.C.E. (Matt 21ff; Luke 1:5), the exact birth year cannot be dated with certainty. He engaged in his public ministry when he was about 30 years old (Luke 3:23), possibly for only a single year, at most three; even here, however, dating remains uncertain, perhaps between the years 26 and 29 C.E. (See the careful assessment in Theissen/Merz, *The Historical Jesus*, 156f.) Neither can the year of Jesus's death be precisely dated, though certain evidence suggests 30 C.E.

- for **Paul**, are Christians not incorporated into living communion with the resurrected and exalted Christ and adopted through the Spirit just as Jesus himself was appointed as the Son of God by the Father at the resurrection?[3]

In this confusing situation, how can even a concise "life of Jesus" be written with any claim to theological and academic integrity? Alongside archaeological discoveries in the traditional sense and the findings of enthusiastic textual archaeology described above with respect to biblical and non-canonical sources (see part 1.1), three additional factors helped move beyond the paradigm of the "second quest" with its fundamental skepticism.

1. What is known as "high Christology" lends inner unity to all the biblical references to Jesus's life despite their perspectival diversity. Scholars now generally agree that worship of Jesus as *kyrios*, as Lord, as the Son of God, and as "God of God" did *not* develop only slowly and gradually in the early church. Nor can it be traced back to any mingling of Jesus-piety with pagan religious conceptions, philosophies, or devotional practices. The message that "God revealed himself in Jesus Christ" developed very quickly after Jesus's death and resurrection, virtually exploding out of Jewish monotheism as a *new* form of monotheism in its own turn.

Martin Hengel, Larry Hurtado, and other notable New Testament scholars have convincingly shown that a piety centered on "Jesus is Lord!" can be extracted from hymns and documentation attesting early Christian worship.[4] "It is understandable that bold christological sketches of this kind were initially presented not in the form of

---

3. Cf. the impressive overview in Gerd Theissen, *Gospel Writing and Church Politics: A Socio-rhetorical Approach*, Chuen King Lecture Series 3 (Hong Kong: The Chinese University of Hong Kong, 2001), 159ff; and the remarks about the christological sketches of several New Testament writings in Kurt Erlemann, *Jesus der Christus: Provokation des Glaubens* (Neukirchen-Vluyn: Neukirchener, 2011), 174ff. See also the detailed contributions in *Seeking the Identity of Jesus: A Pilgrimage*, ed. Beverly Roberts Gaventa and Richard B. Hays (Grand Rapids: Eerdmans, 2008), including Dale C. Allison, Jr., "The Embodiment of God's Will: Jesus in Matthew," 117–32; Joel Marcus, "Identity and Ambiguity in Markan Christology," 133–47; Beverly Roberts Gaventa, "Learning and Relearning the Identity of Jesus from Luke-Acts," 148–65; Marianne Meye Thompson, "Word of God, Messiah of Israel, Savior of the World: Learning the Identity of Jesus from the Gospel of John," 166–79; Richard B. Hays, "The Story of God's Son: The Identity of Jesus in the Letters of Paul," 180–99.

4. See Larry W. Hurtado, *Lord Jesus Christ: Devotion to Jesus in Earliest Christianity* (Grand Rapids: Eerdmans, 2003), 563ff; idem, *How on Earth Did Jesus Become a God? Historical Questions about Earliest Devotion to Jesus* (Grand Rapids: Eerdmans, 2005), 151ff.

speculative prose, but rather in hymns inspired by the Spirit (1 Cor 14:26; cf. Col 3:16; Eph 5:19; Rev 5:9, etc.); the language most appropriate to God's 'inexpressible grace' (2 Cor 9:15) was the hymn of praise inspired by the Spirit."[5] Hengel stresses that Paul justifies the foundational doxological confession "Jesus is Lord" (Rom 10:13; cf. Acts 2:21) with Joel 3:5, where, following the promise of the outpouring of the Spirit on "men and women, old and young, servants and maids," we read: "Then everyone who calls on the name of the LORD shall be saved." "In the original text [Joel 3:5], Kyrios refers to God himself, but for Paul the Kyrios is Jesus, in whom God makes a full disclosure of his salvation."[6]

Hurtado labeled this developing faith as a "binary monotheism."[7] The early Christians viewed monotheism (Deut 6:4) as being as little threatened by the confession to Christ's divinity as it was in Old Testament traditions by the distinction between God and God's word, God and God's wisdom, God and God's Spirit.[8] Among countless scholars from the German- and English-speaking world, little doubt remains that the presence of an "early high Christology," that is, a Christology taking as its point of departure the divinity of Jesus Christ, can indeed be historically assumed. "The resurrected Christ is confessed as *kyrios*, as 'Lord' in the early congregations (. . . 1 Cor 12:3; Rom 10:9f; Phil 2:9–11) and addressed in acclamation and prayer (1 Cor 1:2; 16:22; 2 Cor 12:8)." Early Christians were "identified at every locale . . . as those who 'call on the name of our Lord Jesus' (1 Cor 1:2; cf. Acts 9:14, 21; 22:16)."[9]

---

5. Martin Hengel, *The Son of God: The Origin of Christology and the History of Jewish-Hellenistic Religion*, trans. John Bowden (Philadelphia: Fortress Press, 1976), 76. Concerning this notion and the following, cf. the excellent presentation of christological monotheism in Richard Bauckham, *God Crucified: Monotheism and Christology in the New Testament* (Grand Rapids: Eerdmans, 1998), esp. 25ff.

6. Hengel, *The Son of God*, 77. See his reference to Reinhard Deichgräber, *Gotteshymnus und Christushymnus in der frühen Christenheit. Untersuchungen zu Form, Sprache und Stil der frühchristlichen Hymnen*, SUNT 5 (Göttingen: Vandenhoeck, 1967), 188f.

7. Hurtado, *How on Earth*, 48ff (see part 1.3, note 4); see idem, *One God, One Lord: Early Christian Devotion and Ancient Jewish Monotheism*, 2nd ed. (London: T&T Clark, 2003) 93ff; Rudolf Schnackenburg, *Die Person Jesu Christi im Spiegel der vier Evangelien*, HThK, Suppl IV (Freiburg: Herder, 1993), 340–54.

8. Hurtado, *How on Earth*, 111ff; cf. idem, *Lord Jesus Christ*, 29ff and 134ff (see part 1.3, note 4).

9. Hans-Joachim Eckstein, "Die Anfänge trinitarischer Rede von Gott im Neuen Testament," in Michael Welker and Miroslav Volf, eds., *Der lebendige Gott als Trinität, Festschrift für Jürgen Moltmann* (Gütersloh: Gütersloher, 2006), 86. Alongside Hengel, *Son of God* (see part 1.3, note 5), and Hurtado, *How on Earth*, and idem, *One God, One Lord*, 99ff (see part 1.3, note 7), this consensus was strengthened by James D. G. Dunn's ground-

Alongside references to the crucifixion and resurrection, it is this *universal conviction of Jesus's divine majesty* permeating the background of the Jesus traditions that makes the remarkable coherence comprehensible that we discern between these various portrayals of Jesus within the biblical traditions *despite* their considerable differences in accentuation.[10] It would never occur to anyone that statements about Jesus in the Synoptic Gospels might in fact be speaking about different people. In recent years, this realization has led to extraordinarily interesting, albeit yet unresolved discussions concerning the extent to which the biblical witnesses may indeed be documenting, more than has hitherto been assumed, authentic oral traditions or even eyewitness accounts:

> the period between the "historical" Jesus and the Gospels was actually spanned, not by anonymous community transmission, but by the continuing presence and testimony of the eyewitnesses, who remained the authoritative sources of their traditions until their deaths . . . Gospel traditions did not, for the most part, circulate anonymously but in the name of the eyewitnesses to whom they were due . . . Christians remained . . . aware of the ways the eyewitnesses themselves told their stories. So . . . not oral tradition but eyewitness testimony should be our principal model.[11]

---

breaking investigations *Christology in the Making: A New Testament Inquiry into the Origins of the Doctrine of the Incarnation*, 2nd ed. (London: SCM Press, 1992), 132ff and 263ff; idem, *The Christ and the Spirit: Collected Essays*, 2 vols. (Edinburgh: T&T Clark, 1998) (vol. 1: Christology; vol. 2: Pneumatology), esp. concerning the discussion of the *kyrios* in Acts, vol. 1, 241ff. Dunn trenchantly pioneered the appreciation of the differences in the Synoptic portrayals of Jesus while also revealing the connection to "high Christology" as exemplified in John 1:1ff. His sensibility for the meaning of the Spirit's ministry is also full of insight. – See also part 4.2. – As early as 1913, Wilhelm Bousset showed that many early Christian assertions about Jesus were embedded in liturgical contexts: *Kyrios Christos: A History of the Belief in Christ from the Beginnings of Christianity to Irenaeus*, trans. John E. Steely (Nashville: Abingdon Press, 1970). See also Oscar Cullmann, *The Christology of the New Testament*, trans. Shirley C. Guthrie and Charles A.M. Hall (London: SCM Press, 1959); Ferdinand Hahn, *The Titles of Jesus in Christology: Their History in Early Christianity*, trans. Harold Knight and George Ogg (New York: World Publishing Co, 1969); Werner Kramer, *Christ, Lord, Son of God*, trans. Brian Hardy (Naperville, Ill.: A.R. Allenson, 1966).

10. See C.H. Dodd, *The Founder of Christianity* (London: Collins, 1971), 21f: ". . . the first three gospels offer a body of sayings on the whole so consistent, so coherent, and withal so distinctive in manner, style (and) content, that no reasonable critic should doubt . . . that we find reflected here the thought of a single, unique teacher."

11. Richard Bauckham, *Jesus and the Eyewitnesses: The Gospels as Eyewitness Testimony* (Grand Rapids: Eerdmans, 2006), 8. See even earlier James D. G. Dunn, "Jesus in Oral Memory: The Initial Stages of the Jesus Tradition," in *Jesus: A Colloquium in the Holy Land*, ed. Doris Donelly (New York: Continuum, 2001), 84–145; idem, "Eyewitnesses and the Oral Tradition," *Journal for the Study of the Historical Jesus* 6 (2008), 85–105.

Although more extensive research into transmission strategies and memory cultivation in cultures of the time might certainly provide further answers to these questions, a research program we will outline as "the fourth quest for the historical Jesus" may help as well (see part 1.4).

2. Jesus's positioning within Second Temple Judaism has similarly provided an element of coherence and promoted the quality of historical scholarship.[12] His ministry has been interpreted as, among other things, a reform movement within Judaism intended to strengthen the identity of the Jewish people suffering under foreign rule. Even the development of "high Christology" and the doctrine of the Trinity were explained with the help of conceptual and representational models from biblical and extra-biblical Jewish thought.[13]

An especially striking, sharply articulated profile of Jesus within the context of the Judaism of his time—in significant contrast to Crossan's insights (cf. part 1.1 above)—emerges in Geza Vermes's books on Jesus.[14] Belonging to the Galilean rural population, Jesus saw himself as being sent to the children of Israel (Matt 15:24). He sharply differentiated himself from the Gentiles, to whom he possibly even referred to as "dogs" (Mark 7:27; Matt 7:6). The Pharisees and the teachers of the

12. See Sanders, *Jesus and Judaism* (see part 1.1, note 24); idem, *The Historical Figure of Jesus* (London: Allen Lande/Penguin, 1993); John P. Meier, *A Marginal Jew: Rethinking the Historical Jesus*, 4 vols. (New York: Doubleday, 1991), esp. vol. 1, 205ff; Vermes, *Jesus the Jew* (see part 1.1, note 21); Theissen, *Jesus als historische Gestalt*, 33ff (see part 1.2, note 10); Klaus Berger, *Die Gesetzesauslegung Jesu. Ihr historischer Hintergrund im Judentum und im Alten Testament*, Part 1: *Markus und Parallelen*, WMANT 40 (Neukirchen-Vluyn: Neukirchener, 1972), esp. 574–90; Martin Hengel and Anna Maria Schwemer, *Jesus und das Judentum*, Geschichte des frühen Christentums 1 (Tübingen: Mohr Siebeck, 2007), esp. 39ff and 343ff.

13. See Hartmut Gese, "Natus ex Virgine," in Gese, *Vom Sinai zum Zion. Alttestamentliche Beiträge zur biblischen Theologie*, BEvTh 64 (Munich: Kaiser, 1974), 130–46; idem, "Die Weisheit, der Menschensohn und die Ursprünge der Christologie als konsequente Entfaltung der biblischen Theologie," in idem, *Alttestamentliche Studien* (Tübingen: Mohr Siebeck, 1991), 218–48; Christoph Markschies, "Jüdische Mittlergestalten und die christliche Trinitätstheologie," in Welker/Volf, *Trinität*, 199–214 (see part 1.3, note 9); Hurtado; *One God, One Lord* (see part 1.3, note 7); idem, *Lord Jesus Christ* (see part 1.3, note 4); cf. also part 1.5.

14. Vermes, *Jesus the Jew* (see part 1.1, note 21); idem, *The Gospel of Jesus the Jew* (Newcastle: University of Newcastle Press, 1981); idem, *The Religion of Jesus the Jew* (Minneapolis: Fortress, 1993); idem, *The Changing Faces of Jesus* (London: Penguin, 2001). On Vermes, see Breytenbach, "Jesusforschung: 1990–1995," 236ff (see part 1.1, note 25); I follow his representation here, cf. ibid., 237f and 245f. – See also J. Klausner's 1907 book, published originally in Hebrew, *Jesus of Nazareth: His Life, Times, and Teaching*, trans. Herbert Danby (New York: Macmillan, 1929); and David Flusser, *Jesus*, trans. Ronald Walls (New York: Herder and Herder, 1969).

Law regarded him and those around him as uneducated and religiously unsound. His dealings with the impure, his association with sinners, prostitutes, and tax collectors fit this image. Jesus's conflicts with purification rituals and the temple cult escalated when he went beyond the region of Galilee, and the resistance that arose against him in Jerusalem ultimately led to his execution. The basic contours of Jesus's ministry could indicate that first-century Pharisees in Galilee had lost their religious and moral leadership.

Vermes places much more weight on the exorcisms, expulsion of demons, healing of the sick, and forgiveness of sins than does Crossan. This emphasis on exorcisms, however, does not mean that Jesus's actions and proclamations are no longer historically retrievable, since Jesus's relationship to the Law as a Jew facilitates a reconstruction of his speech and actions. Even his parables about the kingdom of God reveal his efforts to make the coming reality of God's reign realistically accessible to a rural population through the use of familiar images such as seeds, harvests, shepherding, and domestic life. God's reign is much more intelligible from the perspective of its organic growth and development than from any human staging. People themselves must indeed also participate, sowing seeds, kneading dough, filling lamps with oil; but they must also fully trust in the germinating seeds, the sprouting mustard seed, the rising caused by leaven, and the rising morning sun.[15] What we must discern here are minute, subtle, and yet highly consequential differences in the perspectives of Vermes and Crossan on Jesus's person and ministry, differences that can, however, equally reveal to us divergent aspects of Jesus's lived existence.

3. Another enlightening approach to the Jesus quest is offered by the broad investigation of the social history and social psychology of the Jewish community and its setting during Jesus's time and in the decades following his ministry, an investigation that focuses more on the political context of the Roman Empire and the expansion of early Christianity in town settings and among the Gentiles.[16] Social roles and expectations, moral conceptions, and political development in the tensions between

---

15. Cf. Vermes, *Jesus the Jew*, 42ff; idem, *The Changing Faces of Jesus*, 154–65, 193–209; idem, *The Religion of Jesus the Jew*, 137–51.

16. See W.A. Meeks, *The First Urban Christians: The Social World of the Apostle Paul* (New Haven: Yale University Press, 1983; 2nd ed. 2003); *After the First Urban Christians: The Social Scientific Study of Pauline Christianity Twenty-Five Years Later*, ed. T. D. Still and D. G. Horrell (London: T&T Clark, 2009); and the comprehensive work by Gerd Theissen, *Sociology of Early Palestinian Christianity*, trans. John Bowden (Philadelphia: Fortress, 1978); idem, *Gospel Writing and Church Politics* (see part 1.3, note 3).

Jews and Gentiles, Israel and Rome, and rural and urban populations come more sharply into view.

In their extensive contribution to the research of the Jesus quest, Theissen and Merz assess particularly Jesus's "power to attract and provoke far beyond the normal." To the extent he was a charismatic leader who "implicitly attributed to himself a special nearness to God,"[17] he necessarily came into conflict both with traditional messianic expectations as well as those imputed to him. A somewhat vague assertion (cf. 561) suggests that just as Jesus transcended the Torah without contradicting it, so also did he transcend other grand social expectations of his role, particularly the expectation that he was the Messiah. "He activated their messianic hopes, but this very activation of messianic expectations was fateful for him: he was crucified by the Romans because of the messiahship attributed to him by the people" (561). Among what may be called his "exalted titles" (or titles of majesty, such as Messiah, Son of God, Lord), Jesus applied only the title "Son of Man" to himself, in fact "not a title but an everyday expression which was first given messianic connotations by him—however, Jesus linked it with visions of a heavenly being who was like a son of man" (561).[18]

On first glance, Theissen and Merz's reconstruction might seem somewhat differently positioned than those of Crossan and Vermes. Because their conceptions of the kingdom of God detach this kingdom more strongly from Jesus's earthly ministry, they must speak of unfulfilled expectations insofar as this divine kingdom did not in fact arrive following Jesus's death and resurrection. After Easter, however, the lofty connotations attaching to the title "Son of Man" allegedly prompt the consolidation of a "belief in a transformed 'human being' who does not cease to be God's creature even beyond the frontier of death" (562). Theissen and Merz explain (562):

> These new perspectives released a utopian power, so that by the assimilation of all men and women to this "new human being" traditional differences between peoples, classes and sexes could be overcome: differences between Jews and Greeks, slaves and free, men and women (Gal 3:28). Reflection on Jesus today may see him as a kind of metamorphosis of the human.

After Easter, this veneration was allegedly eclipsed by the appeal to Jesus as *kyrios*, with which, according to Theissen and Merz, "Jesus is brought near to God" (563) for those who worship him.

17. Theissen/Merz, *The Historical Jesus*, 560 (see part 1.1, note 5); bracketed pagination in the following discussion refers to this book.
18. See part 1.5.

Although Theissen and Merz also acknowledge the practice of exorcism and communal meals, they emphasize more the notion of a "kind of 'representative popular rule'" perpetuated by the fundamental certainty of a "final shift in the direction of the good" (569). On the basis of this certainty, Jesus was able to inculcate an element of "aristocratic self-confidence" in "ordinary people" (569) through his parables. This uplifting of people, the "fame as a miracle-worker" (570), the "vision of the future rule of God . . . [as] a great shared meal in which Jews and Gentiles were no longer divided by commandments about food and purity" (571), and especially Jesus's direct criticism of the Temple on his entry into Jerusalem led to his death. "The aristocracy which arrested him took steps against him because of his criticism of the temple, but accused him before Pilate of a political crime, of having sought power as a royal pretender" (571).

Images of Jesus deriving from the fascination with archaeological and text-archaeological findings, presentations of Jesus within the context of contemporary Judaism, and socio-historical perspectives that also try to understand the emergence of "high Christology": precisely this field of tension offers an excellent opportunity for assessing the strengths and weaknesses of the numerous more recent representations of Jesus similarly claiming to be based on solid historical scholarship. Along these lines, Joachim Gnilka[19] offers a portrayal of Jesus that, while focusing on him "as a person," is more reserved in attempting any sharper contextual portrayal of his life within the contemporary Mediterranean world or the Galilean environs. Joseph Ratzinger[20] views Jesus as already ministering in Galilee within the context of "we, the Church," a perspective prompting one exegete to remark that we learn more here about "the religious disposition of the pope" than about the historical Jesus.[21] In reality, Ratzinger's presentation positions itself in tension between the *first* and *third* quests for the historical Jesus; it does so, however, while circumventing the *second* quest's skepticism without ever really addressing the complex scholarly and research issues attaching to the *third* quest. Although the pope cites especially German protestant exegetes in

19. Joachim Gnilka, *Jesus of Nazareth: Message and History*, trans. Siegfried S. Schatzmann (Peabody, MA: Hendrickson, 1997); idem, *Jesus Christus nach frühen Zeugnissen des Glaubens* (Munich: Koesel, 1970).

20. Joseph Ratzinger—Pope Benedict XVI, *Jesus of Nazareth: From the Baptism in the Jordan to the Transfiguration*, trans. Adrian J. Walker, vol. 1 (New York: Doubleday, 2007); idem, *Jesus of Nazareth: Holy Week: From the Entrance into Jerusalem to the Resurrection*, trans. Philip J. Whitmore, vol. 2 (San Francisco: Ignatius Press, 2011).

21. See Michael Wolter's review "Joseph Ratzinger, Benedikt XVI., *Jesus von Nazareth*," *EvTh* 68 (2008), 305–9.

his reflections,[22] over broad stretches he is sooner engaged in producing a refined and subtle Gospel harmonization from the perspective of his own, wholly personal capacity for imaginative historical understanding. This approach becomes theologically precarious when the Pope claims to take seriously the christologically mediated revelation of God, on the one hand, but then sooner appears to follow the "revelations" of Aristotle and metaphysics, on the other, and when he mentions God as "the creative logic, the eternal reason" in the same breath.[23]

In the context of the "fourth quest for the historical Jesus," we describe the broad scope of research objectives that lie before us in the domain of serious theological and academic engagement with the life of Jesus. In this context, Ratzinger correctly implies that historical-critical and systematic conceptual approaches must be combined in new ways to facilitate not only historical, but also theological insight.[24]

A particularly fruitful impulse for socio-historical research is Gerd Theissen's essay "Jesus und die symbolpolitischen Konflikte seiner Zeit."[25] Inspired perhaps by Crossan, Theissen argues that we can view historical processes from a wide-angle perspective, as a snapshot, in close-up, and from micro-perspectives.

> If we choose a wide-angle perspective from which we can view the entire period of the principate [the entire earlier period of the Roman Empire], early Christianity seems to have developed during a comparatively stable period.[26] If by contrast we choose a snapshot perspective and observe

22. Martin Hengel, Ulrich Wilckens, Joachim Jeremias, and—in an astonishingly intensive fashion—Rudolf Bultmann.

23. *Jesus of Nazareth*, vol. 2, 192. Concerning his obviously ecclesio-politically motivated departure from any biblical and christological orientation regarding the Eucharistic tradition, see part 5.4. Cf. also *Tod und Auferstehung Jesu. Theologische Antworten auf das Buch des Papstes*, ed. Thomas Söding (Freiburg: Herder, 2011).

24. *Jesus of Nazareth*, vol. 2, xiv et passim; see also Paul Hanson's skeptical perspective over against ecclesiocentric positions in "We Once Knew Him from a Human Point of View," in *Who is Jesus Christ for Us Today?* ed. Schuele/Thomas, 203–18 (see part 0.1, note 7).

25. Gerd Theissen, "Jesus und die symbolpolitischen Konflikte seiner Zeit. Sozialgeschichtliche Aspekte der Jesusforschung," *EvTh* 57 (1997), 378–400; also in idem, *Jesus als historische Gestalt*, 169–93 (see part 1.2, note 10); cf. also Ulrich Luz, "Der frühchristliche Christusmythos. Eine Auseinandersetzung mit Gerd Theissens Verständnis der urchristlichen Religion," in *Neutestamentliche Grenzgänge. Symposium zur kritischen Rezeption der Arbeiten Gerd Theissens*, ed. Peter Lampe and Helmut Schwier, Novum Testamentum et Orbis Antiquus/Studien zur Umwelt des Neuen Testaments 75 (Göttingen: Vandenhoeck, 2010), 31–50; and Annette Merz, "Gerd Theissens Beiträge zur Sozialgeschichte des hellenistischen Urchristentums in der neueren Diskussion," in ibid., 96–113.

26. With the exception of the wars following Nero's death in 68 C.E., there were no civil wars.

Judaism specifically during the period from Pompey the Great to Hadrian, this era appears as a time of crisis for Judaism.[27] The view changes yet again with a close-up perspective focused on the period of the Roman prefects in Judea (ca. 6–37 C.E.) and on Galilee under the rule of Herod Antipas (4 B.C.E.–39 C.E.), during which we encounter remarkably stable conditions. Finally we take a microscopic perspective, which can also bring latent and hidden aspects into our field of vision, and it becomes evident that considerable tension lurked beneath a surface calm. Interpretations of crisis and peace are thus a matter of perspective.[28]

Theissen subtly illuminates the ambiguity of the Jesus movement depending on his choice of perspective. Picking up the ideas of media and political scientist Andreas Dörner,[29] he suggests that one characteristic of Jesus's time is that tensions that previously and subsequently turned into violent conflicts are treated as symbolic-political conflicts. According to Dörner, in *symbolic-political conflicts*, different linguistic media

> [strategically engage] symbolic capital in order to accumulate even more symbolic capital in return, i.e., to increase the descriptive power of one's own position in a given domain; to serve symbolic needs for orientation, meaning, identity, etc. in a political commonwealth or in a partial political culture; to convert symbolic capital into political power and in this way achieve a legitimation or delegitimation of existing conditions, an integration into the community or a mobilization against it.[30]

Theissen emphasizes that apparently both Herod Antipas and Pilate attempted to integrate Galileans and Judeans into the Roman Empire and to weaken or undermine their loyalty to Jewish traditions. Herod's relocation of the capital to Tiberias at the site of a former cemetery intentionally provoked conflicts with Jewish purity laws. Conflicts with the prohibition of images and with Jewish marriage laws provoked the population, which was oriented toward Jewish norms. Pilate stamped coins with pagan cultic symbols and attempted to introduce images of the emperor in Jerusalem; he drew on money from the Temple treasury, apparently routed an aqueduct over a cemetery, and variously incited loyalty

27. Theissen lists the Parthian invasions in 41 B.C.E.; the revolts after Herod's death in 4 B.C.E.; Judas Galilaios's campaign against Roman taxation in 6 C.E.; the Caligula Crisis in 39/40 C.E.; the Jewish-Roman war in 66–74 C.E., which led to the destruction of the Temple and Jewish autonomy; the Jewish revolutions in 115 and 117; and the Bar Kokhba revolt in 132–35, which ended with the destruction and loss of the city of Jerusalem.

28. Theissen, "Jesus und die symbolpolitischen Konflikte," 172 (see part 1.3, note 25).

29. Andreas Dörner, *Politischer Mythos und symbolische Politik. Sinnstiftung durch symbolische Formen am Beispiel des Hermannsmythos* (Westdeutscher Verlag: Opladen, 1995).

30. Dörner, *Politischer Mythos,* 57.

conflicts among the population toward their own traditions. That is to say, politics were employed that "aimed at a careful integration of Jewish Palestine into pagan Hellenistic culture." Theissen concludes that those in power "aroused concrete resentment. Symbolic-political attempts at integration devolved into symbolic-political conflicts."[31] This, however, is only one possible interpretation.

What needs to be examined more closely is whether a *double* strategy guides the political symbolism of those in power when a country is occupied for an extended period. Instead of simple friend-foe structures, what generally develops is a complex myriad of variously potent processes of adaptation and demarcation. Enthusiastic accommodation of the superior ruling powers and embittered resistance even to the point of terrorism are merely the extremes within a broad spectrum of positions that in their own turn can be engaged in multifarious modes of conflict even with one another. Calculated provocations by those in power, in this case the Roman Empire and its representatives, aimed at increased integration or sharper demarcation. Friends *and* enemies become more obvious through such symbolic politics. Prophetic political symbolism "from below" now directs itself against this political symbolism "from above."

These considerations show that during Jesus's time,

> things were fermenting beneath a peaceful surface. . . . Oppositional movements among the people, whose mouthpieces and crystallization points were prophets, were reacting to the politics of acculturation symbols. Three prophets from the time of the prefects are known to us, none of whom, however, appeared until the second half of this period—that is, until after the politics of acculturation through symbols had already commenced: John the Baptist, Jesus of Nazareth, and an anonymous Samaritan prophet.[32]

John the Baptist introduced a purification ritual of baptism for the forgiveness of sins, using it as a symbolic-political gesture to draw attention to the threatening defilement of the entire country by the occupying power. He called out into the desert—this, too, a symbolic-political gesture suggesting a new beginning recalling Israel's exodus from Egypt. This perspectival reversal is combined with an at least indirect criticism of the Jerusalem Temple and along with it the priestly aristocracy, who lived off the Temple cult. Although we have differing

---

31. Theissen, "Jesus und die symbolpolitischen Konflikte," 180 (see part 1.3, note 25).
32. Theissen, "Jesus und die symbolpolitischen Konflikte," 180, 181f.

accounts regarding John's end, he in any case posed a political challenge for those in power.

Theissen suggests that "Herod Antipas's fear of an upheaval was not unjustified. Following the execution of John the Baptist, a new prophet arose, Jesus of Nazareth,"[33] albeit one who replaced baptism with other symbolic actions, namely, exorcisms or the casting out of unclean spirits.

> Exorcisms can be understood as a symbolic protest: the land is being threatened by unclean spirits. They take possession of people and estrange them from themselves. What comes to expression here is the fear of foreign cultural, religious, and military power. . . . By calling one of these demons "Legion" and thereby directly associating it with Roman soldiers (and unclean pigs), the transmitters of exorcism accounts are simultaneously affirming the correlation between belief in demons, exorcisms, and the general social situation in the country.[34]

Jesus's criticism of the existing powers is similarly differently weighted than John's. "John the Baptist combined direct criticism of the rulers with indirect criticism of the temple." Jesus criticizes the leaders only indirectly (with the teaching on divorce, Mark 10:2ff; Matt 5:31ff; Luke 16:18; and by calling Herod a fox, Luke 13:32).[35] However, he criticized the Temple directly—above all through the symbolic action of its purification. Alongside exorcism, temple purification, and temple prophecy, Theissen finds a wealth of other symbolic-political actions in the accounts of Jesus, for example, in the calling of the twelve disciples, who are expressly given leadership over the twelve tribes of Israel according to Matthew 19:28–30. On the one hand, this appointment evokes the memory of Israel's tribal constitution, which during Jesus's time was alive only in oppositional groups like the Essenes. On the other hand, Jesus appoints "ordinary people from the population as rulers and judges of these twelve tribes."[36] Another symbolic-political act was Jesus's entry into Jerusalem as a contrast to the entry of the prefects. Theissen concludes: "There is no doubt: Jesus was able to formulate 'parables' not just with words, but also with deeds. He had mastered the language

---

33. Theissen, "Jesus und die symbolpolitischen Konflikte," 183.

34. Theissen, "Jesus und die symbolpolitischen Konflikte," 183.

35. The same applies to the taxation question (Mark 12:13–17); according to Theissen, Jesus certainly could also have been alluding to Pilate's attempt to covertly introduce banners with Caesar's image into Jerusalem, so that the statement "give to the emperor the things that are the emperor's" might also have alluded to the removal of the images of Caesar from the Holy Land.

36. Theissen, "Jesus und die symbolpolitischen Konflikte," 186.

of symbolic actions, and some of these actions had a symbolic-political character."[37]

We must keep in mind that virtually the entire history documented by the biblical canon unfolded under the pressure of a world power if we are to grasp the crucial significance of this manner of engaging symbolic-political conflict not only within the context of the historical Jesus, but also for the conceptual development and symbolic imagery within the biblical traditions themselves and for the "rationality of religion" at large. Following the Egyptians, Assyrians, Babylonians, Persians, and Greeks, it was now the Romans who controlled the country. The continual presence of militarily and politically superior powers led to varying degrees of accommodation and demarcation that broke down the religious and moral norms and the certainty of expectation within the country. Within the population's relationship with its (currently Roman) occupiers, *relativism* and *apathy* were now added to the tensions otherwise typifying resistance and the interest in preserving life and limb, namely, radical non-compliance, on the one hand, and opportunism, on the other. The "political symbolism of the prophets" spoke to this convoluted mélange, equally addressing normal citizens and the aristocracy as well as differing sensibilities and circumstances of orientation.

At Jesus's time, the Jewish upper class stood in tension between attempts to conform to the Roman Empire and thereby to gain access to the professional opportunities it offered, and efforts to preserve and defend Jewish traditions. In contrast to these options, Jesus proclaimed "the reign of God, the immanent prevailing power of the one and only God, who is already operating in a concealed manner." He offered a new interpretation of the Torah, one that picked up and strengthened traditions while at the same time relativizing them.[38]

Jesus, however, also addressed the people and their conflicts, issues Theissen locates above all in the question of property ownership and taxation. Rather than calling the peasants suffering under the weight of taxation and temple tributes to direct resistance, Jesus instead integrates them in a symbolic-political fashion into a new, metapolitical, but very real community. When, for instance, they are addressed in the Beatitudes, "blessed are the poor in spirit, for theirs is the kingdom of heaven . . . Blessed are the meek, for they will inherit the earth (Matt 5:3, 5)," they were presented with what might well be called symbolic politics of non-violent resistance to tax-collectors and land usurpers. By meddling in the symbolic-political conflicts of his time in precisely the way he did,

---

37. Theissen, "Jesus und die symbolpolitischen Konflikte," 187.
38. Cf. Theissen, "Jesus und die symbolpolitischen Konflikte," 193.

namely, in a form directly benefiting the weak, suffering, and marginalized, and by questioning and indeed eclipsing the professional options of the aristocracy through his proclamation of God's reign, Jesus relativized the differences between the aristocracy and ordinary people: "He formulates many of the values and convictions of the upper class such that they become accessible to all. He gave the little people a consciousness of being elite themselves: the salt of the earth and the light of the world."[39]

Although Theissen's and Crossan's reconstructions of Jesus's life are clearly analogous to each other, they do offer different perspectives—on the one hand, the "grand" symbolic-political disputes that were, however, reflected in interpersonal and familial life; on the other, an exemplary interpersonal ethos that did nonetheless become completely politically engaged. It would be incorrect to insist on one interpretation or the other, since the two perspectives mutually complement each other. In principle, they can be integrated into a more complex portrayal and fruitful research program that we will now introduce as the "fourth quest for the historical Jesus."

---

39. Theissen, "Jesus und die symbolpolitischen Konflikte," 193. See the subtle discussion on the "modes of political social interactions" in Jesus's contexts in Bruce J. Malina, *The Social Gospel of Jesus: The Kingdom of God in Mediterranean Perspective* (Minneapolis: Fortress, 2001), esp. 76ff.

1.4 The "Fourth Quest" for the Historical Jesus: The Illuminating Power of Fourfold Multicontextuality

Most people move fairly effortlessly between different situations. They dress, express themselves, and react differently depending on context. An illustration of the multicontextuality of life does not require us to adduce contrasts as stark as those between a disco and a funeral, or a sports arena and a job interview. Increasing life expectancy, relocation, and career changes often represent trenchant contextual changes in a person's life, prompting changes not only to our way of thinking, but also to the basic patterns of our remembrance and expectations. We ourselves are similarly perceived differently by others depending on context, or appear differently in their perception—even more so when we are not physically present, for instance, when we are present only in reports and testimonies.

When we begin to perceive ourselves, other people, and even historical figures multicontextually, we develop a more complex, but also more acute mental image of a given person or situation. Although we do expect continuity and consistency in life and in the personal development of others, and expect—or at least hope for—character, reliability, and trustworthiness, nonetheless when our expectations are indeed disappointed, we should also consider the possible presence of biographical discontinuity, identity conflicts, and even elements that might be contributing to coerced accommodation. Multicontextual thinking sharpens or trains our individual social, cultural, and historical perception and conceptualization, something that also applies to the search for the historical Jesus.

Jesus ministered in Galilee, in the regions bordering Galilee, and in Jerusalem, among both rural and urban populations. In Jesus's encounter with the centurion of Capernaum (Matt 8:5–13; Luke 7:1–10; John 4:46b–54) and the Syro-Phoenician woman (Mark 7:24–30; Matt 15:21–28), the tension between Jews and Gentiles becomes just as discernible as in the Gospel references to the Roman rulers. In the Capernaum of Jesus's day, a center for his ministry, there was also a division between the spheres of control of Herod Antipas and Herod Philip (both of whom were sons of Herod the Great, who likely died shortly after Jesus's birth), suggesting that here, too, contextual differences might need to be taken into account.

Further, tensions between rich and poor, masters and servants are variously palpable in Jesus's proclamations, as are differences between the pious from among the laity, on the one hand, and religious

87

functionaries and the elite religious leadership, on the other. Jesus's resonance would have been quite different among those with whom he shared communal meals than among those whom he directly or indirectly influenced by his healings, and different yet again among those who were moved primarily by his proclamation of the kingdom of God. Trained Torah scholars likely reacted differently to him than people who were moved primarily by his humanity. His conflicts with those aligned with tradition and temple, namely, with Pharisees, teachers of the Law, elders, and priests, along with his entry into the symbolic-political conflicts between Rome and the religious leaders of Israel increase the complexity of his charisma even more (see part 1.3).

Although we can infer this *initial or first level of multicontextuality* of his lived life only approximately through biblical and extrabiblical witnesses and through specific archaeological evidence, nonetheless numerous contributions to the Jesus quest have paid insufficient attention to it. Instead, they seek a monocontextual image of Jesus (for example, the Jesus of communal meals who recognizes people's basic needs, or Jesus the exorcist and proclaimer of the kingdom of God) rather than taking seriously the notion that even the so-called "concrete history" of Jesus (which can be only approximately reconstructed, though with justifiable or defensible claims to veracity) remains fragmentary and multifaceted. With its unrealistic striving for "mathematical certainty," the "second quest for the historical Jesus" overdrew the difficulties of approaching this concrete history (cf. part 1.2), while the archaeological representatives of the "third quest" excessively downplayed them (cf. part 1.1). Archaeological finds make the level of concrete history considerably more palpable; indeed, its notable successes perhaps even elicited the new wave of the "third quest," or at any rate strengthened it. The level of concrete history becomes accessible to reconstruction via the varying complexity of written sources, among which the Synoptic Gospels stand out.

These written sources constitute the *second level of multicontextuality*. They focus on Jesus's life and ministry from multiple perspectives and present enormous problems for theological and historical research. Because the individual witnesses or witness complexes focus on different contexts in Jesus's life and ministry rather than offering a unified picture of Jesus, they seem implausible to a naïve observer. Within the framework of the "fourth quest for the historical Jesus," these testimonies are to be queried in light of the first level of multicontextuality, namely, concerning how and in which ways they hierarchize, link, and assess or view the various contexts disclosed by that initial level. Do they privilege specific locales in Jesus's ministry, specific typical communication situations? To what extent can deviations in the authors' varying depictions of Jesus be traced back to their *privileging* of specific contexts and graded *subordination* of others?

The complexity of this research task increases dramatically when we consider the previously extremely uncertain settings of the (biblical) authors and their religious, moral, and political audiences. Who is their audience? What is their purpose in writing? Can a consideration of their possible audience explain their arrangement of contexts into a certain complex depiction of Jesus? From the other side, does a presentation of Jesus that has possibly been fashioned with a multicontextually structured hierarchy in mind facilitate speculation about their audience? Which recurring problems and visions do they associate with Jesus's person, life, and ministry? To whom, and in which contexts, do they seem particularly intent on presenting Jesus's person and life? Although it is, of course, possible to gloss over this second level of multicontextuality with the message—one, incidentally, not to be dismissed as simply untrue—that the biblical authors want to proclaim the "good news" to *all people in all times*, one is then no longer moving within the sphere of *historical* research on the life of Jesus.

Moving this search for historical insight forward requires clarifying the complex mutual relationship between the first and second levels of multicontextuality, a clarification that in its own turn requires an assessment of the highly nuanced processes attaching to any quest for truth. Even at this stage, it already becomes clear that although scholarly-theological investigation of the historical Jesus is confronted with an admittedly quite challenging task, one cannot simply take as one's point of departure a situation of allegedly "hopeless confusion" or merely "legendary glosses" with respect to Jesus's life. The biblical authors are not intent on simply relating personal legends of Jesus, though neither do they simply follow the movements of the earthly Jesus in the physical realm. They are not striving to provide conclusive material for archaeological observation with mathematical or at least empirical certainty.

They do, however, ascribe relatively complex positions and actions, memories and expectations to Jesus and his surroundings, evaluating and using them to create a complex depiction of Jesus. Although their profiles differ more or less starkly one from another, they do not thereby move to the level of fantasy. The grand task of historical Jesus research as well is to distinguish between probable references to the contexts of Jesus's ministry, on the one hand, and to the contexts of the textual witnesses and their audiences, on the other. Here one must constantly keep in mind that Jesus's person and ministry cannot be reduced to a monocontextual profile without doing significant harm (specifically for historical research, though certainly also for Christology and the Christian faith!). Neither his ministry nor his proclamation can be reduced to merely a single theme or a single formula. Those who reduce Jesus to a "Mediterranean Jewish peasant" in politically motivated communal meals, or classify him primarily within the realm of the Old Testament men of God and exorcists, remain as one sided as those who insist on hearing in his words solely an existentialist or socio-political message or a metaphysical logos theology.

The *second* level of multicontextuality, however, focuses retrospectively not only on the multicontextuality of Jesus's concrete life, but also on yet a *third* level—that of the *great canonical traditions*. In his proclamation, teaching, and symbolic actions, Jesus often and variously referred back to Old Testament traditions. Which of these references can enduringly and reliably be attributed to the first level of multicontextuality? Which contextual references to the third level of multicontextuality are characteristic of each specific, individual biblical author? To what extent can the second level be articulated by its references to the third? In the search for the historical Jesus, that third level can be related to the first only with considerable caution. Scholars generally agree that Jesus applied only the title "Son of Man" to himself. By contrast, citations from "the law and the prophets" in New Testament texts cannot simply be classified as "authentic words of the Lord." The question is rather which Old Testament traditions, which sovereign titles, and which social expectations of Jesus are adduced cumulatively, as it were, with respect to which contexts involving Jesus's ministry (first level of multicontextuality) or in the various contexts of the biblical witnesses (second level of multicontextuality; see part 1.5)?

The *fourth level of multicontextuality*, the level facilitating the "fourth quest for the historical Jesus," involves *the entire previous history of reception along with the present global multicontextuality within which Jesus's life and ministry are being actively received, on the one hand, and are in their own turn efficaciously active, on the other.* It is with considerable equanimity that one must bear the objection that what we are proposing here is in reality a boundless task. In view of the fourth level of multicontextuality, we must constantly bear in mind that one can proceed only selectively, reductively, and typologically (cf. part 0.4). The "patristic images of Jesus," the "Reformational view of Jesus," the "historical Jesus according to Roman Catholic doctrine," the "Jesus of liberation theology," the "Pentecostal Jesus"—in all these contexts and many more besides, we are presented with a broad collage of images, perspectives, truth claims, and research projects. *This fourth level of multicontextuality can avoid becoming a bottomless abyss by being referred back to its truth claims about the historical Jesus and, in precisely this regard, also to the other three other levels of multicontextuality.* Only then do the various contexts begin to speak, and only then do their religious or religio-critical, ecclesiastical, moral, political, and historically contingent concerns become discernible and, to the extent such obtains, also their scholarly or methodological styles.

We today are quick to maintain that all perception—historical perception included—is determined by specific interests. These interests, however, are rarely ideologically unambiguous, and it is precisely in scholarly (and, for that matter, also ecclesiastical) settings that they are often quite complex and, moreover, consciously or unconsciously quite well disguised. Commitment to a certain interest by no means precludes either a serious search for insight or the question of truth (cf. part 2.2). In fact, even a particularly intense or binding commitment or tie to a specific interest can promote the search for truth—something also true for the quest for the historical Jesus (see part 0.4). Although scholarly research has no monopoly on the historical Jesus, it can and indeed must nonetheless ensure that with respect to historical insight, resulting truth claims are capable of distinguishing between *processes of discovery and processes of invention.*

On the fourth level of multicontextuality, actual or supposed discovery processes must be referred or related back to the other three levels. Are they genuinely guided by interest in historical insight? If so, are specific Old Testament traditions and expectations particularly stressed "so that the scripture might be fulfilled" (third level of multicontextuality)? If so, why? Are particular New Testament authors intentionally emphasized (second level of multicontextuality)? What reasons motivate such preferences? Which contexts of Jesus's life and ministry are particularly targeted by intellectual perception (first level of multicontextuality)? Are contexts intentionally or unintentionally blurred?

Here it is important to remember that historical investigation of Jesus's life represents only *one* of the tasks of Christology. That said, precisely this task is indispensable for any Christology if it is to avoid talking past or talking around the human being Jesus of Nazareth, that is, for any Christology intent on grasping the human being Jesus of Nazareth as precisely as possible.

This Jesus whom we are to encounter multicontextually does not emerge as a natural entity. As Paul aptly put it, we no longer know Jesus "according to the flesh" (*kata sarka*, 2 Cor 5:16), but rather only through various biblical and extrabiblical witnesses, among which the biblical accounts are especially important. They refer to his contemporaneous presence, which even at the time of composition of these witnesses, however, was already in the past, that is, these witnesses already are look-ing *back* at him and his ministry in different contexts. In so doing, they, too, similarly refer back to biblically recounted pasts when they repeat-edly quote Old Testament texts, occasionally with the emphatic addition "so that the scripture might be fulfilled," or when they remark that such and such occurred "in accordance with the scriptures." Sometimes they cite extensively from the Old Testament. One inherent problem—and one that justifiably plagued the second quest for the historical Jesus—is the uncertainty concerning whether the biblical accounts of Jesus's life and ministry really are referring to a past and future that were *relevant from his perspective*, or instead to events that were in the past primarily *from their own*, i.e., the witnesses', perspectives.

Such questions show the importance or even indispensability of the discriminatory power of the four levels of multicontextuality for a nu-anced and (self-)critical search for the historical Jesus. Is Jesus's past, which was already in the past for the biblical witnesses, really only their own, individual current past? The same question applies to the future hopes encountered in the biblical accounts. We know that, as a rule, the biblical authors wrote for a variety groups and audiences, that is, for a multicontextual future. To what extent do these groups and their par-ticular futures determine what they perceive of Jesus, on the one hand, and what they embrace and describe as his past, on the other?

The quest for the historical Jesus must thus not only seek to check carefully what it is among our own current wishes, expectations, moral dilemmas, and religious needs and trends that we might be projecting into Jesus's life; it must not only keep our own current modalities of time distinct from his time and world. It must also seek to distinguish between Jesus's present, past, and future, that is to say, his ministry, teaching, and promises, from the past, present, and future orientations of his great witnesses Paul, Mark, Luke, Matthew, John, and the other New Testament writings. When we seek simple, quick, even mathe-matically certain answers, we can but despairingly conclude that "no one is in a position any longer to write a life of Jesus." By contrast, a consideration of the four levels of multicontextual complexity turns a seemingly unresolvable problem into a highly intriguing, promising challenge. The various biblical witnesses draw from overlapping but also clearly distinct Old Testament traditions and promises. Future life-of-Jesus research must reconstruct these profiles that are relevant for Jesus's life and ministry and in the process also determine with increasing clarity the New Testament authors' intended audiences, that is, their immediate future horizons (archaeological research can be helpful here).

Such should, however, be distinguished from the contexts in which Jesus himself lived and worked. Although there are indeed numerous such contexts, their number is still finite. The fourth quest for the historical Jesus must acquire and articulate an increasingly clear conception of Jesus's multicontextual life and ministry. Although reductions along the lines of Crossan's or Vermes's must certainly be critically assessed insofar as their depictions do indeed enjoy a high degree of probability with respect to *partial* aspects of Jesus's Galilean ministry, the fourth quest must simultaneously sharpen our awareness of the dangers of one-sided reductions.

That said, any theological, exegetical, and historical zeal that might be generated by the fourth quest for the historical Jesus must first respond to the serious critical objection that precisely such a quest is in fact something better suited for theological specialists and the rather rarified air of academic, i.e., intellectualized theology. There are two responses.

First, theologically based research concerning the historical Jesus has always been an academic-theological undertaking and will continue to be a field of inquiry suitable for well trained, historically and exegetically interested and educated scholars. That notwithstanding, the more enduring results—the status of scholarship—can certainly be communicated to broader circles of historically and spiritually receptive individuals. The enduring distinctions attained by the "first quest for the historical Jesus" (cf. part 1.2), for example, have already provided salutary counters to otherwise fictional accounts of Jesus. Although the skepticism of the "second quest" did have a purifying effect, it also contributed to the self-secularization of the western world (cf. parts 0.5 and 0.6). And the "third quest" still risks disintegrating into one-sided historical contextualization, dogmatic usurpation via "high Christology," and socio- and religio-historical reductions to specific images of Jesus.

This proposal to cultivate a "fourth quest" for the historical Jesus intends to preserve the complex concerns of the "third quest" while combining its various epistemological interests. The results of this project—like those of the "third quest" itself—can similarly be made accessible to people beyond scholarly circles both inside and outside the church. Such dissemination, however, is the responsibility of serious publishers and their publications, teachers, pastors, as well as colleges and universities.

Second, the arduously researched historical-critical reconstruction of the historical Jesus is not the only point of access to Jesus Christ within the sphere of the academy or the church. Though such reconstruction is indeed important or even indispensable if faith is to avoid settling for or being deceived by fantastical and arbitrarily constructed images of Jesus, the quest for the historical Jesus itself by no means covers the entire spectrum of appropriate responses to the revelation of God in Jesus Christ.

1.5 Old Testament Christology? Spaces of Messianic Memories and Horizons of Messianic Expectation (Hengstenberg, Vischer, Cazelles, Gese)

New Testament traditions view Jesus in variously concordant or contrasting relationships with Old Testament figures, including Adam,[1] Abraham,[2] Moses, and Elijah,[3] though also Jonah,[4] King Solomon,[5] and David and the latter's descendants.[6] They associate him with the role of king[7] and speak in various ways about his "kingdom" or "reign."[8] They link him to the role of prophet who both proclaims God's word and truth and discloses injustice, falsehood, disaster, ruin, and hopelessness.[9] He is received as a priest and high priest who facilitates contact between human beings and God and between God and human beings despite human sin and guilt.[10]

Jesus being called Messiah[11] and the Anointed positions him within Old Testament traditions of anointed kings, priests, and prophets.[12] Moreover, as Messiah he is also seen in the role of God's chosen servant who is destined for vicarious representative suffering, powerlessness,

1. 1 Cor 15:22, 45ff.

2. Matt 1:1; John 8:56ff; Gal 3:14, 16, 29.

3. Mark 9:4ff; Matt 17:3ff; Luke 9:30ff; John 1:17; 5:46.

4. Matt 12:40f; Luke 11:29, 32.

5. Matt 12:42; Luke 11:31; see also Manfred Oeming, "Salomo-Christologie im Neuen Testament," in *Gegenwart des lebendigen Christus: Festschrift für Michael Welker zum 60. Geburtstag*, ed. Günter Thomas and Andreas Schüle (Leipzig: Evangelische Verlagsanstalt, 2007), 57-76.

6. Rom 1:1–4; Mark 10:46ff; 12:36f; Matt 15:22; 20:30f; 21:9, 15; 22:43ff; Luke 18:38f; 20:41ff.

7. Matt 21:4–5; 27:11ff; Mark 15:2ff, 32; Luke 1:33; 2:11; 19:38; 23:2f, 37f; John 12:13ff; 18:33ff; 19:12ff; 1 Tim 6:14f. See Patrick D. Miller, "The King of Jews," in *Who is Jesus Christ for Us Today?* 3–18 (see part 0.1, note 7); Donald Juel, *Messianic Exegesis: Christological Interpretation of the Old Testament in Early Christianity* (Philadelphia: Fortress, 1992), 59ff.

8. See parts 4.2–4.4.

9. Matt 13:57; 21:11; Mark 6:4, 15; Luke 4:24; 7:16; 13:33; 21:19; John 4:19, 44; 6:14; 7:40; 9:17. This theme is covered extensively in parts 5.5 and 5.6.

10. Heb 2:17; 5:10; 6:20, 7:26; 8:3; 9:11; see William R.G. Loader, *Sohn und Hoherpriester. Eine traditionsgeschichtliche Untersuchung zur Christologie des Hebräerbriefes*, WMANT 53 (Neukirchen-Vluyn: Neukirchener, 1981), 142ff. See also parts 5.3 and 5.4.

11. Mark 8:29; 9:41; 10:46ff; 11:10; 14:61; 15:26; Matt 1:16; 11:20; 16:16, 20; 23:10; Luke 4:41; 9:20; 24:26; John 1:41; 4:25; 7:41f; 10:24, 27; 20:31; Acts 2:26; 3:18–20; 9:22; 17:3; 18:5, 28.

12. Cf. Calvin, *Institutes* ii, 15, 494 (see part 0.5, note 13); *Das Christusereignis*, ed. Johannes Feiner and Magnus Löhrer, Mysterium salutis: Grundriss heilsgeschichtlicher Dogmatik 3/1 (Einsiedeln: Benziger, 1970), 105ff. See also part 4.1.

and pain.[13] The spirit of God rests on him,[14] which he in turn will pour out on his followers.[15] The frequent references in the Synoptics and John to "the Son of Man"—perhaps the only "sovereign title" the historical Jesus applied to himself[16]—enable these New Testament witnesses to express both his lowliness and (following the conceptual world of Dan 7:13) his divine splendor. Old Testament conceptions of "the Son of God," of the one enthroned "at the right hand of God," of the mediator of creation, and of the judge of the world are all applied to him, though such primarily refer merely to major figures and significant roles and expectations; the next task would be to disclose additional, more complicated and subtle referential relationships within different contexts and in reference to particular content and themes.

Does this extremely dense interconnection between New Testament references to Jesus Christ and Old Testament conceptions, images, and promises mean that we should articulate a "Christology of the Old Testament" (perhaps as the third of the four levels of multicontextuality, cf. part 1.4)? Ernst Wilhelm Hengstenberg, an influential representative of nineteenth-century north German confessionalism, argued this very point and published a broadly conceived *Christology of the Old Testament and a Commentary on the Predictions of the Messiah by the Prophets*.[17] Hengstenberg, an experienced Near Eastern scholar, philosopher, and theologian who at twenty-one years of age was already teaching Arabic in Basel and at twenty-two had published a translation of Aristotle's *Metaphysics*, worked through the entire Old Testament in order to show, in hundreds of pages of discussion, that it is full of messianic predictions pointing directly to Jesus Christ. Hengstenberg presents himself as a fervent defender of the revelatory power of the Old Testament. "For whoever truly believes Christ and the Apostles, must acknowledge the divine authority of the Old Covenant, to which they give so clear and definite testimony."[18] Hengstenberg's concerns, however,

---

13. Luke 24:46; Acts 3:18; 17:3.

14. Matt 12:18–21 following Isa 42:1–4; Luke 4:18–19 following Isa 61:1–2.

15. Luke 3:16; Acts 2:33.

16. Cf. Theissen/Merz, *The Historical Jesus*, 610ff (see part 1.1, note 5); see also the contributions in *Jesus und der Menschensohn*, ed. Rudolf Pesch and Rudolf Schnackenburg (Freiburg: Herder, 1975), esp. 11ff, 166ff, 240ff.

17.   Ernst Wilhelm Hengstenberg, *Christology of the Old Testament and a Commentary on the Predictions of the Messiah by the Prophets*, trans. Reuel Keith, 3 vols. (Alexandria [Washington], D.C.: William M. Morrison, 1836). In 1850, the Roman Catholic Johannes Bade published *Christologie des Alten Testaments oder die messianischen Verheißungen, Weissagungen und Typen mit besonderer Berücksichtigung ihres organischen Zusammenhangs* (Münster: J.H. Deiters, 1850).

18. Hengstenberg, *Christology of the Old Testament*, 1:24.

neither contribute clearly to our understanding of revelation nor provide any serious service to Christology.

Emanuel Hirsch rightly recognized that the motivation for Hengstenberg's Herculean endeavor was ultimately a radical biblicism, since for biblicists "the Christian faith [is based] on the Bible as a whole. Whoever infringes on even the most modest Old Testament passage also infringes on Christ."[19] Hengstenberg emphasizes that Israel's theocratic vision risked "becoming extremely contracted and selfish,"[20] that is, of being restricted solely to Israel. For Hengstenberg, the Messiah thus had to emphasize God's omnipotence and propagate God as the Lord of all the nations of the world. He also, however, had to remove any doubt concerning divine guidance from those living in a seemingly hopeless situation. Hence for Hengstenberg the primary purpose of the Old Testament is to prepare for Christ and facilitate the understanding of Christ. In both testaments, the completely infallible Bible proclaims the omnipotence of God and his revelation in the Messiah, Jesus Christ.

Whereas Hengstenberg's presence in European theology today is at best that of a theological historian and an exemplary if problematic confessionalist and biblicist, his *Christology of the Old Testament* is apparently enjoying considerable popularity in the English-speaking world, particularly in the United States. Many editions have been printed; indeed, recently new editions have appeared almost annually.[21]

That said, a "Christology of the Old Testament" written from a biblicist perspective does represent a source of danger. Instead of identifying individual promises of the coming and revelation of the Messiah within various contexts, its systematizing construct instead conveniently ignores historical circumstances and reads the revelation of Christ into the most widely varying contexts. In doing so, it becomes triumphantly ideological and at least tendentiously anti-Semitic.[22]

19. Emanuel Hirsch, *Geschichte der neuern evangelischen Theologie im Zusammenhang mit den allgemeinen Bewegungen des europäischen Denkens*, vol. 5 (Gütersloh: Gütersloher, 1975), 126f; cf. 118ff; cf. also Claude Welch, *Protestant Thought in the Nineteenth Century*, vol. 1, 1799–1870 (New Haven: Yale University Press, 1972), 194–98.

20. Hengstenberg, *Christology of the Old Testament*, 1:20 (see part 1.5, note 17).

21. Most recently: Ernst Wilhelm Hengstenberg, *Christology of the Old Testament, and a Commentary on the Messianic Predictions*, 2 vols. (Benediction Classics, 2011).

22. The presentation by Notker Füglister, "Alttestamentliche Grundlagen der neutestamentlichen Christologie," in *Mysterium Salutis* 3/1, 105ff (see part 1.5, note 12), similarly views the Old Testament as a "history of failures" that ends in an aporia; he suggests that "we can by no means neglect the task of discerning and articulating this *negative aspect* of the Old Testament. It is only against this dark background that the essence of the New Testament, its soteriology and Christology, is properly illuminated, since it is here, after all,

By contrast, the two-volume work by Wilhelm Vischer, *The Witness of the Old Testament to Christ*,[23] written and published during the dictatorship of National Socialism, is in fact shaped by anti-ideological interests. Rather than simply propagate a "Christology" of the Old Testament, Vischer instead shows that an anticipation of Christ's witness can be discerned in many Old Testament passages such that from a Christian perspective, the two testaments can indeed be seen as a unity. Still, Vischer's basic position is ambivalent. On the one hand, he makes the unfortunate blanket statement that "in their preaching of Jesus the Messiah the apostles in no way desire to declare anything else than that which is written in the Old Testament." On the other, he concedes "nor do they wish to give to 'the life of Jesus' in the Old Testament an arbitrary Christian interpretation, and still less to assert the embodiment of some 'Christ-idea.'"[24] His volumes remain a fragmentary collage of citations.

"Christology of the Old Testament" is the subtitle of Henri Cazelles's book, *Le Messie de la Bible: Christologie de l'Ancien Testament*.[25] However, neither the title nor the subtitle really correspond to what Cazelles would like to present. He focuses instead on a fusion of historical investigation and systematic reflections into the "double exit" of a millennium of biblical composition, which on his view issues into both the Torah *and* the person of Jesus Christ.[26] Picking up on the work of Gershom Sholem,[27] Cazelles investigates the biblical traditions by asking how messianic expectations were able to arise in the first place and how they

that this failure is allegedly overcome and the aporia resolved" (ibid., 223). Here a pathetic religiosity is using the Old Testament as a negative foil for its own self-stabilization.

23. Wilhelm Vischer, *The Witness of the Old Testament to Christ*, 2 vols., trans. A.B. Crabtree (London: Lutterworth Press, 1941).

24. Vischer, *Witness of the Old Testament*, 1:11 and 11f; Sidney Greidanus represents a similarly ambivalent position with a homiletic agenda in *Preaching Christ from the Old Testament: A Contemporary Hermeneutical Method* (Grand Rapids: Eerdmans, 1999), esp. 46ff.

25. Henri Cazelles, *Le Messie de la Bible: Christologie de l'Ancien Testament* (Paris: Desclée, 1978).

26. See in this regard Bernd Janowski, "Der eine Gott der beiden Testamente. Grundfragen einer Biblischen Theologie," in Janowski, *Die rettende Gerechtigkeit*, Beiträge zur Theologie des Alten Testaments 2 (Neukirchen-Vluyn: Neukirchener, 1999), 249–84; idem, "Die kontrastive Einheit der Schrift. Zur Hermeneutik des biblischen Kanons," in *Gegenwart des lebendigen Christus*, 77–93 (see part 1.5, note 5); concerning the differences between Jewish and Christian Messianism, see Seán Freyne, "The Early Christians and Jewish Messianic Ideas," 30–41; and Jacob Neusner, "When did Judaism become a Messianic Religion?" 45–56, both in *Messianism through History*, Concilium, ed. Wim Beuken, Seán Freyne, and Anton Weiler (London: SCM, 1993), vol. 1.

27. Gershom Scholem, *The Messianic Idea in Judaism and Other Essays on Jewish Spirituality* (New York: Schocken, 1978).

were eventually disappointed. Following the destruction of the Temple in 70 C.E., messianism allegedly irreversibly came to an end, this then also being the time when news of the appearances of the Resurrected to the disciples, who recognized in Jesus of Nazareth the Davidic, eschatological Messiah, became known to a broader public audience. This particular Messiah is both king and priest of God's people, who in their own turn represent a kingdom of priests:

> His kingdom, however, which is indeed *in* the world, is nonetheless not *of* this world. The Messiah, Jesus, leaves the worldly authorities their positions while he himself gives his Spirit to the church community, which dwells in osmosis with all nations, among whom the Jewish community had already lived after the end of the Davidic monarchy and its royal messianism.[28]

What is outlined here is arguably not an Old Testament Christology at all, but rather a sequence of messianic promises and expectations.

In a study at once both dense and nuanced, Hartmut Gese boldly traces the grand outlines of a "revelation history" that in his view combines the various Old Testament traditions from a primarily messianological perspective.[29] What he finds in the biblical traditions is a development toward an increasingly clear understanding of God's revelatory will. The conception of the Son of God emerged together with the Davidic kingship and existence as a sovereign nation-state. In a sense, the "Davidic kingship on Zion was the curacy of the kingship of God" (144). In this king and at this locale, "God, as it were, approaches the world" (144). Israel shares use of the formula "Son of God" with almost all other forms of sacral kingship. The divine election of Zion, the election of David and Solomon (Ps 89:27f; 2 Sam 7:14) are linked to this formula, and the

---

28. Cazelles, *Le Messie de la Bible* (see part 1.5, note 25), translation here from the German edition: *Alttestamentliche Christologie. Zur Geschichte der Messiasidee*, Theologia Romanica XIII (Einsiedeln: Johannes Verlag, 1983), 189. See also the contributions in *Studien zum Messiasbild im Alten Testament*, ed. Ursula Struppe, Stuttgarter Biblische Aufsatzbände 6 (Stuttgart: Verlag Katholisches Bibelwerk, 1989). Likewise, see Friedrich-Wilhelm Marquardt's creative suggestion that the traditions of the Old Testament contribute substantially to the form of the resurrection hopes that become associated with Jesus Christ: "Just as the resurrected Jesus opened up the scriptures for his witnesses and awoke the memory of the history of the Jewish people, so conversely the scriptures awoke Jesus's new life"; in Friedrich Wilhelm Marquardt, *Das christliche Bekenntnis zu Jesus, dem Juden. Eine Christologie*, vol. 1 (Munich: Kaiser, 1990), 165, cf. 165ff.

29. Hartmut Gese, "The Messiah," in Gese, *Essays on Biblical Theology*, trans. Keith Crim (Minneapolis: Augsburg Publishing, 1981), 141–66. The page references in the following paragraphs refer to this essay. See also John P. Meier, "From Elijah-like Prophet to Royal Davidic Messiah," in *Jesus: A Colloquium*, 45–83 (part 1.3, note 11).

Davidic throne itself comes to be called the "throne of Yahweh" (1 Chr 28:5; 29:23). This honorific title is then transferred to Israel itself in the most varied contexts (e.g., Exod 4:22; Deut 1:31; 32:6,18f; Isa 63:16; Jer 31:9; Hos 11:1; cf. Gese, 145). Gese then suggests that in the New Testament, this installation and enthronement was attributed to "the Son," Jesus Christ (e.g. Rom 1:3f; Mark 1:11 par.; Mark 9:7 par; Mark 15:39;[30] Matt 11:27; Luke 1:32f).

With the collapse of Davidic rule under Assyria in the eighth century B.C.E., messianic understanding changed. God had rejected the house of David, Immanuel had yet to be born (Isa 7:10ff; Mic 5:1,3), and indeed was to be born in "Bethlehem of Ephrathah, [you] who are one of the little clans of Judah." Gese remarks that it "would be possible to try to see the distinction between king and Messiah in the promise given in Isaiah 9:6–7, especially in the four-fold messianic throne name, which surpasses even the figure of David—'Wonderful Counselor, Mighty God, Everlasting Father, Prince of Peace'" (147). The Messiah, as it were, rises above even the king.

During the later postexilic period, Gese discerns yet another "considerable deepening of the messianic concept" in which, on the one hand, an "eschatological return of God to Zion" is envisioned (Zech 9:9f; Isa 12:6; Zeph 3:14f; Zech 2:14) (149) and, on the other, universalized hope focuses on a king of peace who will come humbly riding on a donkey (cf. Zech 9:9–10 with 1 Kgs 1:38).

During the third-century Ptolemaic period, the Messiah took on the form of a martyr, and "the development of the messianic concept in purely Davidic terms as the Son of God came to a certain conclusion" (152). The second and first centuries B.C.E. saw the emergence of the apocalyptic conception of the Son of Man,[31] with the figure of the Son of Man himself oscillating between human and angelic forms; he becomes the royal ruler over an eschatological, truly eternal world kingdom, and, as Gese puts it, the paradoxical situation arises "in which humans belong to the heavenly realm" (154). Gese finds both Mosaic and Davidic prophetic traditions expanded in this figure (Ezekiel; Dan 8:17; but also Exod 24:18), one that then also comes to be associated

---

30. Concerning Mark's Christology, see Donald H. Juel, *A Master of Surprise: Mark Interpreted* (Minneapolis: Fortress, 1994), esp. 33ff and 91ff.

31. Dan 7:15ff, cf. 1 En 37–71 and 4 Ezra 13. See in this regard Theissen/Merz, *The Historical Jesus*, 541–53 (see part 1.1, note 5); Douglas R. A. Hare, *The Son of Man Tradition* (Minneapolis: Fortress, 1990), esp. 213ff; Volker Hampel, *Menschensohn und historischer Jesus. Ein Rätselwort als Schlüssel zum messianischen Selbstverständnis Jesu* (Neukirchen-Vluyn: Neukirchener, 1990), esp. 27ff.

with wisdom theology (Job 28:23ff; Prov 8:30; Sir 24:1–22; Wis 7:22ff, 9:10, 17).[32]

Gese summarizes (160):

> The Son of Man tradition is a transformation of Davidic messianism. Rather than standing alongside the traditional Davidic concept of the Messiah, it instead embraces that same concept by uniting the royal and priestly Davidic Messiah with the Mosaic-prophetic figure that brings revelation, and by then recognizing this universally human mediator of God's revelation as himself being a revelation to mankind.

Gese sees these traditions flowing into the New Testament materials and stresses that what one finds in New Testament Christology is not "additions" from various conceptual sensibilities, but rather "transformations" of messianological traditions for which the Old Testament supplied "the presuppositions of tradition history and revelation history" (166).

Insights articulated during a dispute between Otfried Hofius and Peter Stuhlmacher[33] can facilitate further exploration of the interaction between the first three multicontextual levels (see part 1.4). Although Stuhlmacher finds that the Gospels are already referring to the *earthly* Jesus as the Messiah (John 1:41; 4:25), but simultaneously demonstrating that the reference is "not merely to someone divinely appointed from the line of David, but to the Immanuel promised to Israel in Isa 7:14 (Luke 1:35; 2:6; Matt 1:21–23), the pre-existent Son of God who became flesh (Mark 1:1–2; John 1:1–18)."[34] Although New Testament traditions do clearly acknowledge this distinction, they nevertheless insist that Jesus is the Christ promised in 2 Sam 7:14; Pss 2:7 and 89:28 "(cf. Rom 5:6–8 with Rom 1:2–4; 9:5; 15:8–12 and Heb 1:1–2)."[35] From this perspective, the multicontextuality of Old Testament traditions is fused with messianic expectation. By contrast, Hofius distinguishes "more restricted use" of the term Messiah in reference to "the eschatological salvific king of Israel" from "broader use" that refers more generally to

---

32. See Gese, *Die Weisheit, der Menschensohn* (see part 1.3, note 13); idem, "Die Offenbarung des Gottesreiches und die Erscheinung des Messias. Die Heilserwartung im Alten Testament," in *Weihnachten neu überlegt*, ed. Wolfgang Boehme, Herrenalber Texte 14 (Karlsruhe: W. Boehme, 1979), 18–32; Gerhard von Rad, *Wisdom in Israel*, trans. James D. Martin (London: SCM, 1972), 144f.

33. Otfried Hofius, "Ist Jesus der Messias? Thesen," 103–29; Peter Stuhlmacher, "Der messianische Gottesknecht," 131–54, both in *Jahrbuch für Biblische Theologie 8: Der Messias* (1993) (Neukirchen-Vluyn: Neukirchener).

34. Stuhlmacher, "Der messianische Gottesknecht," 138; idem, *Biblische Theologie des Neuen Testaments*, vol. 1: *Grundlegung. Von Jesus zu Paulus* (Göttingen: Vandenhoeck, 1992), 107ff, 156ff.

35. Stuhlmacher, "Der messianische Gottesknecht," 154.

"eschatological saviors and redeemer figures of various sorts."[36] His intention is to respect historically what we would call the (third level of)
multicontextuality of Old Testament traditions, finding in New Testament witnesses then the creation of a "completely new 'Messianic' concept" that "differs in a fundamentally qualitative way from the royal
messianology documented in Old Testament–early Jewish traditions."[37]
New Testament authors interpreted this messianic concept—which was
to be developed from the perspective of Jesus's cross and resurrection—
"in light of their respective Christologies."[38] That is, the (second level of)
multicontextuality of New Testament traditions must also be respected
as it unfolds in light of the given historical context of the crucifixion (see
especially part 3.3) and the various resurrection accounts (cf. part 2.3).

These differences in assessing continuity and discontinuity between the various traditions can likely not be satisfactorily evaluated
with any claim to historically reliable research through a comparison of
such broad and diverse perspectives. More or less convincing ecclesio-
political and temporally critical concerns (Hengstenberg, Vischer) or
systematic-theological interests (Cazelles, Gese, Stuhlmacher) are variously combined with exegetically and historically oriented research results. The vast network obtaining between the first and second levels of
multicontextuality, on the one hand, and the third (that of recollection
and expectation within Old Testament traditions), on the other, still remains largely obscure and controversial. A bold and impressive outline
of messianic-theological lines of development such as that of Hartmut
Gese clearly exhibits systematic-theological features, and exegetes intent
on proceeding in a clearly focused historical fashion will, like Hofius, resist such outlining of "broad" or "grand sweeps."

How is historically and biblically oriented Christology to deal with
these difficulties? One strategy is to articulate the transitions between
historical and systematic questions regarding the core content of Christology, something I will undertake in the next two parts by focusing on
the two central themes of the resurrection and cross of Jesus Christ.
The crucifixion accounts present Jesus Christ's life in both continuity
and discontinuity with his pre-Easter existence, offering a "sublation"
in the double Hegelian sense of both "preservation," on the one hand,
and "relativizing" or "moving beyond," on the other. Many Christologies have extensively systematized, if not mystified, the accounts of the
crucifixion. As will be seen, a precise examination of Jesus's trial and way

36. Hofius, "Ist Jesus der Messias?" 103 (see part 1.5, note 33).
37. Hofius, "Ist Jesus der Messias?" 128.
38. Hofius, "Ist Jesus der Messias?" 124, cf. 122ff.

of the cross[39] is of particular importance for correctly hearing the nuanced versions of the "message of the cross" and allowing them their full effect. The next question, however, becomes how then to correlate in an appropriate fashion the connection between New Testament witnesses to Christ, on the one hand, and Old Testament traditions, on the other.

On the one hand, given the current research situation it seems prudent to remain attentive to the promising findings of historical and systematic synthesis (Gese) and also to track ongoing exegetical and historical research on specific canonical contextual networks; on the other we have at our disposal a consciously systematic-theological approach that has already long been present in classic Christologies and is, moreover, also ecumenically proven. The "doctrine of the threefold office of Christ," namely, the royal, priestly, and prophetic offices, offers a considerable (if limited) number of connection points with Old Testament traditions (see part 4.1). As will be seen, although this approach is more modest and fragmentary than the grand tradition sweep of "King—Son of God—Messiah—Son of Man," it does offer revealing connections with Jesus's life with respect to his pre-Easter ministry, his cross, and his resurrection. In a way, it functions as a kind of structural repository containing a wealth of historical and systematic connections with which the development of christological doctrine will remain perpetually confronted in its search for insight and truth. The realization that Jesus Christ associates the exercise of his "offices" with the outpouring of God's Spirit and that his witnesses thus receive a share in his life and ministry not only makes the scope of his reign discernible, but also at least partially discloses the dimensions to which references to the "Son of Man" try to allude (cf. parts 4.4; 5.3–5.6).

---

39. Cf. the anticipatory model in Moltmann, *The Crucified God,* esp. chapter 4 (see part 0.1, note 6).

PART 2

The Resurrection

2.1 Debates over the Reality of the Resurrection: Merely Visions? Merely a Myth? (Strauss, Bultmann, Lüdemann)

Hardly any theme associated with the Christian faith evokes as emotional a response as that of the resurrection. As Paul says, "if Christ has not been raised, then our proclamation has been in vain and your faith has been in vain" (1 Cor 15:14). For without faith in the resurrection, Christ's cross simply cannot be understood as a salvific event, and without the resurrection, the entirety of faith itself collapses. That Jesus Christ "not only was, but is,"[1] indeed, that he not only *is*, but is also *present in the power of his creative spirit*—all this hinges on the resurrection. What first turns faith in Jesus Christ into "good news," into a genuine message of salvation, is the confession that the Jesus Christ who is present not only touches human beings through his life and message, but also takes up their lives into his own. That said, hardly any theme is more difficult for healthy human understanding—common sense—to process than precisely that of the resurrection.

Life-of-Jesus scholarship has attempted to make peace on two fronts with healthy human understanding concerning this problem. It maintained, first, that the resurrection was a mere vision on the part of Jesus's disciples; it also suggested, second, that Jesus's followers in fact were merely creating a new myth through their references to the resurrection. The classic nineteenth-century representative of these positions was David Friedrich Strauss. In the twentieth century, it was Rudolf Bultmann, with his program of demythologization, who tried to reconcile so-called "modern thinking" with the resurrection message. More recently, the

---

1. Cf. Joseph Ratzinger—Benedict XVI, *Jesus of Nazareth, Holy Week: From the Entrance into Jerusalem to the Resurrection*, 242: "Whether Jesus merely *was* or whether he also *is*—this depends on the Resurrection" (see part 1.3, note 20).

New Testament scholar Gerd Lüdemann provoked his contemporaries with the thesis that any honest examination of the resurrection had to begin with the fact of Jesus's putrefaction and then understand faith in the Resurrected as the result of visions. All three theologians generated public scandals with these attempts to understand Jesus's resurrection.

The two-volume work *The Life of Jesus, Critically Examined*, published in 1835 and 1836 by a tutor at the Tübingen seminary (the "Stift"), David Friedrich Strauss, generated an immense theological scandal in the wake of which the highly gifted twenty-seven-year-old Strauss, who had studied under Hegel and Schleiermacher in Berlin and Ferdinand Christian Baur in Tübingen, lost his position. Although he later made a name for himself by publishing several brilliant historical biographies and critical works on theology and philosophy, he was never again able to reestablish his academic career. But his *The Life of Jesus, Critically Examined*, which appeared in multiple printings and eventually even in a popularized form "for the German people,"[2] provoked passionate responses throughout Germany. The philosopher Karl Rosenkranz reported from distant Königsberg:

> I was astonished to find even within the rather restricted circle of my own experience that Prussian estate owners spent an entire winter rigorously reading and discussing page after page of Strauss, then later even entering into correspondence concerning disputed points. Clerics hereabouts have frequently come out in nothing less than terroristic opposition to Strauss's assertions.[3]

Two points must be kept in mind if one is to appreciate the sheer extent of the commotion, fright, and indignation this *Life of Jesus* caused in Germany. First, Strauss scrutinized New Testament statements concerning the life and ministry of Jesus quite consciously with an eye on mutually contradictory and divergent portrayals. And since such a vast number of contradictory explications and statements do indeed emerge—beginning with the mutually incompatible birth narratives in Matthew and Luke and extending to the resurrection and ascension narratives—one cannot but conclude that these are *not* historical accounts at all, but rather, as Strauss puts it, "myths" that, like tendrils, are entwined round about what is now a hardly recognizable figure. Regardless of whether miracle

2. *Das Leben Jesu für das deutsche Volk bearbeitet*, 2 vols., 20th ed. (Leipzig: Kröner, 1864) (with Strauss's preface to the first and second editions). A reprint of the original edition of 1835 is being considered by the Wissenschaftliche Buchgesellschaft in Darmstadt.

3. Cited in *Der Protestantismus im 19. und 20. Jahrhundert, Klassiker des Protestantismus*, vol. viii, ed. Wolfgang Philipp (Bremen: Carl Schünemann, 1965), 166.

stories, parables, or prophecies—nothing stands up to his critique. In chapter after chapter, he comes to the same conclusion, namely, that the portrayal of the life and ministry of Jesus is pure invention and fiction, albeit, as he emphasizes, not simply an ordinary bit of fiction. What we have before us here are the "products of the collective consciousness of a certain people or religious circle," and Strauss follows the lead of a rather broad discussion taking placing during his own lifetime in referring to these products as "myths."[4] He speaks in this context about a "primitive-Christian production of myths" in which myths can indeed be expressed by *individuals*, but in which the myths nonetheless elicit broader faith because the individual essentially functions merely as the "organ of universal conviction." Many myths develop "successively and by degrees, under the influence of very different circumstances and events both external and internal."[5]

The second provocation was that after demonstrating the untenability of the natural-historical foundations of the Christian faith, Strauss then also suggested that his contemporaries completely abandon any fixation on Jesus Christ—regardless of whether as a mythological or speculative figure. For, as Strauss puts it in his concluding passages, "this is indeed not the mode in which Idea realizes itself; it is not wont to lavish all its fullness on one exemplar, and be niggardly towards all others."[6] That Christology nonetheless seems tied to the person and history of a *single individual* allegedly derives, Strauss suggests, simply from the limited conceptual capacity of Jesus's own time.

Within the framework of this general assault on Jesus piety and Christology as such, Strauss is also intent on dispensing with faith in the resurrection, emphasizing that even someone as early as the philosopher Celsus during the second century "chose this alternative, deriving the alleged appearance of Jesus after the resurrection, from the self-delusion of the disciples, especially the women, either dreaming or waking; or from what appeared to him still more probable, intentional deception."[7] That said, Strauss does acknowledge that the

---

4. Cf. Strauss, *Life of Jesus*, vol. 1, 27ff, and *Das Leben Jesu*, kritisch bearbeitet, vol. 1, 2nd ed. (Tübingen: Osiander, 1837), 30ff, where he examines historical, philosophical, and poetic myths picking up on the previous work of Friedrich Wilhelm Joseph Schelling, Johann Philipp Gabler, Heinrich Eberhard Gottlob Paulus, Wilhelm Martin Leberecht De Wette, and others. (Texts of translations of Strauss's *Das Leben Jesu* may differ depending on the German edition serving as the basis for the translation, Strauss having edited various passages in subsequent editions. The translation here is based on the German edition indicated above.)

5. Strauss, *The Life of Jesus*, vol. 1, 64, et passim (see part 2.1, note 2)

6. Strauss, *The Life of Jesus*, vol. 2, concluding section 151.

7. Strauss, *Life of Jesus*, vol. 2, 846.

strong faith and enthusiasm with which they proclaimed him as the Messiah
on the succeeding Pentecost, would be inexplicable unless in the interim
something extraordinarily encouraging had taken place—something, in
fact, which had convinced them of his resurrection.[8]

Such by no means proves, however, that this conviction was necessarily
elicited by a real appearance of the Resurrected—or even by some external appearance at all, for that matter. One might just as easily assume,
Strauss maintains, that an inner vision was miraculously generated in
the disciples whose purpose was to render the Resurrected visible to
them according to their own powers and capacity of conceptualization
and the mode of understanding of their own age. Strauss concludes that
we should acknowledge not the *fact* itself of revivification, but rather the
faith in it, along with faith in subsequent alleged appearances of the Resurrected as well, while simultaneously treating the various and sundry
details of these narratives as legendary glosses, that is, as the *fruit* of visions that come to be articulated in the myth.

On June 1, 1941, Rudolf Bultmann delivered his famous (and notorious)
lecture on "demythologization," a lecture that in its own turn ignited a
heated theological discussion that endured for decades.[9] Bultmann's
fundamental thesis is that the New Testament represents or reflects a
mythical view of the world that divides the world into three levels: in the
middle the earth itself, then above it heaven and below it the underworld.
The earth is, on the one hand, the locus of the natural events of quotidian
life, and, on the other, the setting in which supernatural powers come to
bear—those of God and his angels, and of Satan and his demons. Human
history and life are influenced by the intervention of these supernatural
powers, and the portrayals of God's revelation in Jesus Christ and of salvation history similarly correspond to this mythic worldview.

Bultmann finds meaningless and even impossible any expectation
on the part of Christian proclamation that modern human beings accept
this mythic worldview as true. Meaningless because rather than being
something specifically Christian, the mythic worldview as such is "simply
the world picture of a time now past that was not yet formed by scientific
thinking" (3); impossible because a worldview cannot be appropriated by
choice or decision, being instead already given to every human being by
virtue of that person's historical situation (3). Articulations of the world

8. Strauss, *Life of Jesus*, vol. 2, 847.

9. "New Testament and Mythology (1941)," in Rudolf Bultmann, *New Testament and
Mythology and Other Basic Writings*, ed. Schubert M. Ogden (Philadelphia: Fortress,
1984), 1–44. Pagination from this English edition.

come upon us—today we would say: through a paradigm shift—thereafter shaping our worldview whether we want such to be the case or not. Any attempt at reviving the worldview of Jesus's day is doomed to fail. "Criticism of the New Testament is simply a given with modern thinking as it has come to us through our history" (4).

According to Bultmann, elements within New Testament narratives that modern human beings simply cannot constructively appropriate include especially the notion of Jesus's resurrection. Despite even their best intentions, modern human beings simply cannot "understand Jesus' resurrection as an event whereby a power to live is released that we can now appropriate through the sacraments. . . . that the possibility that such a life should be created by a dead person's being brought back to physical life is unimaginable" (7). The notion of resurrection as revivification to actual, corporeal life, however, is not the only element modern human beings cannot constructively appropriate.

> As for the Gnostic scheme of ideas, it is only with great effort that we can even put ourselves into a way of thinking according to which the dead and risen Christ was not simply a man, but a God-man, whose dying and rising again were not an isolated fact occurring only to him as an individual person but rather a cosmic occurrence into which we all are drawn (Rom. 5:12ff.; 1 Cor. 15:21ff., 44b). We certainly cannot think this way ourselves. (8)

Bultmann's intention is to interpret the Christian understanding of being (or existence) from a "nonmythological . . . existential" perspective. He views the true life of human beings as that in which "we lived out of what is invisible and nondisposable and, therefore, surrendered all self-contrived security. This is life 'according to the Spirit' or life 'in faith'" (17). In Bultmann's view, true life in the Spirit and in faith involves "freedom from the world," a distancing of oneself from the world that makes the believers the "lords over all things," thus taking the believer up into an eschatological existence in which that believer becomes a new creature: "The judgment of the world is not a cosmic event that is still to happen but is the fact that Jesus has come into the world and issued the call to faith. . . . Those who believe already have life, they have passed from death to life" (19).

Like David Friedrich Strauss before him, Bultmann is convinced the New Testament presents the Christ event as a mythic event, notwithstanding

> The historical and the mythical here are peculiarly intertwined: the historical Jesus whose father and mother are well known (John 6:42) is at the same time supposed to be the preexistent Son of God, and alongside

> of the historical event of the cross stands the resurrection, which is not a
> historical event. (32)

How is this intertwining to be understood? Bultmann formulates his solution as a question, namely,

> whether the point of such mythological task is not simply to express the
> significance of the historical figure of Jesus and his story, namely, their
> significance as saving figure and salvation occurrence. If this were their
> point, their content as objectifying representations could be given up. (33)

What sense, then, does it make even to speak about the resurrection?
Bultmann again frames his response as a question:

> It (the resurrection) is not a historical event. . . . Can talking about Christ's
> resurrection be anything other than an expression of the significance of the
> cross? Does it say anything else than that Jesus' death on the cross is not
> to be seen as a human death but rather as God's liberating judgment of the
> world, the judgment that as such robs death of its power? (36)

Bultmann never tires of emphasizing that the resurrection is *not* an
"authenticating miracle which one could securely establish so as to con-
vince a doubter that the cross really does have the cosmic-eschatological
meaning ascribed to it" (37). Nor can the resurrection be such an "authenticating miracle" precisely because "a dead person's returning to life
in this world . . . is incredible," and because "the resurrection cannot be
established as an objective fact by ever so many witnesses" (37).

The Easter event is nothing but the emergence of that particular faith
in the Resurrected in which proclamation itself originated. That is, the
Easter event as the resurrection of Christ is *not* to be taken as a *historical*
event. "Christ the crucified and risen one encounters us in the word of
proclamation, and nowhere else" (39). Demythologization, so Bultmann,
grasps what this statement implies; demythologization itself is the process whereby one disengages from the mythical articulation of the New
Testament events. For critics of Bultmann's program of demythologization, however, faith in the resurrection becomes thereby a nebulous theology of proclamation and its "existential" appropriation, which in its
own turn cannot but then turn down the path of "subjectivist faith" (see
part 0.5).

Bultmann clearly explicated his concept of demythologization once
more in 1961.[10]

---

10. "On the Problem of Demythologizing (1961)," in Rudolf Bultmann, *New Testament
and Mythology and Other Basic Writings*, 155-63. Pagination here refers to this English

> By "demythologizing" I understand a hermeneutical procedure that
> inquires about the reality referred to by mythological statements or
> texts. This presupposes that myth indeed talks about a reality, but in an
> inadequate way. (155)

> Myth intends to talk about a reality which lies beyond the reality that can
> be objectified, observed, and controlled. . . . It is the reality that means for
> us salvation or damnation, grace or wrath, and that demands of us respect
> and obedience. (160)

In Bultmann's view, mythological thinking objectifies this "beyond" in a
naïve fashion, whereas "demythologizing seeks to bring out myth's real
intention to talk about our own authentic reality as human beings" (161).
That is, the objectifying discourse of myth is sublated that we might more
appropriately articulate precisely the existential reality that, according to
Bultmann, the myth intended to render discernible on its own terms in
the first place.

In many respects, the provocation caused by the book *The Resurrection
of Jesus: History, Experience*[11] by the Göttingen New Testament scholar Gerd Lüdemann resembles that caused by David Friedrich Strauss's
book. Lüdemann shares with both Strauss and Bultmann a strong inclination for truthfulness and sincerity and an equally strong aversion
against any theology that makes things a bit too easy for itself in that
respect.

> Lack of clarity, cluelessness, though also the disinclination to engage in
> any honest discussion of the topic have disturbed and even tormented
> me [since the beginning of Lüdemann's own study of theology], and I am
> experiencing resistance from every possible quarter yet again now that the
> topic is finally on the table following the publication of my book on the
> resurrection.[12]

Lüdemann emphasizes that he intends to trace out as concretely, vividly,
and sensitively as possible the disciples' experiences between Good Friday and Easter to gain insight into the origins of what is known as Easter

---

edition. Cf. also David Fergusson, *Rudolf Bultmann*, Outstanding Christian Thinkers, 2nd
ed. (London and New York: Continuum, 2000), 107ff.

  11. *The Resurrection of Jesus: History, Experience, Theology* (Minneapolis: Fortress
Press, 1994). Original German: *Die Auferstehung Jesu. Historie, Erfahrung, Theologie*
(Göttingen: Vandenhoeck, 1994).

  12. Gerd Lüdemann, "Zwischen Karfreitag und Ostern," in *Osterglaube ohne Auferstehung? Diskussion mit Gerd Lüdemann*, QD 155, ed. Hansjürgen Verweyen (Freiburg/
Basel/Wien: Herder, 1995), 14.

faith. His searches within the New Testament "Easter visions" for traces of the revivified Jesus repeatedly—and, we must add: justifiably—come up empty, leading to what for him is the disappointing observation that such traces are simply not to be found. He concludes: "Viewed positively, the fact of Jesus's putrefaction is for me the point of departure for all further discussions regarding his resurrection."[13] The issue of Jesus's putrefaction having been clarified for him personally, he next asks what, then, might have prompted the theological assertion that God raised Jesus from the dead. "My answer: *visions*. Viewed from the outside, the Easter experiences are to be characterized as visions. Visions are visual appearances of persons, things, or scenes with no external reality; a vision does not reach the person who sees it through the anatomical sense organs, but is instead a product of the powers of imagination and fantasy."[14] Here Lüdemann offers a popularized theological version supported neither by the intelligent theory of myth underlying Strauss's book nor by the program of demythologization of someone like Bultmann, speculating instead from his own, personal perspective concerning what might have happened to Jesus and his disciples after Jesus's death, concluding that Jesus putrefied, and that the disciples experienced visions.[15]

All three scandal-beset critics of the resurrection—Strauss, Bultmann, Lüdemann—committed an all too frequent error, namely, that of equating Jesus's resurrection with *physical* revivification, which they then call into question, doing precisely what many of the religious fundamentalists do above whom they elevate themselves as "modern human beings" and "honest friends of truth." That is, they share with many fundamentalists an identification of "resurrection" with "physical revivification"—except that they then more or less loudly and radically contest precisely the presupposition *they themselves* have posited, and in so doing, as we shall see, egregiously distort the subtleness of the biblical resurrection accounts. Their references to myth and (subjective) visions fail to recognize the particular reality of the resurrection and of the resurrection

13. Lüdemann, "Zwischen Karfreitag und Ostern," 27.
14. Lüdemann, "Zwischen Karfreitag und Ostern," 27f.
15. For a comprehensive assessment of Lüdemann's assertions, assertions supported neither exegetically nor by historical-critical analysis, cf. *Die Wirklichkeit der Auferstehung*, ed. Hans-Joachim Eckstein and Michael Welker, 4th ed. (Neukirchen-Vluyn: Neukirchener, 2010). – Beginning in 1994, Lüdemann, aided esp. by the public media, sought the approval of what he considered "sincere and honest people," and in 1998 publicly renounced Christianity. Although he pursued legal action against the restriction of his teaching at the University of Göttingen to the "history and literature of early Christianity" and to courses "outside those stipulated for training future theologians," on October 28, 2008, the Supreme Court in Germany ended what was a wholly unsuccessful legal battle.

experience, and their propagation of an "existentialist interpretation" effectively moves toward emptying Christian faith of its content. "Subjectivist faith," which rigorously does without any connection with Jesus Christ and instead seeks "closeness to God" in self-conversation solely within religious interiority, can then appear as a meaningful or even unavoidable alternative (cf. part 0.5).

Wolfhart Pannenberg sought a path out of this dead-end during the second half of the twentieth century by posing the question "Was the resurrection of Jesus a historical event?" In so doing, he inaugurated a new stage in the theological discussion of the resurrection and of resurrection faith.

2.2 The Resurrection as Historical Event (Pannenberg)

In the second volume of his book *Systematic Theology*, Wolfhart Pannenberg quite accurately notes:

> The resurrection of Jesus . . . was not a return to earthly life. It was a transition to the new eschatological life. He is "the first fruits of those that have fallen asleep" (1 Cor. 15:20), "the first-born among many brethren" (Rom. 8:29), "the first-born from the dead" (Col. 1:18; cf. Rev. 1:5), the initiator of a new life (Acts 3:15). (348)[1]

If, however, the resurrection is a transition into new, eschatological life, then how is its *facticity* to be maintained? How reliable are the witnesses to the resurrection? And in the larger sense, how do our references to the "reality of the resurrection" relate to our normal experiential reality? These questions must be answered with persuasive and cogent counter-arguments if we are to refute the views from Strauss to Lüdemann.

Although Pannenberg, like Bultmann and Lüdemann, is intent on proceeding in an intellectually and theologically honest fashion, he deals more cautiously with textual materials than does Bultmann and more precisely with systematic concepts such as experience, reality, and historicity than does Lüdemann. He focuses in a much more concentrated fashion than does Bultmann on the narrative details of the biblical resurrection accounts, in the process coming to the more cautious conclusion that "the appearances reported in the Gospels . . . have such a strongly legendary character that one can scarcely find a historical kernel of their own in them," being so "heavily colored by legendary elements, particularly by the tendency toward underlining the corporeality of the appearances."[2] These encounter narratives, however, while certainly

1. Wolfhart Pannenberg, *Systematic Theology*, vol. 2, trans. Geoffrey W. Bromiley (Grand Rapids: Eerdmans, 1991), 348; cf. also Carey C. Newman, "Resurrection as Glory: Divine Presence and Christian Origins," in *The Resurrection: An Interdisciplinary Symposium on the Resurrection of Jesus*, ed. S. T. Davis, D. Kendall, and G. O'Collins (Oxford: Oxford University Press, 1998), 59–89; Gerald O'Collins, *Easter Faith: Believing in the Risen Jesus* (New York, Mahwah: Paulist Press, 2003), 25ff.

2. Wolfhart Pannenberg, *Grundzüge der Christologie*, 7th ed. (Gütersloh: Gütersloher, 1990), 85. English: *Jesus, God and Man*, trans. Lewis L. Wilkins and Duane A. Priebe, 2nd ed. (Philadelphia: Westminster, 1977), 89; bracketed pagination here refers to this English edition. Cf., however, the more cautious assessment in Pannenberg, *Systematic Theology*, vol. 2, 352ff; see also idem, "Die Auferstehung Jesu und die Zukunft des Menschen," *KuD* 24 (1978), 104–17; idem, "The Historicity of the Resurrection: The Identity of Christ," in *The Intellectuals Speak Out About God: A Handbook for the Christian Student in a Secular Society*, ed. Roy A. Varghese (Chicago: Regnery Gateway, 1984), 257ff. Concerning Pannenberg's theology of resurrection, see Gunther Wenz, "Ostern als Urdatum

not the *only* biblical references to the resurrection, and notwithstanding their legendary coloring, on the whole are indeed intent on giving "proof by means of witnesses for the facticity of Jesus' resurrection" (89), something that becomes especially clear in Paul's grand enumeration in 1 Cor 15:3-9, according to which the Resurrected allegedly appeared first to Peter, then to the twelve disciples, then to more than five hundred "brothers and sisters," then to James the brother of Jesus, then to all the apostles, and finally to "one untimely born," namely, to Paul himself.

Pannenberg challenges the notion that the resurrection testimonies may be dismissed, since one can assume that the witnesses were indeed personally involved and interested in a positive outcome to the event of the cross. The texts, Pannenberg maintains, support the notion that the "appearances of the resurrected Lord were really experienced by a number of members of the primitive Christian community and not perhaps freely invented in the course of later legendary development" (91). One cannot doubt, Pannenberg emphasizes along with Johannes Leipoldt, "that the disciples were convinced that they had seen the resurrected Lord. Otherwise the origin of the community in Jerusalem and with it of the church becomes an enigma" (91).[3] That notwithstanding, these conclusions still say nothing about the *nature* of the disciples' experience.

Since Pannenberg finds no firm basis for historical considerations in the Gospel accounts given their "tendency toward underlining the corporeality of the appearances" (89), he concentrates instead on the light phenomenon, concerning which at least Paul does provide clear testimony. It is here that he finds a point of departure for the facticity of the resurrection, that is, for its historicity. This light phenomenon exhibits five characteristics:

1. It is seen in relationship with the human being Jesus, a relationship that in one fashion or the other becomes clear precisely in that light phenomenon (cf. Gal 1:16; 1 Cor 9:1).

---

des Christentums. Zu Wolfhart Pannenbergs Theologie der Auferweckung Jesu," in *"Der Herr ist wahrhaft auferstanden." Biblische und systematische Beiträge zur Entstehung des Osterglaubens*, ed. I. Broia and J. Werbick (Stuttgart: Katholisches Bibelwerk, 1988), 133ff; and André Kendel, "'Die Historizität der Auferstehung ist bis auf weiteres vorauszusetzen.' Wolfhart Pannenbergs Verständnis der Auferstehung und seine Bewertung der einschlägigen biblischen Überlieferungen," in *Die Wirklichkeit der Auferstehung*, 139ff (see part 2.1, note 15); idem, *Geschichte, Antizipation und Auferstehung. Theologische und texttheoretische Untersuchung zu W. Pannenbergs Verständnis von Wirklichkeit*, International Theology 8 (Frankfurt: Peter Lang, 2001).

3. Johannes Leipoldt, "Zu den Auferstehungsgeschichten," *ThLZ* 73 (1948), 737ff., 737; cf. also Adolf Schlatter, *The History of the Christ: The Foundation for New Testament Theology*, trans. Andreas J. Köstenberger (Grand Rapids: Baker, 1997), 383ff, who draws attention to the biblical texts' concern with localizing the resurrection appearances.

2. What is perceived is a spiritual body, not a person with an earthly body.

3. It likely involved an appearance "from on high," from "heaven."

4. The Damascus appearance happened as a light phenomenon (Acts 9:3f.).

5. Paul's christophany was accompanied by an audition, i.e., by an audible message.

Pannenberg suspects that *all* the resurrection visions were likely of this nature, that is, all were related back to Jesus of Nazareth and all emphasized that he was indeed recognized as such. It must have involved "an extraordinary vision, not an event that was visible to everyone" (93). "An event of this sort must be designated as a vision. If someone sees something that others present are not able to see, then it involves a vision'" (93). Although referring to such an event as a "vision" suggests that the precipitating event was extraordinary in the strict sense of "out of the ordinary," such by no means necessarily implies that the event was *imaginary*. Since biblical traditions attest various sorts of visions— "visions in dreams and visions while awake, visions in ecstasy and visions in a peaceful frame of mind" (94)—it is clear that within the varieties of what is known as the *Sitz im Leben*, reality was indeed attributed to at least a certain "spectrum" of visions. A problem arises, Pannenberg suggests, if one associates *every* vision with a (merely) self-generated fantasy that ultimately has no real connection with objective reality. He similarly warns against applying to religio-historical phenomena, without further qualification, a psychiatric understanding of visions deriving largely from an examination of ill persons.

To demonstrate the historicity of the resurrection and assess the uniqueness of this historical event as such, Pannenberg suggests one must first ask whether the appearances are to be explained "by the enthusiastically excited imagination of the disciples," or, "conversely, the Easter faith of the disciples is to be explained from the appearances" (96). Because the resurrection represents a religio-historical *novum*, psychological explanations are insufficient. What first had to become clear within the context of apocalyptic expectation at that time was that the resurrection, as the Easter message states, happened to Jesus *alone*, and was not the commencement of some universal event affecting all human beings.[4]

---

4. Matt 27:52f alone offers a somewhat dark intimation in this respect: "The tombs also were opened, and many bodies of the saints who had fallen asleep were raised. After his resurrection they came out of the tombs and entered the holy city and appeared to many."

This concentration on the resurrection solely of Jesus is the *first* objection to the assertion of a merely psychic reaction and chain reaction (cf. 96). The *second* objection draws support from the multiplicity of appearances and their temporal dispersal. That the appearances to Peter, James, and Paul are temporally quite distant one from the other, with that to Paul not occurring until three years after Jesus's earthly end in Jerusalem, renders purely psychogenic explanations of the Easter appearances inadequate and instead suggests that attempts at a historical reconstruction would indeed be meaningful. That said, other attendant, qualifying factors must first be clarified and special attention given to the particular understanding of reality inevitably accompanying any historical reconstruction.

An objective and composed examination of the symbolic language in which the resurrection accounts are written is certainly possible if one but avoids understanding "historical" as "that which can be repeated on a naturalistic-empirical level." Much like a political proclamation with very real consequences, so also does the resurrection intervene in the circumstances of human life, positing new historical circumstances in its own turn. With an argument that was already important to Pannenberg at an earlier period and that becomes increasingly dominant in his systematic theology, he emphasizes that "an individual event is never completely determined by natural laws." "Conformity to law embraces only one aspect of what happens. From another perspective, everything that happens is contingent, and the validity of the laws of nature is itself contingent" (98). Against this background, he can concede that the resurrection involves the "beginning of a new aeon," and that "the reality of the new aeon cannot be perceived with the eyes of the old aeon" (99). He then concludes that

> the resurrected Lord is in fact not perceptible as one object among others in this world; therefore, he could only be experienced and designated by an extraordinary mode of experience, the vision, and only in metaphorical language. In this way, however, he made himself known in the midst of our reality at a very definite time, in a limited number of events, and to men who are particularly designated. Consequently, these events are to be affirmed or denied also as historical events, as occurrences that actually happened at a definite time in the past. (99)

By contrast, one can only view critically the propagation of certainty that is allegedly "better" than historical knowledge—for example, "intuitive" certainty deriving solely from faith itself—as an adequate mode of perception for the resurrection.[5] Pannenberg criticizes Bultmann's and oth-

---

5. Cf. Paul Althaus, *The So-called Kerygma and the Historical Jesus* (Edinburgh,

ers' references to the "risk of faith" both in general and specifically in connection with the resurrection. If the resurrection was indeed a real event in the past, then here, too, "the only method of achieving at least approximate certainty with regard to the events of a past time is historical research" (99).

Pannenberg finds another important support in favor of the historicity of the resurrection in the traditions concerning the empty tomb (see in this regard part 2.3). That historicity is supported by the fact that Jewish polemic *shares* with its Christian opponents the conviction that Jesus's tomb was indeed empty (albeit with a different interpretation; cf. 101). That tomb traditions and appearance traditions developed independently of one another suggests the presence of mutually supportive and complementary traditions and enhances the historical probability of the resurrection in the sense described.

The following discussion will move further down the path Pannenberg himself takes but will pay closer attention to the problematical resurrection witnesses that speak about "encounters." A precise examination of these texts reveals that they do *not* assert that Jesus's resurrection was in fact a revivification of the pre-Easter Jesus, nor do these texts give the impression that the post-Easter Jesus Christ lived together with his disciples or with others in the same way as did the pre-Easter Jesus. Although they do emphasize the *continuity* between the pre- and post-Easter Jesus Christ, they also underscore the *discontinuity* between these two stages of his life, suggesting thereby that the Resurrected had a more complex identity we must yet examine more closely. That is, the continuity of his person and his life is not simply that of earthly, physical existence, and to that extent the polemic extending from Strauss to Lüdemann misses the decisive point. It is quite inconceivable that a primary witness to the resurrection could have said, "Please excuse me for not having recognized you at first, Jesus; but how good that you are here again!"

London: Oliver and Boyd, 1959), 38ff, 47ff; and Walter Künneth, *Glauben an Jesus? Die Begegnung der Christologie mit der modernen Existenz* (Hamburg: Witting, 1962), 285 (cf. Pannenberg, *Jesus, God and Man,* 99).

2.3 Light Appearances – Empty Tomb – Resurrection Encounters: The Revealing Complexity of the New Testament Witnesses

The biblical resurrection accounts are paradoxical, asserting at once that the Resurrected stands in both continuity *and* discontinuity with the pre-Easter Jesus. The resurrection was not a physical revivification. Resurrection witnesses reflect this complicated identity by, on the one hand, alluding to the manifest sensual presence of the resurrected Christ—i.e., others can genuinely perceive him with their senses—while simultaneously emphasizing that these were nonetheless *appearances*. The Emmaus story according to Luke 24 is the most trenchant example in this regard.

The eyes of the disciples who encounter the Resurrected on the way to Emmaus are "kept (*ekratounto*) from recognizing him" (Luke 24:16), despite the fact that he speaks with them and interprets the mystery of the Messiah to them "in all the scriptures" (Luke 24:27). Luke 24:30–31 then continues: "When he was at the table with them, he took bread, blessed and broke it, and gave it to them. Then their eyes were opened, and they recognized him." But the passage then abruptly and disconcertingly concludes: "and he vanished from their sight."

Instead of lamenting this conclusion or skeptically viewing the entire event as a ghostly occurrence, the disciples instead retrospectively realize that they had *already* sensed the Resurrected's presence even *before* their eyes were opened by the ritual act of the breaking of the bread during their communal meal. "They said to each other, 'Were not our hearts burning within us while he was talking to us on the road, while he was opening the scriptures to us?'" (Luke 24:32). And then they attest the resurrection of Jesus Christ to others.

This peculiar tension between appearance and sensual manifestness in the encounter with the resurrected Jesus Christ must be taken into account if one is to approach more closely to the particular reality of the resurrection appearances, namely, a feeling or intimation of the presence of the Resurrected (Luke 24:32, at least in retrospect of the encounter) that does *not*, however, extend far enough to constitute or transition into recognition or certainty. After the Resurrected vanishes, that certainty of recognition proves in its own turn to have been a vision, albeit one that now does indeed allow or cause that earlier *intimation* for his presence to transition to legitimate *knowledge*. That is, the Resurrected contemporizes himself in a new form both in the intimation of the presence of the Resurrected that transitions to knowledge, and in knowledge based on a vision. It is a form that exhibits features of sensual manifestness, on the one hand, and yet also is to be identified as an appearance, on the other, since, after all, the Resurrected does indeed vanish or is withdrawn.

One cannot appreciate the subtlety of this constellation (one recurring in several biblical texts; see section C below), however, if one insists on pressing for a decision with respect to the apparent duality inhering within the interior tension, to wit: *either* it is a case of unambiguous recognition, that is, of knowledge based on sensual perception; *or* the entire experience is nothing but phantasmagoria.

To attain a more nuanced understanding of the reality of the resurrection on the basis of the biblical witnesses, our point of departure will embrace a broader spectrum of evidence than does that of Pannenberg, focusing on three groups of narratives: the light appearances, witnesses to the empty tomb, and the appearance encounters, that is, appearances that at least temporarily prompted a consciousness in those who encountered the Resurrected that he was manifestly present in some revivified fashion.

A. Light Appearances

According to the resurrection witnesses, does the physical-biological body of the pre-Easter Jesus reappear? Do those witnesses provide any support for the assertion that through the resurrection, the pre-Easter Jesus was restored such that he could continue his physical, pre-Easter existence—in short, that he was revivified? The first group of traditions unambiguously contradicts this assertion, namely, the light appearances that are so central for Pannenberg's interpretation. It is Paul who, recounting his own "Damascus experience," explicitly attests the resurrection as a light appearance (Acts 9:3–9; 22:6–11; 26:12–18).

Paul recounts that he himself sensually perceived the light appearance.[6] The overwhelming power of this appearance comes to drastically clear expression when Paul reacts to his experience by falling to the ground and going temporarily blind.[7] Paul's letters repeatedly allude to this revelatory experience and its consequences for his life:

- 1 Cor 9:1: "Have I not seen Jesus our Lord?"
- In Gal 1:15–16, he speaks of having been "set . . . apart before I was born and called . . . through his [God's] grace" "to reveal his Son to me, so that I might proclaim him among the Gentiles."

6. Cf. Lüdemann, "Zwischen Karfreitag und Ostern," 28f (see part 2.1, note 12).
7. Acts 9:4, 9; 22:7, 11; according to Acts 26:14, all of Paul's companions also fall to the ground.

- In Phil 3:8, he recounts how his knowing Christ Jesus brought about a complete revaluation of his life and a devaluation of his previous life.

- Finally, in 2 Cor 4:6 he writes: "For it is the God who said, 'Let light shine out of darkness,' who has shone in our hearts to give the light of the knowledge of the glory of God in the face of Jesus Christ."

Lüdemann subtly remarks in this regard:

> In this case, it is likely that at his conversion, Paul saw Christ in a luminous figure, something that accords with his explications of the "man of heaven" (1 Cor 15:49). Paul would, moreover, view his vision of Christ parallel with the emergence of light on the morning of creation to express what happened to him at Damascus.[8]

On the one hand, a luminous figure signaling a second new creation from chaos and in the process manifesting the pre-Easter Jesus in a new form; on the other hand, an instance of human perception that *recognizes* the pre-Easter Jesus in that luminous figure—both belong to the polyphony of resurrection appearances that precipitate the universal and individual certainty that is quickly spreading, namely, that Jesus Christ is risen! He lives!

Pannenberg calls these luminous phenomena "visions," albeit without intending to localize them within merely subjective or even psychopathological categories (cf. part 2.2). By contrast, Joachim Ringleben has advised dispensing completely in this context with any reference to a concept of visions in favor of speaking in a rigorously consistent fashion of "appearances." "The term 'vision,'" Ringleben maintains, "unavoidably displaces the ground of cognition into the visionary subject, whereas 'appearance' displaces it into a self-manifestation or demonstration that additionally— and strictly *eodem actu*—discloses accesses to that appearance."[9] Here Ringleben cites Karl Barth: "He can be perceived only as He comes."[10] It is precisely for the sake of securing the element of facticity and historicity that is so important to Paul, and then from Paul all the way to Pannenberg, that one should employ the concept of "visions"—if at all—only with extreme caution and with the requisite commentary.

---

8. Lüdemann, "Zwischen Karfreitag und Ostern," 29 (see part 2.1, note 12); in a note, he refers to Acts 9:3f.

9. Joachim Ringleben, *Wahrhaft auferstanden. Zur Begründung der Theologie des lebendigen Gottes* (Tübingen: Mohr Siebeck, 1998), 95; cf. 93ff.

10. *CD IV/2*, 144; see in this regard Bertold Klappert, *Die Auferweckung des Gekreuzigten. Der Ansatz der Christologie Karl Barths im Zusammenhang der Christologie der Gegenwart*, 3rd ed. (Neukirchen-Vluyn: Neukirchener, 1981), 287ff.

These light appearances render problematical any attempt to equate "resurrection" with "physical revivification" (cf. part 2.1). They do, however, raise the question of the possible continuity between the pre- and post-Easter life of Jesus. In what way do the accounts of the empty tomb and the personal appearances of the Resurrected take us *beyond* the light appearances in understanding the unique reality of the resurrection?

B. The Empty Tomb

Lüdemann had announced his intention to use the expression "*occupied tomb*" as a kind of battle standard to "hammer home as trenchantly as possible the fact of Jesus's concrete human existence and the brutal facticity of his death," not least in order to bring to bear more forcefully the principle of *reality* in both theology and the church.[11] Any serious discussion of Jesus's resurrection must, Lüdemann maintains, begin with Jesus's putrefaction. "The circumstantial reference to Jesus's putrefaction is for me the point of departure for any further discussion touching on the 'resurrection.'"[12] Although this polemical stance may well appeal to skeptical human understanding, it employs only seemingly historically grounded speculation in circumventing historical research. Were he intent on not losing contact with the biblical traditions, Lüdemann's declared disposition of critical realism would have been better advised to propose that Jesus's corpse had been stolen; such would have enabled him to pick up on the traditions of the empty tomb, traditions supported by both Christian and Jewish materials, albeit with differing reasoning, and allowing in principle differing interpretations.

a) The tomb was empty because the pre-Easter Jesus had been physically revivified and was now at a different locale. This is the interpretation on which most resurrection critics so intently focus. Although the empty tomb simply as such does render this interpretation possible, the question remains concerning how Jesus's restored life then continued physically.

b) The tomb was empty because the corpse had been stolen. Although here one can indeed speculate with Lüdemann that the corpse then

11. Lüdemann, "Zwischen Karfreitag und Ostern," 26 (see part 2.1, note 12). See in this regard Bernd Oberdorfer, "'Was sucht ihr den Lebendigen bei den Toten?' Überlegungen zur Realität der Auferstehung in Auseinandersetzung mit Gerd Lüdemann," in *Die Wirklichkeit der Auferstehung*, 165ff (see part 2.1, note 15); and Ingolf U. Dalferth, "Volles Grab, leerer Glaube? Zum Streit um die Auferweckung des Gekreuzigten," in *Die Wirklichkeit der Auferstehung*, 277ff.

12. Lüdemann, "Zwischen Karfreitag und Ostern," 27.

putrefied at some unknown locale, one still has no "occupied tomb" for a possible autopsy.

c) The tomb was empty as a result of some hitherto inconceivable enrapture or similarly incomprehensible translation.

d) The tomb was empty because an empty tomb was mistaken for the real place of burial. Few interpreters have considered this possibility.

Every interpretation of the empty tomb must acknowledge that according to these witnesses, the empirically and socially perceivable body of the pre-Easter Jesus was (at least temporarily) *removed* or *withdrawn*. In any event, every conceivable explanation of the empty tomb—from the realistically bone-dry (b and d) to the supernaturalistic (c)—involves the notion that the resurrection accounts offer absolutely no material for a pathological examination of a corpse. All the traditions of the empty tomb and every conceivable interpretation of those traditions speak about the removal or withdrawal—however one might conceive such—of the pre-Easter body.

That said, the experience of the absent body by no means suffices to explain the emergence of faith in the resurrection. The empty tomb *alone*—and here virtually the entire history of interpretation concurs—does not yet suffice to awaken resurrection faith. Not even according to the biblical traditions! Not even the appearance of the angel and young man at the empty tomb with the announcement "He has been raised" prompt any dissemination of news of the resurrection.

Individual texts within the biblical traditions clearly exhibit *uncertainty* and *discrepancies* with respect not only to the identity and number of witnesses at the tomb, but also to the messenger appearances.

- In Matt 28:1–8, we read that an "angel of the Lord" descends from heaven, rolls back the stone before the tomb, and sits on it; he is beheld not only by "Mary Magdalene and the other Mary," but also by the guards, "who shook and became like dead men." The chief priests and elders, however, bribe the guards with "a large sum of money" to spread a version of the story according to which the disciples had stolen the body (Matt 28:11–15).

- Mark 16:1–8 maintains that three women go to the tomb, where they find "a young man, dressed in a white robe," sitting at the tomb, who then relates to them the news of the resurrection. They are charged with going to Galilee and passing along this news to the disciples. The story ends with the women fleeing out of sheer "terror and amazement" and saying "nothing to anyone, for they were afraid."

- Luke 24:1–12 mentions the "women" who had accompanied Jesus from Galilee and "*two* men in dazzling clothes" who deliver the resurrection message. The text also, however, reports that the disciples do not believe the women's account: "But these words seemed to them an idle tale, and they did *not* believe them" (Luke 24:11). Peter alone runs to the grave, where he finds only the linen burial cloths, thereafter leaving profoundly disturbed and "amazed at what had happened" (Luke 24:12).

- According to John 20:1–10, Mary Magdalene, on finding the open tomb, fetches Simon Peter and the "other disciple, the one whom Jesus loved"; she breaks down in tears at the theft of the body and says, "They have taken the Lord out of the tomb, and we do not know where they have laid him" (John 20:2b). The disciples confirm the empty tomb, and the narrative remarks that they did not yet "understand the scripture, that he must rise from the dead" (John 20:9). According to the text, it is only the rather obscure, otherwise nameless figure of the "other disciple, the one whom Jesus loved" (John 20:2), who "went in, and he saw and believed" (John 20:8b).[13]

What do these narratives tell us about the empty tomb—apart from the uncertainty concerning details of the course of events, apart from the fact that Mary Magdalene plays a central role, and apart from the consistent assertion that the tomb was empty and that messengers appeared? These traditions concerning the empty tomb are generally viewed as having a high probability of historical veracity, being confirmed or accepted as they are not only by Jesus's own followers, but also—albeit with a different explanation, namely, as resulting from the corpse having been stolen—by groups hostile to those followers. Another consideration militating in favor of their historicity is that the biblical witnesses adduce and lend credence to the witness of women, which at the time was not otherwise publicly admissible.[14]

That said, these tomb narratives reflect anything but a triumphal story of the attested resurrection. Quite to the contrary,

- they mention the propaganda of adversaries, namely, that the disciples themselves had stolen the corpse and were engaged in deception;

---

13. Cf. John 13:23; 19:26f; 20:2; 21:7, 20. See also Jörg Frey, "Beloved Disciple," in *Religion Past and Present*, vol. 1, 682.

14. Thus the argument of Wolfhart Pannenberg, "Die Auferstehung Jesu. Historie und Theologie," *ZThK* 91/3 (1994), following Hans von Campenhausen, "Der Ablauf der Ostereignisse und das leere Grab," in Campenhausen, *Tradition und Leben. Kräfte der Kirchengeschichte* (Tübingen: Mohr Siebeck, 1960), 48–113.

- the women flee from the tomb out of terror and remain silent;
- the women's account meets with incredulity even among the disciples (an "idle tale"!);
- Peter is profoundly unsettled and wonders in astonishment at what has happened;
- Mary reacts with despair at the notion that the corpse has seemingly been stolen.

What are likely genuinely historical traditions concerning the empty tomb demonstrate that at least in the initial stages, the knowledge and proclamation of the resurrection were not well received or given credence. The one message that does remain consistent, however, is that the body of the pre-Easter Jesus disappeared or was withdrawn. That is, there is no palpable, tangible body—putrefied or not.

C. Resurrection Encounters

The resurrection appearances alter the lives and very existence of those to whom they occur, effectively changing their reality.[15] These are not merely passing impressions. Resurrection appearances are, moreover, grounded in reality, since they are also associated back with the pre-Easter Jesus, his life, and his ministry. Rather than simply reappearing in revivified form, however, he is experienced in a decidedly *new* form. Finally, the biblical accounts repeatedly emphasize that these appearances are invariably accompanied by fear, uncertainty, and even doubt.

- According to Mark, the Resurrected appeared in "another" (or different) form (Mark 16:12), and the accounts of the resurrection were not believed. Indeed, according to Mark 16:14 the Resurrected not only appeared to the eleven disciples, but even "upbraided them for their lack of faith and stubbornness."
- According to Matthew, the Resurrected's appearance to the women was accompanied by proskynesis ("and they came to him, took hold of his feet, and worshiped him" [Matt 28:9]). The appearance to the disciples similarly acquires features of a theophany, a divine revela-

---

15. Lüdemann, "Zwischen Karfreitag und Ostern," 33ff (see part 2.1, note 10), quite correctly points out that the encounter with the Resurrected already brings about a complete life change for Paul and Peter; Paul undergoes a drastic transition from being a persecutor of Christians into a believer, and Peter from being a denier and betrayer of Jesus into a believer in the Resurrected. Concerning the practical theological implications here, cf. Ingo Baldermann, *Auferstehung sehen lernen. Entdeckendes Lernen an biblischen Hoffnungstexten*, Wege des Lernens 10 (Neukirchen-Vluyn: Neukirchener, 1999), 102ff.

tion ("When they saw him, they worshiped him" [Matt 28:17a]). The Resurrected's presentation of himself as the divine Lord prompts an appropriate response on the part of the women and disciples, namely, proskynesis. And yet the passage also immediately continues with the words, "but some doubted" (Matt 28:17b).

- In his own turn, Luke ratchets up the tension between sensual manifestness and appearance not only in the Emmaus story, but also in the account of the empty tomb, trenchantly emphasizing that the apostles, rather than believing that account, instead consider it to be a mere "idle tale." He similarly emphasizes that having already received news of the resurrection, the eleven disciples react to the appearance of the Resurrected with fear and terror, believing "that they were seeing a ghost" (Luke 24:38), whereupon the Resurrected then shows them his hands and feet (Luke 24:39–40) and finally even eats something in their presence (Luke 24:41–42). Interpreters who isolate this passage and take it as the measure of all resurrection witnesses cannot but impose the notion of physical revivification (see in this regard part 2.4), notwithstanding Luke, just as he does in the Emmaus story, goes on to say that "while he was blessing them, he withdrew from them and was carried up into heaven" (Luke 24:51; so also Mark 16:19).

- John, too, rather disconcertingly emphasizes to his readers the simultaneous nature of these occurrences as both appearance *and* sensual manifestation. Jesus passes through locked doors to see the disciples, yet also shows them his hands and side, that is, his wounds (John 20:19–20). During a second encounter—again, "although the doors were shut"—the Resurrected tells doubting Thomas to touch his wounds, whereupon Thomas, rather than excusing his stubborn skepticism, instead utters the confession "My Lord and my God!" (John 20:28)

The resurrection appearances are associated with *both* elements—sensual manifestness *and* withdrawal, enduringly accompanied by fear and doubt. Proskynesis *and* doubt, doubt *and* confession to one's Lord and God—these resurrection accounts do not describe quotidian empirical experiences. By emphasizing the elements associated with appearances, the multiplicity of appearances, the withdrawal of the Resurrected even to the point of being withdrawn or transported away *at the very moment of recognition*, and by consistently drawing attention to the presence of *doubt*, these texts overwhelmingly run counter to the notion that the resurrection involved a mere physical revivification of the pre-Easter Jesus. And despite the extremely problematical and disputed character of these events, these texts do not provide evidence that the witnesses fell prey to mere illusions and surrendered to mere fantasies.

These varied and differing witnesses point to a complex historical event, a new reality; the persuasion that Jesus had died and that his mission and person had failed is replaced by a grounded conviction of his living presence. Although it is true that the pre-Easter Jesus does not reappear as a biological, natural-empirical "event," the Resurrected, that is, the post-Easter Jesus, does indeed make his presence known—and does so with incomparably greater force—in the power of his Spirit and with what is initially a rather modest, then increasingly expanding cultural-historical charisma.

This event is as little an "illusion" as was the discovery of mathematics, music, or justice. It is not merely that a new order of things, a new sphere of knowledge or experience, has been disclosed; it is the person and life itself of Jesus that comes to bear in a new and different fashion, so much so that Paul can now speak of a "spiritual body" (1 Cor 15:44).[16] The deeper implications of this reality can be disclosed with the aid of Paul's insights concerning "body" and "spirit" and through continued tenacious questioning concerning the unique reality of the resurrection itself.

---

16. An expression often rather misleadingly translated as "supernatural body" (e.g., Amplified Bible; Germ. *überirdischer Leib*); cf. 1 Cor 15:44ff; concerning John 20, cf. Gregory Riley, *Resurrection Reconsidered: Thomas and John in Controversy* (Minneapolis: Fortress, 1995), 69ff.

2.4 Not Simply "Alive Again" (Wright): Differentiating between "Flesh" and "Body" in Understanding the Real Presence of the Resurrected

It is with an almost tormented voice that biblical resurrection witnesses make it clear that the resurrected Jesus Christ could *not* be recognized by the features typically sufficing for personal recognition, namely, by his face, his build or movements (cf. John 21:4), or his voice. For even when he explicates the messianic secret according to the Old Testament to the disciples on the way to Emmaus, they still do not recognize him (Luke 24:25–27). The ability of the resurrected Jesus Christ to be "recognized" according to the usual features similarly falters within the medium of visions; in this connection, the traditions speak of celestial and luminous appearances, of the disciples' terror when they believe they have beheld a ghost (Luke 24:37), and of abrupt and unexpected appearances of the Resurrected even though doors are locked (e.g., John 20:19). The frequent allegations that doubt and incredulity arise even *after* the Resurrected has been recognized—and even among the disciples themselves—make it perfectly clear that recognition of the Resurrected among the initial witnesses was anything but the result of quotidian personal encounters.

That notwithstanding, an array of witnesses does suggest that certain encounters triggering a recognition of the Resurrected were more typically sense based. Features in such encounters include the Resurrected's scriptural explication (Luke 24:45), the commission and dispatch of the disciples (Matt 28:19), personal and direct address (e.g., John 20:16), and the invitation to a communal meal (John 21:12),[1] then also the presentation of the wounds (Luke 24:39f; John 20:27), the ritual breaking of bread (Luke 24:30), the gift of bread and fish[2] (John 21:13), the strange connection between theophany, proskynesis (Matt 28:9, 17), and the touching of "his feet" (Matt 28:9)—all these examples belong to this group of witnesses that suggest a sensual, manifest presence of the Resurrected.[3] One particular passage in Luke might best support the as-

1. "Jesus said to them, 'Come and have breakfast.' Now none of the disciples dared to ask him, 'Who are you?' because they knew it was the Lord."

2. For theological scholarship, the conspicuous fish motif in Luke and John is as obscure as is the dove motif at Jesus's baptism.

3. By contrast, John 20:17 reads as follows with respect to the encounter with Mary Magdalene: "Jesus said to her, 'Do not hold on to me' . . ." In the encounter with "doubting Thomas," it is similarly uncertain whether the command "Put your finger here and see my hands. Reach out your hand and put it in my side" is what first elicits the premier New Testament confession "My Lord and my God!" (John 20:27–28), or whether it is only the genuinely concrete, bodily touching that does so.

sumption that Jesus was indeed physically revivified and as such present to the disciples in a way quite accessible to sense perception, since according to Luke 24:43 he eats a fish before their very eyes. Yet just as in the majority of other witnesses, so also here does the author emphasize within the narrower context of this specific episode that the resurrection had the character of an appearance (cf. Luke 24:51).

In *The Resurrection of the Son of God*, an impressive book of more than eight hundred pages,[4] Nicholas Thomas Wright builds a strong case for understanding the resurrection as having been not only "bodily," but also "corporeal" (in the sense of "robustly physical"). Although Wright's assertion that the Resurrected was "alive again" (8 et passim) and "still robustly physical" (478 et passim) when he encountered witnesses initially suggests that, like many fundamentalists, Wright understands the resurrection to have been a physical revivification, he also speaks about the Resurrected having a "transphysical" identity (477 et passim). What, however, is the relationship between these statements each to the other and to the reality of the resurrection?

A discussion of Wright's observations and arguments[5] provides an opportunity to examine more closely what the biblical traditions actually say about the corporeal nature of the Resurrected's presence during the forty days (cf. Acts 1:3) after his crucifixion and about his "bodily resurrection."

Wright is quite justified in rejecting a purely spiritualistic reading that explains the resurrection merely as an "extraction" from this wretched world and the natural reality in which human beings find themselves. "What view of creation, what view of justice, would be served by the offer merely of a new spirituality and a one-way ticket out of trouble, an escape from the real world?" (737). From the outset, however, one can and indeed must counter this justified concern with a warning, namely, "What view of creation, what view of justice, would be served by the offer of nothing more than a 'still robustly physical' resurrected body (albeit with various additional and sometimes strange features that Wright calls 'transphysical') and a one-way ticket merely back into the real world without leaving room for the reality of the spiritual body of Christ?"

---

4. N. T. Wright, *The Resurrection of the Son of God* (London: SPCK, 2003); bracketed pagination in the following discussion refers to this edition; the book is the third volume of Wright's trilogy *Christian Origins and the Question of God*; volume 1, *The New Testament and the People of God* (1992), is a comprehensive examination of the Jewish roots of Christianity, while volume 2 bears the title *Jesus and the Victory of God* (1996).

5. For an extensive discussion, see Michael Welker, "Wright on the Resurrection," *Scottish Journal of Theology* 60 (2007), 458–75.

Wright discusses the topic of resurrection in extraordinary breadth: "Life Beyond Death in Ancient Paganism" (32ff); "Death and Beyond in the Old Testament" (85ff); and "Hope Beyond Death in Postbiblical Judaism" (129ff)—that is, it is not merely New Testament traditions that come to expression here. In his own turn, Wright, in more strongly emphasizing the continuity and restitution than the discontinuity and transformation between the "old" and "new" creation, repeatedly states that in connection with the resurrection, creation is "reaffirmed" (128) and "remade" (128), while nonetheless quite rightly warning against confusing the resurrection with the continued existence of an immortal soul or similar notions. Over the course of his examination of New Testament sources, he also emphasizes the resurrection is indeed accompanied by a "transformation" of Jesus's body, referring in the context to a "new, incorruptible bodily life" (271), though this life is, we are told, something different "than simply returning to exactly the same sort of life, as had happened in the scriptures with the people raised to life by Elijah and Elisha" (273). The impression is certainly possible that Wright may be concurring with our critique of his "alive again" and the considerations presented in the discussion below when he says that the "resurrection was not resuscitation, but transformation into a non-corruptible body" (276).

Wright takes issue with a widespread misinterpretation of biblical resurrection witnesses that unfortunately has far-reaching consequences, to wit:

1. with the imputation that the vision of a light phenomenon was a purely subjective experience;
2. with the assumption that all the apostles had such a subjective experience;
3. with the conclusion that this non-objective experience calls into question the notion of a bodily resurrection of Jesus (cf. 393).

As helpful as Wright's overall critical approach is, his own constructive position is not without problems itself, namely, his view that Paul saw a transformed but "still physical body" (398). Wright maintains that the resurrection appearance experienced by Paul was merely "accompanied" by a light, and that Paul himself encountered a "still physical body." This view is not supported by the biblical witnesses. According to Acts 9:7, Paul's companions do not share Paul's full resurrection experience; although they do hear a voice, they see no light. According to Acts 22:9, they see the light but hear no voice. Objectivity must incontrovertibly be attributed to Paul's experience *not* because he encountered a "still physical body," but because he falls to the ground and is temporarily blinded. The partial or incomplete nature of the experiences of Paul's companions in this revelatory episode alone suffices to warn against entertaining too simplified an understanding of the objectivity of the resurrection.

Wright is correct in insisting that the first biblical witnesses did not say that they had seen "signs of the heavenly presence of Christ," but rather that "Jesus of Nazareth had been raised from the dead" (479). He also persuasively observes that the Synoptics, rather than simply adopting Paul's resurrection message, instead draw from *different* oral and perhaps written traditions. He also accurately discerns a remarkable religious dearth and contestability in the various resurrection accounts in the Gospels.

1. They do not draw from any particular wealth of biblical symbolic material in elaborating their resurrection accounts (599; cf. 599ff).
2. Although they associate the resurrection message with a mission calling, they offer no elaborate individual or collective eschatological visions (602ff).
3. Unlike Paul or a vision of the Son of Man such as that in Daniel 7, Jesus is not described as a luminous heavenly figure (604ff).
4. Despite the fact that, as already mentioned, women enjoyed no legal recognition as witnesses at the time—which is likely why Paul also fails to mention them (cf. 607)—all the Gospels extensively recount the presence of women as initial witnesses of the empty tomb and of resurrection appearances (cf. 608).

Wright concludes from these observations that in the Gospels, the resurrected Jesus appears as "one human being among others," albeit with a body "with properties that are, to say the least, unusual" (605). These "unusual" properties include his ability to appear or vanish at will, to enter through closed doors, and the fact that even close friends do not recognize him (cf. 605). But his interpretation that the Resurrected's body was "somehow transformed" (609 et passim), or "somehow different" (611 et passim), falls short and fails to grasp adequately the subtlety and strangeness of the biblical witnesses, which do not portray the Resurrected simply as "one human being among others." Nor does Wright's assertion that the resurrected Jesus had "unusual properties" accurately grasp his new corporeality, since "unusual properties" sooner suggest rare physical features such as an extremely large body. Jesus's body in the resurrection cannot be grasped with expressions such as "unusual."

"Despite perplexity and scepticism," Wright stresses, "billions of Christians around the world regularly repeat the original confession

of Easter faith: on the third day after his execution, Jesus rose again"
(3f). He then queries quite pointedly concerning what precisely happened on that third day, on Easter morning. We must, he says, take
the empty tomb as our point of departure and see that people encountered the resurrected Jesus "alive again," and it is on this basis that
we must accept bodily resurrection in the sense of corporeal, physical presence. Precisely here, however, Wright falls into the trap of a
speculative reconstruction of physical resurrection wholly in the style
of Lüdemann, notwithstanding the latter's insistence on Jesus's decay-
ing corpse while Wright focuses on a "robustly physical" Jesus who
became "alive again." That is, Wright "speculates" himself to the side
of the deceased Jesus in the tomb and, as it were, "sees" him, the clock
ticking, finally rise "on the third day," "alive again," "robustly physical,"
and yet "somehow transformed," "the same and yet different"—which
is why Wright then speaks in a rather obscure and vague sense about
a "transphysical body."

A wholly different view emerges if we translate the expression "on
the third day" *not* as "during the period between hours forty-nine and
seventy-two," but rather "after he had unequivocally died." We must
then countenance a more sophisticated sort of transformation than a
somehow "transformed" revivification, correcting the familiar dualistic
mode of conception in two realms—an intellectual and spiritual "realm
of the mind," on the one hand, and a material and biological "bodily
realm," on the other—in favor of more subtle notions. We must acknowledge that the human body—and not merely in the view of various biblical traditions—is to a considerable extent permeated and characterized
by psychical and intellectual forces. We must also acknowledge that the
material disposition of the body itself (in biblical parlance: its carnality)
constitutes but a single aspect of its existence.

Human beings are "robustly physical" in their "carnal existence."
Here we are dealing with the biological-material level of a person's life, a
life, by the way, that lives indispensably from other lives.[6] Nor do strict
vegetarians constitute an exception, since they necessarily destroy infinitely many plant lives for the sake of sustaining their own. It is in this
light that Paul's seemingly obscure remark acquires its more profound
dimension, namely, that the life of the flesh is "sold into slavery under
sin" (Rom 7:14). Carnal or fleshly existence, existence driven to preda-
tory self-preservation and yet ultimately doomed to futility, repeatedly

---

6. Alfred North Whitehead, *Process and Reality: An Essay in Cosmology, Gifford
Lectures 1927–28*, ed. David R. Griffin and Donald W. Sherburne, corrected ed. (New York
and London: Free Press, 1978), 105: ". . . life is robbery."

prompts Paul's acutely negative judgment, particularly when it threatens to gain the upper hand in a person.[7] Contrary to widespread opinion, however, Paul by no means demonizes such existence en bloc. The human heart is, after all, not of stone, but rather of flesh.[8] Jesus himself "was descended from David according to the flesh" (Rom 1:3; cf. 8:3; 9:5). The concrete, individual, one-time existence of each of us is constituted "according to the flesh."

Paul clearly distinguishes between fleshly (or carnal) and bodily existence (*sarx* and *soma*).[9] The bodily existence of living human beings, though bound to the flesh, is yet filled and permeated by soul and spirit. In the appearances of the Resurrected, the fleshly dimension of the body is almost always absent (hence the repeated references to witnesses *not* recognizing him), whereas the spiritual or intellectual dimension of the body is always present. Such refers *not* to purely intellectual or mental phenomena in the sense of an ensemble of mere memories, recollections, and ideas swirling around in different people's heads, but rather to a precise *bodily self-disclosure in the power of the Spirit*.

Paul occasionally engages quite plastic language in describing such "bodily" self-disclosure "in the Spirit." He—Paul himself—is present among his distant church community not only "in spirit," through his memories and imagination, he can also summon them to "assemble" with him—he being present in spirit though absent in body—to adjudicate together (1 Cor 5:3–6). This reference does not involve some miraculous arrangement; we, too, are quite able to include in our deliberations and decisions those who might be absent in body as if they were

---

7. "For what the flesh desires is opposed to the Spirit, and what the Spirit desires is opposed to the flesh; for these are opposed to each other, to prevent you from doing what you want" (Gal 5:17). Those governed by the desires of the flesh are subject to finitude, transitoriness, and corruption; those governed by the Spirit "will reap eternal life" (cf. Gal 6:8). Paul's letter to the Romans reflects this same sentiment: "To set the mind on the flesh is death, but to set the mind on the Spirit is life and peace" (Rom 8:6). See in this regard Veselin Kesich, *The First Day of the New Creation: The Resurrection and the Christian Faith* (Crestwood: St. Vladimir's Seminary Press, 1982), 127ff; Michael Welker, *The Theology and Science Dialogue: What Can Theology Contribute?* (Neukirchen-Vluyn: Neukirchener, 2012), 7ff.

8. "And you show that you are a letter of Christ, prepared by us, written not with ink but with the Spirit of the living God, not on tablets of stone but on tablets of human hearts" (2 Cor 3:3). The suggestion that this might in fact be merely a chance (or even failed) play on words is refuted by statements concerning the revelatory service not only of the body, but also of the flesh, e.g., 2 Cor 4:11: "For while we live, we are always being given up to death for Jesus' sake, so that the life of Jesus may be made visible in our mortal flesh."

9. Gerd Theißen, "Sarx, Soma and the Transformative Pneuma: Personal Identity Endangered and Regained in Pauline Anthropology," in *The Depth of the Human Person*, ed. Michael Welker (Grand Rapids: Eerdmans, forthcoming 2013).

nonetheless present. "What would this person say or do now were he or she present?"

Jesus's resurrection results in his appearing to witnesses during forty days in a bodily self-disclosure that forces them to grasp and conceive not only the obvious influence on or shaping of the body by the spirit ("the way he speaks, the way she looks . . . "), but also, and more yet, the notion of a bodily presence in the Spirit. This presence genuinely acquires a new, even "robustly physical" form (Wright) insofar as the Resurrected himself creates, in the power of the Spirit, a post-Easter body from his members in the form of these witnesses,[10] namely, the church as the post-Easter "body of Christ."

Paul, then, does not view the body simply as a "material entity and basis" functioning as the mere vessel of what might be considered more interesting and valuable "capacities." *The body is rather a complex, multifaceted organism that combines extremely varying services and functions together.* As such, it is a realm, a sphere in which God intends to "dwell" and through which also to be glorified. "Or do you not know that your body is a temple of the Holy Spirit within you, which you have from God, and that you are not your own? For you were bought with a price; therefore glorify God in your body" (1 Cor 6:19–20).

Paul essentially portrays the body as a *bearer of revelation* through which Jesus Christ is glorified and can be recognized (2 Cor 4:10; Gal 6:17): "It is my eager expectation and hope that I will not be put to shame in any way, but that by my speaking with all boldness, Christ will be exalted now as always in my body, whether by life or by death" (Phil 1:20). Taking as his point of departure the body as a multifaceted organism, Paul provides a detailed illustration of the post-Easter, resurrected Christ and the constitution of his church:

> For just as the body is one and has many members, and all the members of the body, though many, are one body, so it is with Christ. For in the one Spirit we were all baptized into one body—Jews or Greeks, slaves or free—and we were all made to drink of one Spirit. (1 Cor 12:12–13)

In his letters, Paul repeatedly challenges his fellow Christians to understand themselves as cooperating members of the one body of Christ: "Now you are the body of Christ and individually members of it" (1 Cor 12:27; see also Rom 12:4f).

---

10. These considerations illuminate the dark and for many people offensive theme of the shedding of Christ's blood, i.e., of what in the biblical understanding constitutes his vital inner force in fleshly form (see in this regard part 3.5), and the identification of the creation gifts of bread and wine with his body and blood in the establishment of Holy Communion (see part 5.4).

Paul refers to the "edification" and vitality of this body with its many members to illustrate more precisely the activity of the divine Spirit and the meaning of the sacraments of baptism and Holy Communion. The love that the Spirit has poured into the hearts of believers (Rom 5:5) shapes—edifies—them into the body of Christ.[11] In this context, God acts through the Spirit on every individual (fleshly and bodily) human being. The Spirit allots to each person that person's unique gift "just as the Spirit chooses" (1 Cor 12:11). Although the miracle of the organic interplay of individual members in the one body is activated by the Spirit,[12] so also is the common charisma and focused activity of the members of the body.

Once the power of the human body in worship and even in revelation (the body as a "temple of the Holy Spirit," 1 Cor 6:19) is taken seriously—a power Paul himself variously emphasizes—and once it is seen that the earthly body cannot in any case do without the flesh, which Paul clearly differentiates from that body, then all primitive either-or notions concerning the "flesh" and "spirit" cannot but be abandoned.[13] The flesh belongs indispensably to the historical-material basis of the bodily and thus also—according to Paul—higher earthly human existence in the form of heart, soul, and spirit.

That said, the dimension "flesh," as the essentially finite and transient basis of human existence, becomes dangerous when it comes to guide all the "endeavors and desires" of a person. In his harsh statements concerning the flesh, Paul repeatedly alludes to the fundamental carnal-bodily functions of nourishment and reproduction, never hesitating—as is well known—with taking passing shots at gluttony, intemperance, and certain kinds of sexual contact.[14] Although viewed superficially these passages might suggest that Paul was somehow hostile toward the body

11. Concerning the relevance of this figure of the "outpouring of the Spirit," see Michael Welker, *God the Spirit*, 134ff; 228ff (see part 0.6, note 16).

12. John Polkinghorne has proposed acknowledging the personhood of the Spirit in its context sensitivity; cf. John Polkinghorne and Michael Welker, *Faith in the Living God: A Dialogue* (London: SPCK, 2001), 71ff (see the introduction above, note 4); John Polkinghorne, "The Hidden Spirit and the Cosmos," in *The Work of the Spirit: Pneumatology and Pentecostalism*, ed. Michael Welker (Grand Rapids and Cambridge, UK: Eerdmans, 2006), 169ff.

13. See Michael Welker, "Die Anthropologie des Paulus als interdisziplinäre Kontakttheorie," in *Jahrbuch der Heidelberger Akademie der Wissenschaften für 2009* (Heidelberg: Universitätsverlag Winter, 2010), 98–108; cf. also Michael Wolter's observation that "not in a single passage does Paul refer to the Spirit *as* a specific or definite substance, always speaking about it instead *as if* about a substance and *as if* about something material" (Wolter, *Paulus. Ein Grundriss seiner Theologie* [Neukirchen-Vluyn: Neukirchener, 2011], 260, cf. 159ff).

14. Cf. Gal 5:19ff; 1 Cor 5:1; 6:9f, 13ff; 10:8; 11:20; 2 Cor 12:21; Rom 1:26f; 13:13.

or inclined to misanthropy and homophobia, his severe criticism of inclinations of the flesh that threaten to gain an upper hand in fact derive from his concern that those who have been won over for God and the gospel might once more become governed by powers that expose them to the futility and transience of human life, thereby blocking or thwarting their awareness of God's plans for them and obscuring perspectives opened up by the Spirit.

There is no abstract and blanket condemnation of the flesh to be found in Paul's anthropology. Along the same lines, uncritical enthusiasm for vague metaphysical and religious notions such as "pure Spirit" or a "direct human relationship with God in the Spirit" similarly fails to do justice to Paul's sharp powers of observation and his subtle conceptual capacity. The reality of the resurrection should not be sought in a "purely spiritual" dimension.

2.5 Spirit, Holy Spirit, and Real Presence in Spirit and Body

Theology, philosophy, and various forms of spiritual praxis have often propagated the ideal of a *purely spiritual* relationship with God (cf. in this regard part 1.5). Paul does grant to the Corinthians who speak in tongues that they enjoy direct spiritual contact with God: "For those who speak in a tongue do not speak to other people but to God . . . they are speaking mysteries in the Spirit." He does, however, immediately sharply criticize this direct contact with God: "nobody understands them . . . those who prophesy speak to other people for their upbuilding and encouragement and consolation" (1 Cor 14:2–3).[1] Paul emphatically advocates using both understanding and reason (*nous*) not only in interpersonal relationships, but also in prayer, indeed, even for glorifying God: "I will pray with the spirit, but I will pray with the mind also; I will sing praise with the spirit, but I will sing praise with my mind also" (1 Cor 14:15).

Paul drastically insists that in church, he "would rather speak five words with my mind, in order to instruct others also, than ten thousand words in a tongue" (1 Cor 14:19), and urgently warns against a church community that, as it were, becomes utterly unhinged "in the Spirit": "If, therefore, the whole church comes together and all speak in tongues, and outsiders or unbelievers enter, will they not say that you are out of your mind?" (1 Cor 14:23).

In this context, "understanding" and "reason" do *not* refer to excessively complicated intellectual capacities that can be developed solely through arduous transcendental philosophical exercises. *By nous— understanding or reason—Paul instead understands the capacity to produce comprehensible statements associated with clearly focused communicative goals.* Outsiders, for example, should also find the church's instruction comprehensible and be in a position to concur on the basis of their own persuasion (to "say amen"). Emotional efforts at persuasion, be they intellectual or moral, are not positive characteristic signs of the Spirit. Over against powerful traditions that have confused and admixed understanding/reason and Spirit,[2] we must insist on their

---

1. Concerning prophetic speech as proclamation, see Thomas Gillespie, *The First Theologians: A Study in Early Christian Prophecy* (Grand Rapids: Eerdmans, 1994); both Ingrid Schoberth, *Erinnerung als Praxis des Glaubens* (München: Kaiser, 1992), 57ff, 191ff, and Gunda Schneider-Flume, *Glaube in einer säkularen Welt. Ausgewählte Aufsätze* (Leipzig: Evangelische Verlagsanstalt, 2006) 11ff, 71ff, advocate the notion of "narrative recollection" as prophetic speech. See also part 5.5.

2. See Welker, *God the Spirit*, part 5.1 (see part 0.6, note 16).

distinction if biblical references to God's Spirit and the human spirit are to be understood.

References at large to the notion of "spirit" cover a wide spectrum of meanings and can variously connote "mind, intellect, imagination, esprit," and associated notions. This semantic range can extend to great personalities (e.g., "Goethe was a great mind/intellect"), though also refer to spectral phenomena, as in "He saw a ghost, and people feared for his understanding." The word "spirit" as such, however, can certainly also refer to a power, medium, or force that ties together and provides the point of orientation for the thinking, behavior, and actions of a given group, institution, society, culture, or even an entire epoch (cf. esp. "zeitgeist," derived from German *Zeit*, "time, age," and *Geist*, "spirit, mind, intellect"). How can the iridescence attaching to the word "spirit" and its semantic spectrum be brought more clearly into focus?

To articulate more clearly what we know about the human spirit, it is probably best to begin with those particular capacities about which there is general concurrence, namely, with what seem to be quite straightforward mental and cognitive operations. The allegedly simple capacity to recall or imagine external objects and events in what is generally called a person's "inwardness" is ascribed to the human spirit in the sense of intellect or imagination. The alleged "reproduction" or "imaging"[3] of something external within or through a person's inner faculties is an extraordinarily complex phenomenon. An object or complex of objects, or even an entire set of surroundings with all the concomitant diverse signals and shadings can be taken up into the human capacity for recollection and imagination. A wealth of objects, an entire nexus of events and experiences, is "internalized" spiritually or intellectually, and in that sense "spiritualized" or "intellectualized." At the same time, this entire "internalized" complex can be committed to latency, preserved—and summoned forth anew. New content can then be varied and recombined in infinite variety. Indeed, through this capacity for recollection and imagination, human beings rule over a vast spiritual and intellectual realm, their spirit or mind being comparable to an ocean or an entire world. Through this capacity, an enormous wealth of not only optical, but also acoustic-linguistic impressions can be accommodated, organized, and variously associated, combined, and contrasted with the world of intellectually or mentally accessible images and image sequences. Imagined smells, tones, tonal sequences, even mentally translated tactile impressions animate and enrich the internal world of the mind and intellect, a

---

3. Concerning the German terms *Abbildung, abbilden* in this context, see J. Nieraad, "Abbildtheorie," in *Historisches Wörterbuch der Philosophie*, vol. 1, cols. 1–3.

world enhanced by its association with enduring influences and powerful emotions.[4]

The rich interplay of content and other elements of the mind or spirit as well as a prudent selection and demarcation of these elements are equally important, since both determine the quality, power, and extent of mental operations. Religious rituals, literature, science, the formative arts, and music all demonstrate the formed and formative power of the spirit or mind on various levels of experiential internalization and imaginative power. Abstract symbolic systems such as mathematics, internally coherent forms of symbolic applications such as logic, and analytical thinking disclose principles, rules, and organizational nexuses in both the natural world and the world of the mind making it possible to meaningfully order the vast array of intellectual impressions and releasing remarkable powers for manipulating the world around us.

The various intellectual and imaginative capacities of human beings enable them to reconstruct highly complex past situations or even the entirety of specific world circumstances and to imagine and reliably anticipate many future events and event nexuses. These same capacities similarly enable them to communicate over vast distances and to transfer and share not only information, ideas, and stories, but also more or less complex sensations and emotions. Human beings are capable of coordinating extremely multifaceted recollections and expectations and thereby of creating the orientational and organizational power of a shared intellectual world. That notwithstanding, even if these individual capacities for recollection and imagination can indeed provide a point of departure for an initial approach or access to the phenomena of the spirit or mind, it is incorrect to understand the parameters of the human spirit as being restricted to a person's inner dimension or interiority. "The spirit . . . has no center and no periphery, neither depth nor surface, nor any interior; nothing about it is concealed from itself."[5] Through recollecting and imagining, we ourselves share and participate in the ocean of the spirit.

Even these brief considerations provide ample and impressive evidence

---

4. See in this regard, e.g., Max Scheler, *Der Formalismus in der Ethik und die materiale Wertethik. Neuer Versuch der Grundlegung eines ethischen Personalismus*, ed. Maria Scheler, *Gesammelte Werke*, vol. 2, 5th ed. (Bern/Munich: Francke, 1966); 8th student edition, ed. Manfred Frings (Bonn: Bouvier, 2009), 259ff; Wai Hang Ng, *Die Leidenschaft der Liebe. Schelers Liebesbegriff als eine Antwort auf Nietzsches Kritik an der christlichen Moral und seine soteriologische Bedeutung* (Frankfurt: Peter Lang, 2009), 50ff.

5. Andreas Kemmerling, "Zweite Meditation. Das *Existo* und die Natur des Geistes," in *René Descartes. Meditationen über die Erste Philosophie*, Klassiker auslegen 37, ed. Kemmerling (Berlin: Akademie Verlag, 2009), 53.

concerning the power of the human spirit. And indeed, it was in the power of the spirit potentially to combine and thereby enhance the disclosure of both world and self that Aristotle, in his *Metaphysics*, discerned not only the power of reason at work, but also nothing less than the essence of the divine itself.[6] And yet a warning is in order not only against equating spirit, reason, and God within philosophical, theological, and even cultural-historical contexts, but also against any unbroken and thereby essentially reckless glorification of the spirit in and of itself. Any examination of the phenomena of the spirit must take into account the varied and powerful possibilities for engaging—consciously or not—intellectual communication to the detriment of human beings themselves, culture, and nature. All over the world, for example, helpful and healthy ideas and intellectual abstractions and reductions are constantly being introduced and circulated through mass communication; at the same time, however, entire currents of trivializing and banal ideas, conceptual forms, and emotional manipulations are similarly being intellectually disseminated and communicatively and culturally nested. Fanatic, indurate positions and views, disseminated and inculcated through the power of the spirit, acquire thereby sometimes enormous social and political power for attracting and fettering people to those same positions. Brutal intellectual and spiritual dispositions—often unnoticed, and yet insidious—spread out among people and eventually lead to misery and destruction.[7]

Monistic, bifurcated, and dualistic conceptual forms, for example, can be successfully engaged, even in a pan-cultural fashion, to check, restrain, and repress new ideas and creative thinking, since simplified intellectual forms of this sort make it possible to communicate swiftly and predictably ("I and thou," "God and world," "friend or foe," "freedom or dependence"). Precisely these admittedly highly effective intellectual reductions, however, simultaneously severely deform both thinking and experience, cutting them off from the richness of real life with all its formative possibilities and potential (cf. parts 0.3 and 0.5). This sort of reductionist thinking, particularly when accompanied by a powerful emotional response and concomitant basic or rigid convictions, can eas-

6. See Aristoteles, *Metaphysics*, xii; concerning this particular issue, see Michael Bordt, *Aristoteles' Metaphysik XII* (Darmstadt: Wissenschaftliche Buchgesellschaft, 2006); Michael Welker, *God the Spirit*, 283ff (see part 0.6, note 16).

7. Today we can see with unequivocal and frightening clarity how entire societies and even epochs can be poisoned by racism, sexism, and fundamental imperialistic and colonialist attitudes. – Well into the 1960s, scholarly texts and reference works still maintained that because water and air represented "infinite resources," they need not be taken into account as economic factors. This ecological brutality was intellectually—and quite innocently—propagated on a global scale.

ily—and dangerously—blind people or even entire societies, cultures, or epochs, in the process committing them to naïve views of the world or aggressive ideologies. An "evil" or "malicious spirit" then comes to govern people's hearts, liberating many of the previously mentioned (and previously extolled) intellectual and spiritual capacities, though now to the extreme detriment of both human beings and the rest of creation. Hence associating or equating the spirit and intellectual world from the very outset with the notion of "good," or identifying it without further reflection as something unequivocally "salutary to life," not to speak of "divine," is a reckless and slippery undertaking.

These observations, underscoring as they do the *profound ambivalence of the power of the spirit*, prompt us to seek instead a more critical and nuanced understanding of the relationship between the human and divine spirit, something Paul did in an exemplary fashion. He clearly discerns the enormous complexity of the human spirit when, on the one hand, he admires its capacity for establishing contact across spatial and temporal distances—and not just among human beings, but also between human beings and God—and, on the other, sees that the spirit does *not* simply in and of itself lead to clear understanding and articulation or discourse. That is, it does not in and of itself bestow a steadfast heart, lucid understanding, and a clear conscience. That notwithstanding, cogent discourse, or what may seem to be a steadfast heart, a clear conscience, or lucid understanding, can in fact be false and deceived, to wit, perhaps shaped and guided by a "spirit of the world" that blocks one's view and closes one off from God (1 Cor 2:12 et passim). Even so-called "ultimate" and "highest" ideas concerning God, be they ever so clear and impressive, can simultaneously be spiritually impoverished and empty, systematically distorting and contorting one's relationship with God (cf. in this regard parts 0.5 and 5). Hence it is important to avoid associating the power of the human spirit and the human intellectual world facilely and without further reflection with the divine. Although it is true that "God is spirit" (John 4:24)—God is not simply *any* form or shape of spirit.

Once the reality of the human spirit, its power and its ambivalence and even its potential dangerousness, is recognized, one can understand why the examination and discernment of spirits (1 Corinthians 12) represents an important theological task, one of significance not only for communities of faith, but also for their social and cultural environs. It also becomes clear why the popular assertion that the Holy Spirit is a *numinosum*, an ungraspable and incomprehensible power, is in reality a careless and negligent assertion.[8] Those who in matters of the spirit

---

8. I address this position in my book *God the Spirit,* 1ff (see part 0.6, note 16); see

all-too-hastily set their fortunes on the indiscernible, obscure, and numinous, are refusing to engage the task of examining and discerning spirits. But how is one to determine or recognize that a spirit does indeed derive from God or has been sent by God?

The clearest answer the Christian faith can give to this question, albeit an answer hardly satisfactory for many people today, is that *the spirit of God reveals itself as the spirit of Jesus Christ.* It not only allows this particular person to be discerned along with the entire wealth of that person's life and ministry, it also connects the life of believers with the life of the Resurrected, putting them in a position to have a share and participate in that life.[9] Human beings who participate in the life of the resurrected Christ also gain a share in a power that has already shaped and continues to shape the world itself, a power revealed in bodily resurrection of Jesus Christ.

Francis Fiorenza has subtly observed that with the accompanying greeting of peace, breaking of bread, disclosure of scripture, charge of baptism, and missionary sending of the disciples—that with these particular elements, the appearances of the resurrected Christ effectively circumscribe or encompass the fundamental forms of worship in the life of the church and its charismatic powers.[10] The greeting of peace, scriptural exposition, communion, baptism, mission—this polyphony of life in worship is associated with the self-disclosure of the Resurrected in

---

also *Jahrbuch für Biblische Theologie* (2009), vol. 24, *Heiliger Geist* (Neukirchen-Vluyn: Neukirchener, 2011).

9. Loci classici include, e.g., the explication of the third article in Martin Luther, "Large Catechism," 396ff (see introduction, note 2); Karl Barth, *CD I/2*, §16: The Outpouring of the Holy Spirit, 203ff, esp. 214ff, though also the pneumatological passages in *CD IV/1–3*; Thomas F. Torrance, *The Trinitarian Faith: The Evangelical Theology of the Ancient Catholic Church* (Edinburgh: T&T Clark, 1993), 191ff; Oepke Noordmans, *Das Evangelium des Geistes* (Zurich: EVZ, 1960), 57ff. An attempt at establishing a dialogue between the biblically precarious Roman Catholic doctrine of the immortality of the soul, on the one hand, and the resurrection, on the other, can be found in the volume *Auferstehung der Toten. Ein Hoffnungsentwurf im Blick heutiger Wissenschaften*, ed. Hans Kessler (Darmstadt: Wissenschaftliche Buchgesellschaft, 2004); see ibid., esp. the contributions by Wolfgang Beinert, "'Unsterblichkeit der Seele' versus 'Auferweckung der Toten'?" 94ff; and Bernard N. Schumacher, "Die philosophische Interpretation der Unsterblichkeit des Menschen," 113ff. Concerning the kinship between biblically based Jewish and Christian resurrection hopes, see Kevin J. Madigan and Jon D. Levinson, *Resurrection: The Power of God for Christians and Jews* (New Haven and London: Yale University Press, 2008), esp. 1ff, 235ff; James H. Charlesworth et al., *Resurrection: The Origin and Future of a Biblical Doctrine, Faith and Scholarship Colloquies* (New York and London: T&T Clark, 2006); cf. also Michael Welker, "Die Wirklichkeit der Auferstehung," in *Die Wirklichkeit der Auferstehung*, esp. 318ff (see part 2.1, note 15).

10. Francis Fiorenza, "The Resurrection of Jesus and Roman Catholic Fundamental Theology," in *Resurrection*, 213–248, 238ff (see part 2.2, note 1).

his spirit, or more precisely: with his spiritual body (see also parts 5.3 and 5.4).

In the resurrection of Jesus Christ, we encounter the Spirit in "bodily" form, as the "spirit of Christ" in what is now no longer "fleshly" continuity with the life of the pre-Easter Jesus. It is absolutely imperative that one become familiar with this spiritual life if one is to grasp the identity and person of the Resurrected and his power to give form to the spirit. The Resurrected at once both constitutes the fundamental elements of implementation of the life of the church and brings to creative engagement multiple dimensions of his pre-Easter life, mediating the salvific, salutary, exalting powers of the "new creation."

The self-disclosure of the Resurrected stands in both continuity and discontinuity with his pre-Easter life, though also with the activity of the Spirit as attested by biblical traditions. According to early biblical witnesses, God's spirit is experienced as a power of unexpected deliverance. In situations of dire affliction and distress, God's spirit comes over a person destined to become the savior of the people of Israel. The people in whom God awakens a "savior" through the Spirit are described as impotent, without hope, and despairing—though also turned against God. The Apostolic Creed states: "I believe in the Holy Spirit, the communion of saints, the forgiveness of sins, the resurrection of the body, and the life everlasting." Communion of saints—sin—resurrection—eternal life: Although early biblical witnesses to the activity of the Spirit sound similar, they stand in clearly definable and delineated experiential contexts. God's spirit acts through a charismatic, a person over whom the Spirit comes amid and on behalf of the people of God, a person who then brings their sinful apostasy from God to an end and liberates them from distress. God lifts up his people—"So the land had rest forty years" (Judg 3:11; 8:28).[11] The role and activity of the Spirit becomes clearer still in the Old Testament prophetic promises that the New Testament then understands as referring to Jesus.

To Israel and the nations, the "Servant of the Lord" chosen by God (Isa 11:1ff; 42:1ff; 61:1ff) brings righteousness, compassion with the poor and weak, and a universal understanding of God and truth—i.e., justice, compassion, and true worship.[12] But how is such a community genuinely established and maintained? Old Testament traditions see this power in

11. Vgl. Welker, *God the Spirit*, 50ff; concerning the following discussion, cf. ibid., 228ff (see part 0.6, note 16).

12. This enumeration evokes the cornerstones of Old Testament law. Through the person chosen by God and on whom the Spirit "rests," God's spirit brings about the fulfillment of the law. A community and world filled with God's spirit is governed by a striving for righteousness and truth, for protection of the weak, and for loving mutual acceptance.

the Torah, in the Law. By contrast, New Testament traditions speak about the self-disclosure of the resurrected Jesus Christ, about the constitution of the post-Easter body of Christ in the form of his church, about the "outpouring of the divine Spirit" onto people by the exalted Christ and the divine Creator, and about the "coming of the Reign of God." Retrieving these grand perspectives requires that we first focus on the situation of despair the resurrection event itself is addressing, namely, the power of the world that brings Jesus to the cross.

PART 3

The Cross

3.1 The Theology of the Cross: A Reformational Revolution (Luther)

The "theology of the cross" is a revolutionary theology whose full dimensions can be grasped only from the perspective of Jesus's life and the power of his resurrection. It directs itself against any understanding or idea of God that is developed solely within abstract speculation and as such is accessible solely to an intellectual elite, and against those forms of religiosity that would ignore God's concern with suffering, distress, and the diverse self-endangerment of both the world and human beings. The theology of the cross respects not only God's presence in a creation that is radically different from God, but also the seriousness and the judging, saving power of this same presence. Martin Luther positioned this theology programmatically at the very center of the Reformation, in so doing following Paul, who in his letter to the Corinthians declared, "I decided to know nothing among you except Jesus Christ, and him crucified" (1 Cor 2:2).[1]

On February 12, 1519, in an epistolary opinion concerning the communion of will between Jesus and his Father in the Gospel of John (John 6:37–40), Luther writes to Spalatin, secretary to Prince Elector Frederick the Wise:[2] ". . . whoever wishes to think or reflect profitably on

---

1. See in this regard Wolfgang Schrage, *Der erste Brief an die Korinther*, Teilband 1: 1Kor 1,1–6,11, EKK VII/1 (Zürich/Braunschweig and Neukirchen-Vluyn: Benziger and Neukirchener, 1991), 227ff, esp. 228: "If the Crucified is the standard and center, then, as the Pauline letters themselves clearly demonstrate, other elements neither fall under suspicion nor are they prohibited; it is, however, only from the cross itself that everything acquires a different quality and perspective, and only from the cross that everything takes its orientation, including the *theologia resurrectionis*, notwithstanding it is through the resurrection that the significance and meaning of the cross is revealed and articulated for proclamation."

2. Translation adapted from Karl Barth, *Church Dogmatics: I.1 The Doctrine of the Word of God*, Study Edition, § 8-12, trans. G. W. Bromiley, G. T. Thomson, and Harold

God should utterly disregard everything except the humanity of Christ"; Luther emphasizes that "This is the one and only way of knowing God, shamefully neglected by the teachers of the sentences, who, passing by Christ himself, have crept into absolute speculations on divinity . . ."

"No one comes to the Father except through me" (John 14:6b). Christian theologians through the ages have endeavored to embrace the implications of this statement. Luther radically objects to the notion that God's revelation in Jesus Christ can in any way be perceived or grasped through some "absolute speculation" concerning God that ignores the humanity of Christ. God's revelation simply cannot be grasped through metaphysical speculation. Nor, for that matter, is it intended solely for small groups of scholars and ecclesiastical leaders. Instead, it pleased God to reveal himself in his Son—in his Son's life and thus also in his impotence and suffering—and it is with *this* fact that both faith and theology, and all scholars and all ecclesiastical and secular dignitaries, must become engaged.

This concentration on God's revelation in the humanity of Jesus Christ set an educational revolution in motion—one whose foundation was already being laid during the late Middle Ages[3]—wholly comparable to the revolution set in motion by the empirically oriented modern natural sciences.[4] It became quickly clear that this revolution involved not only a renewal of the entirety of theology and piety, but also a reorientation within culture, science, and education. Together with Spalatin, Karlstadt, and Melanchthon, Luther set about planning a university and scholarly reform, initially for Wittenberg, in which scholastic philosophy and theology would be preempted by a return to the original sources of theology, to wit, to the biblical texts themselves, and by the cultivation of Greek and Hebrew philology with the goal of breaking the monopoly of thinking oriented toward speculation and philosophizing. Expanded

---

Knight (Edinburgh: T&T Clark, 2010), 126; original text in Latin, WB 1, No. 145, 328f. Cf. Emanuel Hirsch, *Hilfsbuch zum Studium der Dogmatik. Die Dogmatik der Reformatoren und der altevangelischen Lehrer quellenmäßig belegt und verdeutscht*, 4th ed. (Berlin: de Gruyter, 1964), 26ff.

3. Cf. Berndt Hamm, *Religiosität im späten Mittelalter* (Tübingen: Mohr Siebeck, 2011), 513–43; Thomas Kaufmann, *Geschichte der Reformation* (Darmstadt: Wissenschaftliche Buchgesellschaft, 2009), 88–90, 95–102; *Laienlektüre und Buchmarkt im späten Mittelalter, Gesellschaft, Kultur und Schrift 5*, Mediävistische Beiträge 5, ed. Thomas Kock and Rita Schlusemann (Frankfurt: Peter Lang, 1997); *Laienfrömmigkeit im späten Mittelalter. Formen, Funktionen, politisch-soziale Zusammenhänge*, Schriften des Historischen Kollegs: Kolloquien 20, ed. Klaus Schreiner (München: Oldenbourg, 1992); and esp. Volker Honemann, "Der Laie als Leser," in ibid., 241ff.

4. See in this regard Alfred North Whitehead, *Science and the Modern World, Lowell Lectures 1925* (New York: Free Press, 1967) (multiple reprints), 8.

biblical education, competent translations, and the power of the printing press were all to be engaged for the sake of enabling a broader section of the population to gain direct access to the biblical witnesses to God's revelation. Although such would require an enormous effort on the educational-political front, the results would benefit not only the clerical and ecclesiastical, but also the secular "freedom of a Christian."

An abuse of power on the part of the religious elite ignited what is known as the indulgence dispute. On October 31, 1517, and after considerable hesitation, Luther sent to Archbishop Albert of Mainz and to the diocesan bishop of Brandenburg ninety-five theses conceived as the basis for a disputation with which Luther intended to challenge the theology and practice of indulgences. In his accompanying letter, Luther remarked: "What a horror, what a danger for a bishop to permit the loud noise of indulgences among his people, while the gospel is silenced, and to be more concerned with the sale of indulgences than with the gospel!"[5] In thesis 82, Luther provocatively asked: "Why does not the pope empty purgatory, for the sake of holy love and of the dire need of the souls that are there," that is, why only individuals who are willing to pay, "for the sake of miserable money"?[6] Penitence, Luther maintained, can come solely from knowledge of human sin and guilt and from God's grace, both of which, however, are revealed when Christians are "diligent in following Christ, their Head, through penalties, deaths, and hell" (thesis 94).[7] These theses, originally composed in Latin, were quickly disseminated throughout the scholarly world and also among ecclesiastical leaders. After being translated into German (without Luther's permission), they spread like wildfire throughout Germany.

In March 1518, in the piece *Ein Sermon von dem Ablaß und von der Gnade*,[8] Luther presented his views to a broader audience for the first time in German. The sermon spread immediately, enjoying twelve printings during that same year. But this dispute concerning indulgences and their accompanying theology was not just a discussion concerning a specialized theological topic, nor merely an ecclesiastical-political dispute; it became instead a public indictment of the abuse of church power and the dissemination of false religious doctrine. In this explosive atmosphere, the superiors in Luther's order repeatedly entreated him not to cause his

5. *Luther's Works. American Edition*, vol. 48, ed. Helmut T. Lehmann (Philadelphia: Fortress Press, 1963), 47, cf. 47ff.

6. *Resolutiones disputationum de indulgentiarum virtute*, 1518, WA 1, 625f; translations here and below from *Works of Martin Luther*, trans. Adolph Spaeth, L.D. Reed, Henry Eyster Jacobs, et al. (Philadelphia: A. J. Holman Company, 1915), vol. 1, 29–38.

7. WA 1, 628.

8. WA 1, 239ff; Eng. trans. *Sermon on Indulgences and Grace*.

order any harm and instead to issue a public declaration. In April 1518 he set out on foot for Heidelberg, where the monks of his order were to assemble on April 25. On April 26, a public disputation was held in the Augustinian monastery in Heidelberg concerning theses in which Luther took fundamental issue with scholastic theology.

Five doctors of theology discussed the twenty-eight theses that Luther had presented in what is known as the *Heidelberg Disputation*. The first thesis reads: "The law of God, the most salutary doctrine of life, cannot advance man on his way to righteousness, but rather hinders him."[9] Luther's reasoning is that human beings, being fixated on their own works, do not see the works of God, and, being satisfied with the mere appearance of righteousness, do not see God's actions. God reveals himself not in brilliance, but in suffering and impotence, in a savior who "had no form or majesty" (Isa 53:2), and in dramatic acts: "The LORD kills and brings to life" (1 Sam 2:6). Those who seek divine radiance and their own radiance are misusing God's good law, or, as Luther explicitly says, "the law of God, which is holy and unstained, true, just, etc., is given man by God as an aid beyond his natural powers to enlighten him and move him to do the good" (explication to thesis 2).[10] They misuse it insofar as they put all their stock in their own works, but do so with arrogance and without any fear of God. By contrast, thesis 11 reads: "Arrogance cannot be avoided or true hope be present unless the judgment of condemnation is feared in every work. . . . For it is impossible to trust in God unless one has despaired in all creatures and knows that nothing can profit one without God."[11]

What, however, can a person do in order genuinely to seek God and hope in God? How can a person avoid everywhere "seeking himself in everything" (explication to thesis 16), thereby adding "sin to sin" (thesis 16)?[12] What can a person do to avoid sinking into despair or fatalism in this oppressive situation (cf. thesis 17)?

The answer is that a person must hold to God's revelation, or, more precisely, to the *revelation of God's grace in Christ*, something trenchantly articulated and developed in the famous theses 19 to 21.

Thesis 19:

> That person does not deserve to be called a theologian who looks upon the invisible things of God as though they were clearly perceptible in those things which have actually happened . . . the

---

9. Martin Luther, *Heidelberger Disputation*, in WA 1, 355; LW 31, 39.
10. WA 1, 356; LW 31, 43.
11. WA 1, 359; LW 31, 48.
12. WA 1, 360; LW 31, 50-1.

invisible things of God are virtue, godliness, wisdom, justice, goodness, and so forth. The recognition of all these things does not make one worthy or wise.[13]

Those who do strive for such knowledge will invariably try to creep "into absolute speculations on divinity . . ."

Thesis 20: "He deserves to be called a theologian, however, who comprehends the visible and manifest things of God seen through suffering and the cross."[14] God turned his humanity and weakness toward the world. God wants to be known from suffering. God wants the "wisdom of invisible things" to be rejected by the "wisdom of visible and manifest things." Luther summarizes his thoughts here in the explication to thesis 20: "Now it is not sufficient for anyone, and it does him no good to recognize God in his glory and majesty, unless he recognizes him in the humility and shame of the cross."[15] Luther then defines these two theologies in thesis 21, designating as **theology of glory** the theology that would know God from his invisible nature, from his glory, wisdom, power, and divine nature, and the other theology as **theology of the cross**.

"A theology of the cross calls the thing what it actually is," we read in thesis 21. "A theology of glory calls evil good and good evil."[16] Why, however, does Luther judge the theology of glory so harshly? He does so because it abstracts from God's revelation in Christ; that theology knows neither Christ nor the God who is concealed in suffering. The result, Luther believes, is that it comes to prefer God's magnificent works to suffering, his glory to the cross, and his strength to weakness. Theologians of glory hate the cross and suffering, but love magnificent works, both God's and their own, which is also why they call the good of the cross evil and the evil of a deed good. It is in the explication to thesis 21 that the decisive sentence then follows: "God can be found only in suffering and the cross . . ."[17]

The theology of the cross enables one to acknowledge and bear one's own incapacity for good and to orient oneself, with the fear of God, toward the creative God, then allowing God's influence to come to bear in one's life precisely through the cross and suffering.[18] In thesis 25, Luther

13. WA 1, 361; LW 31, 52.
14. WA 1, 362; LW 31, 52.
15. WA 1, 362; LW 31, 52-3.
16. WA 1, 362; LW 31, 53.
17. WA 1, 362; LW 31, 53.
18. In a nuanced assessment of more recent efforts among historians of the church and theology to discover a variant of mysticism in Luther as well, Berndt Hamm enumerates the important transformations to which Luther subjects all theologies propagating such immediacy to God; see Hamm's article "Wie mystisch war der Glaube Luthers?" *in Gottes Nähe*

emphasizes that it is through this orientation that God's righteousness is infused through faith, and that it is on the basis of this infused righteousness that good works then also follow that correspond to the law. That is, the law commands precisely what faith attains; it is in faith that the law's intention is fulfilled. Prior to faith, however, a revaluation of all values comes about through the cross, through God's revelation in humankind, in misery, and in lowness and humility. By focusing human beings wholly on Jesus Christ in his humanity and suffering, the theology of the cross counters all notions of self-righteous triumphalism, be they emphatic or moderate, and all open and concealed forms of self-trust by instead teaching radical trust in the power of the Spirit and in the God who even from within suffering and distress remains creative.

Although this new theological approach was revolutionary when it appeared and remains so today, it must continually be reaffirmed, renewed, and defended against powerful theologies of glory. After returning to Wittenberg, Luther wrote to Spalatin concerning the *Heidelberg Disputation*, remarking that although many of those present found his theology strange, the interest it elicited among students and indeed all

---

unmittelbar erfahren. Mystik im Mittelalter und bei Martin Luther, ed. Berndt Hamm and Volker Leppin (Tübingen: Mohr Siebeck, 2007), 237–87. On Hamm's view, Luther's theology can be harmonized with mystical traditions only if the latter incorporate the mystical concept of *raptus*, the notion of the believer "being torn out of himself" (269, cf. 269ff). Hamm emphasizes that it is in this *raptus* and *extra nos* of faith that one finds not only the liberating element of Christian freedom, but also the harsh bitterness of the cross (271, cf. 273; see also Martin Luther, *The Freedom of a Christian*, § 30, WA 7). Although Hamm acknowledges the variously "broken" nature of Luther's mysticism (275), he nonetheless finds it worthwhile to come to a better understanding of Luther's enthusiasm for the theology of the mystic Johannes Tauler (see 278f and note 132), since both thinkers were fascinated by the experiential "polarity" of extreme abandonment by and intimacy with God (282). While Tauler, like medieval mysticism at large, focused on the elevation of the "inner person" to a deifying *unio mystica* (282) as the spiritual goal, Luther found the ground of possibility for personal salvific certainty in the word of grace and the Holy Spirit that come "from the outside" (285). These considerations raise the question—one certainly needing further examination—whether it makes sense to present Luther's thinking as a variously "broken" (!) mystical position, as one current scholarly trend would have us believe; cf. esp. Bernard McGinn, *The Harvest of Mysticism in Medieval Germany (1300–1500)* (New York: Crossroad, 2005), who emphasizes Luther's publication and recommendation of the mystical *Theologia Deutsch*. Should we not be more inclined to follow the lead of such diverse theologians (whom Hamm mentions on p. 238 with notes 2 and 3) as Adolf von Harnack, *History of Dogma* (New York, Russell & Russell (1958), VI, 87–108, and — following Barth, Gogarten und Brunner — Walther von Loewenich, *Luther's Theology of the Cross* (Minneapolis: Augsburg Pub. House, 1976), 222, in acknowledging that Protestant faith and mysticism are in reality related as are fire and water? Without a christologically focused theology of the cross, mystical piety could well prove to be a Trojan horse within the realm of Christian piety (cf. part 0.5).

the younger people gave him reason to hope. That notwithstanding, he found much to his disappointment that many of his former supporters and friends, appealing to the authority of the voice of "natural reason," were now turning away from him.[19] If we but consider more closely the enormous challenge presented by the theology of the cross, we can hardly begrudge Luther's former friends' and even his adversaries' retreat to natural reason, which, while not straightaway advocating a theology of glory nonetheless did at least try to water down and weaken the theology of the cross. For what is to prevent this concentration on the cross of Christ from rendering, in its own turn, knowledge of God impossible? What is to prevent God in such "humanity and weakness" from becoming simply unrecognizable as God? Indeed, what is to prevent the cross itself from turning into the message "There is no God!"?

Even Luther's own explications reveal two problematic sources of tension that for centuries have considerably burdened theology and Christology in particular. First, in his explication to thesis 21 he emphasizes that God can be found **only** in the cross and suffering. By contrast, in his explication to thesis 20, he maintains that it is not sufficient for anyone, nor does it do anyone good, to recognize God in his glory and majesty unless he **simultaneously** recognizes him in the humility and shame of the cross. A theology of the cross cannot and must not abstract from the resurrection lest it come to a sad end in a mysticism of suffering that is as bottomless as it is problematical, or in obstinate evocations of paradoxes as alleged "revelations."

The second point to which a problematical imbalance attaches not only in the *Heidelberg Disputation,* but also in others among Luther's writings, an imbalance that has severely burdened not only the theology of the Reformation as such, but also subsequent Lutheran thinking, concerns the law. On the one hand, in theses 1 and 2 Luther insists that God's law is "the most salutary doctrine of life, holy and unstained, true, just, etc. . . . given man by God as an aid beyond his natural powers to enlighten him and move him to do the good." On the other, Luther quite justifiably cites Paul's assertion that God's righteousness has been disclosed "apart from law" (Rom 3:21), and that the law not only makes sin recognizable as such, but indeed can also strengthen it ("the power of sin is the law," 1 Cor 15:56). Rather than articulating these various points by differentiating between them and explicating their interrelationships,

19. Letter to Spalatin concerning the *Heidelberg Disputation* on May 18, 1518, WB 1, 173, Eng. trans. LW 48, 62 (see part 3.1, note 6): "the wisdom of natural reason, which for us is the same as the abyss of darkness. We preach no light than Jesus Christ, the true and only light."

however, Luther's entire critique instead focuses on the polarizing opposition between God's works and human works.

It is especially "mortal sins" that are attacked as "**human works**,"
namely, sins that "seem good yet are essentially fruits of a bad root and
a bad tree" (thesis 5 and explication).[20] Luther refers to these human
works simply as "works of the law," thereby somewhat unclearly picking up expressions from Paul's letters (Romans 1–4; Galatians 3) rather
than analyzing more closely the peculiar problem of how some works, by
seeming to correspond to the law, appear good and yet are nonetheless
bad fruits of a bad tree. What Luther could and should have done at this
point was to distinguish between the good law, on the one hand, and the
law as misused by sin, on the other, and certainly also between the law
that allows us to discern sin and the law that is too weak to disclose even
its own misuse by sin. *This slide into impotence on the part of the good
law is a central theme of every theology of the cross* (see parts 3.3–3.5).
Unfortunately, the *Heidelberg Disputation* exhibits no signs of being capable of drawing these distinctions, nor do countless theologies of law
and the gospel include such. And yet precisely the capacity for making
these distinctions is indispensable for perceiving and understanding
what actually happens on the cross of Christ.

Let us first, however, examine the thesis that God is to be found **only**
in the cross and in suffering. For why does it not now follow that this God
is dead, or, indeed, that there *is* no God? Why does God not become utterly unrecognizable on the cross, though also utterly unrecognizable in
Jesus Christ? For even had God yielded to death only temporarily, such
would, after all, have called God's divinity into question. Even had God
hovered above the entire occurrence, as it were, and then, after three
days, remembered his divine power and resurrected Christ—would such
not undermine our trust in God's beneficence and faithfulness? Indeed,
would such not have called into question even Jesus's true communion
and union with God? What initially appears to be a revolutionary breakthrough, namely, finding God revealed in the life and suffering of Jesus,
on the cross and thus in the depths of human suffering, tribulation, guilt,
and death—proves to be an unfathomable theological problem.

As it turns out, an awareness of the enormous significance of these
problems and of the radical nature of the Reformation revolution awakened two of the nineteenth century's greatest philosophical minds, minds
who then brought the most incisive critique of religion and of Christianity in history to a head, namely, Hegel and Nietzsche.

---

20. WA 1, 357; LW 31, 45.

3.2 Philosophy of the Cross and Philosophy "after the death of God" (Hegel and Nietzsche)

During the twentieth century, the horrors of world wars and genocide, along with the advance of atheism and agnosticism, especially in communist parts of the world, gave new relevance to questions concerning the "death of God" and, along with it, to the theology of the cross.

Several great philosophical thinkers of the nineteenth century assist or even provoke theology to rethink the initiatives of both Paul and Luther from the perspective of late modernity. One of the most influential philosophical considerations of the cross and the death of God is that of Georg Wilhelm Friedrich Hegel, who initiated what is probably the most subtle critique of religion and of Christianity in history. Without Hegel, the more familiar and blunt critiques of religion—those of Feuerbach, Marx, and other leftist Hegelians all the way up to twentieth-century neo-Marxist models—would be inconceivable,[1] picking up as they do Hegel's most important points.

Friedrich Nietzsche, similarly contributing to the rediscovery of the theological and practical implications of the theology of the cross, developed a full, incisive critique of religion and Christianity as a "curse on Christianity,"[2] and as a "war" or even "war to the death"[3] against what he considered to be "the practice of nihilism." The positions of Hegel and Nietzsche suggest differentiating between a *transformational critique of religion* that would radically alter and "sublate" religion itself (i.e., maintain it in an altered form while yet rendering it superfluous as living and lived religiosity), and a *denunciatory critique of religion* that would belittle and disparage it as something absurd. Kant and Hegel developed a transformational critique of religion that, as is evident today, is of con-

---

1. Within the context of the supersession and eventual dissolution of orthodox Marxism, the role of neo-Marxism specifically in philosophy and theology has still not yet been adequately assessed. It did in any event renew interest in both religion and the critique of religion, notwithstanding Marx himself insisted that the critique of religion had come to an end and that the focus should henceforth be on a critique of politics, law, and economic issues (Karl Marx, *Early Writings* [London: Penguin, 1992], 243ff). Marx, Engels, and Lenin all warned against reviving the critique of religion, since religion should be treated with repressive indifference so as to, as it were, dry it out. Cf. Michael Welker, "Gegner des Glaubens. Reflexionen über die Gleichgültigkeit," *Evangelische Kommentare* 12 (1979), 403f, 409f.

2. Thus the subtitle of his work *The Anti-Christ* (see part 0.4, note 35).

3. *The Antichrist*, 8. Cf. idem., *Aus dem Nachlass der Achtzigerjahre*, in Friedrich Nietzsche, *Werke in drei Bänden*, ed. Karl Schlechta, vol. 3 (München: Carl Hanser, 1966), 568.

siderably more consequence than the excited denunciatory forms found in Feuerbach, Marx, or Nietzsche.[4]

The Cross as the Pivotal Point in Hegel's Philosophy and Critique of Religion

Hegel, radicalizing Luther's demand that God himself be recognizable in the cross and in suffering, speaks about how philosophy must establish a "speculative" Good Friday. In this context, several extremely difficult sentences at the end of his piece *Faith and Knowledge* have been repeatedly and—with irritation or enthusiasm—reverently cited in which Hegel demands programmatically that Good Friday not only be understood as a historical event, but also, as "speculative Good Friday," acquire a present existence. Good Friday, which was otherwise historical, must, Hegel insists, be reestablished in all the truth and harshness of its forsakenness by God. Philosophy must, he continues, "give philosophical existence" to the infinite pain that earlier was solely historic and existed only as the feeling that God is dead. And it must do so, he concludes, to "reestablish for philosophy the Idea of absolute freedom and along with it the absolute Passion."[5]

Several important—including theologically important—impulses can be gleaned from these rather obscure statements.

1. The cross of Jesus Christ and Good Friday must not be understood solely as an event that was historical only. If, as Christian faith maintains, it was in Jesus Christ that "the other worldly absolute essence has become man,"[6] then this death on the cross involves not only Jesus of Nazareth, but God himself, and in that case this death cannot be a past event only that concerns but a single, individual human being. That is, this death and Good Friday must be discerned in that particular form and radiance that in fact transcends the ages. This insight is also of considerable theological import.

---

4. More recent initiatives toward a less aggressive transformational critique of religion can be found, e.g., in Jürgen Habermas and Niklas Luhmann; see Michael Welker, "Habermas und Ratzinger zur Zukunft der Religion," *EvTh* 68 (2008), 310–24; idem, "Die neue 'Aufhebung der Religion' in Luhmanns Systemtheorie," in *Theologie und funktionale Systemtheorie. Luhmanns Religionssoziologie in theologischer Diskussion*, stw 495, ed. Michael Welker (Frankfurt: Suhrkamp, 1985), 93–119.

5. *Faith and Knowledge*, trans. Walter Cerf and H. S. Harris (Albany, N. Y.: State University of New York Press, 1977), 190f.

6. Georg Wilhelm Friedrich Hegel, *Hegel and the Human Spirit. A Translation of the Jena Lectures on the Philosophy of Spirit* (1805-6) *with Commentary*, ed. Leo Rauch (Detroit: Wayne State University Press, 1983), 125.

2. This death involving not only Jesus on Golgotha, but also God himself, is of consequence for understanding God's revelation. In his lectures
on the philosophy of religion, lectures he repeatedly gave, Hegel specifically adduces a church hymn by Johannes Rist:[7] "'God himself is dead,'
it says in a Lutheran hymn, expressing an awareness that the human,
the finite, the fragile, the weak, the negative are themselves a moment
of the divine, . . . that finitude . . . [is] not outside of God and do[es] not
. . . hinder unity with God."[8] Hegel distinguishes between the "outward
comprehension" of Jesus's death on the cross and the "contemplation
with the Spirit, from the Spirit of truth, the Holy Spirit."[9] This "highest
idea," Hegel says, takes seriously that in Jesus Christ God himself appeared as a human being. Humanity is in God, being such in ultimate dependence, ultimate weakness, and at the most profound level of frailty as
natural death.[10]

3. Good Friday and the death of God, in this capacity to transcend the
ages, involve not just God himself or the existence of a single individual
human being or even more or less large groups of human beings in the
form of religious communities. This death of God, a death transcending the ages and a death that philosophy grasps speculatively in all its
truth, stands in correlation with an entire age, an entire world, or, more
precisely: must in principle be capable of being identified anew in *all*
ages and *all* regions of the world that are both receptive and capable of
discerning the truth. Hegel identifies this Good Friday and this death of
God in "the religion of more recent times," one based on "the feeling that
'God Himself is dead.'"[11] It is not just the historical Good Friday that is
characterized by the experience of God's distant removal from or even
complete abandonment of the world; the culture of the modern world
also experiences this forsakenness, and, moreover, does so now in a collective fashion, as a publicly shared experience. Hegel, who consciously
develops his philosophy with a contextual orientation, that is, with a conscious reference to his own age,[12] clearly focuses in his considerations of

7. See in this regard Jüngel, *God as Mystery of the World*, 64f (see part 0.1, note 5).

8. G.W.F. Hegel, *Lectures on the Philosophy of Religion*, vol. III: *The Consummate
Religion*, ed. Peter C. Hodgson, trans. R.F. Brown, P.C. Hodgson, and J.M. Stewart (Berkeley: University of California Press, 1985), 326. See in this regard Christian Link, *Hegels
Wort "Gott selbst ist tot*," Theologische Studien 114 (Zürich: Theologischer Verlag Zürich,
1974).

9. *Philosophy of Religion*, vol. III, 321.

10. Cf. *Philosophy of Religion*, vol. III, 326.

11. *Faith and Knowledge*, 190 (see part 3.2, note 5).

12. Cf. G.W.F. Hegel, *Elements of the Philosophy of Right*, ed. Allen W. Wood, trans.

the theology of the cross on this particular atmosphere or mood, one enhanced by the philosophy of the Enlightenment. Precisely this situation, he believes, poses a challenge for philosophy itself.

4. Like many respected scholars of his time who at one time or another studied theology, Hegel, too, had a broken relationship not only with theology, but even more so with the church, something that becomes abundantly clear from his earliest letters to his friends Schelling and Hölderlin on into his later letters to his wife.[13] Although he does devote considerable effort to an examination of religion, thinking through the central themes of Christian faith all the way to Trinitarian theology and the theology of the cross, his goal is consistently a "sublation of religion," that is, a relativizing, supersession, or transformational preservation of religion *within* philosophy itself, or in a subtly religio-critical and thus philosophically oriented socio-cultural movement. Like many of his contemporaries, the young Hegel was enthusiastic about Kant's transformation and moral functionalization of religion.[14] Even in his earliest writings,[15] Hegel raises the question of how religion—perceived as sterile and reactionary—might become a power promoting morality and world change on behalf of freedom. On Hegel's view, however, in the modern era this question can no longer be answered in a genuinely theological and ecclesiastical fashion. To wit, neither theology nor the church can be enduringly saved even through external philosophical modernization. Their existence can now be justified solely in a philosophically radically *transformed*, cultural- and socio-critically *secularized* form.[16]

H.B. Nisbet (Cambridge: Cambridge University Press, 2003). See also Rüdiger Bubner, "Philosophie ist ihre Zeit, in Gedanken erfasst," in *Hermeneutik und Ideologiekritik* (Theorie-Diskussion), ed. J. Habermas (Frankfurt: Suhrkamp, 1971), 210ff.

13. Cf. *Briefe von und an Hegel*, vol. I: 1785-1812, ed. Johannes Hoffmeister (Berlin: Akademie-Verlag, 1970), 16f, 24; vol. III, 202.

14. Cf. Immanuel Kant, *Die Religion innerhalb der Grenzen der bloßen Vernunft* (Königsberg: Nicolovius, 1794); Eng. *Religion Within the Boundary of Pure Reason*, trans. J. W. Semple (Edinburgh: T. Clark, 1838).

15. At their initial publication, these pieces were given the somewhat misleading title (approx.) "theological writings of [Hegel's] youth" (G.W.F. Hegel, *Early Theological Writings*, ed. T. M. Knox [Chicago: Chicago University Press, 1948; repr. 1975]). Concerning the development of Hegel's thought, see Dieter Henrich, *Hegel im Kontext* (Frankfurt: Suhrkamp, 1971), 41ff.

16. When a friend suggested to the young Hegel, who was desperately seeking a job, that he might earn a living teaching theology at a secondary school, Hegel responded: "Must I – who for many years nested on the free cliffs with the eagle and who have been used to breathing pure mountain air – now learn to feed on the remains of dead thought or modern stillborn thought – and vegetate in the foul air of empty twaddle?" Although he does add that he could easily enough imagine lecturing on theology after several years of ongoing philosophical lectures, he then continues: "a) an enlightened doctrine of religion,

5. It is in the chapter on revealed religion in his *Phenomenology of Spirit*, published in 1806, that Hegel offers the clearest presentation of his ultimately religio-critical view of the cross in the revelation event attested by Christian faith.[17] The *Phenomenology of Spirit* takes as its point of departure the notion that even the most trivial perceptions and knowledge represent at least diminished stages of the spirit and its truth claims. Philosophy must penetrate these as yet undeveloped shapes and forms of the spirit; consciousness and more fully developed forms of knowledge must be taken *beyond* whatever current position believes it possesses the truth. Hegel reconstructs the stages of knowledge and its truth claims from the simplest sensory certainty on to consciousness, understanding, self-consciousness, and ultimately to reason, scaling and passing beyond each stage philosophically. More complex communal and praxis-oriented forms of knowledge and communication are then disclosed—ethical behavior, education, morality, and finally religion in its various forms as far as the Christian religion of revelation. At the very end, however, "absolute knowledge" is attained, which in Hegel's conviction philosophy alone can offer, philosophy alone having traversed all lesser forms of the spirit and "sublated" them within itself.[18]

The most perfect of the insufficient manifestations of the spirit is revealed or absolute religion. *Revealed religion*, as Hegel designates Christianity, focuses on cultivating a spiritual community tending to universal expansion, which Hegel here calls a religious "community" (Germ. *Gemeinde*) and distinguishes from the religious "assembly" (Germ. *Gemeine*).[19] In this communal setting, too, a basis for knowing, comprehending, and effectively communicating must be established. Within this cognitive process, this process of knowing, those who know and who

b) . . . for the schools, c) . . . in Bamberg , d) with the prospect that claims be made upon me as a result by the local Protestant Christian Church – the very thought of how this would affect me upon contact makes me shudder in every nerve, as if the Christian Church were a charged galvanic battery, and so on. Lord, let this cup pass from me!" (Hegel, *The Letters*, trans. Clark Butler [Bloomington: Indiana University Press, 1984], 150).

17. G.W.F. Hegel, *Phenomenology of Spirit*, trans. A. V. Miller (Oxford: Oxford University Press, 1977; repr. 2004), 453ff.

18. Cf. Charles Taylor, *Hegel* (Cambridge [Eng.], New York: Cambridge University Press, 1975), 197ff; Hans Friedrich Fulda, *Georg Wilhelm Friedrich Hegel* (München: Beck, 2003), 242ff.

19. Cf., e.g., *Phenomenology of Spirit*, 463f, 473f (see part 3.2, note 17). In his own references to civil society, law, and politics, Jürgen Habermas operates analogously in differentiating between "citizens who understand themselves to be the authors of the law" and "citizens of the society"; cf. Jürgen Habermas and Joseph Ratzinger, *The Dialectics of Secularization: On Reason and Religion*, ed. Florian Schuller (San Francisco: Ignatius Press, 2006).

engage in making themselves understood—communicating—are not engaged in discerning simply an abstract truth, or, as it were, in grasping an "ultimate idea" or "thought" called "God." Instead they should comprehend their own spiritual foundations, themselves, and their world, and should ultimately be in a position to become self-transparent and to shape their own life circumstances commensurate with reason and freedom. The section on revealed religion in the *Phenomenology of Spirit* describes the self-constitution of a spiritual communion, the construction of a communion reflecting the structure of the spirit itself: "the I which is a We and the We which is an I."[20]

The Christian-religious community constitutes itself initially by relating to a real, individual self-consciousness in which it sees God himself revealed—thus does Hegel describe the formation of the "assembly" (*Gemeine*) in its concentration on Jesus Christ. Hegel considers it futile to query whether Jesus called forth this communion or whether the communion itself was responsible for him becoming what he is. It is similarly meaningless to wonder whether an "assembly" would have emerged even *without* Jesus, or whether he was merely an expression of the needs of a group that formed only through its focus on Jesus himself. That is, Jesus and the assembly cannot be conceived independent of each other; together they constitute a "phenomenon of the spirit" and are in the strict sense co-present, mutually constituting each other. Here, however, the spirit actualizes itself in a more sophisticated form, since precisely in this "I" that is "we," and this "we" that is "I," the assembly is not merely related to or oriented toward an individual self-consciousness, to a more or less striking human being; it instead views in that very individual the self-revealing God.

Hegel believes that revealed religion can be comprehended as two contrary movements that in their own turn can be expressed in two statements:[21] *Substance becomes self-consciousness—self-consciousness substantiates itself.* The members of the "assembly" grasp in a more plastic fashion what for them is actually an incomprehensible movement or dynamic. Substance becomes self-consciousness—for them, this means that "God becomes a human being," more specifically *this particular* human being, Jesus of Nazareth. Self-consciousness becomes substance—for them, this means that "the church of Christ spreads throughout the world."[22]

---

20. *Phenomenology of Spirit*, 520.

21. Cf. *Phenomenology of Spirit*, 453f.

22. Hegel himself was interested in refining this notion philosophically and transforming it into a universal program of cultural-political development, thereby picking up from a secular perspective on the Platonic and neo-Platonic doctrine of the apotheosis of human beings and world, the *theosis*-doctrine, which, by way of Paul (2 Cor 5:17; Gal 2:20; 3:26f) and John (John 14:23; 17:21), became a central doctrine in orthodox theology (cf. Dumitru

The assembly both grasps and experiences the reconciliation between God and human beings in these and other plastic representations.
That is, it grasps and experiences it only *partially*, only in a *restricted*
fashion. By contrast, because philosophical reflection recognizes in this
reconciliatory process of revealed religion the movement or dynamic of
the concept, the union of substance and subject, that is, the revelation
and reconciliation of the absolute spirit, it is able to discern and render
completely transparent what is *really* happening in religion. What, then,
does Hegel believe is actually happening in revealed religion?

The assembly focuses on the individual human being Jesus of Nazareth and ascertains that in him, God became a human being. For them,
God is yet a numinous totality (substance) or a "beyond" or otherworldly
being they have intimated in some other fashion or sought through reflection, a being that in any case has here, in a miraculous, inexplicable
fashion, become a real, individual self-consciousness. Because, however,
the assembly *does not yet recognize or discern itself* and its own activity
within this process,[23] the *death of Jesus* is necessary.

6. It is not until Jesus dies that the path is cleared leading to self-
recognition, to a detachment from the merely historical or accidental,
and toward an understanding of what has *really* happened in the event
of reconciliation. The assembly, however, mistaking the *essentia* of that
event with its concomitant *accidentia*, focuses on what the real human
being Jesus said and did, what the first Christians experienced, how they
lived, and so on. Hegel bemoans this "spiritless recollection" that, though
certainly following the right instinct in trying to articulate the reconciliation event as a *concept*, nonetheless consistently strays into a distant
past (namely, the New Testament and early Christendom), where it can
but futilely attempt to become conscious of its own origin and its own
true purpose or destiny.[24]

A "higher formative development of consciousness"[25] is required if
the assembly is to break this habit of clinging to past phenomena and
naturalistic notions and focus on the *true* object of this event. The community (*Gemeinde*) that comes thus into being should ultimately discern
itself as the power that brings about the reconciliation of God and human

---

Stăniloae, *Orthodox Dogmatic Theology*, vol. 2 (Brookline, Mass.: Holy Cross Orthodox
Press, 2000), 191ff; Reinhard Flogaus, *Theosis bei Palamas und Luther. Ein Beitrag zum
ökumenischen Gespräch*, FSÖTh 78 (Göttingen: Vandenhoeck, 1997). Hegel's transformational critique of religion develops this concept within the framework of a grand program
of emancipation that draws on various Enlightenment impulses.

23. Cf. *Phenomenology of Spirit*, 477f.
24. Cf. *Phenomenology of Spirit*, 464f.
25. *Phenomenology of Spirit*, 463.

beings rather than engaging natural images—such as that of father, son, or family relationships in general—in understanding and describing, and ultimately thus obscuring, this momentous event through which the substance becomes subject.

7. According to Hegel, the key to making the transition to that higher cultivation of consciousness is a radical understanding of the *death of God*. The philosophically enlightened and cultivated "community" must come to the realization that it was not just this particular, individual human being, Jesus of Nazareth, who died, but rather also the abstract, otherworldly divine being whom the community perceived as entering *into* that particular, individual self-consciousness. The realization that along with this human being all notions of God and all abstract ideas of God have also died, indeed have been extinguished, the realization that all natural and intellectual notions and portrayals of God have definitively failed—this realization, this insight is the "painful feeling of the Unhappy Consciousness that God himself is dead."[26]

What must be envisioned here is a radical death of God encompassing even the most powerful recollection of Jesus Christ and otherwise every conceivable idea of God. And more radical yet: The cross of speculative Good Friday now *no longer* leaves behind in its wake any central or fundamental concept, no ground of certainty, no ultimate support, no ultimate entity or authority, be it called God, self, substance, subject, or anything else. What happens in this situation of absolute, bleak hopelessness, one utterly lacking any support or orientation, is, as Hegel formulates, the "the return of consciousness into the depths of the night in which 'I' = 'I.'"[27] Consciousness falls back into the undifferentiated unity of substance and subject, into the abyss of pre-reflexive self-consciousness.

8. This return of both individual and universal consciousness into the abyss of itself is the point of "speculative Good Friday." That is, consciousness, by actualizing the God-forsaken character of Good Fri-

---

26. *Phenomenology of Spirit*, 476. Hegel finds that this consciousness includes an ultimate experience of impotence, meaninglessness, absurdity, and injustice that cannot be redressed, yet now such that even the question of God has become meaningless. Cf., however, Jüngel, *God as Mystery of the World*, 53 (see part 0.2, note 2). Hegel's philosophy of the cross, however, does render absurd the kind of latecomer sentimentality the writer Jean Paul Friedrich Richter evokes in his "Speech of Christ, after death, from the universe, that there is no God" (*Flower, Fruit and Thorn Pieces: or the Married Life, Death, and Wedding of the Advocate of the Poor, Firmian Stanislaus Siebenkäs*, trans. Edward Henry Noel [Boston: James Munroe, 1845], 332–40, here 336–38: "O Father! O Father! where is thine infinite bosom, that I may be at rest?"

27. *Phenomenology of Spirit*, 476.

day, attains a state characterized by the utter disintegration, dissolution, and decomposition of any and all notions that might promise support and of any references to ultimate ideas or potential points of orientation—whereby consciousness itself falls into the substance abyss of itself. Self-consciousness, entering into itself, acquires what is initially only dim knowledge of "being in itself." It is then in this suffering and in this ultimate freedom that the despairing assembly *(Gemeine)*, abandoned by God, elevating itself into a community *(Gemeinde)*, acquires the foundation of *substantial subjectivity*. More precisely, every member of the religious community acquires this subjectivity, every member draws the abstract, otherworldly God—the God who has died—into the depths of his or her own self, into pure, speculative devoutness. That notwithstanding, the community "does not possess the consciousness of what it is."[28]

9. This assembly, composed of individuals variously only abstractly reconciled with themselves, would now need to examine this event as the emergence of the community of free subjects. It would need to (a) understand what has actually been "revealed" here; (b) avoid trying to observe it from the outside, and instead find it within; (c) turn its attention toward "its own present world"[29] and concretize and spread the "universal divine Man, the community,"[30] the effected reconciliation of the individual and the social group. The death of God must *not* issue in a mystical return merely to the empty and vague individual self (cf. part 0.5). Instead, the community would need to seize this effected universal reconciliation of individual and universal self, the equality and freedom of all human beings within this fundamental experience that connects them all, in the process recognizing, moreover, that it "has for its father its own doing and knowing."[31] It would need, finally, to transition into actualizing and reflecting this fundamental experience through all the multifarious forms of real life, e.g., in politics, morality, and law.

10. According to Hegel, however, such can be accomplished only by cultivated, trained philosophy or the philosophically enlightened post-religious community. Philosophy itself must educate the religious assembly that submerges this effected reconciliation into the depth of inwardness or displaces it into a distant past and a merely longed-for future; indeed, philosophy must contribute to a veritable metamorphosis or transformation into the post-religious community. "The religious

28. *Phenomenology of Spirit*, 477.
29. *Phenomenology of Spirit*, 488.
30. *Phenomenology of Spirit*, 478.
31. *Phenomenology of Spirit*, 478.

community," Hegel writes (and by "religious community" he under-stands what is generally understood as the church community), "is the uncultivated consciousness whose experience is all the harsher and more barbarous the deeper its inner Spirit is. . . . Not until consciousness has given up hope of overcoming that alienation in an external, i.e. alien, manner does it turn to itself . . . (and its) present world," thereby climb-ing down out of the intellectual world of religion and metaphysics, or up out of religious inwardness and into the real world.[32]

Hegel's students argued concerning what he meant by the "sublation of religion." Does "sublation" (Germ. *Aufhebung*) in this sense mean pri-marily the *preservation* of religion? Such was the opinion of *right-wing Hegelians*, especially the theologians among them, who focused on the shade of meaning "to keep, save" attaching to the derivative German verb *aufheben*. That is, in their view Hegel intended precisely this notion of "preservation" of religion, and in this context, namely, an age in which religion was confronted with manifold difficulties, his philosophy offered religion a basis for survival.[33] Hegel himself seems at least at first glance to support this interpretation in his lectures on the philosophy of reli-gion, emphasizing that "the content of philosophy, its need and interest, is wholly in common with that of religion. The object of religion, like that of philosophy, is the eternal truth, God and nothing but God and the explication of God."[34] The only difference is the *form* of activity, since philosophy is concerned with *observation of content leading to compre-hension*, theology with representations without concepts, that is, with merely representational observation. Hegel is convinced that "(r)eligion must take refuge in philosophy,"[35] if it is to endure at all, a conviction that persists through his entire theoretical development.

By contrast, in his later lectures Hegel is less consistently hopeful that a philosophically transformed religion and church might become a contemporaneously efficacious political force, or that the "assembly" in the form of a philosophically educated "community" might contribute to shaping in a reasonable and liberating fashion the concrete life cir-

32. *Phenomenology of Spirit*, 488.

33. Thus more recently the position of Hans Küng, *The Incarnation of God. An In-troduction to Hegel's Theological Thought as Prolegomena to a Future Christology* (New York : Crossroad, 1987), 430ff.

34. G.W.F. Hegel, *Lectures on the Philosophy of Religion. One-Volume Edition: The Lectures of 1827*, ed. Peter C. Hodgson (Berkeley: University of California Press, 1988), 78. – "Philosophy is only explicating itself when it explicates religion, and when it explicates *itself* it is explicating religion. . . . Thus religion and philosophy coincide in one. But each of them, religion as well as philosophy, is the service of God" (ibid., 78f) .

35. Hegel, *Lectures on the Philosophy of Religion,* vol. III, 162 (see part 3.2, note 8).

cumstances of its age. The lecture on philosophy of religion concludes rather somberly: "When religious truth is treated as historical, that spells an end to it. . . . not the speculative truth [prevails]! Where the gospel is not preached to the poor, who are the ones closest to infinite anguish—there the salt has lost its savor."[36] Hegel, in a mood of almost political resignation, then describes the position and task of philosophy itself: "it forms an isolated order of priests – a sanctuary – who are untroubled about how it goes with the world . . . and whose work is to preserve this possession of truth. How things turn out in the world is not our affair."[37]

The more gifted among Hegel's students, what are known as the *leftist Hegelians*, were not content simply to make do with this resigned view, understanding the expression "sublation of religion" as referring instead primarily to its *removal*, an *elimination* of religion, initially through its *functionalization* and *transformation*.[38] They greatly regretted, moreover, Hegel's enduring interest in a speculative idea of God,[39] fearing it might in fact constitute a restitution of theology otherwise inconsistent with Hegel's thinking. "He who clings to Hegelian philosophy also clings to theology."[40] They also criticized the attempt, intentional or not, "to restore Christianity, which was lost and wrecked, through philosophy,"[41] and viewed the "death of God" as the prerequisite for entering into a post-religious age and a post-religious world. They experimented with conceptual approaches and programs critically focused on religion (Ludwig Feuerbach), politics (Bruno Bauer), the me-

---

36. *Lectures on the Philosophy of Religion,* vol. III, 160.

37. *Lectures on the Philosophy of Religion,* vol. III, 162 (dated 1821).

38. Cf. the wittily sarcastic piece by Bruno Bauer, *The Trumpet of the Last Judgement against Hegel the Atheist and Antichrist: An Ultimatum,* Studies in German Thought and History 5, trans. Lawrence Stepelevich (Lewiston, N.Y.: E. Mellen Press, 1989).

39. "God is attainable in pure speculative knowledge alone and is only in that knowledge, and is only that knowledge itself, for He is Spirit; and this speculative knowledge is the knowledge of the revealed religion. Speculative knowledge knows God as Thought or pure Essence, and knows this Thought as simple Being and as Existence, and Existence as negativity of itself, hence as Self, as the Self that is at the same time this individual, and also the universal, Self. It is precisely this that the revealed religion knows" (*Phenomenology of Spirit,* 461).

40. Ludwig Feuerbach, "Preliminary Theses on the Reform of Philosophy," in *German Socialist Philosophy,* ed. Wolfgang Schirmacher (New York: Continuum Publishing Company, 1997), 55. Cf. J.C. Janowski, *Der Mensch als Maß. Untersuchungen zum Grundgedanken und zur Struktur von Ludwig Feuerbachs Werk,* ÖkTh 7 (Zürich, Köln, Gütersloh: Benziger and Gütersloher Verlagshaus, 1980), 211ff.

41. Feuerbach, *Principles of the Philosophy of the Future,* trans. Manfred Vogel (Indianapolis: Hackett Publishing Company, 1986), 34. Cf. Jüngel, *God as Mystery of the World,* 97 (see part 0.2, note 2).

dia (Arnold Ruge), and finally also economics (Moses Hess, Friedrich Engels, Karl Marx) in attempts to get beyond Hegel by promoting a liberation-theoretical transformation of philosophy into concrete praxis that alters culture itself.[42] Anyone who examines Hegel's program in an unabbreviated fashion cannot but appreciate in them—rather than in the right-wing Hegelians—the heirs who more clearly discerned the deeper implications of Hegel's thought.[43]

That notwithstanding, Hegel's considerations of a philosophy of the cross did indeed prove to be quite fruitful for twentieth-century theological discussions. The cross stands for the radical experience of God's absence, an absence that does not just affect Jesus of Nazareth and his surroundings, both near and far. This experience of God's absence does not consist merely in an individually or collectively shared, insurmountable skepticism or even profound indifference toward any and all ideas and notions of God or their secularized forms. What Hegel envisions is a substantial, concretely historical sublation of God that in fact commences with Christianity itself; this position takes seriously the proclamation of the death of God that finds in God himself the experience of the obliteration of the fleshly (*sarx*) existence he had taken on (cf. part 2.4), along with the loss of all the acknowledgment and expectational hope focused on him. Hegel's philosophy of the cross, however, also encompasses the universality of God (i.e., an existence not just in the beyond, nor only in ideas and feelings, but even as far as the reality of the flesh and indeed even unto death). But it simultaneously includes the annihilation of this existence within an acutely real forsakenness by God—and not merely as a sensed, felt, alleged, or desired abandonment or absence. As such, this philosophy presses toward a life of conviction: "let us save ourselves."[44]

---

42. Cf. Dieter Henrich, "Karl Marx als Schüler Hegels," in Henrich, *Hegel im Kontext*, 187ff (concerning this book see part 3.2, note 15); see also the poem Hegel composed toward the end of his life to his student Heinrich Stieglitz (*Hegel: The Letters*, trans. Clark Butler and Christiane Seiler, 680 [see part 3.2, note 13]): "That empty grievances should not dissipate this word, / That these spirits may bear it to the people and put it to work!"

43. It is not enough simply to reduce Hegel to a "philosopher of subjectivity." Hegel, rather than merely pursuing a program à la Fichte, consistently focused on a development toward what in his view was a society organized according to the rule of law and freedom, a development, moreover, that proceeded by way of education, associations, and institutionalizations. See in this regard Michael Welker, "Das theologische Prinzip des Verhaltens zu Zeiterscheinungen. Erörterung eines Problems im Blick auf die theologische Hegelrezeption und Gen 3,22a," *EvTh* 36 (1976), 225–53; cf. also Hegel, *Elements of the Philosophy of Right*, 10ff (see part 3.2, note 12).

44. Eugène Pottier, *The Internationale*, from second stanza ("sauvons-nous nousmêmes").

Nietzsche's philosophizing "after the death of God" and contra the cross's power of fascination

"Book Five: We Fearless Ones" in Nietzsche's book *The Gay Science* begins with the words: "How to understand our cheerfulness. – The greatest recent event – that 'God is dead'; that the belief in the Christian God has become unbelievable – is already starting to cast its first shadow over Europe."[45] Nietzsche, with grim determination—despite being intent on philosophizing cheerfully "after the death of God"—thus concludes his late piece *Ecce Homo* with a question to which he dramatically devotes an entire paragraph:

"9. – Have I been understood? – *Dionysus versus the crucified.* . . ."[46]

According to Nietzsche, no one previously was able to conceive a "more dangerous bait" than the Crucified, "(s)omething to equal the enticing, intoxicating, benumbing, corrupting power of that symbol of the 'holy cross,' to equal that horrible paradox of a 'God on the Cross,' to equal that mystery of an unthinkable final act of extreme cruelty and self-crucifixion of God for the salvation of mankind?" This instrument of "revenge and revaluation of all former values," Nietzsche maintains, has previously repeatedly triumphed "over all nobler" ideals.[47]

What are we to make of this tension between Nietzsche's satisfied ascertainment of the death of God and, by contrast, his irritable critique of religion, his "curse on Christianity" with its central symbol of the cross? Nietzsche is, on the one hand, an incisive critic of any and all forms of dual-world or two-world models. He repeatedly and with indefatigable expressions of aversion enumerates examples of the theoretical and practical deceit and trickery that in his view religions have perpetrated by fixating human beings on the most varied forms of the "beyond," "transcendence," and "higher worlds." To that extent, he is quite one with Luther's critique of the metaphysical "theology of glory" (see part 3.1) and with Bonhoeffer's theological critique of religion (see part 0.1). On the other hand, he does move beyond the classical critique of religion in both philosophy and theology in a threefold respect.

45. Friedrich Nietzsche, *The Gay Science*, ed. Bernard Williams, trans. Josephine Nauckhoff (Cambridge: Cambridge University Press, 2001), 199.

46. Friedrich Nietzsche, *The Anti-Christ, Ecce Homo, Twilight of the Idols, and other Writings*, ed. Aaron Ridley, trans. Judith Norman (Cambridge: Cambridge University Press, 2005), 151.

47. Friedrich Nietzsche, *The Genealogy of Morality*, ed. Keith Ansell-Pearson, trans. Carol Diethe (Cambridge: Cambridge University Press, 2006), 51-52.

1. Nietzsche also discovers in countless philosophical theories and conventional secular worldviews traces of this parareligious *two-world thinking*. With detective-like acumen, he relentlessly tracks down the mutual enhancement at work between various religious models, theologies, philosophies, on the one hand, and non-religious worldviews, on the other, and then castigates unholy alliances that, by fixating human beings on fantasies and delusions, diverts or distracts them from acquiring solid, reliable knowledge and the capacity for shaping their own lives.

2. Nietzsche, however, directs an equally severe attack against all forms of religious and worldview *monism*. Monism, too, deceives us with covert two-world thinking by attributing to a "false world" any perspective that does *not* share its own view of the *one* reality, the *one* truth, the *one* nature, the *one* rationality, and so on.[48] Hence, in Nietzsche's view any fundamental concepts assuming that a simple unity attaches to totality or a simple fundamental disposition to reality are to be subjected to criticism: concepts such as the world, being, thing, and so on. Quite along the same lines, any fundamental concepts positing or assuming that any sort of unity accompanies our perception of reality or that our comprehension of reality can be universally shared and reapplied are subjected to scathing criticism: such include reason, morality, common sense, general consciousness, and so on. These concepts merely represent refuges for religious narrow-mindedness, instruments of torture for healthy human perception. Such is the case, Nietzsche explains, because totalizing or universally applicable concepts of this sort can exist only relative to a given position or a given perspective; that is, they are contextually determined, experientially determined, and shaped by specific interests, and are, moreover, chosen by our "will to power." Such considerations do indeed make Nietzsche's theory the "turning point" to post-modernism.[49]

3. Nietzsche also, however, turns against religious, philosophical, and worldview positions that historically have repeatedly protested against prescriptions for and prohibitions against *thinking itself* imposed by

48. Cf. Friedrich Nietzsche, "How the 'True World' Finally Became a Fable. The History of an Error," in *Twilight of the Idols or How to Philosophize with a Hammer*, in *The Anti-Christ, Ecce Homo, Twilight of the Idols, and other Writings*, 171ff (see part 3.2, note 46).

49. Jürgen Habermas, *The Philosophical Discourse of Modernity: Twelve Lectures, Studies in Contemporary German Social Thought* (Cambridge, Mass.: MIT Press, 1987), 83. More precisely, Nietzsche becomes the model for "soft post-modernism," which equates pluralistic organizational forms with diffuse "plurality," and contextual connections with relativism; see in this regard Michael Welker, *Kirche im Pluralismus*, 2nd ed. (Gütersloh: Kaiser, 1995), 13ff.

"rulers"—be they priests, professors, or politicians—and against any invocation of otherworldly powers and transcendentally grounded organizational frameworks. He similarly attacks all religious, philosophical,
and political notions, values, and morals nourished by the ressentiment
and attunement of survival and self-preservation strategies on the part
of broad societal strata. It is not without a certain measure of irritation
that Arthur C. Danto, one of the leading authorities on Nietzsche today,
acknowledges that "(h)is difficult philosophical stance involved both a
criticism of common sense (the view of the 'herd') as well as a defense of
it against all 'life-denying' philosophical and religious criticism."[50]

On the one hand, Nietzsche staunchly defends common sense—understanding based on concrete perceptions and authentic experience—
against religious and metaphysical abstraction and speculation, and
against hierarchically, autocratically imposed and justified modes of reasoning and thinking. That is, he defends "concretely lived life," concrete
human concerns with survival, and experientially based strategies of
self-preservation against religious and philosophical values and morals.
On the other hand, however, he levels the harshest criticism imaginable
against mass culture and the "herd mentality" focused solely on optimiz-
ing one's capacity for survival and on merely stabilizing the satisfaction
of needs.[51]

On the one hand, Nietzsche brings to bear—especially against religion, metaphysics, and intellectualism of whatever sort—a peculiar sort
of vitalism, a glorification of the impulse for self-preservation that accompanies concretely lived life. On the other hand, he attacks as extremely
dangerous sources of anarchy and decadence the Judeo-Christian traditions that are interested precisely in protecting lived and endangered
life, describing the systems of morality based on those traditions as that
particular "general revolt of the downtrodden, the miserable, the malformed, the failures."[52] *And this "general revolt" positions itself, with
extraordinary historical charisma, under the sign of the cross!*

4. Christianity, presenting itself beneath the symbol of the cross, is

---

50. "Nietzsche," in *A Critical History of Western Philosophy*, ed. D. J. O'Connor (London: Free Press, 1964), 384ff, 387.

51. Concerning these "herd-animal" ideals, see Nietzsche, *Nachgelassene Fragmente*,
in Nietzsche, *Sämtliche Werke. Kritische Studienausgabe (KSA)*, ed. Giorgio Colli and
Mazzino Montinari, 2nd ed. 2002 (München and Berlin / New York: dtv and de Gruyter),
vol. 13, 65ff; concerning the oft-repeated identification of Christians with "herd animals,"
cf. ibid., 192, 481.

52. *Twilight of the Idols*, 185 (see part 3.2, note 46); cf. Nietzsche, *The Antichrist*,
ibid., 4f et passim.

dangerous, and the battle against it urgent. Nietzsche describes Christianity as a purely degenerative movement under the sign of the cross, as

> . . . a degeneracy movement composed of reject and refuse elements of every kind . . . it is from the first an agglomeration of forms of morbidity crowding together and seeking one another out — It is therefore *not* national, *not* racially conditioned; it appeals to the disinherited everywhere; it is founded on a rancor against everything well-constituted and dominant: it needs a *symbol* that represents a curse on the well-constituted and dominant . . . it takes the side of idiots and utters a curse on the spirit. Rancor against the gifted, learned, spiritually independent: it detects in them the *well-constituted*, the *masterful*.[53]

It should be pointed out that Nietzsche does nonetheless accord a grudging measure of respect to Paul—whom he otherwise profoundly hates—for having discovered and propagated one important expression of the "will to power," namely, love. In Nietzsche's view, Christianity constructs its edifice on an important power code, that of petit-bourgeois love.

> The reality upon which Christianity could build itself was the small Jewish family of the Diaspora, with its warmth and tenderness, with its readiness to help and to stand up for each other, . . . with its unenvious saying No, deep within, to everything which has the upper hand and possesses power and magnificence. *To have recognised this as power*, to have recognised this *psychological* state as communicative, seductive, infectious for heathens too – that is the *genius* of Paul.[54]

Nietzsche believes that Christianity, as also the various philosophies and worldviews that secularize its values, picks up and propagates a morality that effectively undermines and denies or negates life, its intoxication with transcendence and metaphysics as well as its decadent herd morality also inculcating false developmental trajectories and false notions of perfection.

For Nietzsche, such "herd virtues" include trust, respect, a sense for truth, sympathy, impartiality, uprightness of character, and toler-

53. Friedrich Nietzsche, *The Will to Power*, trans. Walter Kaufmann and R. J. Hollingdale, ed. Walter Kaufmann (New York: Vintage Books, 1968), 96.

54. Nietzsche, *Will to Power*, 107 (translation altered): "We are divine through love, we become 'children of God'; God loves us and wants nothing whatever from us save love; this means: no morality, obedience, or activity produces that feeling of power and freedom that love produces . . . Here is the happiness of the herd, the feeling of community in great and small things, the living, as the sum of the feeling of life. Being helpful and useful and caring for others continually arouses the feeling of power; visible success, the expression of pleasure underlines the feeling of power; pride is not lacking, in the form of community, the abode of God, the 'chosen.'"

ance. He vehemently objects to this mob rule that supports such "social mishmash" and the establishment of equal rights, and that with its ethos of equality and sympathy cannot but drag down every culture.[55] His charges against this Jewish-Christian ethos based on the preservation and strengthening of the weak include crimes against life, assaults on healthy, emergent life, violation of instincts that promote life, self-abuse, and anarchy.

> The Christian and the anarchist: both are decadents, neither one can do anything except dissolve, poison, lay waste, bleed dry, both have instincts of mortal hatred against everything that stands, that stands tall, that has endurance, that promises life a future.[56]

Nietzsche views this contagious fundamental disposition of Christianity, one perpetually inspired anew by the symbol of the cross and oriented toward the protection of the weak, as

> . . . the most fatal seductive lie that has yet existed, as the great unholy lie: I draw out the after-growth and sprouting of its ideal from beneath every form of disguise. I reject every compromise position with respect to it — I force a war against it. Lower-class people's morality as the measure of things: this is the most disgusting degeneration culture has yet exhibited. And this kind of ideal still hanging over mankind as "God"![57]

Nietzsche's allegation is quite accurate that protection of the weak and advocacy on behalf of the poor and disadvantaged occupy a central or even indispensable role in Judeo-Christian traditions. That notwithstanding, his failure to grasp and reconstruct clearly the most important sources and origins of this concentration on the protection of the weak also prevents him from comprehending the enormous, life-affirming power of mercy, a power capable of shaping not only family ethos, but, even more, the coexistence of larger communities or even an entire people or nation (see in this regard part 4.4). Whereas Nietzsche views mercy as a shrewd accomplishment or cunning trick with whose assistance the weak, those who have come up short, and, as Nietzsche himself puts it, the "malformed" and those unworthy of life, band together to bring down the strong, powerful, handsome, and those otherwise worthy

---

55. Cf.. Nietzsche, *Nachlass*, 708f; 14[182].

56. *The Antichrist*, 60 (see part 3.2, note 46).

57. Nietzsche, *Will to Power*, 117 (translation altered) (see part 3.2, note 53). ". . . it is indecent to be a Christian these days"; "What miscarriages of duplicity modern people are, that in spite of all this they are not ashamed to call themselves Christians!" (*The Antichrist*, 34-5 [see part 3.2, note 46]).

of life, we encounter a wholly different understanding in the biblical traditions (cf. parts 4.3 and 4.4).

Hegel's philosophy of the cross claims that the cross, as the cross of Jesus Christ, the incarnate God, is in fact not merely a past event that concerns Jesus of Nazareth alone. It is an occurrence instead in which God reveals himself—as the God who enters into natural death. This occurrence also forces one to come to terms with radical atheism not only during Jesus's own age and not only in the form of the philosophy of modernity, but also prompted for all time by religion itself and the truth disclosed within it. In this sense, Hegel provided important points of discussion not only for the twentieth-century theology of the cross, but beyond it as well, even though he himself considered further substantive or useful development to be possible only *contra* theology and the Christian faith. In any event, theology is confronted with the necessity of coming to terms with the cross of Christ as an event that spans all ages and cultures and involves the real absence and questionability of God.

Nietzsche's philosophizing "after the death of God," with his attacks on Christianity and its central symbol of the cross, rages against the inexhaustible resonance and enthusiasm that the message of God's love and mercy under the sign of the cross elicited and continues to elicit. Although Nietzsche does indeed acknowledge the considerable charismatic power of this message, he also considers it to be disastrous because it generates and strengthens not only illusory religious (wishful) thinking, but also a very real ethos of love for one's neighbor, an ethos of charity, service to one's neighbor and especially to the helpless, weak, and sick (cf. part 4.4). Nietzsche considers this humanism—Christian or not—to be detrimental to life and decadent. It represents a historically extremely influential counterprogram to the sort of "ascendant life" and *Übermensch* Nietzsche (albeit rather vaguely) envisions. Both Hegel's and Nietzsche's critical points were picked up by the twentieth-century theology of the cross and, notwithstanding their religio-critical intentions, then theologically "sublated" and transformed in their own turn.

3.3 Theologies of the Cross after Bonhoeffer: New Testament Multi-dimensionality and Speculative Reduction (Moltmann, Jüngel, Dalferth, Kitamori)

"The return of talk about the death of God to theology" during the second half of the twentieth century was "prepared if not initiated" by Dietrich Bonhoeffer and his letters from prison.[1] Eberhard Jüngel also finds that Bonhoeffer shares "in the problems as seen by the young Hegel" in the "working through of modern atheism and the effort to arrive at a Christian concept of God."[2]

Although in his letters from prison Bonhoeffer does indeed incorporate into his views concerning Jesus's cross and God's suffering key points from Luther and Hegel, then developing them further, nonetheless in National Socialism he confronted a far more brutal form of atheism than did Hegel; nor is he interested primarily in developing a mere *concept of God*, and certainly not a primarily philosophical one (cf. parts 0.1 and 0.3). Although Bonhoeffer doubtless believed that an example of modern life without God can also be found in the cool scientific and cultural atheism of his age, he suffered primarily from the aggressive, misanthropic, explicit and implicit atheism of Nazi ideology in Germany, atheism that extended even into the church itself, and from its devastating consequences. The atheism revealed through the cross is something far more than merely an intellectual or worldview problem. Bonhoeffer warns against turning "the cross and/or suffering into a principle."[3]

The God who in the midst of life is "in charge," who makes us capable of living amid the polyphony of life,[4] "consents to be pushed out of the world and onto the cross." He delivers the world over to its

---

1. Jüngel, *God as Mystery of the World*, 57, 57ff (see part 0.2, note 2); concerning Bonhoeffer, see also parts 0.1 and 0.3.

2. Jüngel, *God as Mystery of the World*, 57; cf. earlier Moltmann, *Theology of Hope*, 171 (see part 0.4, note 24); and idem, *The Crucified God*, 32ff (see part 0.1, note 6).

3. Bonhoeffer, DBWE 8:492 (see part 0.1, note 1). Michael Plathow, "Die Mannigfaltigkeit der Wege Gottes. Zu D. Bonhoeffers kreuzestheologischer Vorsehungslehre," in idem, *Ich will mit dir sein. Kreuzestheologische Vorsehungslehre. Aufsätze zu Gottes Mitsein im Kreuz* (Berlin: Köster, 1995), 87–105, has persuasively demonstrated that Bonhoeffer combines the theology of the cross with the doctrine of providence.

4. Cf. part 0.3 for documentation. Bonhoeffer could and, it seems, should have mentioned the doctrine of the Holy Spirit in this context. One point needing clarification is the extent to which he is prevented from doing so by a clearly discernible Hegelianizing pneumatology in his early writings (*Sanctorum Communio*, DBWE 1:143ff,150ff [see part 0.5, note 17]) and by difficulties in distinguishing clearly between the objective spirit and the Holy Spirit (ibid., 208ff, 135ff).

own power and in so doing confronts it with its most profound impotence, with a forsakenness that results in multifarious and severe self-endangerment. Jüngel clearly sees that the God who consents to be pushed out of the world nonetheless remains related to it.[5] That notwithstanding, this relationship is not to be understood merely as one of loving and saving concern, but rather also as one of judgment that reveals to the world its forsaken state under the power of sin. In this situation, nothing more can be expected from the emancipatory power of the post-religious "community" in which Hegel was yet able to trust. And against this same background, Nietzsche's vision of the *Übermensch* who has divested himself of the binding powers of love and mercy can but make us shudder.

More recent theological discussion of the theology of the cross has both critically and constructively picked up impulses from Luther, Hegel, and Nietzsche in various forms. Jürgen Moltmann, for example, has worked toward a biblically oriented Christology of discipleship, picking up Luther's critique of speculative theology and outlining a decidedly Christian alternative to Hegel's secularizing-emancipatory program, in the process also passionately affirming the ethos of love and mercy so resolutely rejected by Nietzsche. Eberhard Jüngel, to take another example, seeks with Hegel to transfer the event of the cross onto the level of thought itself, trying to conceive God—though now beyond theism and atheism—or work toward a concept of the God who according to Luther reveals himself precisely on the cross; Jüngel, however, hardly deals at all with Hegel's practical emancipatory program or Nietzsche's raging criticism of any emotionalizing or moralizing theology of the cross. Ingolf Dalferth, picking up Jüngel's question concerning knowledge of God, critically objects to a theology of the cross that focuses on practical discipleship, combining this critique with far-reaching queries concerning any Christology whose content is oriented toward the "Nazarene" and "good person." Kazoh Kitamori, finally, addressing attempts to articulate God's revelation on the cross in a primarily reflexive fashion, provides guidance for devotion with respect to the "pain of God" as revealed on the cross. We will systematically examine the most important points attaching to these various programs for a theology of the cross, programs interrelated and critically juxtaposed one to the other in what is often a rather complex fashion (see part 3.4).

---

5. "The relationship established by departure must not necessarily be negative either. It can even imply an intensification. Thus, for example, the departure of the Johannine Christ is what first makes it possible to approach him properly" (Jüngel, *God as Mystery of the World*, 61 [see part 0.1, note 5]).

Jürgen Moltmann: Theology of the Cross and Discipleship of the Cross

As early as an excursus in his *Theology of Hope*,[6] and especially in his book *The Crucified God*,[7] Jürgen Moltmann picks up various key points from Luther, Hegel, and Bonhoeffer that prove fruitful for a theology of the cross, though in so doing he also points out and tries to address their respective weaknesses and positional problems. In Luther, Moltmann focuses on the assertion that it is God himself who wants to be recognized in the Crucified:

> The one who knows God in the lowliness, weakness and dying of Christ does not know him in the dreamed-of exaltation and divinity of the man, who seeks God, but in the humanity which he has abandoned, rejected and despised. And that brings to nothing his dreamed-of equality with God, which has dehumanized him, and restores to him his humanity, which the true God made his own. (213)

Moltmann concludes that if with Luther we seek to recognize God in the Crucified, then we must with Hegel also resolutely acknowledge the enduring relevance of the event of the cross, relevance that transcends the ages. As such, the cross cannot be relevant *solely* in a specific realm of history, nor *solely* in partial spheres of theology and piety; its significance must instead be discernible for the *totality* of human reality.[8] Although we must indeed complement Luther's revolutionary insight with what we have learned in the wake of Hegel's considerations, we cannot, according to Moltmann, simply concur with Hegel's assertion that in Jesus Christ we encounter essentially the incarnation of God *in a human self-consciousness*, and that the cross brings about primarily the fall of human self-consciousness into the "night of the I=I." Over against Hegel, Moltmann emphasizes the unique, *one-time nature* of the event of the cross, the singularity of Jesus of Nazareth, and God's revelation precisely in this one-time event. The uniqueness, the singularity, of the cross of Jesus Christ on Golgotha must not be surrendered even though this very

6. "The 'Death of God' and the Resurrection of Christ," *Theology of Hope*, 165–72 (see part 0.4, note 24).

7. *The Crucified God* (see part 0.1, note 6); parenthetical pagination in the text refers to this book. Concerning additional christologically relevant books by Moltmann (*The Way of Jesus Christ: Christology in Messianic Dimensions* [San Francisco: Harper, 1990]; *Jesus Christ for Today's World* [Minneapolis: Fortress Press, 1994]), see part 4.2.

8. Such also includes its ethical charisma. Cf., however, Moltmann's only weakly developed critique of Luther to the effect that he, Luther, was unable to deal critically in a *philosophia crucis* with the work philosophy of Aristotle or to combine an ecclesiastically reformational with a socio-critical theology of the cross (cf. 72f).

event, as Hegel quite correctly sees, involves an event of world-historical efficacy. It is not that the absolute substance reveals itself in a human self-consciousness that just happens to be connected to Jesus of Nazareth. Rather, the living God reveals himself in this particular human being, in this particular Crucified, so that he, God, might become active in a creation-historical fashion *in* him and *through* him.[9]

This combination of singularity and universal significance becomes discernible as soon the *multidimensionality of the event of the cross* as attested in the New Testament and its concomitant charismatic power are grasped, in which respect Moltmann at least indirectly picks up certain impulses from Bonhoeffer. When Jesus of Nazareth dies on the cross of Golgotha, it is not just a single human self-consciousness that dies in the night of abandonment by God. Moltmann makes three distinctions in this regard, namely, that Jesus dies

- as the "blasphemer" at odds with the Jewish religion,[10]
- as the "rebel" at odds with Roman power,[11] and
- as the "godforsaken" in tension with God the Creator and Father.[12]

We can leave in abeyance for the moment the question whether these three dimensions adequately grasp the person Jesus of Nazareth, his calling, and the conflicts that led to his execution (see in this regard part 3.4). These distinctions do in any event establish connections to the historical crucifixion of Jesus, thereby countering the risk of seeking knowledge of God in the Crucified solely—as Luther objects—in a speculatively conceived self-relation on the part of God or in a metaphysically reflected

9. Moltmann, *Theology of Hope*, 171f (see part 0.4, note 24): ". . . the god-forsakenness of the cross cannot, as in Hegel, be made into an element belonging to the divine process and thus immanent in God. A theology of the dialectical self-movement of absolute Spirit would then be only a modification of the dialectical ephiphany of the eternal as subject."

10. 128ff, with reference to Lev 24:16 and picking up on W. Schrage, "Das Verständnis des Todes Jesu Christi im Neuen Testament," in *Das Kreuz Jesu Christi als Grund des Heils*, ed. Ernst Bizer et al. (Gütersloh: Gütersloher, 1967), 51–89.

11. 136ff, following Oscar Cullmann, *Jesus and the Revolutionaries* (New York: Harper & Row, 1970), 31; also Martin Hengel, *Was Jesus a Revolutionist?* (Philadelphia: Fortress Press, 1971), 14ff; with reference to idem, *The Zealots: Investigations into the Jewish Freedom Movement in the Period from Herod I until 70 A.D.* (Edinburgh: T. & T. Clark, 1989); idem, "Gewalt und Gewaltlosigkeit. Zur 'politischen Theologie' in neutestamentlicher Zeit," *KuD* 18 (1972), 18–25.

12. 145ff. In making these distinctions, Moltmann picks up on the testimonies of the Synoptics concerning the crucifixion of Jesus; at the same time, he is interested in developing the theology of the cross "in all the three areas in which the ancient world used the term theology, and in which even today men are inescapably religious: in mythical theology, in the form of demythologization, in political theology, in the form of liberation; and in philosophical theology, in the form of understanding the universe as creation" (73).

or mystically intimated, intensive relationship between God and human beings.

Analogous to Hegel's philosophical vision of a "community" that, having awakened from the night of speculative Good Friday, sets about overcoming alienation and reshaping the real world, so also does Moltmann speak about how the cross and resurrection initiate "the overcoming of the history of man's sorrow and the fulfillment of his history of hope" (278). Moltmann, however, does not understand this history as a movement of the collectively understood "divine human being, the community," on its path toward innerworldly *theosis* (see part 3.2), but rather within the framework of a discipleship of Christ that yet awaits a theologically and ethically more precise disclosure.

> If his future in God and his being sent into the world for the future of God are manifested in the appearances of the risen Christ, then at the same time the significance of his cross and his way to the cross must also be manifested backwards; otherwise the identity of his person would not be maintained, and resurrection faith would be a way of separating oneself from the crucified Christ and the recollection of his career. (180)

The singularity of this person and this life, and the universality of the Resurrected's presence in the power of God's spirit must not be sundered. Moltmann's focus on the multidimensionality of the biblical witnesses to the ministry of the Crucified and his suffering prompt him to raise questions concerning the "psychological" and "political" liberation of human beings (cf. 291, 317), thereby enabling him to address in an exemplary fashion concrete examples of discipleship to the Crucified. This focus can be viewed as an attempt to carry through in a socio-ethical context as well Bonhoeffer's trust in God's presence even amid the most profound human suffering and collective self-endangerment.

Moltmann's intention here is to counter the sort of contemplative mysticism associated with a theology of the cross that so easily arises when one emphasizes—with Luther—that God can and wants to be known *solely* in the cross and in suffering. In this way, he seeks to prevent or thwart a theology of assuagement or devoted resignation that understands the cross essentially as religious instruction according to which one must come to terms with suffering, distress, and death in as tranquil or even-tempered a fashion as possible. Instead, in the light of the resurrection the "theology of the cross" must unfold as a "theology of following the cross" (cf. 65ff) that also testifies through concrete Christian praxis to God's saving and liberating presence amid the sufferings of the age.

Eberhard Jüngel: Conceiving God in differentiated unity with the Crucified

Hegel developed his theory of the cross as the core of a practical-philosophical program, one that inspired his students especially within the Hegelian left all the way to orthodox Marxism. At the same time, he wanted to articulate the notion of "substance becoming subject," along with all its consequences, within a process-oriented philosophical idea of God. It is this second impulse in particular that Eberhard Jüngel has addressed. In his main work, *God as Mystery of the World*,[13] though even earlier as well, in his programmatic essay "Vom Tod des lebendigen Gottes. Ein Plakat,"[14] he turns against the facile "syntactical connection" of the words "God" and "death" of the sort found in at least some variants of so-called "theology *after* the death of God" (43).[15] It is in view of this particular theme that Jüngel in his turn addresses the problem, a problem to which he refers in language influenced by if not entirely coincidental with Martin Heidegger as the "overcoming of the metaphysical concept of God."[16] Countering a false theistic concept of God—something Bonhoeffer's "critique of religion" also opposed—requires examining the christological origins of references to the death of God and inquiring concerning the meaning of the death of God for God himself.[17]

Jüngel comes to the conclusion:

> The essential act of death is essential to God himself, albeit not as something alien or that alienates from God . . . But such that God himself tolerates negation within himself that creates within his being space for other being.

13. See part 0.2, note 2. Parenthetical pagination in the text refers to this edition.

14. In Eberhard Jüngel, *Unterwegs zur Sache. Theologische Bemerkungen* (München: Kaiser, 1972), 105ff (henceforth cited as "Tod des lebendigen Gottes").

15. Several American theologians, e.g., Gabriel Vahanian, *The Death of God: The Culture of our Post-Christian Era* (New York: Braziller, 1961); Thomas J. J. Altizer, *The Gospel of Christian Atheism* (Philadelphia: Westminster, 1966); Richard L. Rubenstein, *After Auschwitz: History, Theology, and Contemporary Judaism*, Johns Hopkins Jewish Studies, 2nd ed. (Baltimore and London: Johns Hopkins University Press, 1992); though also Dorothee Sölle, *Christ the Representative: An Essay in Theology after the Death of God* (Philadelphia, Fortress Press (1967), 10, picking up on Hegel, Nietzsche, and Jean Paul, spoke about the historical event of the death of God, an event that within secular modernity or certainly in the world after the Holocaust could allegedly no longer be denied.

16. "Tod des lebendigen Gottes," 109 (see part 3.3, note 14).

17. Here Jüngel (and Moltmann as well) not only pick up on impulses from Bonhoeffer's critique of religion, they are also standing in the tradition of Karl Barth's pioneering doctrine of election, which emphasizes that there "is no such thing as Godhead in itself . . . In no depth of the Godhead shall we encounter any other but Him (scil. Jesus Christ)" (*CD* II/2, 115, cf. 150f et passim).

It is for others, namely, for *us*, that God did, after all, enter into death. God's no to himself is his yes to us.[18]

Among other things, what follows from this is that God's eternal being is not to be conceived as *simplex esse*, and other metaphysical divine predicates need to be questioned as well. "God's eternal being is both more differentiated and more temporal than we are capable of conceiving."[19] In his book *God as Mystery of the World*, Jüngel retrospectively acknowledges Hegel in emphasizing that

> this distinction between God and God based on the cross of Jesus Christ has destroyed the axiom of absoluteness, the axiom of apathy, and the axiom of immutability, all of which are unsuitable axioms for the Christian concept of God. (373)

Picking up on Hegel's positions and those of post-Hegelian critiques of religion, though also on Luther's position, Jüngel articulates his own theological program as two questions:

- "Can theology appropriately talk about the death of God without ceasing to be theology?"
- Can "theology which avoids talk about the death of God" still be theology? (44-45)

These considerations sooner *indirectly* focus on the socio-ethical charisma accompanying the discipleship of the cross that is so important to Moltmann and so detested by Nietzsche.[20] Jüngel develops his theology of the cross primarily in connection with the question "Where is God?" and makes it clear that this particular question acquires a quite different profile in the biblical traditions, on the one hand, and in modernity, on the other. Biblical traditions take as their point of departure the assertion that God, when not present, is hidden and in that sense absent.

> But once absent, he certainly is not now nothing, but rather the hidden God, who as hidden still is the only true God, who is the only one in whom faith is to be put. Right faith cries with its question for the right God. This is the meaning of the quotation from Psalm 22 on the lips of the dying Jesus. "My God, my God, why hast thou forsaken me" (Mark 15:34) is the most agonizing variant of the biblical question "Where is God?" (51)

---

18. "Tod des lebendigen Gottes," 120 (see part 3.3, note 14).

19. "Tod des lebendigen Gottes," 120.

20. This nexus emerges as at least a potential problem in view of the way Luther associates a new approach to a theology of the cross, on the one hand, with a critique of the law and works righteousness, on the other.

By contrast, modern sensibility is not prepared to accept the concealed nature of the true God, assuming instead that God in fact has no true locus and as such cannot but be met with "the indifferent shrug of one's shoulders" (54). Over against such vague references to God, theology must confront modern culture with God's presence *beyond* the alternative of "presence or absence"; it can do so by focusing on the crucified God.

In light of the cross, Jüngel conceives God as the "mystery of the world."[21] The event of the cross of Jesus Christ makes it necessary to discern the unity of God with the mortal human being, specifically the "identification of God" with the one human being Jesus on behalf of all others.

> That the God who is love must be able to suffer and does suffer beyond all limits in the giving up of what is most authentically his for the sake of mortal man, is an indispensable insight of the newer theology schooled by Luther's Christology and Hegel's philosophy. Only the God who is identical with the Crucified One makes us certain of his love and thus of himself. (373)

Jüngel incisively articulates in an abstract concept of love both the relationship between God and human beings and the orientation toward discipleship offered to human beings by the revelation on the cross. Love, Jüngel maintains, is the "still greater selflessness within such great self-relatedness" (374).[22]

Like Hegel, so also does Jüngel stress that the end of Jesus's earthly presence is what first makes it possible to understand his being as "God's coming." That is, precisely the withdrawal of the pre-Easter Jesus is what renders possible God's revelation as the "becoming present of an absent one as absent" (349 et passim). Although this assertion sounds rather obscure and paradoxical, the point is that God reveals himself precisely in the withdrawal of the pre-Easter Jesus and in the latter's contemporization in a *new* form, albeit a form that simultaneously maintains the absence of the pre-Easter Jesus. In light of Jesus's resurrection appearances and the self-contemporization of the exalted Christ in the power of the Spirit,[23] the content of this nexus or correlation can now be articulated more clearly theologically.

Jüngel now asks why it is precisely the history of Jesus's life and suffering that turns out to be the "trace" ultimately leading to the "founda-

---

21. Here, too, traces of Barth's doctrine of election are discernible; cf. *CD II/2*, 20ff, 30, 146ff et passim.

22. See in this regard parts 4.2 and 4.4.

23. See in this regard parts 2.3–2.5.

tion" of faith in the triune God. He points out how the announcement of God's reign occupies a central position in Jesus's own proclamation, a reign whose "eschatological future appeared to be combined with the present in the person of Jesus himself" (350).[24] It is precisely because this proclamation of God's reign characterized—or even defined—his existence as a human being that his life moved inevitably toward a violent death. Along with God's reign, Jesus thereby also proclaims God's "majestic act," as Jüngel formulates following Peter Stuhlmacher,[25] "with which he asserts himself over the world" (353).[26] God's will, however, proves to be a will to love, and to a love that is at once also love of one's enemies. What comes about here is a "new obviousness of reconciliation""(356). This is the same praxis of love, mercy, and forgiveness that draws both Nietzsche's hatred and his grudging respect for the efficacious power generated by the proclamation of the reign of the Crucified.

Even the earliest Christian confessions of faith present "the death of Jesus not as an event merely among men, but rather as an event between this one man and God, so that Jesus' God-forsakenness is now seen as God's most authentic work" (362). They emphasize that in the death of Jesus something happens in God himself that has enormous consequences for both the world and human beings. Jüngel's interpretation is that in Jesus's death, God differentiates himself from himself, though the "differentiation of God from God may not be understood as an opposition which is coerced on the being of God" (363). He then cites Goethe: "No one is against God unless it is God himself"[27] (363). God distinguishes himself from God. Jüngel in his own turn finds this self-differentiation effected insofar as it is precisely by identifying himself with the deceased Jesus that God defines himself.

24. So also Pannenberg, *Systematic Theology*, vol. 2, 326ff (see part 2.2, note 1).

25. Peter Stuhlmacher, "The Gospel of Reconciliation in Christ: Basic Features and Issues of a Biblical Theology of the New Testament," in *Horizons in Biblical Theology*, vol. 1, no. 1 (1979) 161–90, here 161ff; see also idem, *Jesus of Nazareth, Christ of Faith* (Peabody, Mass.: Hendrickson Publishers, 1993), 12ff; idem, *Die Verkündigung des Christus Jesus, Neutestamentliche Beobachtungen* (Wuppertal: Brockhaus, 2003).

26. Jüngel adduces the proclamations of God's reign in the classic parables of the prodigal son (Luke 15:11–32), the laborers in the vineyard (Matt 20:1–16), the good Samaritan (Luke 10:25–37), the Pharisee and the tax collector (Luke 18:9–14), and the unforgiving servant (Matt 18:21–35). He emphasizes the power Jesus claims to forgive sins (Mark 2:5; Luke 18:10f) "as is made concrete in the symbolic act of table fellowship with sinners," in "the healing of sick, those who are excluded from the temple ceremonial," and in taking issue with "the cultic Torah . . . in favor of the direct encounter with those who are lost and lawless" (356).

27. "Nemo contra deum nisi deus ipse." Johann Wolfgang Goethe, *Truth and Poetry: From My Own Life*, ed. Parke Godwin, vol. 2 (New York: Appleton, 1855), part 4, book 20, 107.

God defines the human being Jesus as the Son of God (Rom 1:4). "The kerygma of the Resurrected One proclaims the Crucified One as the self-definition of God" (364). Jüngel suggests that several things are in fact happening when God identifies with the Crucified and simultaneously differentiates himself within himself. First, God is opening up his own being for "the other," that is, for creaturely existence as such. At the same time, however, God subjects the divine life to death such that the divine life takes up death into itself. In this context, Jüngel speaks about a "death which was turned around on the cross of Christ" (364). That is, because death is no longer ultimate or final, death itself is "turned" into the divine life.

Jüngel's theology of the cross combines a theological consideration of Jesus's proclamation and death with speculative reflection on God's "self-relation" after the model of modern anthropology and the philosophy of reflection. He associates the cross with an opening on God's part "for the other," which he posits as death (which is overcome within God's self-relation) and as a salvific event (within God's self-relation) "for us"; that is, Jüngel attempts to combine God's self-relation—interpreted in terms of Trinitarian theology—with a radical experience of differentiation within God's self-relation—interpreted in terms of a theology of the cross. This attempt at clarification is far removed from Hegel's thought, which passed through a comprehensive critique of the reflexive philosophy of subjectivity and the efficacious power of its various forms.[28] That said, the overall conceptual results of this position are unfortunately also theologically deficient, since such reference to God's "selflessly" opening self-relation cannot really adequately or clearly articulate the salvific power of the resurrection and the Holy Spirit.[29]

---

28. Cf. even Hegel's early piece *Faith and Knowledge* (see part 3.2, note 5), though also Hegel's recurring critique of Aristotle's intellectualism, a thinker Hegel otherwise highly esteems. The philosophy of reflection, Hegel asserts, persists in the conceptual model of the individual: "This element of thought itself, however, is abstract, that is, is the activity of an *individual* consciousness. The spirit, however, is not only as an individual, finite consciousness, but as a *universal*, concrete spirit in and of itself. This concrete universality, however, encompasses all the developed modes and aspects within which it is and becomes an object commensurate with the idea" (G.W.F. Hegel, *Vorlesungen über die Geschichte der Philosophie III*, Theorie Werkausgabe, vol. 20 [Frankfurt: Suhrkamp, 1971], 481). Although the philosophy of reflection can indeed incorporate the Aristotelian concept of spirit, it cannot incorporate those of Hegel and certainly not the conceptual shapes of the Holy Spirit. Cf. Welker, *God the Spirit*, 283ff (see part 0.6, note 16); cf. also part 2.5.

29. Cf. Jüngel's rather sparse explications concerning "God as Event of the Spirit" (374ff), in which the figure of the "relation of the relations" (375) und a rhetoric of "the fire of love" (375) must fill in for the lack of any considerations concerning a soteriological pneumatology.

Ingolf Dalferth: A Renewal of Kerygma Theology?

On the one hand, Ingolf Dalferth views his own christological reflections in continuity with Jüngel's program of understanding God in unity with Jesus and Jesus as the Crucified, of then comprehending this unity with Jesus as God's "being for us," of conceiving this being as love, and of understanding that message as gospel.[30] On the other hand, he enumerates a whole array of fundamental problems generated by the implementation of this program (cf. 54ff).[31] According to Dalferth, the double task of grasping both the distinction and the interrelation between Jesus Christ and God and, simultaneously, the distinction and interrelation between Jesus Christ and us human beings, is enormously difficult (cf. 59).[32]

One danger he sees is that Jesus might, for example, be grasped metaphorically as a "God-man," the resulting metaphors then being "understood *mythically* and interpreted *metaphysically*" (66). Here Jesus risks becoming an "eschatological special case" "with whom we have nothing to do," and any references to the "Son of God" would merely amplify the difference between us and Jesus into what for us at least is an "unbridgeable" gulf (66). By contrast, if Christology focuses on the "true human being," then "the christological metaphors are read as statements concerning the *norm of what it means to be human*" (67), in which case, differences between Jesus and God are preserved as those between creature and creator, and those between Jesus and us are understood as the "*perfect* and *failed* realization of human existence intended by God" (67). Any suspicion that this path merely idolizes a human being is countered by an emphasis on his divinity (cf. 64). The objection that this response in its own turn merely again amplifies the difference between Jesus and us into an "unbridgeable" gulf is countered by an emphasis on the "*exemplary character*" of his life as a human being (64).

It is precisely here, however, that Dalferth sees the loss of Christology and its displacement by a "*Christian ethics of life and discipleship*" (64). Dalferth disdainfully criticizes this development that positions the "*good person*" (63) Jesus at the center. Over against the "Christology of example" that emerges in various Jesulogies that find in Jesus the "exemplary model of the friend, helper, new man, feminist, etc." and even today are

---

30. "Gott für uns. Die Bedeutung des christologischen Dogmas für die christliche Theologie," in *Denkwürdiges Geheimnis. Beiträge zur Gotteslehre, FS Eberhard Jüngel*, ed. Ingolf U. Dalferth, Johannes Fischer, and Hans-Peter Großhans (Tübingen: Mohr Siebeck, 2004), 51, 73ff; parenthetical pagination in the text refer to this essay.

31. See the more thorough discussion in part 5.2.

32. Cf. Ingolf U. Dalferth, *Der auferweckte Gekreuzigte. Zur Grammatik der Christologie* (Tübingen: Mohr Siebeck, 1994), 13ff, 139ff (cited as *Der auferweckte Gekreuzigte*).

still regnant at the forefront of discussion (67)—all of which in his view represent little more than uncontrolled post-christological growth—he recommends a drastic cure.

He conceives what he describes as a *"strict Christology of revelation"* that focuses "not on Jesus as such, but on Jesus as the locus of God's revelation" (64).[33] "It is not *the Nazarene himself* and *as such* that carries theological weight, but rather the *will and activity of God* that becomes discernible through and in him" (65). Dalferth's assurances that he is here *not* advocating that revelation be historically emptied are as casually incidental as they are feeble (cf. 65). Christology, he says, has "no particular doctrine of the person of Jesus to develop that would be anything other than a *doctrine of God*" (74).

Dalferth's Christology culminates in the message that God's presence is so ubiquitous that human beings "can live with God in the world, are never without God, and hence also need not die without God. God is *God for us*, and *that* is the good news that comes to expression in the gospel" (75). Dalferth describes this God as a ubiquitous *creator ex nihilo*: "Wherever God acts, something new emerges from nothing. And God acts perpetually and everywhere where something is, in every time and at every place in the world."[34] It is difficult not to find in these considerations simply a new version of kerygma-theology that has been radically emptied of christological content (see part 1.2). Over certain stretches, Dalferth's explications seem like an incipient "retrieval" of Christology and theology of the cross back into metaphysics—accompanied now by

---

33. Cf. "Gott für uns," 65: Theologically, Jesus is to be adduced "exclusively as the actual locus of God's revelation." Joachim Ringleben, *Jesus. Ein Versuch zu begreifen* (Tübingen: Mohr Siebeck, 2008), appropriates this language in his assertion that "God produces himself at the locus of Jesus" (653 et passim), though he does consistently and justifiably emphasize that this "locus" is shaped by the life of Jesus that in its own turn is shaped by the resurrection, transformed by the Spirit, and preserved in a new form (ibid., 632ff; and earlier Ringleben, *Wahrhaft auferstanden*, 113ff, 142ff [see part 2.3, note 4]). – Dalferth, *Der auferweckte Gekreuzigte*, 129, had yet maintained that the "reign of God proclaimed by Jesus becomes the horizon of understanding and theological interpretive vehicle of his life that discloses that life as a form of presence of the reign of God. In a reverse fashion, Jesus's own life as experienced both historically and eschatologically then becomes the soteriological interpretive vehicle of God's reign by explicating it as a reign of salvific love." Cf. ibid., 58f et passim. This more substantive christological content is increasingly vanishing in favor of a concentration on "God as the reality of the possible" (I. U. Dalferth, *Radikale Theologie*, Forum theologische Literaturzeitung 23 [Leipzig: Evangelische Verlagsanstalt, 2010], 239 et passim), on "creation" that states that "everything real and possible is owed to God" (ibid., 244), on a "new view of the entire world" that teaches us to see "everything in a new and different way" (ibid., 255) and directs us to the "task of perpetual reorientation" (ibid., 279) in the form of a constant differentiation between old and new.

34. *Der auferweckte Gekreuzigte*, 59.

arid kerygmatic assurances—designed to make Christianity's "universal claims" more presentable.[35] Jesus Christ as the "locus of revelation" is emptied or replaced— apart from the arid kerygma—by the God who incessantly and everywhere ("everywhere where something is") creates or prompts something new to come into being from nothing. What yet remains obscure, however, is why this particular God is to be called "love" and not simply "incessant perpetual renewer." Whereas the "second quest for the historical Jesus" at least *lamented* our inability to grasp the historical content of the life of Jesus and his person, Dalferth now envelops this concern with the aura of a mistaken theological orientation. The historical emptying of the "locus" of revelation goes hand in hand with its pneumatological deflation.

A potential alternative to Dalferth's radical reductionism, however, can be found contextually close to this attempt to retrieve the theology of the cross back to within the horizon of a doctrine of God and theology of creation.

Kazoh Kitamori: Theology of the Pain of God

In his book *Theology of the Pain of God*, written before and during the Second World War and published in 1946,[36] the Japanese theologian Ka-

---

35. Cf. *Der auferweckte Gekreuzigte*, 312 et passim. In his book *Jenseits von Mythos und Logos. Die christologische Transformation der Theologie* (Freiburg: Herder, 1993), Dalferth, likely following Rev 21:5, was already advocating the thesis that everything becomes "new" in the encounter with Jesus as the Christ. In light of these assertions, Hartmut Rosenau, "'Was sagen die Leute, wer ich sei?' (Mk 8,27) – Überlegungen zu einer sapientialen Christologie," *Marburger Jahrbuch Theologie 23, Christologie*, ed. Elisabeth Gräb-Schmidt and Reiner Preul, Marburger Theologische Studien 113 (Leipzig: Evangelische Verlagsanstalt, 2011), 138, called for a "more precise description," suggesting instead that everything acquires thereby its intrinsic essence. Ulrich Kühn, *Christologie*, UTB 2393 (Göttingen: Vandenhoeck, 2003), 62f, taking issue with Dalferth, *Der auferweckte Gekreuzigte*, found that despite Dalferth's emphasis on the necessity of allowing "the identity of Jesus with the Resurrected and his soteriological significance for us even during his earthly life to radiate and become comprehensible," (Dalferth, 91), nonetheless such a position rigorously abandons any point of departure for "Christology from below." Kühn finds in Dalferth "a 'steep' about-face back to the Reformational approach to a theology of the cross, albeit one that yet leaves open the problem of a historical approach to the reality of Jesus of Nazareth of the sort that has become of fundamental importance for the contemporary understanding of truth." In this speculatively extreme version, a theology based on perpetually new creation (or sooner: on perpetual renewal) and recommended as being "radical" risks ultimately turning into a sterile theology of what Hegel called "bad infinity."

36. Kazoh Kitamori, *Theology of the Pain of God* (Richmond: John Knox Press, 1965); parenthetical pagination in the text refers to this edition; concerning the relationship between Kitamori and Moltmann's conceptual approach, see Peter Fumiaki Momose, *Kreu-*

zoh Kitamori describes a God who, rather than incessantly ("everywhere where something is") prompting something new to arise from nothing, instead is intimately related in pain to creation, which in its own turn, and quite separate from God, is subject to self-endangerment, infinitude, and death. Over against the "'soprano' . . . of the love of God" to which western theologians are so inclined (24 et passim), he emphasizes along with Hajime Tanabe that "[t]he absolute, which transcends man's sin without pain and suffering, may be called love, God, mercy, or Buddha, yet it does not satisfy our religious needs" (29). Instead, he describes the cross and incarnation as two paths from the historical Jesus toward the pain of God, and "from the pain of God toward the historical Jesus" (34). In his pain, this compassionate God[37] turns his love toward sinners who turn their backs, love that overwhelms through forgiveness (cf. 37, 40). Those sinners who turn their backs on God, however, are those who experience and indeed then usually try to repress the pain of finitude, the "reality of darkness" (148 et passim).[38]

Kitamori emphasizes that the "task of witnessing to the gospel is to vitalize the *astonishing fact* of the gospel" (44) that both theology and the church must learn anew. He himself, Kitamori tells us, first learned this profound astonishment by way of Jer 31:20 and from a passage from the letter to the Hebrews (2:10): "It was fitting that God . . . should make the pioneer of their salvation"—the Son—"perfect through sufferings."[39] "The little word *eprepen* thundered in my ears as though it would shake the entire universe" (45). God's essence consists of God's pain as revealed on the cross, pain that characterizes his elementary relationship to creation, which in its own turn is radically differentiated from God. Kitamori describes God's love as the newly creative power through which

---

zestheologie. Eine Auseinandersetzung mit Jürgen Moltmann, Ökumenische Forschungen: 2, Soteriolog. Abteilung, vol. 7 (Freiburg/Basel/Wien: Herder, 1978), esp. 91ff.

37. Kitamori repeatedly cites Jer 31:20 and Isa 63:15, even concluding his book with a meditation on them (151ff).

38. It is worth noting that it was precisely from Germany and Japan that more broadly discussed drafts of a theology of the cross emerged following the Second World War. Kitamori himself stresses that in his own theology, he combines a biblical and Lutheran education with an orientation toward classical Japanese drama, the latter of which is centered in the tsurasa, tragic pain (cf. 135f, 148); cf. also the reflections on the "power of God in the suffering Christ" in Arthur C. McGill, *Suffering: A Test of Theological Method* (Philadelphia: Westminster, 1982), 93ff; see also Douglas John Hall, *God & Human Suffering: An Exercise in the Theology of the Cross* (Minneapolis: Augsburg, 1986), 104ff; Paul S. Fiddes, *The Creative Suffering of God* (Oxford: Clarendon, 1988; paperback 1992), 144ff.

39. NRSV: "It was fitting that God, for whom and through whom all things exist, in bringing many children to glory, should make the pioneer of their salvation perfect through sufferings."

God overcomes sinners through forgiveness and thereby gives them, too, the power of forgiving love, even to the point of loving one's enemy (cf. 121f). "The pain of man corresponds with that of God which is the content of the gospel. . . . This change into light from darkness is possible only by man's response to God's action" (147f).

Although a theology of the cross must take this pain of God into account, it cannot in so doing reduce its message to merely a basic impression or a more or less complex core idea if its intent is *also* to articulate itself as a theology of the resurrected Crucified.

3.4 The Cross Reveals Not Only the Suffering, but also the Judging and Saving God

Although Jesus Christ's death on the cross is a revelatory event, it is not such simply in and of itself, since death by crucifixion sooner merely leaves an observer speechless. In light of the resurrection, however, and in light of Jesus's pre-Easter ministry, the cross is indeed an extremely complex revelatory event. The disturbing collaboration between representatives of the global power Rome, Jerusalem's religious elite, and certainly also enflamed and functionalized public opinion[1] results in Jesus being nailed to the cross. The "rulers of this age," Paul writes, "crucified the Lord of glory" (1 Cor 2:8). Because it was as an impoverished itinerant preacher that this Lord of glory had proclaimed the coming of God's reign, those rulers failed to recognize him. And yet he symbolically initiated that very reign by actively turning to human beings in teaching, healing, acceptance, and table communion. It is through his resurrection that he is revealed as the divine Lord (see part 2.5).

What, then, does the cross reveal in the light of Jesus's resurrection and his pre-Easter life, and in the shadow of the powers that collaborated to bring about his execution?

The cross reveals the terrifying, godforsaken situation of human beings, a situation they themselves, however, do not recognize as such. The representative world, in a curious mixture of anxiety, fear, and aggressivity, turns against God's presence in the life and ministry of Jesus.

The cross discloses a situation that could not but plunge the world into profound despair were the world truly to grasp it; as it is, however, the world is able simply to pass over or disregard it in dull unconsciousness, with a shrug of the shoulders, or even gleefully. The cross of Christ is the expression of the godforsaken condition of human beings, a condition they yet try to disguise even though they themselves have brought it about.

Although Jewish and Christian thinkers have associated Auschwitz and the cross within the context of extreme suffering and godforsakenness,[2] doing so is misleading in at least two respects. First, since Auschwitz represents the mass murder of countless people, the brutal annihilation of millions of Jews, any association between these

---

1. Cf. Mark 15:11, 13f; Matt 27:20, 22f; Luke 23:18, 21, 23; John 19:12, 15.
2. Cf., e.g., Ignaz Maybaum, *The Face of God after Auschwitz* (Amsterdam: Polak & Van Gennep, 1965); Paul van Buren, *Discerning the Way* (New York: Seabury Press, 1980).

two events risks evoking the notion that the Germans were trying some-how to compare or even balance out this horror with the death of Jesus Christ. Second, the cross discloses a situation of *global* hopelessness and consternation. That is, whereas large parts of the world did indeed rise up and oppose the abominations of the Nazi dictatorship—albeit not em-phatically enough against the persecution and murder of the Jews—in the event of the cross, by contrast, both foes and friends, occupiers and the occupied, foreigners and indigenous, pagans and Jews alike acted in concert. Even the "rulers of this age" who were in conflict with one an-other were unified at least in this context.

The cross reveals the diastasis of God and humankind, God and world.

By killing the "Lord of glory," the world succeeds in cutting itself off from God. Rather than remaining merely a possibility, diastasis, the falling apart of God and world, actually comes about here. The cross reveals the radical difference between God and world, God and human beings, a difference early dialectical theology emphasized so strong-ly: "How these two things fall apart, how abstractly they stand facing each other!"[3] All Christian references to this distinction between God and human beings, to this tension that human beings simply cannot overcome on their own initiative, though also all references to God's hiddenness and distance cannot but take the cross as their point of departure if they are to avoid downplaying or otherwise making light of the religious dimensions at work here. To wit, the cross radically calls into question or indeed even puts an end to any and all lighthearted theologies that make their peace with the "dear Lord," that try to en-gage God and human beings in a kind of enduring but unproblematic partnership, or that otherwise propagate a peaceful ongoing relation-ship between God and human beings.

The cross reveals the profundity of the sin of the world. It stands for the triumph of the powers of the world over the presence and revelation of God.

The cross reveals that understanding the phenomenon of sin solely as individual self-relatedness and individual self-glorification dangerously downplays it,[4] since it is on the cross that the ghastly violence of the pow-

3. Karl Barth, "The Christian in Society," in Barth, *The Word of God and Theology*, trans. Amy Marga (New York: T & T Clark International, 2011), 35.

4. Cf. Sigrid Brandt, "Sünde. Ein Definitionsversuch," in *Sünde. Ein unverständlich gewordenes Thema*, ed. Sigrid Brandt, Marjorie H. Suchocki, and Michael Welker, 2nd

ers of the world is revealed, powers that compromise religion, law, politics, and public morality and opinion in opposing and even veiling God's presence.[5] It becomes clear in light of the cross of Jesus Christ that even God's "good law" can turn into an instrument of lies and deception under the power of sin.[6] Jesus Christ is crucified in the name of religion, of global power politics, with reference to both Jewish and Roman law, and with the approval or even under the pressure of public opinion.[7] The distinctions between the political, religious, and legal norms and orientations, whose task would in fact be to promote the search for justice, are leveled, and even the distinctions between nations and traditions, between occupiers and subjects, friends and foes, are effectively abolished beneath the cross. The entire representative world is allied in this triumph of the "will to the distancing of God,"[8] against the divine revelation in the loving ministry and proclamation of Jesus. The cross reveals how human beings distance themselves both individually and collectively from God's loving presence, or even oppose that presence with violence while yet giving the appearance of justice, being pleasing to God, political necessity, and public consensus.

The cross reveals the danger that God's revelation might not reach human beings because God may well withdraw from them.

Eberhard Jüngel's distinction between the modern notion of God's *absolute* absence over against the biblical notion of God's *relative* ab-

---

ed. (Neukirchen-Vluyn: Neukirchener, 2005), 13–34 (cited henceforth as Brandt, "Sünde"). Cf. also part 3.5.

5. Cf. Barth, *CD IV/3*, "The Falsehood of Man," esp. 434ff.

6. See in this regard Michael Welker, "Warum Moral und Medien der Sünde gegenüber hilflos sind. Gedanken im Anschluß an 1 Kor 2,1–10," in Brandt/Suchocki/Welker, *Sünde*, 189ff (see part 3.4, note 4); also Welker, "Ist Barths Sündenlehre in gesellschaftlichen und kulturellen Kontexten relevant?" *Zeitschrift für Dialektische Theologie* 27 (2011), 60–76.

7. Hengel and Schwemer, *Jesus und das Judentum*, 591ff and 601ff (see part 1.3, note 12), illuminate the complicated interplay of powers between the family of Annas, the high priest, who installed all five of his sons as well as his son-in-law Caiaphas in this office, and Jewish capital jurisdiction, furthermore also that between the administrative power the Roman emperor bestowed on the prefect Pilate and the manipulation of public opinion by a group from among the inhabitants of Jerusalem in the Barabbas episode, an episode mentioned by all the Gospels (Mark 15:6–15; Matt 27:15–26; Luke 23:13–25; John 18:39f). Ratzinger makes extensive use of this reconstruction in *Jesus of Nazareth*, vol. 2, 167-201 (see part 1.3, note 20).

8. Hans-Georg Geyer coined this expression (Germ., *Wille zur Ferne Gottes*); cf. idem, *Andenken. Theologische Aufsätze*, ed. H. T. Goebel, D. Korsch, et al. (Tübingen: Mohr Siebeck, 2003), 107ff, 215ff.

sence (the image of God "turning his countenance away" or "withdraw-ing his Spirit") enables us to articulate more precisely what is meant by the "death of God" (part 3.2) and the "crucified God." Biblical insight into God's relative absence makes it possible to distinguish between the notion of God's *absolute* death, on the one hand, which would under-mine any and all ideas of God, and the real danger of a *relative* death of God, on the other. What emerges here is the serious danger that God and world, God and humankind, "have died to each other" in a wholly disas-trous sense, a death of God quite in the sense of the expression, "This person is dead for me—I have absolutely no relationship or connection with this person now, nor do I want any." God has died for human be-ings; that is, he is null and void for them. It is, however, in precisely the same sense that God's own judgment on the world is pronounced from the cross: For God, human beings themselves have died; that is, they have been delivered over to their own nullity.

The cross not only reveals the danger that the world might close itself seamlessly off from God, utterly renouncing or even taking up a posture of opposition against God, it also reveals the danger that God, too, might no longer seek and find access to that very world.

The cross, however, also reveals God's own suffering; it re-veals not only the suffering of Jesus Christ, but also that of the triune God who through the sending of Jesus simultaneously seeks to reveal his proximity to human beings.

Jesus Christ's death both as a human being and as a criminal not only severely calls into question and strains the credibility of all his sovereign predicates and claims and promises, it also destroys every conceivable perspective from which one might yet entertain any notion of Jesus's communion with the Creator and with God's spirit. We can refer to this situation as **God's inner disruption or as disruption within God.** Through the cross, God is confronted with the death and sin of the world in a way that calls into question not only Jesus's life, but also the divine life itself. **What sort of God is it that fails within its own divine revelatory will?** What sort of God moves off into the furthest possible distance from human beings precisely while seeking the greatest possible proximity to them?

The cross reveals the abyss in which the very deity of God is most profoundly called into question.

The sacred God is desecrated through the direct confrontation with sin and death. The creative God is confronted with chaos. The revelation of divine love in Jesus Christ founders on organized hatred and violence. The beneficent normative and orientational powers of the law through which God intends the world to be governed are perverted and corrupted. The cross reveals a suffering or impotence on God's part; it reveals not only the suffering and death of Jesus Christ, but also the suffering and impotence residing deep within the deity itself.[9]

Insofar as the cross reveals God's pain and impotence, so also does the inner communion between Creator, Spirit, and Jesus Christ become discernible over against a world that closes itself off from God.

The deity that reveals itself is the deity that has entered into the abyss of human misery and horror, subjecting itself not only to natural death, but also to the abyss of extreme separation from God, which various biblical traditions call "hell." The cross reveals God's descent into hell. It reveals that God himself is no stranger to hell, that God suffers from hell and allows the divine life itself, in the figure of the crucified Resurrected, to be enduringly characterized by this very suffering.

Because human beings not only close themselves off from Jesus, who proclaimed the coming reign of God and even embodied such in his own person and life, but also turn against and similarly close themselves off from the creative, living God and the divine Spirit, the cross of godforsakenness reveals the profound communion between Jesus and God, whom Jesus calls his Father and with whom he lives in the power and communion of the Holy Spirit. This situation, however, is one of paradoxical communion amid disunion of the sort similarly coming to expression in the tension between trust and despair in God in the words the Crucified himself speaks: "My God, my God, why have you forsaken me?" (Matt 27:46; Mark 15:34, picking up Ps 22:2).[10]

An awareness of the deeper dimensions of God's revelation on the cross also casts a clearer light on the resurrection itself. In the resurrection, the creative God reveals himself in the midst of the enormous separation

9. Cf. in this regard Kitamori, *Theology of the Pain of God* (see part 3.3, note 36). Although Paul Gavrilyuk, *The Suffering of the Impassible God: The Dialectics of Patristic Thought*, paperback ed. (New York: Oxford University Press, 2006), esp. 135ff, has justifiably warned against viewing this disruption within God as belonging to the *essence* of God; however, his concerns should not prompt a renewal of the metaphysical notion that God is incapable of suffering.

10. The possible significance for a theology of the Trinity of the Crucified's statements about "surrendering the spirit" (cf. Mark 15:37; Luke 23:46; John 19:30b) remains unclarified.

from God in which human beings find themselves; that is, in the resurrected Jesus Christ, God discloses himself in the midst of human beings' sinful self-isolation. The resurrection, rather than deriving from human preconditions, is solely God's own creative and re-creative deed. God engages those who are anxiously fearful, doubting, and unhappy along with those who are hardened and indifferent, and gives them a share in this demonstration of his presence. God turns the fortunes of those who are lost, has mercy with humanity and creation under the power of sin, and does so by saving, lifting up, and exalting them.

In the power of the creative Spirit and the presence of the resurrected Crucified, hopelessness turns into joy, doubt into faith, temptation into certainty, and lack of direction into new discipleship. Insofar as human beings are included in what happens here, it is explicitly the activity of God's spirit, the Holy Spirit, that comes to expression and comes to bear. "The event of the crucifixion of Jesus Christ does not merely bring the deity of the Father as well as the Son into question. It refers both to the work of the Spirit, who as the Creator of life raises Jesus from the dead."[11] With the resurrection, God opens up the divine life for human participation and involvement in a previously wholly inconceivable fashion.[12]

The witnesses become concrete bearers of the presence of the resurrected Christ and thus also of the presence of the creative God on this earth. From within the hopeless situation of the cross and the inner disruption of the divine life itself, the creative deity and the power of the Spirit emerge within the life of the Resurrected that now, as it were, enmeshes and binds the faithful into the divine presence.

Hence it is in multiple respects that the cross is a revelatory event. In light of the resurrection and the pre-Easter path of Jesus all the way to the cross itself, it is revealed as an event that in its own turn reveals sin, judgment, the renewal of the world, and the saving of human beings, the latter of whom are now chosen from within their hopelessness to become

11. Wolfhart Pannenberg, *Systematic Theology*, vol. 1 (Grand Rapids, Mich.: Eerdmans, 1991), 314. See in this regard also the profound reflections of Sergius Bulgakov, *The Lamb of God* (1933) (Grand Rapids and Cambridge, UK: Eerdmans, 2008), 316ff, 382ff, 402f. Cf. 1 Cor 15:44ff; Rom 1:4; 8:11; 1 Tim 3:16b.

12. What happens here cannot be grasped adequately by the image of an "opening" of a bipolar self-relation on the part of God (cf. part 3.3). See also Hilarion Alfeyev, *Christ the Conqueror of Hell: The Descent into Hades from an Orthodox Perspective* (Crestwood: St. Vladimir's Seminary Press, 2009), 17ff, 203ff; idem, *The Mystery of Faith: An Introduction to the Teaching and Spirituality of the Orthodox Church* (London: Darton, Longman & Todd; Oxford [England]: St Stephen's Press, 2002). See also Hans Urs von Balthasar, "Theologische Besinnung auf das Mysterium des Höllenabstiegs," in *"Hinabgestiegen in das Reich des Todes." Der Sinn dieses Satzes in Bekenntnis und Lehre, Dichtung und Kunst*, ed. Hans Urs von Balthasar (Munich and Zurich: Schnell & Steiner, 1982), 84ff.

the bearers of God's very presence. It is not without reason that the cross of Christ stands at the very center of the church and at the center of the Christian faith itself. Whenever faith does not emerge ever anew from the cross and the crucified Christ, Christian piety and the church lose their seriousness, their gravity, and their orientation.[13]

---

13. Cf. parts 0.1 and 3.1. Picking up on the dispute between Gregory of Nyssa and Eunomius, John Behr, *The Mystery of Christ: Life in Death* (Crestwood: St. Vladimir's Seminary Press, 2006), 33ff, discloses God's demonstration of power precisely in kenosis and the cross.

3.5 Sin and Atonement – Sacrifice and Victim – Vicarious Substitution "for us" (Brandt, Gese, Janowski)

Biblical traditions associate the suffering, dying, and cross of Jesus Christ with the general notion of sacrifice (e.g., Eph 2:14; 5:2; Heb 9:14, 26ff; 10:10ff) and atonement (Rom 3:25; 8:3), furthermore with the sacrifice of the lamb (e.g., John 1:29, 36; Acts 8:32; 1 Cor 5:7; Rev 5:6–22:1, 3 passim) and its blood (John 6:54ff; Rom 3:25; 5:9; 1 Cor 10:16; 11:25; Eph 1:7; 2:13; Col 1:20; 1 Pet 1:19; 1 John 1:7; 5:6ff; Heb 9:12ff; 10:19; Rev 1:5) for the sins of the world. The attendant conceptual world and ideas are largely profoundly alien to people today, on occasion appearing not only offensive, but wholly incompatible with the notion of salvation and redemption. A careful examination of the event of the cross can lead us out of this conundrum.

The power of sin in the abuse of politics, religion, law, and public morality and opinion

Under the Romans at the time of Jesus, crucifixion was viewed as an especially disgraceful form of political capital punishment, one imposed particularly on "the lower classes, i.e., slaves, violent criminals and unruly elements in rebellious provinces."[1] Martin Hengel has, however, also pointed out that by contrast, it was above all high-ranking officials and military commanders who were crucified among the Persians and Carthaginians. Against this background, the inscription on the cross "Jesus of Nazareth, King of the Jews"—according to John in three languages and initiated by Pilate[2]—might well be an expression of derision or even sarcasm directed equally against the Jews and Jesus.[3]

Crucifixion during that period, however, was not only a particularly disgraceful form of capital punishment, but also a particularly gruesome one. The various forms of torture, at least floggings of the disrobed condemned person, were public and often lasted for days, and the profoundly degrading execution itself was designed to demonstrate the power of the occupiers and also to serve as a deterrent to the public.[4] Unlike the film by Mel Gibson and other voyeuristic and sadistic crucifixion fan-

---

1. Martin Hengel, *Crucifixion: In the Ancient World and the Folly of the Message of the Cross* (London: SCM Press, 1977), 87, 46ff.

2. John 19:19f; cf. also Matt 27:37; Luke 23:38.

3. It might also, however, express a remnant of respectful diffidence toward Jesus and his life, an element of ultimate awe as reflected in all the accounts of Pilate's behavior prior to the condemnation and surrendering over of Jesus.

4. Cf. Hengel, *Crucifixion*, 22ff, 87 (see part 3.5, note 1). Cf. Matt 27:26, 30; Mark 15:15; see also 14:65; John 19:1–3.

tasies, the biblical witnesses themselves do not go into extensive detail concerning the gruesome acts carried out against Jesus. What they do portray more extensively is Pilate's indecisiveness in imposing the death penalty on Jesus in the first place.[5] Nor is Jesus denied a burial, something otherwise frequently the case with crucified persons.[6]

That notwithstanding, the overall impression characterizing the canonical traditions is one of profound disgrace. According to Paul, the "message about the cross" is "foolishness" and a "stumbling block" for Jews and Gentiles (1 Cor 1:18, 23). Is it not then absurd to maintain, as does Paul himself, that "the power of God and the wisdom of God" are revealed here (1 Cor 1:24)? Understanding the message of the cross as well as *the way God deals with the power of sin* (cf. part 3.4) requires that we first examine the detailed Gospel portrayals themselves rather than immediately contextualizing the cross *solely* within the perspective of a single individual (juxtaposed, e.g., with a creative God who does not simply abandon a person in his or her hour of death). For the Gospels portray an extremely complex religio-moral-political weave of circumstances that ultimately lead to Jesus's crucifixion.

Primary culpability for Jesus's death is regularly attributed to the Pharisees and scribes who persecute Jesus during his public ministry, ensnare him in captious disputations, and "conspire how to destroy him," and also to the "chief priests and the elders," who incite the crowd against Jesus before Pilate.[7] The chief priests and the entire high council "were looking for false testimony against Jesus that they might put him to death" (Matt 26:59; Mark 14:55, 64). A fear of the people on the part of Jesus's persecutors, however, is also repeatedly emphasized (e.g., Luke 19:47), as was earlier the case among those hounding John the Baptist. The chief priests finally succeed in "stirring up the crowd" against Jesus (Matt 27:20; Mark 15:11ff; Luke 23:13ff.), and Pilate, even against his own intuition (Mark 15:10ff), his legal expertise (Luke 23:13ff; John 18:31, 38), and the advice of his wife (Matt 27:18ff), gives in to the pressure of the increasingly agitated crowd, though also because his own loyalty to the Roman emperor is vehemently called into question (John 19:12, 15). Rather than risk allowing Jesus to live, his Jewish persecutors utterly ignore the fact that, at their own insistence, a condemned crimi-

5. Cf. Matt 27:11–26; Mark 15:1–15; Luke 23:1–25; John 18:28–19:16.

6. The crucified's corpse was generally left out for wild animals and birds of prey to devour. Cf. Hengel, *Crucifixion*, 87f (see part 3.5, note 1).

7. Matt 12:14; 26:4, 59; 27:1, 20; Mark 3:6; 14:1; Luke 19:47; 22:2; John 5:18; 7:25; 8:37, 40; 10:33; 11:53. Especially in John, these attributions of culpability are accompanied by fierce polemic against "the Jews," though the Synoptics are similarly generous with negative portrayals of the Jewish religious elite.

nal will be set free, and that in order to coerce Pilate they themselves are now feigning loyalty to the Gentile emperor and hostile world power. That is, the freeing of a condemned criminal and feigned loyalty to the Gentile emperor and hostile world power solely for the sake of coercion seem less dangerous to them than that Jesus might live. "Away with him! Away with him!"[8]

The event of the cross parades before us a horrific nexus of blindness and self-deception: indecisive and intimidated, ultimately likely indifferent political leadership, a blinded religious elite similarly acting more out of considerations of maintaining power, inflamed public opinion ("Today: hosanna! Tomorrow: crucify him!"), a manipulated system of justice, abused legal and religious norms—these witnesses confront us with a bewildering weave of entanglements that make a mockery of any query concerning justice or search for truth. In short, it is the world under the power of sin.

However things may stand with the historical soundness of these details, the message itself is unmistakable that Jesus was subjected to concerted persecution by the Pharisees, scribes, chief priests, and elders. That said, examinations of Jesus's life and ministry too frequently abstract from the fact that he did indeed minister during the period of Roman occupation, that the Temple and Torah constituted key religious points of crystallization for his own people, and that accordingly his critique of the Temple and his tendency to relativize the authority of the law could not but provoke massive opposition among the religious elite of his age. To understand why that elite opposed Jesus with such vehemence, we must take seriously the extent to which the Roman occupiers essentially emasculated their power. In this same struggle, the "crowd," the "people," and public opinion play an important if vacillating role. It is similarly quite possible to understand Pilate's wavering behavior toward Jesus and then his ultimate condemnation and surrender of Jesus to his persecutors quite without any proper legal condemnation.[9] Pilate was, after all, responsible for maintaining calm and order in the province and in Jerusalem, calm and order demonstrably threatened by Jesus, his followers, and the public reaction he provoked. Perhaps Pilate initially hesitated because he saw that Jesus was in fact innocent; perhaps his own moral compass and the visionary-moral sensibility of his wife held him back. Indeed, given the symbolic-political conflicts of his age (see

---

8. Luke 23:18; John 19:15; see Ratzinger–Pope Benedict XVI, *Jesus of Nazareth*, vol. 2, 185f, 199f (see part 1.3, note 20) concerning Barabbas.

9. Cf. Karl Barth, *Rechtfertigung und Recht*, Theologische Studien 104, 4th ed. (Zürich: EVZ, 1970), 5-48, 14f.

part 1.3), perhaps he was not particularly disinclined even to allow this "provocation Jesus of Nazareth" to continue on for a while. In any event, it was only after the religious elite and "public opinion" exerted pressure on him by threatening him with a popular uprising and by questioning his very loyalty to the Roman emperor that he gave in to the unreasonable demand that Jesus be killed. This *complex normative entanglement* did not abate at least temporarily until Jesus was indeed condemned to die on the cross.

Participants include religious representatives intent on preserving the identity of the people by way of the Temple and Torah, and on inculcating respect for these same religious institutions. Their fear of seeing precisely those institutions devalued by Jesus, though also their anxious apprehension in the face of the public acclamation he elicits, prompt them to begin manipulating the mob and witnesses and to feign loyalty to the global power Rome and its emperor in pursuing their goal. Pilate, of course, is also involved in this tangled nexus, being responsible in any case for maintaining public order and yet not disinclined to provoke the repressed people himself—while simultaneously fearing public opinion and the danger of being seen as not quite as loyal to his emperor as might be deemed appropriate. **This situation—with its weave of anxious concerns for stabilization and the preservation of the status quo, of fearful anxiety and feelings of impotence, and of inconstancy and aggressivity—offers a trenchant example of what the biblical traditions call "sin."** Individuals, at once both suffering and malicious, fearful and aggressive, are inextricably entangled in this complex nexus of force fields.

One of the grandest and most far-reaching errors in theological judgment has been consistently to underdefine "sin" as "self-relatedness" or "self-centeredness." Such alleged "sinful" self-relatedness has then been juxtaposed with the catchy but unfortunately excessively primitive conceptual figure of "relationality and interaction" with "one's neighbor and God." In an insightful typology, Sigrid Brandt[10] has demonstrated that from the classic doctrine of sin presented by Julius Müller[11] on to Paul Tillich[12] and late-twentieth-century feminist theology,[13] sin has consis-

10. Brandt, "Sünde," 13ff (see part 3.4, note 4). The titles in the following notes (12–13, 15) are cited from this piece.

11. Julius Müller, *The Christian Doctrine of Sin*, trans. William Urwick, 2 vols. (Edinburgh: T. & T. Clark, 1868); originally published in German in 1844.

12. Paul Tillich, *Systematic Theology*, vol. II (Chicago, Illinois: University of Chicago Press, 1958), 55-58, 66f; idem, *Symbol und Wirklichkeit* (Göttingen: Vandenhoeck, 1962), 33.

13. Cf. e.g. Judith Plaskow, *Sex, Sin and Grace: Women's Experience and the Theolo-

tently been defined in an almost contrary fashion as "self-transgression," "self-alienation," "selflessness and self-surrender." Karl Barth, in his own grandly conceived and decidedly christologically oriented doctrine of sin, identified not only self-centered "pride," but also indulgent "sloth" and "falsehood" as fundamental forms of sin.[14]

Is sin accordingly to be understood as self-relatedness or as a failure to maintain and guide the self? Or as both? Over against this rather vague constellation, some complain that this theological fixation on the—self-related or selfless—individual self fails to discern the true nature of sin, and that we should focus instead on misguided relationships of interdependence or on contextual relationships of oppression if we are to discern clearly the nature of sin.[15]

Modernity put an end to the dispute concerning false alternatives by developing a secular, egalitarian morality wholly uninterested in references to "sin," the fundamental conviction being that the threatening word "sin" refers to those particular religious, moral, political, and legal transgressions viewed as being especially reprehensible by a specific stratum of functionaries or a specific public group. The lengthy and ultimately futile church battle against "sin" precisely at the front of sexual morality, a battle unfortunately all too often also accompanied by an element of double morality, contributed not inconsiderably to rendering any references to sin obsolete and ultimately essentially incomprehensible.

Egalitarian forms of morality, forms welcomed by most modern enlightened and democratic societies, subject *all* actual or alleged negative phenomena and modes of behavior to universal and public moral reasoning. Although references to extreme cases such as irreparable violence against children as "sin" are tolerated within this framework, the overall tendency is to avoid this particular mark of indignation. The result is that the seriousness of references to "sin" is ratcheted down, with such acts as dietary transgressions or even modest traffic violations qualifying as "sin."[16] By contrast, the understanding presented in the biblical

---

gies of Reinhold Niebuhr and Paul Tillich (Lanham, New York, London: University Press of America, 1980).

14. CD IV/1, 358ff, IV/2, 378ff, and IV/3, 368f.

15. See Brandt, "Sünde," 17f (see part 3.4, note 4), who in this context refers to, among others, Bonhoeffer, Sanctorum Communio, DBWE 1:109–15 (see part 0.5, note 17); Marjorie H. Suchocki, The Fall to Violence: Original Sin in Relational Theology (New York: Continuum, 1994), esp. 161–65; James Cone, God of the Oppressed (New York: Seabury Press, 1975), 17, cf. 16–38; and Leonardo Boff, When Theology Listens to the Poor (San Francisco: Harper & Row, 1988), 110.

16. See also the more thorough interpretation in Brandt, "Sünde," 14f.

traditions is as complex as it is terrifying. Paul casts a particularly harsh and dramatic light on this understanding in the statement "I am of the flesh, sold into slavery under sin" (Rom 7:14; cf. 7:25). The irrefusable urge for self-preservation at the cost of the lives of others is initially to be retarded and its effects channeled by God's beneficent law. The law obligates human beings to follow an ethos of peaceful coexistence with their neighbors,[17] thereby channeling their behavior into directions salutary to life through an orientation toward justice, protection of the poor, and cultic cognition of God.[18] That same law, however, can itself become dangerously perverted by falling under the power of sin, an urgent situation to which Old Testament prophecy and the development of the legal traditions already doggedly direct our attention.[19] Those traditions reflect the realization that any abuse of the law not only endangers individuals in a society, but ultimately constitutes a *systematic self-endangerment of society as a whole*. The law, which is essentially "sacred and good," is perverted into the "law of sin" (Rom 7:23ff; 8:2; 1 Cor 15:56). Though the law's intent is unconditionally good, deriving as it does from the spirit of God (Rom 7:12,14), though it contains the "embodiment of knowledge and truth" (Rom 2:20), and though it can and should aid us in recognizing sin (Rom 7:7), instead it veritably seduces us into sinning, then even glosses sin over.

The cross of Christ reveals the impotence of the law and its devastating effects under the power of sin. It reveals the entanglement in which the world now finds itself, a world oriented toward Jewish and Roman law, religious and political rationality, and public morality and opinion—a world that in a destructive admixture of feelings of impotence and consciously or unconsciously brutal self-affirmation closes itself off against Jesus, his message, and the revelation of God's presence. The helplessness and the radical need for deliverance in the face of the power of sin become particularly clear in the way interpretation and the theology of the cross refer back to the tradition of atonement offering.

---

17. A particularly striking illustration is the Decalogue, the Ten Commandments (Exod 20:2–17; Deut 5:6–21); see in this regard Patrick D. Miller, *The Ten Commandments, Interpretation* (Louisville: Westminster John Knox, 2009); Frank Crüsemann, *Bewahrung der Freiheit. Das Thema des Dekalogs in sozialgeschichtlicher Perspektive*, Kaiser Traktate 78 (München: Kaiser, 1983); Hermann Deuser, *Die zehn Gebote. Kleine Einführung in die theologische Ethik* (Stuttgart: Reclam, 2002).

18. Cf. Michael Welker, "Theologie und Recht," *Der Staat* 49 (4/2010), 573–85.

19. See in this regard Michael Welker, "Recht in den biblischen Überlieferungen in systematisch-theologischer Sicht," in *Das Recht der Kirche*, vol. 1, *Zur Theorie des Kirchenrechts* (FBESG 49), ed. Gerhard Rau, Hans-Richard Reuter, and Klaus Schlaich (Gütersloh: Kaiser, 1997), 390–414.

"Atonement as salvific event" and its enduringly alien character

References to "atonement" are even less universally accessible than those to "sin." Christian theology was long characterized by a paradigm that said, God is merciful, but God is also just. Since human beings had through sin withdrawn from God's righteousness and indeed even taken up a position contrary to it, they merited both temporal and eternal punishment. Although God wanted and still wants to have mercy on them, as both a compassionate and a just God he needs some counterbalance (compensation, recompense, satisfaction) in return. Because sinful human beings are in no position to provide such, however, God selects his own Son, a "sinless lamb" (John 1:29, 36; Rev 5:6 et passim), and delivers him over to a bloody death in order to save human beings.[20]

Apart from the resultant and successful religious stabilization of the kind of thinking that is of central importance for the law and marketplace ("Pay what you owe"), virtually every point of reference in this conceptual figure was unclear and offensive. The images of God underlying these ideas were especially difficult to understand and were a source of enormous difficulties for Christian piety.[21]

Hartmut Gese's innovative approach in his pioneering essay "The Atonement"[22] initiated a long and fruitful discussion that once again addressed the topics of sin, atonement, and sacrifice in a constructive theological fashion[23]—despite constant irritation repeatedly provoked by

20. Cf. Anselm, *Cur deus homo*, book I, 12–13; book II, 19; see in this regard Gustaf Aulén, *Christus Victor: An Historical Study of the Three Main Types of the Idea of the Atonement* (London: SPCK, 1961), 100ff; also J. Christine Janowski, "'Stellvertretung.' Polysemie, Ambivalenzen und Paradoxien," in *Stellvertretung. Theologische, philosophische und kulturelle Aspekte*, ed. J. Christine Janowski, Bernd Janowski and Hans P. Lichtenberger, vol. 1, Interdisziplinäres Symposion (Tübingen 2004; Neukirchen- Vluyn: Neukirchener, 2006), esp. 187ff, and the reference to J. G. Walch, ibid., 188 (essay henceforth cited as "Stellvertretung," the book as *Stellvertretung*).

21. Cf. J. Denny Weaver, *The Nonviolent Atonement* (Grand Rapids and Cambridge/ UK: Eerdmans, 2001).

22. In Hartmut Gese, *Essays on Biblical Theology* (Minneapolis: Augsburg Pub. House, 1981), 93-116.

23. It was Gese's student Bernd Janowski who, in his dissertation (*Sühne als Heilsgeschehen. Traditions- und religionsgeschichtliche Studien zur priesterschriftlichen Sühnetheologie*, WMANT 55, 2nd ed. [Neukirchen-Vluyn: Neukirchener, 2002]), initially picked up and broadly grounded Gese's theses. This initial publication was then followed by contributions from various New Testament scholars, e.g., Otfried Hofius, "Sühne und Versöhnung. Zum paulinischen Verständnis des Kreuzestodes Jesu," in idem, *Paulusstudien*, WUNT 51 (Tübingen: Mohr Siebeck, 1989), 33–49; and Peter Stuhlmacher, "Sühne oder Versöhnung? Randbemerkungen zu Gerhard Friedrichs Studie: 'Die Verkündigung des Todes Jesu im Neuen Testament,'" in *Die Mitte des Neuen Testaments. Einheit und*

populist theology[24] and not a few critical suggestions and corrections. More strongly than others who address this topic, Gese views atonement in connection with the profound entanglement, opacity, and hopelessness otherwise characterizing sin. Atonement, Gese finds, intervenes in an assistive and salutary fashion in human life precisely where that life has been "forfeited." It intervenes where human beings themselves are unable, on their own initiative and power and despite even the best moral, medical, legal, and other human means, to thwart being "given over" or "falling prey" to death. Atonement intervenes in a person's life where that person "stands in an irreparable plight, irreparable because it encompasses the limits of existence itself. Nothing can any longer be made good."[25] Atonement responds to the question

> Is there any possibility of release from this plight for a person who is so guilty as to reach the limit of existence, or for a nation in a similar situation? Is there any possibility for a new life beyond an irreparable event?[26]

That is, atonement is neither a reconciliation nor an appeasement of God, for it emerges and enters in precisely those situations where human beings have already forfeited any possibility for such appeasement, let alone reconciliation. Only a truncated understanding of sin and a false understanding of atonement can suggest that human beings, in the midst of their enslavement to death, might yet be in a position to reconcile and appease God—for example, through an offering of some sort. Gese de-

---

Vielfalt neutestamentlicher Theologie, FS E. Schweizer, ed. U. Luz and H. Weder (Göttingen: Vandenhoeck, 1983), 291–316; then also systematic-theological and interdisciplinary contributions, e.g. Günter Bader, "Die Ambiguität des Opferbegriffs," NZSTh 36 (1994), 59–74; Ingolf U. Dalferth, "Die soteriologische Relevanz der Kategorie des Opfers. Dogmatische Erwägungen im Anschluß an die gegenwärtige exegetische Diskussion," in *Altes Testament und christlicher Glaube, Jahrbuch für Biblische Theologie* 6 (1991) (Neukirchen-Vluyn: Neukirchener, 1991), 173–94; Eberhard Jüngel, "The Sacrifice of Jesus Christ as Sacrament and Example," in idem, *Theological Essays II*, trans. J. B. Webster (Edinburgh, Scotland: T & T Clark, 1995), 163-190; *Opfer. Theologische und kulturelle Kontexte*, stw 1454, ed. Bernd Janowski and Michael Welker (Frankfurt: Suhrkamp, 2000); Sigrid Brandt, "Hat es sachlich und theologisch Sinn, von 'Opfer' zu reden?" in ibid., 247–81 (cited as Brandt, "Hat es . . . Sinn, von 'Opfer' zu reden"); idem, *Opfer als Gedächtnis. Auf dem Weg zu einer befreienden theologischen Rede von Opfer*, Altes Testament und Moderne 2 (Münster/Hamburg/London: Lit, 2001).

24. See e.g. Klaus-Peter Jörns, "Abschied vom Verständnis der Hinrichtung Jesu als Sühnopfer und von dessen sakramentaler Nutzung in einer Opfermahlfeier," in idem, *Notwendige Abschiede. Auf dem Weg zu einem glaubwürdigen Christentum* (Gütersloh: Gütersloher, 2004), 286ff.

25. Gese, "The Atonement," 95 (see part 3.5, note 22).

26. Gese, "The Atonement," 95; cf. Janowski, *Sühne als Heilsgeschehen*, 359 (see part 3.5, note 23).

scribes cultic atonement as *liberation*, granted by God, from the often involuntary and even unnoticeable, and yet for precisely that reason powerful and dangerous enslavement to death, and as the *experience* of this liberation as mediated to human beings in the cult. Such comes about through ritual offering.

This act, however, rather than taking place merely incidentally within the framework of quotidian life, instead interrupts what is understood as the normal course of life in accordance with the instruction of the law. The offerings examined by Gese and Janowski (the central text being Leviticus 16), consist in the ritual slaughter of domestic animals, animals kept for human nourishment and sustenance in the broadest sense. As such, they represent important elements of human property and capital in ancient Israel, and in an even more concrete sense, as potential nourishment and as various other means of subsistence they represent "bearers of the concrete possibility of life" in the context of trade. That is, those who offer up such a domestic animal are in fact surrendering part of their concrete possibilities for sustenance in the broader sense.[27]

In this cultic offering, a concrete part or element of a person's overall life sustenance is consciously surrendered, in effect part of the concrete foundation of that person's future and continued existence, as well as, of course, part of the person's wealth. And what ultimately comes about through this ritual is an identification between the person making the atonement offering, on the one hand, and the offering itself, on the other, an identification Gese and Janowski describe in considerable detail and which in the meantime has become the subject of a controversial discussion. The sacrifice is life that is destined for my own life, in a wholly concrete sense part of the material foundation of my life, part of what ultimately makes my existence possible, and part of my—also physical or material—future.[28] Through the cultic sacrifice, this surrendering of

27. The surrender of (moreover, unblemished) domestic animals for the offering likely represented a not inconsiderable economic hardship for most Israelites, something the amelioration regulations in Leviticus 5 also address. To wit, if, e.g., someone overhears a "public adjuration" and yet does not speak up, or if someone incurs guilt by uttering a rash oath or touches the carcass of an unclean animal—even inadvertently—or touches human uncleanness—in such cases, a person is already obligated to offer a head of small livestock. Leviticus 5, however, is demonstrably aware of this hardship, since Lev 5:7 immediately adds that "if you cannot afford a sheep, you shall bring to the Lord, as your penalty for the sin that you have committed, two turtledoves or two pigeons." And Lev 5:11 then reduces even further from turtledoves or pigeons to choice flour.

28. Gese and Janowski experimented with expressions such as "subject transferal" and "vicarious substitution for existence." Concerning the critical discussion of these issues and attempts to disclose a theological concept of atonement within the biblical traditions

an element of one's *concrete or real life possibilities* becomes an experience of the surrendering of *life realities*, of *real life*. The animal in my possession, one yet of various potential use, dies by means of a violent intervention in its life, experiencing thus totally and irretrievably what the offerant experiences partially and retrievably, namely, the surrendering of life. It is in the ritual slaughter and blood rite that the conscious experience of such surrender of life is now carried through.

Blood is viewed as *the inner bearer of life* (Lev 17:11; Deut 12:33), as the power of life, and the letting of blood is associated with *death* for the sacrificial animal, and with an *experience of death* for the offerant. Although the restriction of one's own life possibilities by the animal sacrifice is experienced through the bleeding, expiring animal as the surrender of concrete life reality, this same experience of death is simultaneously associated with renewed *certainty of life*, albeit not such that is culpably acquired, but rather such *that is both willed and granted by God*. The blood of the bearer of life is spilled not arbitrarily, but rather commensurate with the law, within the framework of the cult, and therefore such that it comes into contact with the sanctuary.[29] The cultic bearing and experiencing of death is justified insofar as the blood is permitted and indeed is intended to be sprinkled on the altar, the curtain of the Holy of Holies, indeed on the locus of God's very condescension. The offerant's certainty of life, this external perspective on death itself, is not only granted by God, it is also borne by God, and as such is *sanctified*. It is over against this surrender of life and in the face of death that life certainty and salvific certainty now come together.

This experience of life certainty and salvation is appropriated in the cultic offering in an evidentiary fashion that can hardly be eclipsed. To wit, what is mediated through this cultic act is a manifest experience that permeates all sense perception virtually to the point of physical participation, and it is this unequivocally elementary evidentiary experience of certainty that liberates the offerant from the uncertainty of an "existence between life and death." Such uncertainty obtains both with respect to one's own life reality and with respect to the presence of salvation, and it is precisely from this *double* situation of uncertainty that atonement now provides liberation.

God makes such cultic atonement possible. Leviticus 17:11, the "sum

---

incorporating the notions of wisdom and new creation, see Brandt, "Opfer," 133ff (see part 3.5, note 23).

29. See Gese, "The Atonement," 107f (see part 3.5, note 22): "The decisive factor for the cultic act of atonement is that this sacrifice of life . . . is a surrender of life to what is holy, and at the same time an incorporation into the holy, given expression throughout contact with blood."

of cultic atonement theology,"[30] follows immediately on the prohibition against consuming blood ("anyone . . . who . . . eats any blood, I will set my face against that person . . . and will cut that person off from the people") and reads as follows: "For the life of the flesh is in the blood; and I [God] have given it to you for making atonement for your lives on the altar; for, as life, it is the blood that makes atonement." Janowski understands this passage as meaning that the general prohibition against consuming blood is ultimately grounded in the fact that *Yahweh* provided Israel with blood as a means of atonement for the sacral realm, blood being the *bearer of life*.[31] God himself gives Israel this blood so that the life substance set free in the cult—commensurate with the law—can carry out, in a vicarious substitutionary fashion, the self-surrender of the offerant to the holy. This "offering of the life contained in blood makes it possible for the forfeited human life to be redeemed, in a figuratively or symbolically concrete fashion, through the vicarious substitutionary death of the sacrificial animal; that is, it makes atonement possible."[32] It is this particular offering ritual that is now transferred to the "lamb of God," that is, to Jesus Christ, whose death discloses the sinful process in which not only individuals and groups, but the entire representative world as such are entangled. In connection with his pre-Easter life and proclamation, on the one hand, and his resurrection, on the other, this revelation now provides a way out of hopelessness and to new life.

Atonement theology is one means of interpreting what happens on the cross. Those who object to the alien nature of such means need but recall the way contemporary electronic media constantly bombard us with programs involving crime and crime prevention, programs more often than not also including portrayals or other references to murder. Moreover, allegedly "enlightened" attempts to distance or otherwise neutralize the strange attraction exerted by ritually dramatized death are at the very least somewhat half-hearted.[33] Atonement theology, however, is

30. Janowski, *Sühne als Heilsgeschehen*, 242 (see part 3.5, note 23).

31. Ibid., 246.

32. Ibid., 247; similarly Gese, "The Atonement," 107 (see part 3.5, note 22).

33. René Girard, in *The Scapegoat* (Baltimore: Johns Hopkins University Press, 1986) and *Violence and the Sacred* (Baltimore: Johns Hopkins University Press, 1977), maintains that religious violence in the form of sacrifice in fact provides the ultimate key to understanding cultural development and the stabilization of social order. See in this regard William Schweiker, "Heilige Gewalt und der Wert der Macht. René Girards Opfertheorie und die Theologie der Kultur," in *Opfer*, ed. Janowski/Welker, 108–25 (see part 3.5, note 23); Brandt, *Opfer als Gedächtnis*, 19ff (see part 3.5, note 23); J. Ch. Janowski, "Stellvertretung," 177ff, 203ff (see part 3.5, note 20). Girard finds in all human societies a mechanism of "desire" at work oriented toward the notion of the rival, desire that both infects that rival and is in turn infected by him. With the aid of sacrificial offering, this "mimetic crisis," i.e.,

not the only biblical interpretive tool applicable to what happens on the cross. Emphatic reference has justifiably been made to the multivalence of the phenomenon "offering," especially to the important distinction in English (not evident in German *Opfer*) between the course or process of offering (in the sense of *sacrifice*), on the one hand, and what is actually offered (*victim*), on the other, a perspective that is in fact quite useful in distinguishing, with respect to the event of the cross, between God's own revelatory activity and the culpable activity of human beings.

Sacrifice and *victim*

In her publications on the general thematic complex "offering,"[34] Sigrid Brandt has disclosed several problematic perspectives concerning the varied aspects of what is broadly understood by the notion of "sacrifice," including references to persons who have met a violent death, the reduction of "sacrifice" to a sin or atonement offering, the widespread identification of "offering" and "gift" or "oblation," and attempts to articulate the concept within a simple dynamic of "offerant-oblation-recipient" (cf. 357). Differentiating her own position from that of Marcel Mauss,[35] Brandt remarks:

> Gifts are worldly goods presented or offered—frequently with an eye on reciprocity—within the framework of standardized relationships of exchange; they generally also represent goods that the offerant can afford

---

this infected and infecting desire that moves tendentiously toward a war of all against all, is turned around. This "counterpart mimesis," so Girard, turns into a "mimesis of reunification"; that is, the sacrificial offering focuses these adversaries on an "other" over against them (and thereby reunites them), the religious offering presenting ritually before them precisely that which all of them do and for which they all strive, namely, the transition from adversary mimesis to reunification mimesis. Violating the sacrificial offering, Girard continues, endangers the balance and harmony of the social group. Here a single mechanism is taken as the interpretive key to the dynamic of all cultural development. (Cf. the more subtle interpretive key in the sequence "hunt down—kill—divide and distribute" in Walter Burkert, *Homo necans: The Anthropology of Ancient Greek Sacrificial Ritual and Myth* [Berkeley: University of California Press, 1983], 29ff; idem, *Anthropologie des religiösen Opfers. Die Sakralisierung der Gewalt*, C. F. von Siemens Stiftung, Themen 40, private printing, 2nd ed. [1983], 25ff). This view, however, distorts not only the perception of the social nexus of life, but also the complex phenomenon of sacrificial offering.

34. Brandt, *Opfer als Gedächtnis* (see part 3.5, note 23), parenthetical pagination in the text refers to this edition; idem, "Hat es . . . Sinn, von 'Opfer' zu reden" (see part 3.5, note 23); idem, "War Jesu Tod ein 'Opfer'? Perspektivenwechsel im Blick auf eine klassische theologische Frage," in *Das Kreuz Jesu. Gewalt – Opfer – Sühne*, ed. Rudolf Weth (Neukirchen-Vluyn: Neukirchener, 2001), 64–76.

35. Marcel Mauss, *The Gift: Forms and Functions of Exchange in Archaic Societies* (New York: Norton, 1967).

to relinquish. By contrast, sacrifices are offerings or investments of life and life resources that frequently breach the notion of reciprocity, breaking through the calculations potentially associated with gifts, and clearly affect substance to a greater extent. The latter make life possible . . . or set it free. Systems of gift giving organize and regulate communal life. Systems of sacrifice organize and regulate life at the cost of other life. (358)

What Brandt clarifies here is that a valuable present from the hands of a propertied or wealthy individual can be characterized as a "gift," while a comparable present from the hands of a poor person can be character- ized as a "sacrifice," the latter affecting as it does the "substance" of life and thereby constituting a presentation of a portion of the person's life resources.[36] Augustine, reflecting on the sacrifice of Jesus Christ,[37] dis- tinguished between the person to whom the offering is presented, the of- ferant, the offering or sacrifice itself, and the person for whom it is sacri- ficed. Brandt expands this schema and distinguishes between 1. offerant; 2. executor; 3. recipient; 4. victim; 5. beneficiary (360). Even though in any given concrete (religious or secular) implementation of this schema the offerant and executor or recipient and beneficiary can be the same person, this overall schema of act and observation is useful for under- standing the process and in identifying misconstrued forms, something Brandt demonstrates with numerous examples, including from politics and competitive sports (cf. 366ff, 384ff).

One additional important distinction is that between the complex event as such—the sacrifice—and the sacrificed offering at its center—the victim, a distinction obscured in some languages (e.g., in Germ. *Opfer*). It is similarly important to note that even in Old Testament traditions, sacrifices or offerings are not necessarily associated with the surrender of bodily existence. Brandt demonstrates, for example, that in Psalms 40, 50, 51, and 69, other forms are already replacing more material or con- crete cultic offerings, stipulating that *sacrifices* do not involve bodily ex- istence being extinguished, but rather being engaged for the fulfillment

36. Risto Saarinen, *God and the Gift: An Ecumenical Theology of Giving* (Collegeville: Liturgical Press, 2005), offers a subtle analysis of the general phenomenon of gift–forgiv- ing–sacrifice. Concerning the development of a concept of gift incorporating the tempo- ral factor (in emphatic contrast to both Mauss and Brandt), see Pierre Bourdieu, *Practial Reason: On the Theory of Action* (Stanford: Stanford University Press) 1998, and Jacques Derrida, *Given Time: I. Counterfeit Money* (Chicago: University of Chicago Press, 1992).

37. Cf. Aurelius Augustinus, *The Trinity, The Fathers of the Church*, vol. 45 (Wash- ington: Catholic University Press of America, 1963), iv, 14. Similarly the sacrificial schema in Henri Hubert and Marcel Mauss, *Sacrifice: Its Nature and Function* (London: Cohen & West, 1964), 19, which they develop within the framework of their examination of Vedic and Jewish sacrifice.

of God's will (Psalm 40) within the context of public thanksgiving (Psalm 50) or public extolling of God (Psalm 69), and as part of an acknowledgement of one's own guilt before God and of surrender to God's purifying and re-creative activity (Psalm 51) (cf. 111ff). The stipulation one finds in the psalms that both *thanksgiving* and *praise of God* qualify as *offering or sacrifice* is not merely a figure of speech. It is precisely with respect to thanksgiving and praise that reference to the *perception and observation schema "offering, sacrifice"* demonstrates why these institutions fully accord with the category "offering or sacrifice" and are thus also quite justifiably designated and presented as such[38] (cf. 111–20).

In numerous cultic and even non-cultic offering accounts, the *victim* (the sacrifice or material presented) is "consecrated," that is, liturgically dedicated. "The fact that the victim, at the time of the offering act, is 'consecrated' means that it is *displaced or enters into a new sphere*" (363). This "consecration liberates (in a positive or negative sense) *life* or *energy* for the benefit of the offering recipient" (365). Against this background, Brandt now suggests viewing even the incarnation itself in connection with the sacrifice of Jesus Christ. In Jesus Christ, God enters into the creaturely sphere, an act through which, insofar as God thereby renders himself "exchangeable," is also associated with a sacrificial assignation of his life. Although God does not thereby intend that Jesus be victimized by human beings on the cross, he does risk such happening.[39] Even in the face of Christ's victimization by human beings on the cross, God remains faithful to his communion with human beings, communion revealed in the incarnation itself (and in the accompanying surrender of his life = sacrifice).

According to Brandt, the *"multidimensional social dynamic between God and human beings"* articulated in such references to offering (sacrifice) can be further explicated such that

> Jesus Christ's life comes to expression *from God, through God, and for God or his name for the benefit of human beings*. . . . New Testament

38. This refinement and expansion of perception is also important for an adequate understanding of the "priestly office." See in this regard Stephan Winter, "Die Opferkategorie im Kontext von Ordinationen und Personenweihen," in *Das Opfer. Biblischer Anspruch und liturgische Gestalt*, ed. Albert Gerhards and Klemens Richter, Quaestiones Disputatae 186, 2nd ed. (Freiburg/Basel/Wien: Herder, 2000), 286ff; also parts 4.1, 5.3, and 5.4.

39. Thus Günter Thomas, "Das Kreuz Christi als Risiko der Inkarnation," in *Gegenwart des lebendigen Christus*, ed. Thomas/Schüle, 151–79 (see part 1.5, note 5), following Niels H. Gregersen ("Faith in a World of Risks: A Trinitarian Theology of Risk-Taking," in *For all People: Global Theologies in Contexts*, ed. E. M. Wiberg Pedersen, H. Lam, and P. Lodberg [Grand Rapids: Eerdmans, 2002], 214ff) and theoretical reflections on risk-taking in Niklas Luhmann (*Risk: A Sociological Theory* [New York: W. de Gruyter, 1993]). See also Pannenberg, *Systematic Theology*, vol. 3, 642ff.

christological-ecclesiological statements about sacrifice can be understood or interpreted as meaning that *human beings themselves are now included in Jesus Christ's life from God, through God, and for God or his name for the benefit of human beings, thereby acquiring participation in that very life.* (409; cf. ibid. for additional distinctions)

Brandt maintains that the letter to the Hebrews, as a "primary New Testament witness to the sacrifice of Jesus Christ," articulates this relational nexus. This letter designates as *the* premier "sacrifice" (NRSV: "offering")—the sacrifice through which human beings themselves are sanctified once and for all—the fact that the Son of God came into the world to fulfill God's will through living, bodily communion of existence with his siblings, though especially through proclamation of God's "name" (Heb 2:12; 10:10) (cf. esp. 182ff). This letter's understanding of the christological offering or sacrifice in this sense thus quite follows the intention of the Old Testament's understanding of offering, which, Brandt maintains, aims primarily at establishing the "commemoration of God in the world" (cf. 394ff and 433ff).[40]

The particular strength of Sigrid Brandt's contribution is that, on the one hand, she tries to do justice exegetically to the differentiated conceptual worlds of both the Old and the New Testaments, while, on the other, disclosing various inner-canonical developmental tendencies and systematic interpretive possibilities that prevent any *one* sacrificial tradition or conceptual figure from being isolated and taken as the framework for a universal articulation of the complex phenomenon "sacrifice." Although more recent discussion has shifted the thematic focus from "sacrifice" to "vicarious substitution" in trying to gain a broader interpretive framework, such must remain mindful not to surrender the still useful illuminative capacity of the offensive conceptual world of sin–atonement–sacrifice.

---

40. Prompted by Rita Nakashima Brock ("And a Little Child Will Lead Us: Christology and Child Abuse," in *Christianity, Patriarchy, and Abuse: A Feminist Critique*, ed. Joanne Carlson Brown and Carole R. Bohn [Cleveland: Pilgrim Press, 1989], 42–61), Brandt considers whether the image of the twelve-year-old Jesus in the temple might function as a new guiding image for the sacrifice of Jesus Christ. The unreserved dedication of the twelve-year-old in the temple to the "'commemoration' of the name of God" in the world along with his vulnerability and defenselessness—through which he already becomes "a potential victim of the sacrificial powers of this world"—are features that fundamentally characterize the New Testament understanding of Jesus Christ's "sacrifice" and that can be reappropriated by the imagination precisely with the help of this image (435f).

Vicarious Substitution "for us"

Bernd Janowski has examined the inner complexity of sacrificial rituals, the rich symbolic worldview accompanying them, the multifarious aspects of the phenomenon of sin to which those rituals are reacting, and the pedagogy of stepwise approaches to God's sanctity or holiness within these rituals.[41] He has also tried to view the conceptual world of sacrifices within the framework of the phenomenon of the need for vicarious substitution and of vicarious-substitutional perception. Like Christoph Gestrich,[42] his point of departure is that references to "vicarious substitution" can refer, on the one hand, to the *"representation* of a person or entity" and, on the other, to the *"relief or release* of a person from certain tasks or obligations for a certain period of time." In this context, he sketches out a broad *"typology of vicarious substitution"* whose varied relational nexus includes, for example,

> the king as "representative" or "mediator" of God (Jer 26:19; Psalm 72 et passim); the human being as the image of God (Gen 1:26, 27; 5:1,3; 9:6); the prophet as Israel's "intercessor" (Exod 32:*7–14, 30–34; Jer 15:*10–20 et passim); the scapegoat as "ritual bearer of misfortune or disaster" (Lev 16:20–22; cf. in substance Zech 5:5–11); the servant of God as a "suffering righteous person" (Isa 52:13–53:12); an image as a "substitution" or "contemporization" of the original (substitutionary, cultic, divine image).[43]

Janowski's attempt to incorporate his initial theological reflections on atonement into a broader biblical-theological and christological context is clear, whereby the "expression 'enter in our stead' . . . which doubtless finds its most trenchantly efficacious articulation in the traditions of the suffering Servant of God . . . and the death of Jesus," is for Janowski the "formula" that most appropriately and adequately renders the notion of vicarious substitution.[44] The conclusion of Jesus's life as a "surrender of life," Janowski maintains, illuminates "his *entire life* as sacrifice and

41. See Bernd Janowski, "An die Stelle des anderen treten. Zur biblischen Semantik der Stellvertretung," in *Stellvertretung*, 65 (see part 3.5, note 20) with respect to Leviticus 16, Leviticus 4f; 8–10, and Lev 14:3–7.

42. Christoph Gestrich, *Christentum und Stellvertretung. Religionsphilosophische Untersuchungen zum Heilsverständnis und zur Grundlegung der Theologie* (Tübingen: Mohr Siebeck, 2001); idem, "Das ontologische Fundament und das Potential der Stellvertretungskategorie," in *Stellvertretung*, 149ff, esp. 163ff (see part 3.5, note 20).

43. Janowski, "An die Stelle des anderen treten," 54, 54f (see part 3.5, note 41); see also idem, *Ecce Homo. Stellvertretung und Lebenshingabe als Themen Biblischer Theologie*, Biblisch-Theologische Studien 84 (Neukirchen-Vluyn: Neukirchener, 2007).

44. Janowski, "An die Stelle des anderen treten," 68.

surrender."[45] By contrast, Stephan Schaede has explicitly warned against "emphatic use of the notion of vicarious substitution in theology," viewing this expression instead as a "signpost pointing to a [yet outstanding] descriptive task" that would need to disclose the systematic nexus between such varied concepts as *substitutio, vicariatio, procuratio, repraesentatio,* and *intercessio.*[46]

The fact that every Christology must necessarily concentrate on the theology of the cross should not, then, mislead us into appropriating the *entirety* of the thematic wealth of God's revelation in Jesus Christ solely in a theology of sacrifice and surrender. Otherwise the weight of the resurrection, the saving and elevating presence of the Resurrected himself in the power of the Spirit, and certainly various important features of his life witness and his proclamation of the reign of God—features full of saving promise and the power of new creation—risk losing their contours or being obscured.[47] On the other hand, Christology invariably forfeits its depth and seriousness if it excludes the themes of sin, atonement, and sacrifice for reasons of false sentimentality or out of conceptual incapacity, and certainly also if it disparages such concepts. The point of incorporating such concepts is to grasp those particular dimensions of the profound normative entanglement that precisely the cross of Christ discloses or illuminates as the power of sin, revealing nothing less than a dynamic of comprehensive blindness, the mendacity and hopelessness of political, legal, and moral leadership and of religious orientation, and the breakdown of prophetic wisdom and understanding. That same cross, however, simultaneously points out the path of divine salvation leading out of this enormous distress and need.

45. Janowski, *Ecce Homo,* 90 (see part 3.5, note 43).

46. Stephan Schaede, "Jes 53, 2Kor 5 und die Aufgabe systematischer Theologie, von Stellvertretung zu reden," in *Stellvertretung,* 147, cf. 144–46 (see part 3.5, note 20); see idem, *Stellvertretung. Begriffsgeschichtliche Studien,* BHTh 126 (Tübingen: Mohr Siebeck, 2004).

47. Jörns, "Abschied vom Verständnis der Hinrichtung Jesu als Sühnopfer" (see part 3.5, note 24).

PART 4

The Exalted Christ and His Reign

4.1 From the Threefold Office of Christ – King, Priest, Prophet (Calvin) – to the Threefold Gestalt of Christ's Reign

Many reasons might prompt a person *not* to believe in God, even when many people may be living that very faith in a person's immediate surroundings. Many reasons might similarly prompt a person to fall away from faith in God, into unbelief, even without the impetus of dramatic personal experiences involving misfortune, suffering, and distress. The wretchedness, infirmity, instability, and seeming futility and meaninglessness of human life can fundamentally call into question any trust a person may have in a powerful, loving God and beneficent Creator. Profound doubts in the existence of God and his beneficent, creative activity are strengthened by our realization that creaturely life lives unavoidably at the cost of other life, and that illness and natural catastrophes (even according to biblical witnesses) are an unavoidable part of God's creation.

Once, moreover, we become aware that precisely the influential and potent Christian churches and communities of faith have participated extensively in the rejection, distortion, and destruction of natural, cultural, and social life on this earth, more factors seems to militate *against* than *for* belief.[1] And once life on this earth and religion as such are viewed in such gloomy light, it helps faith very little to refer to God's world "beyond," in which everything is allegedly so different and so much better.

God's revelation in Jesus Christ, centered on the "message of the cross," sooner strengthens such reservations through the unsparing confirmation that, as matter of fact, the world does indeed stand under the

---

1. See in this regard the particularly shrill voice of "new atheism" in Richard Dawkins, *The God Delusion* (Boston: Houghton Mifflin Co., 2006); cf., however, also Alister McGrath, *The Dawkins Delusion: Atheist Fundamentalism and the Denial of the Divine* (London: SPCK, 2007).

power of sin and death. That is, God's revelation, mediated through Jesus Christ and his cross, sooner emphasizes and even intensifies those particular experiences of impotence and aggressivity, malice, and deception that in our world seem not only ineluctable, but possibly even willed by God (cf. parts 3.4 and 3.5). Nor does some divine roll of the drums liberate us from the accompanying hopelessness and paralysis. Although the message of the resurrection is often enlisted to portray God's revelation in Jesus Christ in just this way, then also being associated with the miracle of revivification, the biblical traditions themselves present a quite different witness (cf. parts 2.3 and 2.5). In the power of the Spirit and in the advent of his reign, the resurrected Christ reveals the loving, creative fashion in which God deals with the fragility and manifold self-endangerment of his creation. That is, God does *not* simply overrun endangered creaturely life through some form of absolute dominion and domination. Nor does he awaken and fortify faith through eloquent assurances that his divine power cannot but be the purest goodness and love. Instead, people are won over to the Christian faith through the subtle, often "hidden" presence of the Resurrected in the power of the Spirit. It is through the—usually inconspicuous—coming of the divine reign that God bestows and effects faith and hope in the midst of a creation that is so clearly or even *drastically* different from him. That said, however, just what is this "reign of God" about which we are speaking here? And why and how does it acquire its salutary, efficacious form in and through Jesus Christ and his spirit?

Biblical traditions frequently refer to "God's reign" or the "kingdom of heaven"[2] and to his "coming," which the pre-Easter Jesus predicts and proclaims and for which the post-Easter church communities pray. Several of the few texts that do speak explicitly about the "reign of Christ" stand sooner on the periphery of the canon and seem to be referring to an eschatological reality beyond earthly time and history.[3] By contrast, other traditions emphasize the presence of Christ's reign even now, in this present age and world: God the Creator and Father "has rescued us from the power of darkness and transferred us into the kingdom of his beloved Son, in whom we have redemption, the forgiveness of sins" (Col

---

2. See Klaus Koch and Jens Schröter, "Kingdom of God; I. Old Testament; III. New Testament," in *Religion Past and Present*, vol. 7, 187-91.

3. "In the presence of God and of Christ Jesus, who is to judge the living and the dead, and in view of his appearing and his kingdom [or reign], I solemnly urge you" (2 Tim 4:1). See also 2 Tim 4:18: "The Lord will rescue me from every evil attack and save me for his heavenly kingdom"; 2 Pet 1:10f: "be all the more eager to confirm your call and election . . . For in this way, entry into the eternal kingdom of our Lord and Savior Jesus Christ will be richly provided for you."

1:13f). They speak about the "kingdom of Christ and of God" (Eph 5:5) and about how divine dominion has been transferred to the Son, who will destroy "every ruler and every authority and power" until God's final and complete eschatological revelation (1 Cor 15:23–28), emphasizing how the Son, invested with full power of divine dominion, will exclusively reveal the loving Creator and Father.[4]

Through Jesus Christ and in the power of the divine Spirit, God's reign reveals the loving, preserving, salvific, and uplifting activity of the Creator and the triune God. Although Christian theologians have regularly tried, in a reverse fashion, to understand God's revelation in Christ and in the power of the Holy Spirit from the perspective of "creation" and "Creator," representatives of biblical, Reformation, and dialectical theology have steadfastly pointed out the folly of all such attempts. The weakest among these allegedly "creation-theological" initiatives have taken as their point of orientation a metaphysically conceived mechanistic power over (or of) the universe and then engaged implausible or unpersuasive imagery such as that of the "divine watchmaker" in their explications. The more successful contributions have tried to associate the "ground of being" (Tillich), "all-determinative reality" (Bultmann), the "reality of the possible" (Dalferth), and similar notions with a more or less persuasive understanding of "love." These seemingly creation-theological approaches have generally been motivated by the desire to make the Christian faith seem plausible toward the outside as well, that is, over against other religions and likely also various philosophies and secular worldviews. Unfortunately, these initiatives have articulated neither persuasive connections with God's revelation in Jesus Christ nor pneumatologically or phenomenologically satisfying concepts of love nor even sufficiently differentiated concepts of "creation" or "new creation." Even where these positions managed to avoid an understanding of creation colored largely by a feeling of mechanistic hopelessness, God was usually reduced to the idea of an absolutely omnipotent, merciful God who was, however, wholly incapable of responding to the gnawing question of theodicy or of generating the kind of elation elicited by the Holy Spirit.

How, then, is one to grasp the power of the creative and re-creative God and Holy Spirit in and through Jesus Christ? One must first realize that the resurrected and exalted Christ *is not present apart from the Holy Spirit* and that it is *through the divine Spirit that he includes his witnesses in his post-Easter life* (parts 4.2 and 2.5). It is precisely

---

4. Cf. Matt 11:27; Luke 10:22; cf. Matt 28:19, though also John 1:12; 17:1–3; Rom 1:4; 2 Thess 1:9; Jude 1:21ff; Rev 1:6 et passim.

through these witnesses, who as "members" constitute the post-Easter and post-Pentecostal body of Christ, that the Resurrected acquires the "robustly physical" existence that N. T. Wright quite justifiably advocates. Calvin, in his own grand Reformation dogmatics, trenchantly emphasized the notion that the Holy Spirit was not given to Jesus Christ alone (*privatim*), but rather "that he might pour out his abundance upon the hungry and thirsty!"[5] The resurrected and exalted Christ is not to be found without the Holy Spirit and without the witnesses gifted with that Spirit.

The second key Calvin offers enables us to grasp the differentiation and concretion of the efficacious influence of the resurrected and exalted Christ, the power of his spirit, and the coming of his reign *in connection with his pre-Easter life.*

Although both the continuity and the discontinuity between the pre- and post-Easter life of Jesus now become clear, it is not just the connections with Jesus's pre-Easter life, the crucifixion, and the resurrection that become discernible. Instead, the broad commemorative spaces and expectational horizons of *Old Testament traditions* now similarly come into clearer focus within this orientation toward the Resurrected and Exalted (see part 1.5). And finally, this key also discloses the particular broad ecumenical consensus in more recent Christology.

Calvin's second key christological insight reads as follows: "To know the purpose for which Christ was sent by the father, and what he conferred upon us, we must look above all at three things in him: the prophetic office, kingship, and priesthood."[6] This doctrine of the threefold office (*munus triplex Christi*), also known as the doctrine of the "three offices," enables us to grasp the complex wealth of both the public and eschatological ministry of Jesus Christ, disclosing as it does a nexus of relationships with Old Testament traditions, threads of continuity between the pre- and post-Easter ministry of Jesus Christ, on the one hand, and the activity of the anointed kings, priests, and prophets, on the other, to which the New Testament witnesses in their own turn constantly allude.[7]

---

5. Calvin, *Institutes*, 500 (II, 15,5; cf. also II, 15,2) (see part 0.5, note 13); see also Dumitru Stăniloae, *The Experience of God, Orthodox Dogmatic Theology*, vol. 4: *The Church: Communion in the Holy Spirit* (Brookline, Mass.: Holy Cross Orthodox Press, 2012), 27ff; cf. in this regard the more extensive discussion in part 4.2, cf. also 2.5.

6. Calvin, *Institutes*, 494 (II, 15,1); Isaak August Dorner, in his monumental *History of the Development of the Doctrine of the Person of Christ*, Division Second, from the end of the fourth century to the present time, vol. II, trans. D. W. Simon (Edinburgh: T. &. T. Clark, 1881), 220ff, demonstrates that Calvin's considerable accomplishments in the field of dogmatics could go utterly unrecognized by even significant theologians.

7. See esp. the contributions of Hartmut Gese (cf. part 1.5).

Schleiermacher,[8] Barth,[9] Wainwright,[10] and other important theologians of the Reformed and Methodist traditions have picked up and developed this doctrine. This doctrine was introduced into Lutheran theology by Johann Gerhard[11] and similarly found its way into Roman Catholic dogmatics[12] as well as that of Orthodox churches.[13]

Edmund Schlink offers the following commentary:

> The spread of the doctrine of Christ's *munus triplex* involves an ecumenically singular phenomenon insofar as this particular doctrinal piece acquired its dogmatic shape *after* rather than *before* the various churches separated; that is, it cut directly through these church schisms in establishing its statements concerning the salvific work of Jesus Christ as a *common* doctrine.[14]

Classic theologians order, prioritize, functionalize, and otherwise interpret this threefold office in varying ways. Calvin initially speaks about the *prophetic office* by virtue of which God never leaves his people "without useful doctrine sufficient for salvation" and through which he orients that people toward "the Mediator's coming."[15] Jesus Christ not only offers us the doctrine in which "all parts of perfect wisdom are contained," but also, through the outpouring of the Spirit, grants to each member, sons and daughters alike, participation in the body of Christ (Joel 3:1).[16] Through the *kingly office*, God's intention is "that

8. Friedrich Schleiermacher, *The Christian Faith* (London: T&T Clark, 1999), §§102–5.

9. Barth, *CD IV/1*, 211ff; *IV/2*, 154ff; *IV/3*, 12ff, 48ff, 180ff.

10. I would like to thank Niko Koopman for helpful conversations on this topic as well as for referring me to findings in his as yet unpublished work, namely, that the doctrine of the threefold office might be further structured through analogous functions of the three offices themselves. Geoffrey Wainwright, *For Our Salvation: Two Approaches to the Work of Christ* (Grand Rapids: Eerdmans, 1997), 109ff, similarly distinguishes in all three offices a "christological, baptismal, soteriological, ministerial," and "ecclesiological use."

11. Johann Gerhard, *Loci theologici*, 1610–22, Loc. IV, ch. 15.

12. Matthias Joseph Scheeben, *Handbuch der katholischen Dogmatik*, vol. 5,2, 2nd ed. (Freiburg: Herder, 1954), 226–305; see also the remark in Thomas Aquinas, *Summa theologiae*, III, 22 art. 1 ad 3.

13. Dumitru Stăniloae, *Orthodox Dogmatic Theology*, vol. 3: *The Person of Jesus Christ as God and Savior* (Brookline, Mass.: Holy Cross Orthodox Press, 2012), 85ff, 103ff; Stăniloae, *Orthodox Dogmatic Theology*, vol. 4, 33ff (see part 4.1, note 5); P. Trempela, *Dogmatikē tēs orthodoxu katholikēs ekklēsias* (Dogmatics of the Orthodox Catholic Church; in Greek), vol. 2 (Athens: Adelphotes Theologon "Zoe," 1959), 143–203; see also already Eusebius of Caesarea, *Hist. Eccl.* I,3 (see part 0.4, note 16).

14. Edmund Schlink, *Ökumenische Dogmatik. Grundzüge* (Göttingen: Vandenhoeck, 1983), 414.

15. Calvin, *Institutes*, 495 (II, 15,1) (see part 0.5, note 13).

16. Calvin, *Institutes*, 496 (II, 15,2).

through the hand of his Son he will be the eternal protector and defender of his church." At the same time, Calvin emphasizes that Christ is the "eternal" king of an eternal, spiritual reign, and especially that the faithful will be preserved and kept for eternal life. Here, too, however, the faithful are granted participation in this dominion through baptism and through the outpouring of the Spirit.[17] Calvin interprets the *priestly office* following the letter to the Hebrews, chapters 7–10, maintaining that Jesus Christ intercedes on our behalf as chief priest before God, offering himself as a sacrifice. At the same time, we are ourselves, in the power of the Spirit, priests "*in him,*" presenting our offerings to him in both prayer and praise while "freely enter[ing] the heavenly sanctuary."[18]

The way one arranges, prioritizes, and determines the content of each of these threefold offices depends largely on whether one's point of orientation is primarily *Jesus's pre-Easter life* or the *exalted Christ*:

> Hence Jesus exercised the *prophetic* office in his identity as the earthly Jesus through his proclamation, and as the exalted through his apostolic sending and, in an ongoing fashion, through the gospel itself. He exercises his *priestly* office as the earthly Jesus in his self-surrender to death, and as the exalted through intercession with God on behalf of his followers. Nor was it just through his installation to dominion as the exalted that his *royal* office came about, since it already obtained during the dominion of the earthly Jesus over the powers of nature and forces of destruction.[19]

---

17. Calvin, *Institutes*, 497 (II, 15,3); cf. 496-501 (II, 15,3–5).

18. Calvin, *Institutes*, 502 (II, 15,6). – Schleiermacher initially speaks about Christ's prophetic office, which consists in "teaching, prophesying, and working miracles." He takes his orientation especially from the pre-Easter Jesus, who, he emphasizes, is the "climax and the end of all prophecy," just as he similarly represents the zenith and end of the priestly office (Schleiermacher, *The Christian Faith*, 441, 445, 465 [see part 4.1, note 8]). With regard to the priestly office, Schleiermacher distinguishes between Jesus Christ's "perfect fulfillment of the law (i.e. His active obedience)" and his "atoning death (i.e. His passive obedience)," and finally "His intercession with the Father for believers" (ibid., 451). Christ's royal office brings to an end all "political religions as well as theocracies" through his "purely spiritual lordship of His God-consciousness." Through this office, "everything which the community of believers requires for its well-being continually proceeds from Him" (ibid., 473, 466). – Karl Barth initially intends to address the high-priestly office, then the royal, and finally the prophetic office, though he does replace cultic conceptual figures with legal ones by summarizing his presentation of the high-priestly office in the expression "the judge judged in our place" (Barth, *CD IV/1*, 211; cf. 211ff; 274ff; in this context, he remarks that alongside legal and cultic imagery, one might, following the New Testament, also have introduced financial or military imagery [ibid., 273f]); cf. the critique in Brandt, *Opfer als Gedächtnis*, 294ff (see part 3.5, note 23); detailed discussion in parts 4.4, 5.3, 5.5.

19. Schlink, *Ökumenische Dogmatik*, 414 (see part 4.1, note 14).

The widely varying prioritization of these offices even among classic theologians might initially seem to diminish the value of this doctrine,[20] which does indeed allow one to address a wealth of the most varied systematic and dogmatic interests. How can it respond to the charge that, by allowing such arbitrary interpretations, it unfortunately also lends itself to abuse on behalf of all sorts of agendas? Daniel Migliore has proposed taking as one's orientation for Christ's threefold office his pre-Easter life and proclamation, his cross, and his resurrection.[21] The following discussion will pick up on this proposal while yet considering, in the case of each individual office, Calvin's attention to its pneumatic resonance and charisma. An orientation toward the pre-Easter life and toward Jesus's ministry lends clear contours to the *royal* office, an orientation toward Christ's cross illuminates the functional spectrum of the *prophetic* office, and witnesses to the resurrection and the ensuing appearances of the Resurrected disclose the wealth attaching to the *high-priestly* office.

Because the three offices interpenetrate one another and are thus *perichoretically* connected,[22] it is more appropriate to refer to the "threefold office" than to the "three offices." Because, moreover, pneumatic charisma attaches inseparably to the threefold office, its doctrine should be closely tied to that of the *threefold gestalt of the reign of Christ* or the *threefold gestalt of the reign of God.*[23]

The resurrected Christ's intention is to reveal the triune God and thereby himself as the divine word, as the eternal logos, though also the Holy Spirit and the loving Creator, who also creates anew. In this revelation, he does not want to be "without his own," though "his own" must

20. Cf. Martin Kähler, *Die Wissenschaft der christlichen Lehre von dem evangelischen Grundartikel aus im Abrisse dargestellt*, 2nd ed. (Leipzig: A. Deichert'sche Verlagsbuchhandlung, 1893), 332f.

21. See Daniel L. Migliore, *Faith Seeking Understanding: An Introduction to Christian Theology*, 2nd ed. (Grand Rapids: Eerdmans, 1999), 155.

22. See Stăniloae, *Orthodox Dogmatic Theology*, vol. 3, 86ff (see part 4.1, note 13); concerning the concept "perichoresis," see Eberhard Jüngel, "Perichoresis/Circumincession," in *Religion Past and Present*, vol. 9, 714f.

23. Paul Tillich, *Systematic Theology*, vol. III, 15ff (see part 0.4, note 37), proposed replacing the familiar metaphors of "level" and "stratum or layer" with that of "dimension," which allows prioritization without having to fix a specific hierarchy in describing life processes. Although such might also make it possible to speak of the "three dimensions of God's reign," the problem is that it is usually accompanied by *spatial* associations. As will be seen, in the various churches, though certainly also from various external perspectives on the Christian faith, one can observe differing prioritization of the activities and charisma associated with the threefold office and of the corresponding dimensions or shapes of God's reign. Excessively obscuring any two dimensions or too strongly integrating them into the remaining one will result in a problematic understanding of discipleship and distort the understanding of revelation.

not, as will be seen, be reduced simply to the constituted churches. As becomes especially evident with respect to the prophetic and royal gestalt of God's reign, the reign of Christ is both more extensive and more comprehensive than simply the sphere of activity of the churches.

Ascribing too much importance to any one office is a risky venture. Although strongly emphasizing, for example, the royal office or the corresponding gestalt of God's reign in theology and the church may well generate energetic diaconal notions of discipleship, it risks fostering humanistic self-secularization with respect to piety and the churches themselves.[24] Although strongly emphasizing the prophetic office and the prophetic gestalt of God's reign may well liberate confrontational political and astute academic-analytic forms of theology and piety, it risks ending in moral breathlessness and spiritual exhaustion.[25] And finally, granting strong privileges to the priestly office and the corresponding gestalt of the reign may well contribute to the development of strong spiritual and ecclesiastical profiles, it risks fostering ecclesiocentric self-isolation and liturgical calcification.[26]

By remaining mindful of the perichoretic relationship between the three forms in this sense, the doctrine of the threefold office of Christ or of the threefold gestalt of God's reign offers an important point of theological orientation, directing us away from these unfortunately widespread but unbalanced prioritizations. It provides a christological point of orientation, enabling us to distinguish between the creative and re-creative activities of God in the power of the Spirit and the "coming" of the divine reign, on the one hand, and other notable ideas associated with creation, concepts of the spirit, and sundry other related movements, on the other.

24. Cf. part 4.4.
25. Cf. part 5.5.
26. See in this regard parts 5.3 and 5.4.

4.2 Spirit-Christology and Jesus Christ as "the Reign of God in Person": "The Resurrected is not without his people." The Challenges of Pentecostal Theology

Because Christ, the Messiah, the Anointed, was anointed not with oil, but with the Holy Spirit, he is endowed with divine power in a unique, singular fashion; Calvin stresses this point in his work on dogmatics, the *Institutes of the Christian Religion*, maintaining that Christ is called the *Anointed of God* because on *him* rests "the spirit of wisdom and understanding, the spirit of counsel and might, the spirit of knowledge and the fear of the LORD" (Isa 11:2). In addition, however, Christ was also anointed with the Holy Spirit that he might through the Spirit grant to "his own" participation in his power.[1]

Calvin emphasizes what is known as the "outpouring of the Spirit" by the "one anointed by the Spirit," an experience that was already of seminal importance for the early church. It is not merely that the spirit of God "rests" on or "came over" Jesus Christ; it also grants to his witnesses genuine participation in that divine strength and power.[2] The worldwide twentieth-century Pentecostal movement and charismatic renewals, with approximately a half billion members the largest faith movement in human history, positions this event of "baptism by the Spirit" at the very center of their faith.[3]

Frank Macchia, one of the leading contemporary Pentecostal theologians, has referred to "Spirit baptism" as the "crown jewel" of his church and its theology.[4] At the same time, he describes a tense conflict among Pentecostal theologians, a conflict which in his opinion has allowed this

---

1. Calvin, *Institutes*, 500 (II, 15,5, cf. II, 15,2) (see part 0.5, note 13); cf. the citation documented in part 4.1, note 5. Calvin provides the following commentary: "The father is said 'not by measure to have given the Spirit to his Son' [John 3:34 p.]. The reason is expressed as follows: 'That from his fullness we might all receive grace upon grace' [John 1:16 p.]" (ibid., 500, cf. 495f [II, 15,5, cf. II, 15,2]).

2. Cf. James D. G. Dunn, "Towards the Spirit of Christ: The Emergence of the Distinctive Features of Christian Pneumatology," in *The Work of the Spirit*, esp. 7ff (see part 2.4, note 12); cf. idem, *Jesus Remembered* (Grand Rapids: Eerdmans, 2003), 355ff, 655f.

3. Cf. Peter Zimmerling, *Die charismatischen Bewegungen. Theologie – Spiritualität – Anstöße zum Gespräch* (Göttingen: Vandenhoeck, 2001), esp. part 1.1; David Martin, *Tongues of Fire: The Explosion of Protestantism in Latin America* (Oxford and Cambridge, USA: Blackwell, 1993), esp. the reflections on 271ff concerning the general influence on religiosity in America, Roman Catholicism, and theories of secularization..

4. See Frank D. Macchia, *Baptized in the Spirit: A Global Pentecostal Theology* (Grand Rapids: Zondervan, 2006), 20ff, 57ff; idem, "The Kingdom and the Power: Spirit Baptism in Pentecostal and Ecumenical Perspective," in *The Work of the Spirit*, 109ff (see part 2.4, note 12).

strong concentration on Spirit baptism to recede, something brought to expression in the question whether theologically the gift of the Spirit is to be understood primarily as *"sanctification" in the sense of acceptance into communion with Christ*[5] or is sooner to be grasped as the *endowment with spiritual gifts (charismata) to be engaged in building up the body of Christ.*[6] This tension has allegedly often been traced back to differing prioritization with respect to the writings of Paul (sanctification and communion with Christ) and Luke (bestowal of spiritual gifts).[7] More recent theological discussion within Pentecostal churches and charismatic movements at the turn of the millennium, however, has allegedly indeed managed to overcome this tension and restrictive view, the key having been to associate Spirit baptism with a concentration on the exalted Christ and his reign. The outpouring of the Holy Spirit not only endows those associated with Christ through faith with his spirit, it also both incorporates them into his dominion and gives them a part in his post-Easter life and ministry. It is at this point that the oft-sought and invoked "Spirit Christology" must be engaged.[8] Spirit Christology combines a concentration on Jesus Christ and on the outpouring

---

5. Pentecostal theology joins other theological traditions insofar as it does not understand "sanctification" as a movement from one "high voltage crisis experience" (Macchia, *Baptized in the Spirit*, 30) to the next. Concerning a christological interpretation of Spirit baptism, see Barth, *CD IV/4*, esp. 13ff.

6. Cf. in this regard C. van der Kooi, *Tegenwoordigheid van Geest. Verkenningen op het gebied van de leer van de Heilige Geest* (Kampen: Kok, 2006), esp. 53ff.

7. Cf. the thorough examination in James D. G. Dunn, *Baptism in the Holy Spirit*, Studies in Biblical Theology, Second Series 15 (London: SCM Press, 1970).

8. Although Dunn tried quite early to prepare this path exegetically (James D. G. Dunn, *Jesus and the Spirit: A Study of the Religious and Charismatic Experience of Jesus and the First Christians as Reflected in the New Testament* [Philadelphia: Westminster, 1975], esp. 301ff), such attempts have often faltered because of the rather narrow focus of their key conceptual figures. In Dunn himself, the concept of consciousness predominates, in Paul W. Newman (*A Spirit Christology: Recovering the Biblical Paradigm of Christian Faith* [Lanham, New York and London: University Press of America], 1987) that of "interpersonality." Concerning the background of such reductions, see Welker, *God the Spirit*, 283ff (see part 0.6, note 16); idem, "The Spirit in Philosophical, Theological, and Interdisciplinary Perspectives," in idem, *The Work of the Spirit*, 221ff (see part 2.4, note 12). Although Jürgen Moltmann, *The Way of Jesus Christ* (see part 3.3, note 7) initially began to develop a Spirit Christology oriented biblically toward the notion of "Christ's Birth in the Spirit" and "Christ's Baptism in the Spirit" of Christ (73ff), he extended the arc of his discussion to the messianic ministry and to a theology of God's reign (94ff), in the process unfortunately losing sight, however, of the explicitly pneumatological lines of thought (cf. 149ff) and underestimating the potential value of the doctrine of the threefold office (cf. 136f). That notwithstanding, the following considerations do share many of his original intentions. See also Peter C. Hodgson, *Winds of the Spirit: A Constructive Christian Theology* (Louisville: Westminster John Knox, 1994), 267ff.

of the Spirit through him with efforts to identify the dynamic forces of God's reign within the piety and church community influenced by that concentration,[9] and its theology of God's reign similarly discloses both present and future eschatology for Pentecostal theology.[10] Picking up impulses not only from Johann and Christoph Blumhardt[11] and Jürgen Moltmann,[12] but also from various theologies of liberation, numerous Pentecostal theologians engage "the kingdom of God motif as an integrating concept to bring together personal piety, communal worship, and social praxis." At the same time, Macchia similarly acknowledges that the "kingdom also fits well with the Pentecostal penchant for power encounters and divine victories over the powers of darkness, especially through spiritual gifts."[13] This insight in its own turn must be distinguished from that particular preoccupation or even enthusiasm—found in Pentecostal churches as well—for end-time catastrophes and speculations concerning the "second coming of Christ in judgment."

What is known as "dispensationalism" speculates concerning God's commission with respect to the "fullness of time" (Col 1:25; Eph 1:10; 3:2) in a series of judgments on the Jews and Gentiles under the conditions of increasing godlessness, a notion whose "modern" representative was especially John Nelson Darby (1800–1882) and which still finds many adherents and imitators even today.[14] How can this position be

9. Donald W. Dayton, *Theological Roots of Pentecostalism* (Grand Rapids: Zondervan, 1988), 48–54.

10. Cf. D. William Faupel, *The Everlasting Gospel: The Significance of Eschatology in the Development of Pentecostal Thought* (Sheffield: Sheffield Academic Press, 1996), 13–18; cf. also part 4.3.

11. Frank D. Macchia, *Spirituality and Social Liberation: The Message of the Blumhardts in the Light of Wuerttemberg Pietism,* Pietist and Wesleyan Studies (Lanham: Scarecrow, 1993).

12. Moltmann, *Theology of Hope* (see part 0.4, note 24); idem, *The Coming of God: Christian Eschatology* (Minneapolis: Fortress Press, 1996).

13. Macchia, *Baptized in the Spirit,* 42, 45 (see part 4.2, note 4); cf. Steven J. Land, *Pentecostal Spirituality: A Passion for the Kingdom* (Sheffield: Sheffield Academic Press, 1993), 62ff; Samuel Solivan, *The Spirit, Pathos and Liberation: Towards a Hispanic Pentecostal Theology* (Sheffield: Sheffield Academic Press, 1998); cf. in this regard *Pfingstbewegung und Basisgemeinden in Lateinamerika. Die Rezeption befreiungstheologischer Konzepte durch die pfingstliche Theologie,* Weltmission heute 39, ed. Michael Bergunder (Hamburg, 2000); Rudolf von Sinner, "Zwischen Weltflucht und Dominanz: Pfingstbewegung und Bürgerrechte in Brasilien," ThLZ 137 (2012), 507-22.

14. Cf. *The Collected Writings of J. N. Darby,* ed. William Kelly, 34 vols. (London: Morrish, 1867–1900); between 2000 and 2010 alone, reprints of many of his works were also published electronically under STEM (Sound Teaching on Electronic Media). This "sound teaching" is being disseminated in more recent publications; see Stanley Howard Frodsham, *The Coming Crisis and the Coming Christ* (Springfield: Gospel, 1934); David Wilkerson, *Racing toward Judgment* (Old Tappan: Revell, 1976); Jerry Falwell, *Nuclear*

engaged in serious theological discussion?[15] Neither a Christology of the dominant *kyrios* (Christ descending vertically from above)[16] nor any enthusiasm for a mighty advent of the reign of God can counter this fixation on a Christology and theology of the reign of God oriented toward an end time defined by conflict, since both can be effortlessly integrated into precisely such a position.[17]

Efforts at combining a Spirit Christology with a theological eschatology focused on the reign of God can render such fixation on an apocalyptic "beyond" superfluous by clearly articulating the figure of the outpouring of the Spirit and the concrete effects of such outpouring among human beings themselves. In the Old Testament, it is the prophet Joel who offers a visionary promise of how God's spirit will be poured out on men and women, old and young, male and female slaves (Joel 3:1ff), a revolutionary notion in a patriarchal society in which males alone had a say, in a society of slaveholders of the sort that was quite natural in antiquity, and in societies in which only the "elderly" or "elders" were listened to or in which, by contrast, those who belonged to the "older generation" were dismissively or even hostilely treated. The account of the Pentecostal outpouring of the Spirit in Acts 2:1ff, however, now finds that what the prophet Joel predicted has indeed come to pass: God's spirit is indeed being poured out on men and women, young and old, male and female slaves alike. In addition, however, it is now poured out not just on Israel, but on people from other nations, traditions, and languages as well. What takes place is an incredible hearing and understanding of God's great deeds, and in the midst of all the differences between people, nations, and cultures, what is ultimately established is a *universal communion of the Spirit*.

For Christian faith, this differentiated community of the Spirit is mediated through the resurrected and exalted Jesus Christ, his spirit, and his reign. Through his spirit, Christ bestows various gifts (*charismata*) that serve the edification of a living community and a dynamic search for truth and justice. Paul uses the image of the "body of Christ" whose vari-

---

War and the Second Coming of Jesus Christ (1983); Tim LaHaye, *The Beginning of the End* (Wheaton: Tyndale, 1991); Marilyn Hickey, *Armageddon* (Denver: Marilyn Hickey Ministries, 1994). Fundamentalist and evangelical forms of piety are being combined with science fiction, e.g., in the novels of Tim LaHaye and Jerry B. Jenkins and the attendant film versions in the series *Left Behind* and *Finale*. The apocalypse serves as the script, and the struggle with the anti-Christ plays a central role.

15. Cf. N. T. Wright, *Surprised by Hope: Rethinking Heaven, the Resurrection, and the Mission of the Church* (New York: Harper, 2008), esp. 118ff.

16. Barth, "The Christian in Society," 31ff (see part 3.4, note 3).

17. Cf. part 4.4 concerning *Barmen III*.

ous members act together with different gifts and talents. Jesus Christ himself is the head of this body, and because this body is wholly characterized by his person, his life, and his ministry, so also does his reign bear the features of his person, whence also his body has since Tertullian similarly been called "the reign of God in person." Spirit baptism, the outpouring of the Spirit, lends to this reign a complex constitution and form, since those endowed and filled by the Spirit are neither posited as consistently equal nor organized and related through any simple hierarchy. Such is the case because in the life of any body, in any given situation the eyes may well be more important, in the next situation perhaps the ears, later perhaps the hands, and in still other situations the feet (cf. 1 Cor 12:12ff). In this organic-pluralistic interplay, God's spirit effects a communion of believers based on freedom.[18]

A key insight the later Barth shares with Luther helps us grasp the inner constitution of Christ's dominion along with the activity of his spirit and reign:

> When we say Jesus Christ we say Jesus Christ *and His own*—those who are co-elected by Him as the Son of God and in Him as the Son of Man. We say Jesus Christ *and His community*, Jesus Christ as the Head *of His body*, Jesus Christ in both His heavenly *and* also His earthly-historical form of existence. His existence takes *both* the one form *and* the other.[19]

That is, not only must Spirit Christology and the coming of his reign be associated with a richly differentiated, polyphonic, dynamic, and freedom-based human community, that differentiated community must *also* be respected and appreciated as humanity that has been "elevated" by God.

> . . . human essence can only be called an essence which in its creatureliness is sharply distinct from that of God, and in its perversion alien and opposed and hostile. But this is not the case in respect of this One. In Him it is certainly distinct from God as concerns its creatureliness. But it is also bound to Him. And its godlessness and opposition and hostility are not only denied but removed and replaced by His perfect fellowship with God.[20]

18. See in this regard Welker, *God the Spirit*, 147ff, 228ff (see part 0.6, note 16); idem, *Kirche im Pluralismus*, 53ff, 104ff (see part 3.2, note 49); cf. also Noordmans, *Das Evangelium des Geistes*, 38ff (see part 2.5, note 9); Ted Peters, *God – the World's Future: Systematic Theology for a Postmodern Era* (Minneapolis: Fortress, 1992), 233ff.

19. Barth, *CD IV/2*, 59 (my emphasis); cf. in this regard also the solid presentation—despite insufficient attention to pneumatological issues—of the correlation between resurrection and exaltation in Walter Kasper, *Jesus the Christ* (London: Burns & Oates; New York: Paulist Press, 1976), 146ff.

20. Barth, *CD IV/2*, 117.

These insights preclude both a purely "other-worldly" eschatology and Christology as well as any sort of negative end-time anthropology intoxicated with regnant notions of "struggle" and "annihilation." Macchia replaces the visions of struggle and destruction evoked by such apocalyptic eschatologies with the promise from 1 Cor 2:9f:[21] "'What no eye has seen, nor ear heard, nor the human heart conceived, what God has prepared for those who love him'— these things God has revealed to us through the Spirit."

An experience of the rich, vibrant, freedom-based life of the "body of Christ" *even* in the midst of persecution, struggle, and the challenging finitude of this world makes it possible to sense and foster the enormous wealth of this way of organizing or viewing life. Following the lead of Walter J. Hollenweger,[22] Macchia stresses the importance of the "orality of liturgy, narrativity of theology and witness, maximum participation in reflection, prayer, and decision making within reconciling communities."[23]

Pentecostal theologians frequently invoke the biblical imagery of bride and bridegroom and a "hymn to love" in portraying the connection between the outpouring of the Spirit, Spirit baptism, the initiation of the coming reign, and the search for a more perfect revelation of Christ, on the one hand, with the uplifting and energizing of his community, on the other.[24] The divine love in which human beings themselves variously come to participate is revealed in the arc extending from God's surrender on the cross to the triumphant outpouring of the Spirit by the Creator and the exalted Christ. In this field of tension between Good Friday and Pentecost, divine love is revealed to the world as profound surrender and the salvific power of transformation. The multifarious ways the reign of Christ grants participation in this love include experiences and acts of diaconal service (cf. part 4.4), worship and sacramental communion and celebration (see parts 5.3 and 5.4), and the liberating, prophetic search for truth and justice (cf. part 5.5).

---

21. After Isa 64:4 and 65:16. Cf. Richard B. Hays, *First Corinthians*, Interpretation (Louisville: John Knox, 1997), 44f.

22. Walter J. Hollenweger, "Priorities in Pentecostal Research: Historiography, Missiology, Hermeneutics, and Pneumatology," in *Experiences in the Spirit*, ed. J. A. B. Jongeneel (Bern: Peter Lang, 1989), 9f.

23. Macchia, *Baptized in the Spirit*, 51 (see part 4.2, note 4); cf. ibid., 56: "Whether experiential or doctrinal, Spirit baptism can function in multiple ways to guide the Pentecostal movement towards a Trinitarian, Christo-formistic, pneumatologically rich and diverse, and eschatologically robust version of Christian life and thought."

24. Cf. Macchia, *Baptized in the Spirit*, 270, following William J. Seymour, *Behold the Bridegroom Cometh, The Apostolic Faith* (Los Angeles), Jan. 1907, 2.

4.3 The Coming Reign of God as Emergent Reality and the Power of Free, Creative Self-withdrawal on Behalf of Others

"What must I do to enter the kingdom of God?" What must I do "to inherit eternal life"?[1] According to the Synoptics, Jesus initially responds to these questions by referring to the law, especially to the Decalogue, the Ten Commandments: "You shall not murder; You shall not commit adultery; You shall not steal; You shall not bear false witness; Honor your father and mother; also, You shall love your neighbor as yourself." That is, to inherit eternal life or enter into the kingdom of God, one must first of all follow the law. And yet certain other biblical texts seem to emphasize an element of discontinuity precisely between the law and God's reign: "The law and the prophets were in effect until John [the Baptist] came; since then the good news of the kingdom of God is proclaimed, and everyone tries to enter it by force."[2]

Although these words seem not only to distinguish unequivocally between two stages, namely, between the law and the reign of God, and also to support the conventional theological distinction and opposition between the "law that demands" (till John) and the "gospel that gives" (after John), the following sentence immediately contradicts this view: "But it is easier for heaven and earth to pass away, than for one stroke of a letter in the law to be dropped."[3] The relationship between the "law and prophets," on the one hand, and proclamation of the reign of God as gospel, on the other, is to be understood not as one of opposition or mutual negation, but sooner in the sense of "sublation," as a relationship of relativization and preservation. That is, the reign of God and proclamation of the gospel *preserve* the intention of the law.

Both the law and the reign of God are oriented toward an *"ethos of free self-limitation,"* as Wolfgang Huber has formulated it.[4] The rest of

---

1. Matt 19:16ff, esp. 18f; cf. Mark 10:17ff, esp. 19; Luke 18:18ff; cf. 10:25ff with reference to Exod 20:12–16, Deut 5:16–20, the "second table of the Decalogue," and Lev 19:18. This section draws on material from Michael Welker, "Das Reich Gottes," *EvTh* 52 (1992), 497–512.

2. Luke 16:16.

3. Luke 16:17; see also Matt 5:17ff; cf. in this regard Bertold Klappert, *Worauf wir hoffen. Das Kommen Gottes und der Weg Jesu Christi*, Kaiser TB 152 (Gütersloh: Kaiser, 1997), 90ff.

4. Wolfgang Huber, *Konflikt und Konsens. Studien zur Ethik der Verantwortung* (München: Kaiser, 1990), 205ff; see idem, "Selbstbegrenzung aus Freiheit. Über das ethische Grundproblem des technischen Zeitalters," *EvTh* 52 (1992), 128ff; idem, *Gerechtigkeit und Recht. Grundlinien christlicher Rechtsethik*, 3rd rev. ed. (Gütersloh: Gütersloher, 2006), 197ff, 380f et passim.

Jesus's response to the question "How can I enter into the kingdom of God?" intensifies *the ethos of free self-limitation* into an *ethos of free, creative self-withdrawal*:[5] "If you wish to be perfect, go, sell your possessions, and give the money to the poor, and you will have treasure in heaven; then come, follow me."[6] This ethos of free, creative self-withdrawal for the sake of the poor and weak as well as for the sake of discipleship to Christ similarly picks up the intentions of the law, especially laws governing mercy, which focus both on the protection of the weaker members of society and on self-withdrawal (including such as is publicly expected) on their behalf.[7] Discipleship to Christ and participation in the reign of God preserve the intention of Old Testament law to anchor protection of the weak in the law itself and in so doing make it routine, or habitual, and indeed guarantee its efficacy, since it is only in this way that justice in the strict sense is attained.[8] That said, the expectations of the law are now clearly radicalized.

The law itself had previously fixed such self-limitation and the limited free self-withdrawal on behalf of others, the latter notion being viewed, moreover, as wholly compatible with the continuation of the previous life of the subject of such self-withdrawal, for example, freeing slaves in the seventh year, renouncing exploitation of the weaker and usurious interest taking,[9] and leaving the gleanings of the harvest[10] and the full tithe of produce for the poor and needy.[11] By contrast, the path to eternal and valid life and to participation in God's reign demands free self-withdrawal on behalf of the poor which, insofar as one's own property is to be surrendered, radically alters a person's life as previously lived. Participation in the reign, treasure in heaven, access to eternal life and to a worthy life, none of which can be relativized at any time or in any situation—all this is associated with free, creative self-withdrawal on behalf

---

5. This emphasis on the *freedom* and *creativity* of self-withdrawal is important over against ideologies of self-sacrificing "self-surrender" (cf. part 3.5).

6. Matt 19:21; Mark 10:21; Luke 18:22; cf. Luke 12:33.

7. The call to discipleship might also pick up intentions of cultic law, whose content includes establishing both creaturely and publicly accessible contact with God. See in this regard Michael Welker, "Security of Expectations: Reformulating the Theology of Law and Gospel," *Journal of Religion* 66 (1986), 237ff; idem, "Moral, Recht und Ethos in evangelisch-theologischer Sicht," in *Marburger Jahrbuch Theologie XIII*, ed. W. Härle and R. Preul (Marburg: Elwert, 2002), 67–81.

8. See in this regard Heinrich Bedford-Strohm, *Vorrang für die Armen. Auf dem Weg zu einer theologischen Theorie der Gerechtigkeit* (Gütersloh: Gütersloher, 1993); Welker, "Theologie und Recht," 573–85 (see part 3.5, note 18).

9. See, e.g., the regulations in the Book of the Covenant, Exod 21:2ff; 22:20ff.

10. See Lev 19:9f; 23:22; 24:21f.

11. See in this regard Deut 14:28f; 26:12–15.

of the poor that *far* transcends the expectations of the laws of mercy. The disciples, commensurately shocked—and, according to Luke, "those who heard it"—ask, "Then who can be saved?"[12]

As we now see, access to God's reign in the form of free, creative self-withdrawal on behalf of others picks up and radicalizes the original intent of the law to establish justice, mercy, and the knowledge of God. As the parables of the unforgiving servant and the laborers in the vineyard demonstrate,[13] access to and participation in God's reign can be characterized not only by this radicalization of mercy toward the poor, but by additional forms of such free self-withdrawal on behalf of others as well, including the forgiveness of debt, compensation according to fundamental need rather than actual services rendered, though certainly also a willingness to accept a form of merciful justice that grants equal status to those who might have accomplished or are only capable of accomplishing less than their fellow human beings.

Such ethos of free, creative self-withdrawal that goes beyond the law of mercy and comes to expression in the forgiveness of debt, in compensation that secures livelihood independently of quantifiable accomplishment, and in the unenvious acceptance and recognition of such—this particular ethos, this continuation and transcending of the intention of the law, however, provides but the *first part* of the answer to the question "What must I do to enter the kingdom of God?"

This sphere of free, creative self-withdrawal for the sake of others must not focus merely on *active* approaches, that is, on the concrete *praxis* of self-withdrawal, for *access to God's reign is characterized no less by experiences of mercy we have ourselves received*, of forgiveness or compensation beyond our own expectation. As the parable of the unforgiving servant illustrates, it may be just such an experience of free self-withdrawal *on the part of others* for *our sake*, on *our behalf*, that first opens a person's eyes to the reign of God. That is, those who have *actually experienced* such free self-withdrawal on the part of others on their behalf acquire access to this sphere by, in their own turn, responding to that experience by practicing precisely the same such mercy and forgiveness toward others and in so doing providing them with the means to secure a humane life. In this sense, the requests "Your kingdom come" and "forgive us our debts, as we as we forgive our debtors" are merely different perspectives on the same insight.

This same insight—understanding God's reign as a twofold experi-

---

12. Matt 19:25; Mark 10:26; Luke 18:26.
13. Matt 18:23ff and Matt 20:1ff; see also the parable of the prodigal son (Luke 15:11ff) and the context of the requests in the Lord's Prayer (Matt 6:10–12; Luke 11:2–4).

ence of free self-withdrawal, namely, of our own on behalf of others and of others on our behalf—is what first renders truly comprehensible why access to God's reign can be illustrated by the paradigm of *becoming like children* (Matt 18:3ff; Mark 9:33ff; Luke 18:17). Because a child is perpetually dependent on the solicitude and care of people in its immediate surroundings, it also perpetually experiences their self-withdrawal on its behalf. At the same time, it is generally forced to accommodate to those surroundings to a greater extent than are adults. The child, however, usually accomplishes such accommodation in a wholly naïve fashion that *precedes* any *explicit* self-relation and decision making. As such, however, in every relationship the child lives to a far greater degree than adults in a *correlative nexus* of self-withdrawal with others. From the perspective of the twofold direction of self-withdrawal discussed above, we can now also see why according to the Synoptics the rich—who cling to wealth and property—have difficulty entering into God's reign.[14] On the one hand, their concern with preserving and indeed maximizing their possessions is constantly in conflict with the ethos of free self-withdrawal on behalf of *others*. On the other hand, that very wealth diminishes the concrete chances of the wealthy to experience free self-withdrawal on the part of others on *their* behalf. God's reign cannot but remain difficult for them to discern.

That is, the petition that God's reign come focuses on a sphere of power decisively characterized by this direct experience of free self-withdrawal on the part of others on *our* behalf, on the one hand, and our own free self-withdrawal on behalf of *others*, on the other. Nor should this sphere of power be understood only as the otherwise rare occurrences of extreme ethical accomplishment. To the contrary, such loving concern for children, the ill, the weak, and the infirm is quite frequently accompanied by precisely this free, creative self-withdrawal on their behalf, just as familial love and gratitude and even large parts of educational and health systems in many societies are characterized by precisely this ethos. And yet can the coming of God's reign really be comprehended *this* broadly? Is that reign genuinely present in such infinitely many contexts of practiced and received care and love?

The classical systematic conceptual approaches through which God's reign is generally articulated can be interpreted as differing answers to three questions, each of which addresses two possibilities.

First: "Is God's reign present or future?" Second: "Is God's reign immanent or transcendent?" And third: "Is God's reign intersubjective ('within and between you,' as Luther puts it) or externally discernible?"

14. Cf. Mark 10:23ff; Matt 19:24; Luke 18:24f; though also Luke 12:16ff.

Present—future, immanent—transcendent, internal—external. Although most of the combinations associated with these possibilities have indeed been attempted at one time or another in church and cultural history,[15] not every alternative has needed to be decided. One combination that has acquired considerable moral and political influence—even into its secularized forms in left-wing Hegelianism and neo-Marxism—goes as follows: God's reign is immanent and external, and is both future and present. It has also been possible simply to ignore a given duality entirely, as in the abstract-eschatological position for which God's reign is transcendent and future but neither internal nor external.

Although such considerations may well seem like little more than theological glass-bead games, these various understandings of God's reign—be they ever so incompatible or even mutually wholly exclusive—have at different times profoundly inspired and moved people and even entire cultures. Not only have they influenced Christian piety and the way Christians have perceived themselves and the world and shaped their very lives, they have also defined regulations of church governance along with religious and secular morality, political ideology, and even historiography and prophecy.[16]

One can already discern in the early church shifts from one conception to a new, mutually incompatible one. The apostolic fathers are wholly inclined to support a doctrine according to which the reign of God is "future" and "other-worldly."[17] Moralizing features attaching to the expectation of God's reign along with spiritualizing interpretations draw the notion of this reign into the present, though "present" by no means immediately implies externally discernible immanence.[18] Eusebius of

---

15. Günter Klein, "'Reich Gottes' als biblischer Zentralbegriff," *EvTh* 30 (1970), 642–70, using a table illustrating the relational dualities "this-worldly—other-worldly" and "present—future," has described the four positions as follows: The "Orthodox understanding" defines God's reign as other-worldly and future, whereas more recent eschatology—likely referring to Jürgen Moltmann's Theology of Hope—views it as this-worldly and future. Herbert Braun, by contrast, views it as this-worldly and present, Günter Klein as other-worldly and present.

16. Ernst Staehelin examines the various understandings of God's reign over the course of church history in *Die Verkündigung des Reiches Gottes in der Kirche Jesu Christi*, vols. 1–7 (Basel: Reinhardt, 1951–65). – The EKU study *Die Bedeutung der Reich-Gottes-Erwartung für das Zeugnis der christlichen Gemeinde. Votum des Theologischen Ausschusses der Evangelischen Kirche der Union* (Neukirchen-Vluyn: Neukirchen, 1986), 17, cf. 11, 30 et passim (cited here as *Reich-Gottes-Erwartung*) offers an overview of the most important versions. See also R. Mau and M. Beintker, "Herrschaft Gottes / Reich Gottes," v and vi, TRE, vol. 15 (1986), 218ff.

17. *Reich-Gottes-Erwartung*, 76.

18. "According to Clement of Alexandria, Christians who have attained the level of 'gnostics' participate in God's reign," whereas according to Origen God's reign is a present

Caesarea, under the "overwhelming influence of the historical turn" associated with Constantine, was the first to teach the "immanence of God's reign within the world empire."[19] But where is God's reign? After all, earlier it was future-other-worldly, and now it is present-this-worldly. Mystical and speculative thinking, however, also militated against this particular conception, and it was especially the collapse of the western empire and the fall of Rome that made it necessary to bid farewell to Eusebius's imperial theology. Such by no means meant a permanent dismissal of the notion that God's reign might indeed be actualized *within the Christian empire*, however, and eleventh-century reformers advocated anew the "conviction of the imperial reality of God's dominion."[20] God's reign is an externally discernible, immanent entity whose realization has either already come about or is urgently to be effected. Without this conception of the externally immanent, present reign of God, phenomena such as the demands made to the English king by the reformer Martin Bucer "to create a Christian state according to the laws of life followed by the citizens of the Christian empire,"[21] or the "reign of God in Münster,"[22] and even the attempt during the English revolution under Oliver Cromwell to "establish a reign of God on earth"[23] are all incomprehensible. The politically at least indirectly extremely influential approaches of left-wing Hegelianism all the way to Karl Marx can be understood as secularized forms of this imperial theology.

But again, where is the reign of God? Within the broad spectrum of configurations extending from future, transcendent, and internal, to present, immanent, and external—that is, within the broad spectrum extending from the immortality of the soul to religiously interpreted, current socio-political developments—this reign seems at once to be both impalpable and all-too-easily accessible. Is God's reign merely the plaything of theological opinion, of pious or sanctimonious wishful thinking, or of historical and cultural shifts? Over against such confusion, one can nonetheless indeed clarify *why God's reign can and indeed must be described as both future and present, immanent and transcendent, and internally and externally discernible.*[24]

---

spiritual reality that is nonetheless "radically distinct from external reality" (*Reich-Gottes-Erwartung*, 77f).

 19. *Reich-Gottes-Erwartung*, 78.

 20. *Reich-Gottes-Erwartung*, 79.

 21. Cf. Martin Bucer, *De regno Christi* (1550), cited in *Reich-Gottes-Erwartung*, 82.

 22. *Reich-Gottes-Erwartung*, 83.

 23. *Reich-Gottes-Erwartung*, 84.

 24. Concerning the various aspects, see also Tillich, *Systematic Theology*, vol. III, esp. 356ff (see part 0.4, note 37).

Put polemically, we must take leave of these "arrival-departure" notions of God's reign. That is, we must recognize why it is wholly misleading to ask whether it has already arrived or is not yet there, whether it is arriving at this very moment or will not come until later, or even never. We must recognize that God's reign is instead a *perpetually emergent reality*.

What is actually meant by the expression "emergence" can perhaps best be understood from the perspective of the familiar expression that "the whole is more than the sum of its parts." This assertion, or more precisely, the word "more," generally elicits something akin to secular devotion. The expression "emergence" grasps this numinous "more" along with its correlation with the so-called "parts" in view of both striking and simultaneously "creeping" *alterations* to the "whole." New ideas emerge, changing, for example, a given situation of dialogue or making it necessary to recast the regnant scholarly landscape. A new political power emerges, requiring a redefining of our global situation. All these examples take account of a surprising or unexpected change in the previous configuration that now acquires clear contours and either is accompanied by or requires new powers of self-organization. What emerges is a new "quality," one that cannot, however, be derived from the features of the previous components and that nonetheless consists solely in the interplay of precisely those components.[25] In common parlance, we then simply say that "*the conversation* took a surprising turn," "*scientific study* reorganized," or "*the world* changed." In reality, however, such changes can be traced back to the fact that by way of a multiplicity of specific, altered instances of interaction between elements or parts of the whole, a *fundamental* change in the interaction of those same parts came about, leading to a *new* shape of the whole itself. This fundamental change within the interaction of the so-called parts is then perceived as a change in that which is "more" than those parts. Now, the expression

---

25. This "modern" definition of emergence, as articulated in *Emergenz: Die Entstehung von Ordnung, Organisation und Bedeutung*, stw 984, ed. Wolfgang Krohn and Günter Küppers (Frankfurt: Suhrkamp, 1992), 389, asserts that microscopic interplay brings about a new quality on the macroscopic level. In the "classical" sense, emergence is allegedly the rise of new strata of being (life over against inanimate nature or spirit over against life) that can in *no way* be derived from or explained or predicted on the basis of features attaching to lower levels. – See also *Emergenz. Zur Analyse und Erklärung komplexer Strukturen*, stw 1917, ed. Jens Greve and Annette Schnabel (Frankfurt: Suhrkamp, 2011), esp. Renate Mayntz, "Emergenz in Philosophie und Sozialtheorie," in ibid., 156ff; also the contributions in the section "Theologies of Emergent Complexity and their Critics" in *The Oxford Handbook of Religion and Science*, ed. Philip Clayton and Zachary Simpson (Oxford: Oxford University Press, 2006), 749ff; and (following A. N. Whitehead and S. Alexander) G. H. Mead, *The Philosophy of the Present* (La Salle: Open Court, 1959), 65ff.

"emergence" grasps what we are calling the "change" in the whole—the change that produces the new "more"—in view of the configurational alterations among the parts and in view of the changes within their mutual interplay. Engaging the term requires comparing two or more correlations between entities or events in view of configurational changes that lead to the so-called "new whole."

God's reign is a world-changing power and a discernible reality notwithstanding the difficulty we have in determining and defining it. This perplexing situation becomes clearer, however, once we see that God's reign is in fact an *emergent reality* that challenges human beings ever anew *to grasp the mutual interplay of free, creative self-withdrawal as unavailable qualitative changes to concrete life contexts.*

It is precisely that, however, that human beings find so difficult to do. For they see that this mutual interplay is both concrete and constantly in motion, both inconspicuous and thereby constantly at risk, and that as such it provides no clearly determinable foundation or point of orientation for their own lives. It is quite true that experiences of free, creative self-withdrawal on the part of others on behalf of their fellow human beings, and of our own free self-withdrawal on behalf of others often surprise and delight us in a wholly unexpected fashion, coming about in our lives as something miraculous and radiant. Even in a larger sense, circumstances we perceive as gracious and accommodating, loving and peaceful, are frequently characterized by precisely such mutual willingness to engage in free, creative self-withdrawal on behalf of our fellow human beings. That notwithstanding, many people shrink at the notion of actually trusting or allowing this determinative power to alter the quality of their life circumstances. Why, however, are they unable to acknowledge and accept such free self-withdrawal on behalf of their fellow creatures as a fundamental experience and disposition, penetrating and shaping as it does every facet of our life circumstances?

The answer provided by the parables of God's reign is that although we can certainly contribute to *shaping* the processes in which such free, creative self-withdrawal on behalf of others takes place, those processes are inherently *unavailable* to us and beyond our reach. That is, such free self-withdrawal takes place in *emergent* processes. God's reign is present, immanent, and externally discernible insofar as it alters the interplay of concrete life circumstances in an *emergent* fashion. At the same time, however, it remains future insofar as it is by no means exhausted by such alterations to concrete life circumstances, but rather continues its activity as a driving force that in effect engages human beings in its service while remaining wholly inaccessible to their control or manipulation. To the extent it remains fundamentally future in this sense, God's reign can thus quite justifiably be called "transcendent."[26] Within this complex disposition of what can be called the "coming" reign, God's power exerts quite real influence within the reality of concrete life circumstances. Because of this same subtle and complex disposition, however, counterforces can and indeed do thwart and distort the emergent coming of this reign to a high degree.

The coming of God's reign cannot be concretely predicted. *Free* self-withdrawal on behalf of others remains contingent, and precisely the sort of hardened, unfree life circumstances that might be changed *solely* by self-withdrawal, *solely* by a change of direction or conversion on the part of the strong, seem as a rule to be characterized by particularly tenacious powers of resistance. Any change in their fundamental orientation seems highly improbable, and even where such occurs, sooner fortuitous, singular, and serendipitous. Hence one sign for the Synoptics that God's reign has indeed come is the exorcism of the demonic powers that exclude free volition on the part of those overcome by such powers, powers that possess such people not only to their own detriment, but also quite to the horror of people around them.[27]

The helplessness of those close to people affected by such suffering is trenchantly described, for the powers at work here transcend even the collective resolve of well-meaning persons. And yet even though one can neither plan nor anticipate nor even learn how to eliminate such forces, nonetheless rescue from this collective helplessness and what seems to be unavoidable concrete suffering and distress is no illusion. In fact, the assuagement of multiple forms of concrete suffering is sooner characteristic of the coming of God's reign. What becomes clear is that it is precisely the power of free self-withdrawal in acts of mercy, forgiveness, and many other forms that is genuinely able to sunder rigidified circumstances of suffering, distress, and powerlessness.

This strange nexus in which God's reign is obviously present and yet difficult to grasp and impossible to anticipate comes to expression is those statements that, in speaking about its presence, emphasize that it cannot be concretely fixed in space and time. The best-known of these passages is probably Luke 17:20f: "Once Jesus was asked by the Pharisees when the kingdom of God was coming, and he answered, 'The kingdom of God is not coming with things that can be observed; nor will they say, "Look, here it is!" or "There it is!" For, in fact, the kingdom of God is among you.'"

26. See also Dietrich Ritschl's reservations about solving otherwise outstanding theological problems or problematical phenomena through hypothetical displacement into the future (*The Logic of Theology: A Brief Account of the Relationship Between Basic Concepts in Theology* [Philadelphia: Fortress Press, 1987], 257f).

27. See in this regard Welker, *God the Spirit*, 195ff (see part 0.6, note 16).

Jesus's parables are particularly effective in illustrating the inconspicuous nature of God's reign and its power, its concealed and yet at-
tractive nature, its persistent emergent coming, as well as the multifarious forms in which its presence is both thwarted and distorted. In fact,
those parables might well be viewed as a *typology of human resistance
to the coming of God's reign.* Because the elements of God's reign are
inconspicuous and easy to overlook and underestimate—as illustrated by
the parables[28] of the mustard seed[29] and yeast[30] and the various seed
parables[31]—it comes as no surprise if the uninitiated perceive "nothing
at all" or perhaps only bare earth in a freshly tilled field. Nor, however,
is it surprising if others are even now perceiving here their daily bread
for the immediate future and the imminent basis of future life. People
can perceive germs of hope or problematical growth in the same seeds.
That is, different experiential and anticipatory horizons can not only
prompt people to perceive emergent processes quite differently, such
can also shape their respective practical responses. After crop failure, for
example, many people may well view the growth of even *un*affected seed
differently than after a successful harvest. Quite along the same lines,
people perceive acts of free self-withdrawal differently depending on differing attendant contexts—or variously overlook and ignore them relative to such contexts.

Free, creative self-withdrawal, however, can often seemingly lead nowhere. Many instances of free self-withdrawal on behalf of others seem
to elicit no discernible mutual interplay or interaction or any tangible
life transformation at all. From the perspective of the parable of the
sower, this means that the news of the reign, the announcement of the
emergent coming of this new sphere of divine power, this interpenetra-
tion of human life by that same power, is neither discerned nor understood—and simply remains infertile. When, however, even in the midst
of the inconspicuousness of its concrete activity God's power is nonetheless discerned—there one can indeed anticipate that the good seed will
eventually be enormously fruitful. The parables of the treasure and the

---

28. Concerning the hermeneutical function of New Testament parables, see Christian
Link, *Die Welt als Gleichnis. Studien zum Problem der natürlichen Theologie* (München:
Kaiser, 1976), 288ff; concerning the connection between proximity and unpredictability
with respect to the coming of the reign, see Helmut Merklein, *Die Gottesherrschaft als
Handlungsprinzip. Untersuchungen zur Ethik Jesu,* FzB 34, 2nd ed. (Würzburg: Echter
Verlag, 1981); idem, *Jesu Botschaft von der Gottesherrschaft. Eine Skizze,* Stuttgarter Bi-
belstudien 111 (Stuttgart: Katholisches Bibelwerk, 1983), esp. 51ff.

29. Mark 4:30ff; Matt 13:31f; Luke 13:18f.

30. Matt 13:33; Luke 13:20f.

31. Mark 4:26ff; 4:1ff; Matt 13:1ff; Luke 8:4ff.

pearl[32] additionally illustrate the overwhelming sense of joy elicited in those who do indeed come to recognize the sometimes obscure reign of God, and who as a result come to consider it something highly, indeed incomparably, desirable.

These parables, however, do not merely disclose the manifold difficulties in *discerning* and *recognizing* God's reign, a reign whose concrete emergence, because it is so varied, is thus also inconspicuous. As Matthew emphasizes in his parables of the weeds and the fishnet,[33] actively offensive counterforces and fortuitous, unexpected events that do not share the intentions of God's reign similarly hinder or thwart its advent and obscure its discernment. These parables conclude with the promise that valid, eternal life will be accordingly separated out eschatologically from invalid, forfeited life. Here, too, the connection with the law is unmistakable.[34] After this separation of valid from invalid life in God's reign, the *righteous* will "shine like the sun."[35] By contrast, those who cause sin and are "evildoers" lead rejected lives that are invalid and have no permanence (Matt 13:41). Other parables—for example, those of the entrusted money or the ten virgins—additionally adduce laziness and imprudence among those who in fact are already anticipating God's reign.[36] Finally, the parable of the royal wedding banquet[37] describes the refusal of those caught up in the business of the world to devote either time or energy to this joyous event. What drives such people is not free self-withdrawal on behalf of others, but rather self-reduction on behalf of quotidian concerns and business—even though the potential joy of participating in valid life can be palpably anticipated.

The parables of Jesus illuminate these varied hindrances to the revelation of God's reign as well as the self-hindrances people create for themselves, people who stand so helpless precisely before the concrete proximity and discernible joy of that reign. They live in a culture that sanctifies self-assertion without consideration—or with as little consideration as possible—of others; truly a case of "writing on the wall." And yet another fundamental feature in these parables is much stronger than any threat or evocation of judgment. For the parables express how God's reign is indeed inconspicuous and difficult to grasp, and enumer-

32. Matt 13:44ff.

33. Matt 13:36ff; 13:47ff.

34. Cf. Eberhard Jüngel, *Paulus und Jesus. Eine Untersuchung zur Präzisierung der Frage nach dem Ursprung der Christologie,* HUTh 2, 4th ed. (Tübingen: Mohr Siebeck, 1972), 197ff.

35. Matt 13:42; cf. also 13:49.

36. See Matt 25:1ff.

37. Matt 22:1ff; Luke 14:15ff.

ate the manifold distortions and irritation, conscious and unconscious ways people find to refuse and resist its coming. In so doing, however, these parables encourage human beings to surrender these wholly unnecessary self-hindrances, and as such they become comprehensible as announcements of God's love toward human beings, as loving and caring challenges to seize this joy in God's power that because of its emergent concreteness and proximity is yet so inconspicuous.

With their petition in the Lord's Prayer "Your kingdom come," repeated ever anew at Jesus's own instruction, human beings show that this challenge has not gone completely without resonance. With this petition, human beings express ever anew their willingness to enter into a renewal of the world through the power of free, creative self-withdrawal on behalf of others.

4.4 The Kingly Presence of Christ with His Own and the Liberating Power of Love: Diaconal Existence and Christian Humanism

The coming reign of God is revealed by the life of the resurrected and exalted Christ, something that becomes comprehensible in his threefold gestalt as king, priest, and prophet even though the "kingly dominion of Jesus Christ" can be understood in quite differing ways. My kingdom, my kingship, Jesus says, "is not from this world" (John 18:36), a statement Calvin believed intended to admonish us that Christ's kingly office is of a "*spiritual character*" and to remind us of the "*eternity of Christ's dominion.*"[1] Here the reference to that royal dominion is associated *not* with a cheerful, pleasant life here, but rather with heavenly life in the beyond!

That notwithstanding, Christ's reign can also be associated already with life on this *present* earth, in the here and now, to wit, in a form of discipleship that includes a willingness to suffer. That is, life in discipleship to Christ must not only reckon with the quotidian conflicts and suffering normally associated with human existence as such, but also—at least in some ages and in some contexts—bear additional persecution and tribulation.[2] But does the testimony of Jesus's own life really deliver such a message, namely, that under this king things will go badly for you in *this* world, whereas *there*, in an eternal heavenly beyond, you will be compensated? The life of the pre-Easter Jesus does not strengthen such an understanding. In the form of healings, concrete table communion[3] and edifying, comforting teaching, through the ethos of justice, mercy, and love as lived by Jesus himself, through inspired passion in the search for truth and the establishment of peace, and certainly also through the realization that "in spite of persecution"

---

1. "For this reason we ought to know that the happiness promised us in Christ does not consist in outward advantages – such as leading a joyous and peaceful life, having rich possessions, being safe from all harm, and abounding with delights such as the flesh commonly longs after. No, our happiness belongs to the heavenly life!" (Calvin, *Institutes*, 496, 498 [II, 15,3, 4] [see part 0.5, note 13]).

2. This consideration can lead to an understanding of Jesus Christ as a "mediator" in a "double function," e.g., in that of the "concealed king" and the "revealed king." Cf. Emil Brunner, *The Mediator: A Study of the Central Doctrine of the Christian Faith* (Philadelphia: Westminster Press, 1947), 548ff, 561ff.

3. Concerning the considerable significance of "life together," *convivence*, see Sundermeier, *Konvivenz und Differenz*, esp. 43ff (see part 0.4, note 26); idem, *Den Fremden verstehen. Eine praktische Hermeneutik* (Göttingen: Vandenhoeck, 1996), 198ff; also Dietrich Bonhoeffer, *Life Together*, DBWE 5 (Minneapolis: Fortress Press, 1996).

we receive "the word with joy inspired by the Holy Spirit" (1 Thess 1:6; cf. Rom 14:17), life in discipleship to Christ does indeed become a life of inspired joy and elation.

Such varied perspectives on life in the reign of this king are similarly associated with varying notions of his royal existence. On one side of the spectrum, we find the doctrine of Christ the *pantocrator*, as universal ruler, the Almighty, an epithet picked up from Rev 1:8 and Matt 28:18[4] and attributed to other deities in antiquity as well. Christ as *pantocrator* is a vivid theme especially in Byzantine art, his image frequently filling the apse of Orthodox churches or positioned at the center of iconostases, his raised right hand symbolizing the tranquil sovereignty of the power of blessing, and the open book of Gospels in his left hand attesting his exalted teaching authority.

The church celebrates the "King of kings" (1 Tim 6:15) in the "divine liturgy" of John Chrysostom[5] following Jerusalem temple theology.[6] The royal and priestly-cultic functions of the exalted Christ flow together in the celebrated entry of what is known as the "king of the gods" and the concomitant divine revelation.[7] By contrast, the close connection between royal and prophetic function is articulated in theologies of Christ's "royal dominion" similar to those developed during twentieth-century struggles with the National Socialist dictatorship in Germany, with the German Christians, the racist South African churches, and the oppression of large portions of the population in Latin America during the twentieth century. Although the Barmen Theological Declaration (1934) does not explicitly mention the "king," it does indeed speak about the "word and work of the Lord" and about Jesus Christ as the presently active Lord.[8] The Belhar Confession of 1982,[9] developed in South Africa in

4. Though also generally following the *kyrios*-confession (cf. part 1.3); cf. also 1 Cor 15:27f and Rev 12:10; also Eberhard Busch and Bernd Wannenwetsch, "Kingly Reign of Christ," in *Religion Past and Present*, vol. 7, 196-98.

5. Chrysostom, *The Orthodox Liturgy, being the Divine Liturgy of S. John Chrysostom and S. Basil the Great* (London: Society for Promoting Christian Knowledge, 1939). The Chrysostom liturgy became the regnant liturgical form from the Constantine turn onward (11th/12th century).

6. See in this regard the excellent presentation in Gregor Etzelmüller, . . . *zu schauen die schönen Gottesdienste des Herrn. Eine biblische Theologie der christlichen Liturgiefamilien* (Frankfurt: Otto Lembeck, 2010), 39ff.

7. Cf. in this regard also part 5.3 and Karl Christian Felmy, *Die orthodoxe Theologie der Gegenwart. Eine Einführung* (Darmstadt: Wissenschaftliche Buchgesellschaft, 1990).

8. Barmen VI and Barmen III; cf. *Die Barmer Theologische Erklärung. Einführung und Dokumentation*, ed. Martin Heimbucher and Rudolf Weth, 7th rev. ed. (Neukirchen-Vluyn: Neukirchener, 2009); Arthur C. Cochrane, *The Church's Confession Under Hitler* (Philadelphia: Westminster Press, 1962), 237-42.

9. The English version has been published by Piet Naudé, *Neither Calendar nor Clock:*

dialogue with the Barmen Theological Declaration,[10] declares in conclusion that though authorities and human laws may well prohibit it, the church is nonetheless called to live and act in obedience to Jesus Christ, its only head, a position it solemnly underscores in section 5.2, a section consisting of but a single sentence: "Jesus is Lord."[11]

The Barmen Theological Declaration consistently emphasizes acknowledging and accepting Christ's dominion in trust and obedience. As Barmen I puts it, "Jesus Christ, as he is attested for us in Holy Scripture, is the one Word of God which we have to hear and which we have to trust and obey in life and in death." Barmen II then states that it is through Jesus Christ that we experience "a joyful deliverance from the godless fetters of this world for a free, grateful service to his creatures," and Barmen III, in this same context so thoroughly focused on Jesus Christ and his dominion, concludes:

> The Christian Church is the congregation of the brethren in which Jesus Christ acts presently as the Lord in Word and sacrament through the Holy Spirit. As the Church of pardoned sinners, it has to testify in the midst of a sinful world, with its faith as with its obedience, with its message as with its order, that it is solely his property, and that it lives and wants to live solely from his comfort and from his direction in the expectation of his appearance.

The considerable deficits of this particular conception of Christ's royal office and "christocratic brotherhood" become clear when we see how far Barmen III lags behind the biblical verse with which its authors prefaced its third thesis. That guiding verse is found in the fourth chapter of the letter to the Ephesians and reads essentially as follows according to Barmen III: "*Let us instead be upright in love and grow in every way in him who is the head, Christ, from whom the whole body is joined and knit together*" (Eph 4:15–16).

Remarkably, the biblical text does not speak about "growing in the head," but rather "toward the head": "*Being truly in this love, let us grow in every way toward him who is the head, Christ*" (Eph 4:15). The Barmen Declaration variously tempers the dynamic tension and dynamic coexistence between the head and the members. The rather circumstantial wording of Eph 4:16 reads as follows:

Perspectives on the Belhar Confession (Grand Rapids and Cambridge, U.K.: Eerdmans, 2010), 219–23.

10. See in this regard Dirk J. Smit, "Barmen and Belhar in Conversation: A South African Perspective," in idem, *Essays on Being Reformed, Collected Essays 3* (Stellenbosch: SUN MeDIA, 2009), 325–36; Naudé, *Neither Calendar nor Clock*, 65ff, 122f.

11. See Naudé, *Neither Calendar nor Clock*, 223.

> . . . from whom [i.e., the head, from Christ] the whole body, joined and
> knit together by every ligament with which it is equipped, as each part is
> working properly, promotes the body's growth in building itself up in love.[12]

That is, the letter to the Ephesians explicitly emphasizes the *polyphonic
interplay of the members (joints and ligaments) of the body of Christ.*
Although the members of the body do indeed receive from Christ,
their head, the energy and orientation for growth, they *also* receive,
through the Holy Spirit, their own strength and dignity with which
to engage their activities within that interplay, something that must
not be overshadowed or, certainly, obscured by emphasis on Christ's
dominion "from above." And although one can doubtless understand
and empathize with Barmen's concern that such concentration on "his
own" might diminish or even obscure or endanger the "clear line" and
concentrated impact of the influence of this true king and prophet in
the struggle with hostile powers,[13] any abstraction from the interplay
of the members of the body of Christ or any diminishing of its significance in his dominion distorts our view of the royal Christ—a view it
was intended rather to sharpen. It similarly distorts our perception of
his royal office and the gestalt of the accompanying reign. In a word,
the exalted Christ is not interested in acting in an *isolated* fashion.
"His own"—these are the actual members of his body, not merely an
ensemble of extras or a chorus that merely accompanies his life and
ministry in the background.

In light of Jesus's pre-Easter life, *the royal dominion of Christ* and
his own acquires clear contours and develops *a clear message of freedom and diaconal love. In light of the outpouring of the Spirit, this same
royal dominion revolutionizes hierarchical and monarchical organizational forms in the ecclesiastical sphere and, indirectly, also political*

---

12. NRSV. Cf. (in German) Rudolf Schnackenburg, *Der Brief an die Epheser*, EKK X
(Köln and Neukirchen-Vluyn: Benziger and Neukirchener, 1982), 173, cf. 192ff as well as
the "annotation of the Protestant partner" Eduard Schweizer, 195f.

13. It is in this sense that the somewhat nervous christocentric rhetoric in the work of
Karl Barth is to be understood, e.g., when he interprets the Resurrected's otherwise rather
tranquil assurance that "All authority in heaven and on earth has been given to me" (Matt
28:18) with almost anxiously fearful agitation: "To Me – who give you this commission
and this office with it – to Me is given all power in heaven and on earth" (*CD II/2*, 434). So
also in the emphatic description of the "royal man," cf. *CD IV/2*, 154ff; cf. 268: "The given
fact of His existence as the royal man, and His effective power and lordship, cannot be allowed to sink into the background, becoming the content only of a completed christological
statement which we have now conveniently left behind to construct a second statement of
which Christ is no longer the subject but we ourselves at a certain distance from Him—the
Christian as a being which is certainly in relationship to Christ, but has also its own independent existence."

forms of rule and organization, since this king is at once both brother and friend, or indeed even one who is poor and outcast. With its radically democratic and post-patriarchal organizational concepts, this royal dominion may well seem uncomfortably complex and unclear to some, while others may find in it an exemplary model of orientation for church communities and civil organizations with its emphatic affirmation of freedom.

The royal gestalt of God's reign is characterized by a praxis of love and by the freedom mediated by that love. This praxis in its own turn is governed by loving acceptance, healing, liberating teaching and education, and the concern with giving everyone access to such.

Love and forgiveness, in both continuity and discontinuity with Torah traditions, are characterized by *free, creative self-withdrawal* [14] on behalf of others.[15] This free, creative, and—in love certainly also joyous—self-withdrawal on behalf of one's fellow human beings is also an extraordinarily powerful factor promoting and encouraging *freedom.* The goal of this love, love inadequately defined by *eros, agape,* and *philia,*[16] is for "all things [to] work together for good" (Rom 8:28) with respect to the beloved person. That person's feet are to be placed in an "expansive space." For understanding the reign of God, it is also of central significance that it is *not just the obligation* to engage in behavior and acts conducive to freedom that first gets our attention and wins over our hearts, but rather the joyous and grateful *personal experience of the free self-withdrawal on the part of others on our own behalf,*[17] one reason children are thought to enjoy a

---

14. Cf. Huber, *Gerechtigkeit und Recht,* 316f et passim (see part 4.3, note 4); Bedford-Strohm, *Vorrang für die Armen* (see part 4.3, note 8); Michael Welker, "Routinisiertes Erbarmen und paradigmatische Öffentlichkeit. 'Generalisierung von Altruismus' in alttestamentlichen Gesetzesüberlieferungen," in *Altruismus. Aus der Sicht von Evolutionsbiologie, Philosophie und Theologie,* Loccumer Protokolle 30/92, ed. Hans May (Loccum, 1996), 143–60.

15. Christian Grappe, *Le Royaume de Dieu. Avant, avec et après Jésus* (Geneva: Labor et Fides, 2001) provides an excellent examination of the connections between the various Old Testament notions of God's reign, Jesus's own proclamation and ministry, and early Christian life praxis. Concerning the topic of God's reign, the torah, and Jesus's position over against Jewish law, cf. Gunther Wenz, *Christus,* Studium Systematische Theologie 5 (Göttingen: Vandenhoeck, 2011), 239ff; also Karl-Heinrich Bieritz, *Grundwissen Theologie: Jesus Christus,* KT 148 (Gütersloh: Kaiser, 1997), 47ff.

16. Michael Welker, "Romantic Love, Covenantal Love, Kenotic Love," in *The Work of Love: Creation as Kenosis,* ed. John Polkinghorne (Grand Rapids/London: Eerdmans, 2001), 127–36.

17. Cf. Wilfried Härle, *Dogmatik,* 3rd ed. (Berlin, New York: de Gruyter, 2007), 237ff; idem, *Ethik* (Berlin, New York: de Gruyter, 2011), 328ff, 388ff. However, see also Heinz Schmidt, "Reich Gottes und soziale Entwicklung. Grundelemente einer diakonischen Theologie," in *Gegenwart des lebendigen Christus,* 339–61 (see part 1.5, note 5); Rudolf Weth,

particularly close proximity to the reign of God (cf. 4.3).[18] Such an ethos of liberating joy and gratitude, however, is also of fundamental significance for an ethos of humane diaconate.[19] Unfortunately, social routines too often obscure this grateful sensibility for the enormous potential of free, creative self-withdrawal in many contemporary contexts.

Such grateful awareness of the enormous potential of free, creative self-withdrawal in the context of family, friends, education, medical care, and civil and social organizations should similarly raise our awareness of the strong direct and indirect formative power of the *munus regium Christi*. That is, it is not just in the shadow of distress and tribulation, but certainly also in the light of gratitude that we should focus on the powerful diaconal, pedagogical, therapeutic, constitutional, ecclesiastical, and intercultural global challenges prompting us to both pray for *and* become engaged on behalf of the continued "coming" of the reign of Christ. It is through myriad, often inconspicuous acts of love and forgiveness that the reigns of God and Christ acquire contours among us.

Nor is it merely the *direct* witnesses who acquire a portion and participation in this often inconspicuous but immensely powerful royal reign. William Schweiker, picking up on and developing further initiatives introduced by the Niebuhr brothers[20] and James Gustafson,[21] has illustrated quite clearly how "Christian humanism"[22] not only influences

---

"Ecce homo – Vom neuen Sehen des Menschen in der Diakonie. Biblisch-theologische Impulse zum diakonischen Menschenbild," in ibid., 363–90.

18. Cf. Matt 10:14; Marcia J. Bunge, "Children, the Image of God, and Christology: Theological Anthropology in Solidarity with Children," in *Who is Jesus Christ for Us Today?*, 167–81 (see part 0.1, note 7); idem, ed., *The Child in Christian Thought* (Grand Rapids, Cambridge, U.K.: Eerdmans, 2001); idem, ed., *The Child in the Bible* (Grand Rapids, Cambridge, U.K.: Eerdmans, 2008).

19. Cf. J. H. Wichern's emphasis on "grateful love" as a fundamental form of diaconal life together (Johann Hinrich Wichern, *Schriften zur Sozialpädagogik [Rauhes Haus und Johannesstift]*, Sämtliche Werke, vol. IV,1, ed. Peter Meinhold [Berlin: Luth. Verl.-Haus, 1958], 119 et passim); Theodor Strohm, *Diakonie und Sozialethik. Beiträge zur sozialen Verantwortung der Kirche*, ed. Gerhard K. Schäfer and Klaus Müller, Veröffentlichungen des Diakoniewissenschaftlichen Instituts 6 (Heidelberg: Heidelberger Verlagsanstalt, 1993), 138ff.

20. See, e.g., H. Richard Niebuhr, *Christ and Culture* (New York: Harper & Row, 1951); Reinhold Niebuhr, *The Self and the Dramas of History* (New York: Charles Scribner's, 1955), esp. chap. 19.

21. James M. Gustafson, *Christ and the Moral Life* (New York: Harper & Row, 1968).

22. Cf. William Schweiker and David E. Klemm, *Religion and the Human Future: An Essay on Theological Humanism* (Oxford: Blackwell, 2008); William Schweiker, "Flesh and Folly: The Christ of Christian Humanism," in *Who is Jesus Christ for Us Today?* 85–102 (see part 0.1, note 7); idem, *Dust That Breathes: Christian Faith and the New Humanisms* (Oxford and Malden: Wiley-Blackwell, 2010), esp. 84ff, 207ff; Liu Xiaofeng, "Sino-Christian Theology in the Modern Context," 70ff (see part 0.4, note 31).

other religious and secular forms of behavior and practices involving love and engagement on behalf of our fellow human beings, but is in its own turn similarly influenced by them. That is, the scope of Christ's reign, promoting human freedom at large, is considerably more extensive than all the churches of all the regions of the world and even of all ages. "Just as you did it to one of the least of these who are members of my family, you did it to me"—whether you discern my own presence in them or not.[23] Those who, by contrast, restrict Christ's dominion to "word and sacrament" fail to recognize this breadth of its liberating presence in the power of the Spirit. That said, it is similarly incorrect to adduce some abstract, universal moral continuum as a realm allegedly superior to a "merely Christian" ethos, since any such value-free moral realm is itself ultimately a mere construct.[24]

Because the Barmen Theological Declaration is largely silent concerning Jesus Christ's promised presence among the poor or even among the distressed and the "least of these who are members of my family" (Matt 25:31–46), it is similarly silent concerning the church's own diaconal service. Such becomes evident in a particularly oppressive fashion insofar as the declaration is utterly silent concerning the persecution and systematic murder of Jews, Sinti and Romani, the physically and mentally handicapped, and other human beings.

By concentrating on the Lord who acts "in word and sacrament," Barmen redirects attention to the priestly office, whereas in the struggle with the Nazi dictatorship it is the prophetic office that moved into the foreground.[25] Unfortunately, this double concentration within Christ's royal dominion on the priestly and prophetic offices distorts or obscures the fact that the dominion of the exalted Christ *also* stands in continuity with Old Testament legal traditions, with messianic promises, and certainly also with God's special—and not merely appellative!—intervention, as repeatedly attested throughout the entire Old Testament canon, on behalf of the hard-pressed, the disadvantaged, and the oppressed.[26]

---

23. Cf. Matt 25:40 and 25:34ff; John F. Hoffmeyer, "Christology and *Diakonia*," in *Who is Jesus Christ for Us Today?* 150–66 (see part 0.1, note 7). See also Alfeyev, *Christ the Conqueror of Hell*, 214 (see part 3.4, note 12). Viewed in this light, the proximity to the Eastern Church is closer than Alfeyev thinks: "Unlike the West, Christian consciousness in the East admits the opportunity for salvation not only for those who believe during their lifetime but also for those who were not given to believe but pleased God with their good works."

24. See in this regard the instructive discussion between Judith Butler, Jürgen Habermas, Charles Taylor, and Cornel West in *The Power of Religion in the Public Sphere*, ed. Eduardo Mendieta and Jonathan VanAntwerpen (New York: Columbia University Press, 2011).

25. Cf. part 5.5.

26. Although this interconnection between the charismatic powers of the offices of Christ (the forms of his reign) can doubtless provide creative initiatives, it can also gloss

Any concentration on the royal office must always apply a critical corrective when that office is transformed into the priestly or prophetic office if the royal office is to emerge clearly within the context of its service of love, diaconate, and humanistic charisma. A similarly critical corrective must be applied to any attempts to disregard those members of its body or more distant witnesses who participate in that royal office and acquire a portion of the royal gestalt of God's reign *through the Spirit*. And finally, such corrective must also be applied to any attempts to at-

---

over spiritual and theological questions. A commensurate and adequate understanding of the exalted Christ and his reign emerges *only* if the differences between the royal, priestly, and prophetic forms of the reign of Christ, their contrasts, connections, and various modes of interplay are kept in mind. By contrast, playing these forms off against one another can impose a "tragic" turn (see below) on the attendant spiritual, theological, and ecclesiastical relationships. Jon Sobrino, picking up on the work of Ignacio Ellacuría, maintained that "even *now*, the resurrection of Jesus is shaping present history through the outpouring of the Holy Spirit" (Jon Sobrino, *Der Glaube an Jesus Christus. Eine Christologie aus der Perspektive der Opfer* [Ostfildern: Matthias Grünewald, 2008], 40 [*Christ the Liberator: A View from the Victims* [Maryknoll, N.Y.: Orbis Books, 2001]). Sobrino developed his own Christology and his doctrine of the church in the light of "discipleship/following" focused on "giving life to the poor" (ibid., 92, cf. 499 et passim) and on turning the church into the true church, that is, into the church of the poor (idem, *The True Church and the Poor* [Maryknoll: Orbis, 1984], esp. chaps. 4, 5, 10). Concentrating primarily on the royal and recalcitrant prophetic dimensions of discipleship, and picking up on Matt 5:48 ("Be perfect, therefore, as your heavenly Father is perfect"), his occasional use of metaphorical language can expose him to the charge of having mixed up God's activities with those of human beings. "Giving life to the poor"—cannot only God himself do that!? It was in this sense that Joseph Ratzinger accused Sobrino of having effected a "transformation of the biblical message" that would certainly "manifest itself in an almost tragic fashion when one considers the concrete effects such attempted imitation of God has *already* had and indeed continues to have" (Jon Sobrino, "Brief an den Generaloberen des Jesuitenordens – Dezember 2006," in *Die Freiheit der Theologie. Die Debatte um die Notifikation gegen Jon Sobrino*, ed. Knut Wenze [Ostfildern: Matthias Grünewald, 2008], 32).

Benedict XVI, in his encyclicals in the style of the political theology of Carl Schmitt, invoked — in a decidedly and unequivocally more precarious fashion — a political world authority, universally recognized and with efficacious power at its disposal, with the task of solving all contemporary economic, military, social, and ecological problems, a vision associated with a program of a "purification" of reason through opening up to transcendence and to the supernatural truth of love. Klaus Tanner quite correctly observed that the pope tried to undergird these propositions with an "ontological-metaphysical understanding of natural law" drawing on logos speculation in the early church (Klaus Tanner, "Politische Theologie nach Benedikt XVI.," in *Politische Theologie*, 65ff, 74ff [see part 0.4, note 24]). Were this speculation genuinely to be incorporated into a perspective on discipleship to Christ, here the "doctrine of the church" would likely be positioned within the realm of the "priestly form of God's reign." Young Ratzinger had indeed critically assessed such traditions of natural law and even as cardinal had invoked them only with a measure of skepticism (cf. Michael Welker, "Zukunftsaufgaben Politischer Theologie. Über Religion und Politik nach Habermas und Ratzinger," ibid., 83ff).

tribute to this particular office and this reign a merely *heavenly* or *transcendent* existence.

None of these considerations, however, means that the connection and unity between the three offices and three forms of God's reign are to be challenged or the eschatological breadth of Christ's royal influence called into question. That said, however, the indispensable emphasis on the eschatological breadth of Christ's influence and his reign must be ever mindful not to overlook or even downplay the fact that Christ's royal presence *also* influences or radiates out into clearly secularized and political forms of life. *Whenever and wherever human beings today strive to bring about education and healthcare for everyone, to shape free communities and civil societies, and never cease emphasizing and insisting on unconditional respect for human rights and human dignity—in such cases, consciously or not, forces deriving from Christ's royal and prophetic ministry invariably constitute part of their underlying motivation and orientation.*

Quietly but persistently, the royal office—or the royal gestalt of God's reign—works together with the prophetic office—its prophetic gestalt—toward the establishment of radical-democratic forms of life and society, and in this context the interplay or cooperation of Judeo-Christian traditions and impulses, on the one hand, with Enlightenment critique and the secularization of precisely these impulses, on the other, has proven to be extraordinarily fruitful. Indeed, this religio-secular interaction and cooperation, in which the Christian faith sees the spirit of the exalted Christ at work, has come to provide the model in an increasing number of regions in the world.

4.5 The Public and the Eschatological Christ

This present Christology advocates complementing the doctrine of the threefold office of Christ with a doctrine of the threefold shape or form of Christ's reign, and in so doing to pick up Calvin's view of Jesus Christ, the Messiah, the Anointed, as having been anointed with the Holy Spirit so that "his own" might *also* have a portion and participate in his spirit and his offices (cf. part 4.1). That is, Jesus Christ has no intention of keeping the divine Spirit simply for himself, nor does he confer it merely on a few select dignitaries or officeholders or those canonized by the church. Here the *dynamic* presence and *expansive* influence and efficacy of the resurrected and exalted Christ and the outpouring of the Holy Spirit with the constitution of the entire post-Easter body of Christ become discernible—particularly if one bears in mind the threefold gestalt of Christ's reign—in all their extensive interrelations. Here as well, Luther's and Barth's central insight that the resurrected and exalted Jesus Christ is not found apart from "his own" acquires a much clearer and more animated profile.

These considerations also throw new light on the "Christology of the Spirit" that during the past few years has often remained so puzzling and yet has repeatedly been in demand. For this doctrine of the threefold gestalt of Christ's reign can easily incorporate the various Pentecostal concerns with combining a doctrine of sanctification centered on Jesus Christ, on the one hand, with a differentiated doctrine of spiritual charismata in discipleship to Christ, on the other (part 4.2)

Those who have long promoted the development of a "public theology" will likely be especially inclined to welcome a Christology in which Christ's dominion in the power of the Spirit can be perceived and articulated in such a differentiated fashion. The various concerns associated with this programmatic formula can be examined and clarified, and their various contexts and interrelations discerned in the light of this christologically focused threefold gestalt of God's reign.

The concept of public theology has been engaged polemically against reductionist forms of theology that would concentrate Christ and his dominion solely on *individual* human beings and their *personal* salvation. On the other hand, church worship with its public proclamation in free societies, theological doctrine as such, ecclesiastical communiqués, and the church's more or less marked diaconal service in various countries throughout the world make it rather easy to demonstrate the unequivocally *public* character of church ministry and activities and the accompanying theology. All of which begs the question: what sort of theology would *not* always be public theology in any case?

Wolfgang Huber has submitted a clear proposal that both intensifies and articulates more precisely the expectations made on a public theology:

> By "public theology" I understand that particular theological activity that would examine the theological relevance of questions of life together and its institutional implementation and determine the contribution Christian faith makes toward shaping our present world and lives in a responsible fashion. By "public theology" I at once am also referring to a form of theology that, rather than retreating into a specialized "innertheological" language, instead strives to be universally comprehensible itself while simultaneously seeking out communication with other disciplines.[1]

According to Huber, then, public theology begins with questions of life together and identifies contributions from and relevant points of contact with the Christian faith in this larger context, then articulates these contributions in a language at once both public and interdisciplinary.[2] Monological statements in the context of worship, instruction concerning the content of faith, and diaconal charisma and ministry alone do not yet constitute genuine public theology, which, as Habermas put it, must translate *elements of orientation* such that they are then applicable in civil society and other scholarly disciplines.[3] Simply asserting the relevance of theology and church and then demanding that life at large accommodate itself to religious expectations and standards does not yet produce a genuine public theology.

Those particular forms of public theology that present themselves in an emancipatory context and incorporate an element of cultural, social, or societal critique generally acquire more sharply normative profiles and as a result are also more controversial. Variations of political theologies (the "new political theology" dating back to the 1980s), feminist theologies, liberation theologies, post-colonial or decolonializing theologies claimed and still claim to be publicly engaged.[4] The doubts they have always raised usually involve the question whether they maintain a legitimate connection and relationship with Jesus Christ and his spirit or are sooner defined by moral, cultural-critical, and political-critical spirits.

---

1. Huber, *Gerechtigkeit und Recht*, 12f (see part 4.3, note 4).

2. Cf. Wolfgang Vögele, *Zivilreligion in der Bundesrepublik Deutschland*, Öffentliche Theologie 5 (Gütersloh: Kaiser, 1994), 418ff.

3. Jürgen Habermas, "'The Political': The Rational Meaning of a Questionable Inheritance of Political Theology," in *The Power of Religion*, 25ff (see part 4.4, note 24).

4. See in this regard Jürgen Moltmann, "Politische Theologie in ökumenischen Kontexten," in *Politische Theologie*, 1ff (see part 0.4, note 24); Elisabeth Schüssler Fiorenza, "Die kritisch-feministische The*logie der Befreiung," in ibid., 23ff.

Such queries, which can intensify into shrill denunciations of liberation theologies as Marxist-inspired developments,[5] are positioned in the tension between, on the one hand, a disastrous sort of petty faith incapable of genuinely appreciating the breadth of Christ's dominion, and, on the other, potentially quite justified apprehensions that various political, moral, and religious concerns and spirits might be being admixed and even confused.

The concept of "public theology" also came to include concepts and drafts focusing on analyses of civil society and civil religion, analyses that, though often sociologically quite interesting and revealing in and of themselves, nonetheless only in rare instances exhibited any genuine theological, christological, and pneumatological substance or innovation.[6] And finally, the desire not only to raise one's voice in the discussion of contemporary political and moral issues, but also to lend that voice a certain measure of religious emphasis also identified itself as a form of "public theology."

The work of David Tracy can serve as an illustration of the considerable challenges to any Christian public theology as well as the problems invariably attending the development of its christological profile and the difficulties in doing justice to these challenges. Beginning in the late 1970s, Tracy was already emphasizing that any public theology must necessarily develop a positive relationship with pluralism in society, and must clearly understand that it is speaking within or from three different public perspectives (or "publics"), namely, society, academy, and church.[7] These different publics in turn demand the development of different forms of theology.[8] It quickly became clear that such concentration on but three publics (society [more precisely: civil society], the academy

---

5. Cf. Jon Sobrino, "Brief an den Generaloberen des Jesuitenordens – Dezember 2006," 32 et passim (see part 4.4, note 26).

6. Noteworthy examples include Robert N. Bellah, "Civil Religion in America," in *Beyond Belief: Essays on Religion in a Post-Traditionalist World* (Berkeley, Los Angeles: University of California Press, 1970; paperback 1991), 169–92; Peter L. Berger, *The Sacred Canopy. Elements of a Sociological Theory of Religion* (Garden City, N.Y.: Doubleday, 1967); Niklas Luhmann, *Funktion der Religion* (Frankfurt: Suhrkamp, 1977), Eng. trans. of chapter 2: idem, *Religious Dogmatics and the Evolution of Societies* (New York/Toronto: Edwin Mellen Press, 1984); Eilert Herms, "Die Bedeutung der Weltanschauungen für die ethische Urteilsbildung," in *Theologische Ethik der Gegenwart. Ein Überblick über zentrale Ansätze und Themen*, ed. Friederike Nüssel (Tübingen: Mohr Siebeck, 2009), 49ff.

7. See David Tracy, *The Analogical Imagination: Christian Theology and the Culture of Pluralism* (New York: Crossroad, 1981), 3ff.

8. Tracy experiments with fundamental theology and systematic and practical theology (Tracy, *The Analogical Imagination*, 54ff).

[science and other scholarly disciplines], and the church) was insufficient for analyzing late-modern societies.[9] The notion of "civil society," for instance, does not entirely cover the various publics associated with political, media-related, legal, therapeutic, and economic processes of organization and communication. Hence a truly public theology within a pluralistic context must work with more sophisticated socio-analytical models if it is to be successfully implemented commensurate with socio-analytical requirements.

Although Tracy himself addressed these issues only during a limited period, ultimately opting for the simple "plurality" of moral, political, and religious engagement instead of an analysis of structured societal pluralism,[10] he could have chosen a clear *theological* alternative had he but examined the possibility of applying a latent *christological orientation* to his original point of departure with the (merely) three publics, in which case he might then have analyzed societal pluralism within a theological and christological framework.[11]

What do we find when we concentrate on the *public* Christ and his reign? Christ's royal office or the royal gestalt of God's reign both inside and outside the churches exhibits an unstoppable dynamic; a grand current of what individually are often quite inconspicuous deeds of free, creative self-withdrawal, love, acceptance, loving concern, and forgiveness sets into motion enormous emergent processes and developments. Even though this—in the broadest sense diaconal—activity exerts considerable influence on both social and political circumstances, it is nonetheless difficult to determine its contours or profile when it does not appear in more clearly recognizable institutionalized and organized forms. The christological power of orientation similarly comes to be associated with the dynamics of family, friendship, neighbors, socio-morality, and professional therapeutic contexts. In his 1933 essay "The Church and the Jewish Question,"[12] Dietrich Bonhoeffer considered the possibility that under extremely problematical and dangerous social and societal circumstances or developments, "direct political action on the part of the church" might be in order, action consisting not merely in "bind[ing] up the wounds of the victims beneath the wheel," but in "seiz[ing] the wheel itself," albeit a revolutionary step that in its own turn presupposes ap-

9. See in this regard Welker, *Kirche im Pluralismus*, 13ff (see part 3.2, note 49).

10. David Tracy, *Plurality and Ambiguity: Hermeneutics, Religion, Hope* (San Francisco: Harper & Row, 1987).

11. What would have emerged in any case is that the academy is too narrow to grasp adequately the prophetic dimension of God's reign, and that only certain parts of the communicative processes attaching to civil society are genuinely theologically relevant.

12. DBWE 12:361–70.

proval by an "evangelical council."[13] And indeed, broad areas of activity within the royal gestalt of Christ's reign both inside and outside the church do serve to bind the wounds of victims beneath the wheel and attempt to prevent further victims from falling beneath that same wheel if at all possible.

It is the prophetic office and the prophetic gestalt of God's reign that tries to brake the wheel and bring it to a stop, doing so through a broad spectrum of activities extending from quiet, reflective discourse and instruction to loud public protest, symbolic political actions, and non-violent resistance. It would be incorrect to acknowledge *only* the diaconal or *only* the prophetic form of discipleship in the power of Christ's spirit as relevant for public theology, though equally incorrect to deny theological and christological legitimacy to *either* form from the outset.

If as our point of departure we take the public Christ and his reign, this public efficacy and power cannot really become theologically interesting *as such*. That is, God's reign also acquires form or contours in what is the often inconspicuous experience of individuals, in encounters with them, and in ministry and action on their behalf. Any potential theological interest in public ministry and action must always ask itself whether it is invoking Jesus Christ merely to reinforce pending actions that from other perspectives as well may be morally and politically desirable. What is ultimately decisive for any public theology taking a christological orientation is whether it is fully in accordance with the eschatological presence and directive of Christ, which in its own turn contains and will reveal the entire wealth of his pre- and post-Easter life.

The eschatological presence and directive of Christ, his eschatological person, is not simply to be equated with what is known as the end-time Parousia (the so-called return of Christ). We encounter Christ's eschatological person in the past, present, and future with his coming reign, and we both expect and indeed hope for his complete revelation in his perfected reign. Because, as our examination of God's reign has revealed, it is at once both a *present* and a *future* reality, one must not play present and future eschatology off against each other.[14] The coming of God's reign is in fact emergent, and within this emergent occurrence, the respective preponderance of Christ's royal, priestly, and prophetic dominion is sometimes more and sometimes less clearly discernible. A competent discernment of spirits is constantly required if one is to avoid confusing Christ's reign, on the one hand, with the dominion of other spirits, on the other, or if one is to avoid polarizing the two one against

13. DBWE 12:365–67.
14. Cf. part 4.3.

the other, and instead to demarcate them clearly, constructively, and critically one from the other.[15]

It is not, however, only in temporal and historical perspectives that we encounter the eschatological person of Christ, his reign, and his deity, for God's complete, perfected reign, for which faith itself hopes, encompasses all ages and regions of the world. Biblical traditions warn unequivocally and with utter clarity against false prophets who allege or will allege, "'Look! Here is the Messiah!' or 'There he is!'"[16] The same applies to any spatial or temporal predictions concerning his arrival. The Parousia of Jesus Christ will not occur at any natural location on this earth nor along our familiar temporal continuum. The resurrected and exalted Christ will reveal himself in his fullness, entering into all ages and all the regions of the world just as we, too, hope with our entire lives to be judged and saved beyond earthly death.

Faith is able to take a perspective on life that, while surpassing or transcending natural experience, is by no means absurd, something illustrated simply enough by the question, "Who was and who is this beloved person whom I just lost or whom I lost long ago?" Is it the child I know only from stories and pictures? Is it the shadowy, indistinct recollection from my own youth? Is it the familiar, accustomed person in all his or her developments and changes with whom I shared a portion, long or short, of my own life's path? Or is it the frail, dying person into whose eyes I gazed with such immense sorrow? Eternity-eschatology preserves the living entirety of this person (and not just as recollected in punctiliar moments). This entire corporeal existence is kept and preserved not in the flesh, nor in nature, but in the spirit. Hence it is both quite accurate *and* profoundly misleading when our confessions speak about a "return" of the eschatological person of Jesus Christ. The historical Jesus will not return, nor the Resurrected in his post-Easter appearances before the first witnesses. The eschatological person of Jesus Christ, however, imprinted by the entire coming reign, will indeed stand in continuity with both the pre-Easter Jesus and the post-Easter Resurrected. He will be a familiar, trusted and trustworthy judge and savior. Statements concerning the final theophany are of necessity of an extremely visionary nature.[17] If we are to understand the revelation of Jesus Christ's divine

15. See in this regard Bonhoeffer, "The Empirical Form of the Church," in *Sanctorum Communio*, DBWE 1:208–82 (see part 0.5, note 17); Schleiermacher, *The Christian Faith*, 453-57 (see part 4.1, note 8).

16. Matt 24:23ff; Mark 13:21f; Luke 17:23f.

17. See Michael Welker and Michael Wolter, "Die Unscheinbarkeit des Reiches Gottes," in *Reich Gottes*, Marburger Jahrbuch Theologie XI, ed. W. Härle and R. Preul (Marburg: Elwert, 1999), 103–16; concerning the extremely difficult concepts of "sitting

identity, we must avoid being satisfied with merely impressive demonstrations of his public relevance and instead try to grasp the connection between the public Christ with the power of his spirit and God's power of creative renewal, something we can do by focusing on the priestly and prophetic dimensions of his ministry and his reign.

---

at the right hand of God" and, in a more universally religious sense as well, of "salvation," see Konrad Stock, "Zur Rechten Gottes," in *Gegenwart des lebendigen Christus*, 261–69 (see part 1.5, note 5); Christoph Markschies, "'Sessio ad dexteram.' Bemerkungen zu einem altchristlichen Bekenntnismotiv in der Diskussion der altkirchlichen Theologen," in idem, *Alta Trinità Beata. Gesammelte Studien zur altkirchlichen Trinitätstheologie* (Tübingen: Mohr Siebeck, 2000), 1–69; Jan Assmann, "Das Heil: Religiöse Zukunftsvorstellungen im kulturellen Gedächtnis," in *Gegenwart des lebendigen Christus*, 463–78 (see part 1.5, note 5).

PART 5

Truly God–Truly Human

5.1 God's Revelation in Jesus Christ: The Nearness and Depth of the Incarnation – The Richness and Breadth of Salvation. The Path of this Christology

God has revealed himself in Jesus Christ! Jesus Christ reveals God himself! These statements both disclose and guarantee to faith God's love and beneficent inclination toward human beings along with his unconditional proximity. That said, however, the fascination prompted by this promise of God's proximity in Jesus Christ is hard pressed in the face of human experience and reflection. Though piety may well be moved by the cross of Jesus Christ, and though people be genuinely or even profoundly touched by the iconic presence of Jesus in the imagery of the child in the manger and the dying Jesus on the cross, the gnawing question persists, namely, how this person and this life can be the source from which the gospel emerges that in its own turn so profoundly moves human hearts and supports, shapes, and fundamentally renews and alters their very lives, such that the grand proclamation concerning "saving and redemption" through Jesus Christ is genuinely credible. Does not God become unrecognizable *precisely* in the lowliness and impotence of both manger and cross? When we consider Jesus Christ and his life, what becomes of the sovereignty and majesty, or indeed the saving power and creativity we normally associate with the word "God"? However we may try to grasp God through names or concepts, are not the person and life of Jesus Christ far too paltry, far too meager to reveal anything as lofty as the deity?

An additional challenge is presented by the subtle queries in reference to internal tensions within the confession itself. To wit, what, exactly, does the expression "has revealed" mean in the assertion that God *has revealed* himself in Jesus Christ?

- Is the statement referring to a past event?

- Or does it refer to an occurrence whose efficacy *continues* into the present?

Some languages, including English, can express this tension quite succinctly and clearly with different forms of the past tense:

> *God revealed himself in Jesus Christ!* – i.e., a concluded event in the past.
>
> *God has revealed himself in Jesus Christ!* – i.e., an occurrence that continues into the present.

If faith decides in favor of a *past* occurrence, it can quite convincingly maintain the notion of *incarnational proximity and kenotic depth* (i.e., God's becoming human in Jesus and his self-debasement even to the point of impotent death on the cross). In Jesus Christ, a real human being lived among other human beings and died a real human death. Unfortunately, this position confronts faith with the dilemma of explaining how one can speak of a revelation of *God* that remains efficacious even today if, after all, it involved a human life that was lived almost two millennia ago—even assuming we acknowledge the considerable charisma that life yet possesses. What does that past life have to do with the grand promises we still associate with it today? In this light, how can the convictions of faith still be maintained, namely, that through Jesus Christ God wants to liberate, save, and redeem human beings of all epochs from the power of sin and death? Or that through and in Jesus Christ human beings and indeed all creation acquire a portion and participation in divine, eternal life?

If the presupposition is that God's revelation refers solely to a past event—then how sustainable are the promises associated with Jesus Christ and that revelation? How can we then speak about God's *continued* creative and saving activity in and through this revelation in Jesus Christ? Does this presupposition not then empty *soteriology* (the doctrine of Christ's redemptive work) and *eschatology* (the doctrine of Christian hope, God's reign, and eternal life) of any genuine content? Does not Christian faith itself lose its *soteriological richness and eschatological breadth*? That is, does it not become spiritually empty and hollow?

Under the pressure of these considerations at the latest, faith becomes inclined toward a different option, assuring us then that the verb "to reveal" in the statement "God has revealed himself in Jesus Christ" is to be taken not in the sense of simply "God revealed," as an occurrence that was concluded once and for all in the past, but in an ongoing, *present* sense that remains efficacious and powerful even today, that is, as an event that continues in full force up to the present and even beyond, namely, for all time. Faith may perhaps invoke the words from the letter to the Hebrews in adding that "Jesus Christ is the same yesterday and today and forever" (Heb 13:8), the "reflection of God's glory and the exact imprint of God's very being," and that through him the world itself is created (Heb 1:2f). Such corresponds as well to the emphasis in the letter to the Colossians that "in him [Jesus Christ] all the fullness of God was pleased to dwell," and that "by him all things in heaven and on earth were created" (Col 1:16, 19f). Faith can similarly invoke John's assertions that "the Father and I are one" (John 10:30; cf. John 1:1 and 10:38), and that "I am the way, and the truth, and the life. No one comes to the Father except through me" (John 14:6). Those who believe in Jesus Christ and, through him, in God, attain nothing less than "eternal life" and "glory" (John 17:2ff, 22ff; cf. also Matt 11:27; Luke 10:22; Acts 4:12 et passim).

And yet the more wholeheartedly faith emphasizes this charismatic radiance of the person, life, and ministry of Jesus Christ—radiance that saves and preserves us yesterday, today, and in all eternity—and his unity with the Creator, all the more unbelievable can precisely that become which fascinated faith in the first place about God's revelation in Jesus Christ, namely, the element of incarnational proximity and kenotic depth. Here Christian faith in God's revelation in Jesus Christ seems to be standing before a difficult alternative. If God genuinely did disclose himself in this particular human life, and if God genuinely did move into such close proximity to human beings in another human life, then we must indeed take seriously the historical distance between then and now. Almost two thousand years ago, "the Word became flesh and lived among us, and we saw his glory" (John 1:14). More precisely, not *we*, but rather the initial witnesses saw—perhaps—his glory. If, on the other hand, we are intent on expressing God's revelation in its present salvific and future redemptive power, and if we emphasize the power and glory of the Christ event as such, then the incarnational honesty and kenotic seriousness seem to disappear.

Much suggests that this particular dilemma stands at the center of most of the crises faced by the Christian faith even today (cf. parts 0.4–0.6). How can we reconcile the power of fascination exerted by the child in the manger and the man dying on the cross, on the one hand, with our religious notions of human life sheltered, preserved, saved, and elevated by God? How can we assert that this particular human being, Jesus Christ, and his suffering revealed God himself? Should we not instead turn to the more or less successful universal concepts of God as, for example, the "ground of being" (Tillich), the "whence" of our feeling of "absolute dependence" (Schleiermacher), or the "reality determining all else" (Bultmann, Pannenberg)? This particular dilem-

ma—ultimately between a christologically and biblically oriented faith
and its corresponding theology, on the one hand, and a more universal
"faith in God," essentially a form of religious theism, on the other—this
dilemma becomes even more acutely urgent in an age of globalization
in which, more than ever before, people are confronted with literally
countless notions, concepts, and images of God that mutually relativize
one another. In such a setting, the problems attending the so-called
"special status" of Christianity among religions, with its concentration
on God's revelation in Jesus Christ, become more trenchantly evident
than ever.

The religiosity and theology of modernity have reacted to this problematical state of affairs by associating the revelation of God's proximity
with a form of piety that, rather than relating directly to Jesus Christ, instead tries to discover and discern God within human self-consciousness.
It is allegedly in the innermost recesses or depths of self-consciousness
that God comes intimately near to us and we to God. Although a few theologians have tried to assure us that in this way we are in fact acting commensurate with Jesus's own disposition toward God and, by extension,
with Jesus's own self-consciousness,[1] as a rule this piety and theology
simply eliminates and, indeed, surrenders any overt references to God's
revelation in Jesus Christ, leaving behind a fundamental religious disposition focused on what it takes to be the interplay between God's proximity and distance within the innermost interiority of self-consciousness
(cf. part 0.5).

The advantage of this reflective piety seemed to be that it could be
attributed not just to Christianity, but to *all* religions. Even weakly religious and otherwise secularized people could be won over to this position
and even counted as "anonymous Christians."[2] In reality, such thinking
has sooner promoted the self-secularization of Christianity in the West,
a development widely observable in many Christian churches. What is
actually at work here is a systematic theological "self-emptying" accom-

---

1. A few isolated but particularly perceptive theological thinkers have recognized the
problems facing this notion of grasping oneself in "pure self-consciousness" and tried to
associate this failure with Jesus's cross. Cf. the final section in Friedrich Gogarten, *Die
Verkündigung Jesu Christi. Grundlagen und Aufgabe*, 2nd ed., Hermeneutische Untersuchungen zur Theologie 3 (Tübingen: Mohr Siebeck, 1965); see also the critical assessment
in Welker, *Der Vorgang Autonomie*, 129ff (see part 0.5, note 14).

2. Karl Rahner, "Anonymous Christians," in *Theological Investigations*, vol. VI, tr.
Karl-H. and Boniface Kruger (London: Darton, Longman & Todd), 390-98 et passim. See
in this regard Nikolaus Schwerdtfeger, "Der 'anonyme Christ' in der Theologie Karl Rahn-
ers," in *Theologie aus Erfahrung der Gnade. Annäherungen an Karl Rahner*, ed. Mariano
Delgado and Matthias Lutz-Bachmann, Schriften der Diözesanakademie Berlin 10 (Berlin:
Morus, 1994), 72–94.

panying a massive decline in religious training that in its own turn has been accompanied by uncertain and insecure religious experimentation, inflationary symbolic kitsch ("What is this little flower trying to say to us today?"; "For today's worship service, let us reflect on 'water.'"), and a banalizing of piety and church life, a development onto which conservative cultural critics have pinned the epithet "Christophobia," a kind of anxiety in the face of Christ and Christianity. Significantly, it was not a fundamentalist Christian hailing from the "Bible belt" in the USA, but rather an orthodox Jew and brilliant legal scholar born in South Africa who introduced into the public forum an effective critique of the cultural and historical amnesia resulting from such religious educational demise, remarking that Europe was being controlled by Christophobia that was blocking (or at least seriously thwarting) not only any reference back to Europe's own cultural, intellectual, and spiritual foundations, but also any cultivation and creative further development of those same foundations.[3]

The Path of this Christology

This present Christology seeks an alternative to the open or concealed dissolution of Christian faith that comes about in subjectivist faith and theistic metaphysics.

One of its most important insights is that *several* paths must be taken in the search for truth and understanding. When, for example, we really want to get to know or get better acquainted with other people, life paths, historical situations, and so on, we invariably seek out *several* paths offering different points of access, something that by extension, of course, also applies to any effort to come to know or understand the living God and revelation in Jesus Christ.

1. The quest for the historical Jesus takes us down the first of these paths. Christology intent on embracing God's revelation in this human being cannot and must not ignore this question. The historical Jesus is neither a stone in the middle of the desert nor a mere vessel for "Christology from below" that seeks a point of departure in an abstract notion of "humanity," self-consciousness, a feeling of certainty concerning God, or similar merely seemingly "kerygmatic" entities. Although the historical Jesus is an elusive if charismatic person whom we encounter in historical contexts whose contours are similarly difficult to pin down, nonetheless our query and search for reliable knowledge of this person and this life are not at all meaningless, and the sometimes irritating and often

---

3. Cf. the reference to Weiler, *Ein christliches Europa* (see part 0.4, note 3).

enough also futile search for more promising historical and scientific methods of inquiry should *not* prompt us to overlook or dismiss those particular modes of scholarly and scientific inquiry that do indeed take the quest further.

What is known as the "third quest for the historical Jesus" set in motion a development that yielded unquestionably valuable scholarly results from which this present Christology has greatly profited (cf. parts 1.1–1.3). Even faith that is not particularly interested in any direct way with scholarship as such should take note of at least the most important results and claims of these developments and come to terms with their implications. Part 1 of this book proposed various lines of query in the search for truth about the historical Jesus that might also be pursued in the future (part 1.4). That is, on the one hand, the current status of the search has been described with its various results; on the other, suggestions have been made concerning how through both assessing and defending these results and claims one might keep the overall quest for the historical Jesus open and invigorated.

2. Queries concerning the historical Jesus cannot alone yield Christology.

> He would have disappeared from historical memory as yet another first-century messianic pretender whose claims were shown in the end to be delusory. Yet we have all heard of Jesus. *Something* must have happened that continued his story. All the New Testament writers are clearly convinced that this "something" was the resurrection.[4]

The reality of the resurrection, however, is no less complex than the life of the historical Jesus. Quite to the contrary, the life of the Resurrected maintains his pre-Easter existence with all its rich charisma in a new form. In his "royal dominion," the Resurrected encompasses the entire fullness of his pre-Easter life. Many of the paths taken by "discipleship" pick up on Jesus's life in the power of his resurrection. Although the church similarly understands itself as the "body of Christ," as the bearer of his post-Easter existence, the diaconal power of the life of Jesus and of the exalted Christ radiates considerably further out than merely into the institutionalized churches.

Demonstrating this requires that Christology explain that the resurrection was *not* a physical revivification, a mistaken notion found particularly (and emphatically) among fundamentalists and agnostics (and sometimes confused theologians as well; cf. part 2.1) who, having posited

---

4. Polkinghorne, *Science and Religion in Quest of Truth*, 121 (see introduction, note 4).

such a "resurrection," then, depending on their camp, either fanatically defend or derisively or indignantly deny it. This understanding, however, does not hold up to sound exegesis. That is, a certain level of knowledge and insight has also been attained with regard to the resurrection, a level below which one's position should not fall and yet one that does leave open further questions concerning the reality of the resurrection and of the divine Spirit that theology must address in the future (cf. parts 2.2–2.3).

Remaining issues include anthropological, pneumatological, and epistemological questions concerning the reality of the Spirit and concerning an understanding of the body that does justice to its status as both a natural and a psycho-pneumatological entity. Here theology is well advised to seek dialogue with philosophy, psychology, and the natural sciences, since what is involved is nothing less than the stirring question concerning intellectual, cognitive, and spiritual realities. Theology must consult and examine philosophical, psychological, and other scientific findings concerning cognitive or spiritual realities even if a theology of the Resurrected cannot be derived from the perspective of these particular disciplines and findings. Theology must instead begin with the transformation of Jesus's pre-Easter life into his post-Easter life if it is to stay the course of Christology in the stricter sense (parts 2.4–2.5).

3. Jesus's pre-Easter life and his resurrection serve God's revelation, and with this revelation ultimately also the saving, redemption, and elevation of both humanity and creation. The *soteriological* significance of revelation, however, emerges in its full seriousness and depth only if we realize that Jesus's earthly life moves toward his death on the cross, and that the resurrection involves nothing less than God's victorious confrontation with the powers and authorities that bring the world under the power of sin and Jesus onto the cross. What that cross ultimately reveals is that in his revelation, God has entered not only into an individual human life (incarnation), but also into the full depth of creaturely distress, including unfathomable suffering and the entanglement of human culpability (kenosis). What also becomes clear, however, is that the institutional and organizational forms that claim to guide human life through an orientation toward truth and justice—forms normally viewed as "benevolent powers," namely, politics, law, religion, morality, and public opinion—all work together on the cross *against* God's revelation (parts 3.3–3.4).

The discussion of sin and atonement, sacrifice and vicarious representation, introduces a whole array of phenomena that with these terms try to grasp the generation of the most extreme situations of distress and the most dangerous concealment. This difficult conceptual world requires further discussion and disclosure. It is at this point that theology cannot avoid dealing with nothing less than the very boundaries of the possibilities of moral, legal, political, and religious guidance and initiative. The various phenomena associated with "systemic distortion," to which the symbol of the cross as well as what have become largely incomprehensible references to "sin" are alluding, must yet be disclosed and articulated within incipient, still tentative dialogue with the scholarly disciplines of law, politics, and the social and cultural sciences (part 3.5).

A "theology of the cross" must similarly address not only God's own sympathetic suffering, but also God's creative and re-creative dealings with the presumptions and arrogations of human power, with sin, and with the curse of death. Here, too, this present Christology offers new conceptual approaches.

4. A nuanced christological disclosure of Jesus's pre-Easter life, his resurrection, and his cross makes it possible to develop more fully what is known as "high Christology," the doctrine of the exalted Christ and his divinity, picking up on both the biblical traditions themselves and classic theological positions. Calvin's doctrine of the "threefold office of Christ," namely, the royal, priestly, and prophetic, offers an important stimulus for this Christology, a doctrine intimately connected with the realization that the resurrected Christ "pours out" his spirit precisely so that his witnesses will come to participate in his royal, priestly, and prophetic ministry (cf. part 4.1). This doctrine of the threefold office organizes and structures the plethora of often diffuse expectations made on the Messiah, the Anointed. Old Testament kings, priests, and prophets were anointed at being installed in their offices, and as anointed office bearers they were charged with executing those offices and with doing justice to the expectations made on them by both God and human beings. By contrast, because Jesus Christ is far more than merely an office bearer, occasional references to him as an "official" evoke false associations; even the frequent asseveration in more recent theology that Christology must "overcome" the classic separation of person and office falls short of the mark, failing as it does to grasp adequately the task associated with the doctrine of the pre- and post-Easter Jesus Christ.

As Calvin quite rightly emphasizes, Christ does not exercise his own threefold office "without his own"; the resurrected and exalted Christ "pours out his spirit" in order to fill his witnesses with his own powers. This present Christology's discussion of the "threefold gestalt of Christ's reign" (cf. parts 4.4, 5.3–5.5) illustrates the breadth of the Messiah's ministry and activity, which in its own turn quite possibly takes in certain aspects of the conceptual world associated with the "Son of Man," equipped with heavenly power (see in this regard part 1.5).

The resurrected and exalted Christ must be perceived and understood in both continuity and discontinuity with the pre-Easter Jesus. The doctrine of the threefold office discloses that it is in Christ's royal dominion that the influence and ministry of the pre-Easter Jesus and his proclamation of God's coming reign acquire their *post-Easter* form, through which both Jesus and his followers—"his own"—continue and develop further his diaconal ministry, his message of love, and his nonviolent changes to various forms of human dominion and rule. It is in this gestalt of God's reign, a form showing that an ethos of love, of free, creative self-withdrawal on behalf of others, is stronger than the powers of self-preservation, that the Resurrected now rules in the power of his spirit, which he bestows on "his own" and in which he constitutes the royal gestalt of his reign. It is in this free, creative self-withdrawal that human life on behalf of other life grows, as it were, beyond itself, overcoming finitude in an exemplary fashion and defying the threats of the power of that finitude. "For love is strong as death" (Song 8:6).[5] The level of understanding attained by this consideration of the *royal* gestalt of God's reign must be maintained—though this present Christology similarly marks out other, additional paths of understanding that might be taken. Though the classical doctrine of the threefold office has often run aground or become somewhat rigid in its classification and arrangement of the various functions of the "office bearer"—the doctrine of the threefold shape or form of God's reign must focus on the dynamic interrelation of the processes of life and development as defined or contoured by the person of Jesus himself and the charisma of his spirit.

5. The worship presence—in the narrower sense—of the resurrected and exalted Christ is revealed in his priestly office or in the priestly gestalt of his reign. Within the context of a truly christological, pneumatological, and biblical orientation, worship services, though perhaps rigidified within crippling liturgical and rhetorical routines in some western industrial nations, can still offer an enormously dynamic sense of the mediated and received experience and knowledge of God to their congregations, a sense that can, moreover, become clearer still in light of the sacraments of baptism and Holy Communion. Here theological reflection is charged with grasping the pivotal change of dominion that comes about in baptism and the luminous power of the presence of the Resurrected in Holy

5. Paul Mendes-Flohr revealed to me the considerable significance the Song of Solomon has not only for the connection between religious and familial thinking and experience in Jewish theology, but also within Sabbath culture.

Communion, for what these central sacramental events disclose is nothing less than a nuanced experience of the presence of the triune God.

Understandably, some churches focus on discipleship to Christ through diaconal service, while others find their fundamental point of departure and high point in liturgy and the celebration of Holy Communion—this present Christology culminates in a presentation of Christ's prophetic office and the prophetic gestalt of God's reign (parts 5.5–5.6), which complements and expands the reign's diaconal charisma, refining, moreover, our sensibility for the multifarious hindrances to Christ's royal dominion, not only outside, but inside the institutionalized churches as well. It stirs ever anew our passion for questions of truth, the quest for justice, and our engagement on behalf of truth and justice even to the point of non-violent resistance. It is through the prophetic gestalt of God's reign, however, that the priestly dimension also acquires its gravity. The institutions of worship celebration, pastoral care, doctrine, and proclamation must all constantly be protected against the dangers of overly self-confident, detached rituals and rhetorical routines. On the one hand, the prophetic form of discipleship to Christ embraces the contemporary questions and tribulations that affect human beings and their surroundings; on the other hand, it simultaneously maintains a sense for the expansiveness and creativity of the revelation event itself in the sense evoked by Paul: "I consider that the sufferings of this present time are not worth comparing with the glory about to be revealed to us" (Rom 8:18).

5.2 The Value and Limits of the Classic Doctrine of the Two Natures (Nicene Creed, Chalcedonian Definition, Barth, Tillich, Bonhoeffer, Coakley)

From the perspective of the resurrection, the cross proves to be a revelatory event that reveals far more than the suffering God. It discloses that those particular earthly powers that are indispensable for human communal life and thus also generally viewed without question as being benevolent—namely, religion, law, morality, politics, and public opinion—that precisely these powers can be subject to corruption and as a result become extremely dangerous. These powers, though seeming to ensure justice, maintain morality, even act in a way pleasing to God, preserve religiously inviolable values and lend an ear to the voice of healthy public opinion, can nonetheless work together in bringing about disaster and ruin—just as was the case when they united in bringing about Jesus's death on the cross. Instead of simply opposing these powers as such, the resurrected and exalted Christ unmasks their fateful and disastrous activities under the power of sin. At the same time, he summons and enables human beings to become engaged in the grand countermovement characterized by mutual service, by worship-centered assembly and sending, by the prophetic search for justice and truth, and by an assurance of that very truth. From the perspective of the cross, the resurrected and exalted Christ reveals that God can create something new and good from what is bad and malevolent; it is in that sense that the cross and resurrection reveal God's creative and re-creative activity.

It is not merely the self-endangerment and self-destruction in which human beings and human society engage that the cross reveals, nor merely their imprisonment—their active and passive entanglement—under the power of sin; the cross and resurrection also reveal that and how God deals with powers that while *seeming* to protect and help us, in fact either knowingly or unknowingly lead us to ruin. Nor is this event to be taken merely as a judgment on certain institutions and social powers. It also judges individual human beings and their religiosity, their morality, their political loyalties, and their allegedly healthy common sense. It judges us as human beings who support these very powers, as human beings who while believing we are being protected by those powers repeatedly and ever again also suffer under them.

The cross and resurrection, revealing not only the sin of the world but also God's mighty but still disputed dealing and reckoning with that sin, do *not* refer us to a numinous God who somehow lives and acts and holds sway in some transcendent background. It is as the *radically re-creative*

God that God reveals himself in overcoming the absolute self-entanglement and hopeless condition of the world as disclosed on the cross. The radically re-creative God alone can lead out of the bondage to sin into which human beings have fallen. It is the resurrected and exalted Christ that reveals the "God of God, Light of Light, very God of very God" as formulated in the confession of faith of the First Council of Nicaea (325).[1] This particular formulation was picked up by the expanded confession we know as the Nicene Creed, though the latter in its own turn essentially did not acquire its finished form until the year 381 in Constantinople, which is also why it bears the rather circumstantial title Niceno-Constantinopolitan Creed (*Nicaeno-Constantinopolitanum*).[2] Unlike the western Apostles' Creed,[3] this confession has since 451 been viewed in both the East and West as authoritative, a status it has maintained unbroken—albeit with one significant textual variation[4]—up to the present.[5]

1. "Creed of Nicea (325)," in *Creeds of the Church: A Reader in Christian Doctrine from the Bible to the Present*, ed. John Leith, rev. ed. (Richmond, VA: John Knox Press, 1973), 30–31; cf. Henricus Denzinger, *Enchiridion Symbolorum. Definitionum et Declarationum de Rebus Fidei et Morum* (Freiburg: Herder, 1955), 29f (hereafter cited as Denzinger).

2. Philip Schaff, *Creeds of Christendom*, vol. 1, *The History of the Creeds* (New York: Harper, 1877), 28–29 (Nicene Creed of 325 and Constantinopolitan Creed of 381 juxtaposed); Denzinger, 41f.

3. Schaff, *Creeds of Christendom*, 1:21–22 (old Roman form and received form juxtaposed); Denzinger, 1ff; attested since the 6th century.

4. See in this regard *Spirit of God, Spirit of Christ: Ecumenical Reflections on the Filioque Controversy*, ed. Lukas Vischer (London: SPCK; Geneva : World Council of Churches, 1981), esp. the contributions by André de Halleux, "Towards an ecumenical agreement on the procession of the Holy Spirit and the addition of the filioque to the creed," 69-84; Boris Bobrinskoy, "Filioque yesterday and today," 133-148; Jürgen Moltmann, "Theological proposals towards the resolution of the filioque controversy," 164-173; Dumitru Staniloae, "Procession of the Holy Spirit from the Father and his relation to the Son, as the basis of our deification and adoption," 174-186. Concerning the fertile differences between Staniloae and Moltmann with respect to the *filioque* issue, see Daniel Munteanu, *Der tröstende Geist der Liebe. Zu einer ökumenischen Lehre vom Heiligen Geist über die trinitarischen Theologien J. Moltmanns und D. Staniloaes* (Neukirchen-Vluyn: Neukirchener, 2003), esp. 108ff, 162ff. See also Bernd Oberdorfer, *Filioque. Geschichte und Theologie eines ökumenischen Problems*, FSÖTh 96 (Göttingen: Vandenhoeck, 2001); Kathryn Tanner, *Christ the Key, Current Issues in Theology*, 3rd ed. (Cambridge, UK: Cambridge University Press, 2011), 188ff.

5. See John Norman Davidson Kelly, *Early Christian Creeds* (New York: D. McKay Co. [1972]), 296ff; see the assessment of this study in Alois Grillmeier, *From the Apostolic Age to Chalcedon (451)*, trans. John Bowden, 2nd ed. (London: Mowbray, 1975), 480ff; idem, *Fragmente zur Christologie. Studien zum altkirchlichen Christusbild*, ed. Theresia Hainthaler (Freiburg/Basel/Wien: Herder, 1997), 112ff; Lewis Ayres, *Nicaea and its Legacy: An Approach to Fourth-Century Trinitarian Theology* (Oxford: Oxford University Press, 2004; reprint 2006), 85ff.

Jesus Christ is "God of God, Light of Light, very God of very God." The Nicene Creed clarifies this by explicating the unique relationship between Jesus Christ and God the Creator, on the one hand, and the unique relationship between Christ and the earthly world, on the other. Jesus Christ is not created, but is rather of one essence with the Creator (*homoousios*). He is the uniquely born Son of God, and was so "before all worlds" or ages. This same Son of God, begotten of God before all ages, is, however, simultaneously a true human being, born of the young woman Mary, and a human being who really, physically lived on this earth, was crucified under Pontius Pilate, suffered, and was buried.

The *Nicaeno-Constantinopolitanum* presents this interrelation between divinity and humanity as a descent from heaven on behalf of us human beings and our salvation, then as resurrection and exaltation into heaven to participate in the dominion of the Creator, and finally as his anticipated "coming in glory" to judge the living and the dead. Amid all this movement down from heaven, back up to heaven, to divine dominion, to participation in that dominion, and back down in glory for judgment—in all this movement, Christ is the Lord of all human beings, exercising his divine lordship, maintaining a reign that "shall have no end."

In his own interpretation of the second article of the Apostles' Creed in the *Small Catechism*,[6] Luther summarizes this point with existential urgency, emphasizing that the second article confesses that Jesus Christ, truly God and truly human, is "my Lord," who appropriated *me* for himself "in order that I might be his, live under him in his kingdom, and serve him in eternal righteousness, innocence, and blessedness." And Christ effected this appropriation of human beings for himself through his suffering and his death, through which he "delivered me from all sins, from death, and from the power of the devil." Christ's divinity is stated once quite succinctly with respect to his unique relationship with the Creator, then also with respect to his movement "between heaven and earth" (incarnation, resurrection, ascension, and Parousia for judgment), and finally through the establishment of God's eternal reign, for which human beings are appropriated through Christ's own dying and resurrection. This orientation toward spatial movements "from above" and "from below" then became the abstract orientational foundation for numerous Christologies.

The ancient church's grand creeds strictly adhere to the notion that Christ's true humanity be stressed along with his divinity, a position,

6. *The Small Catechism of Dr. Martin Luther*, trans. H. Wetzel (Woodstock, Va.: n.p., 1872), 5.

however, necessarily prompting some extremely awkward doctrinal formulations that initially demanded the articulation of an (ultimately Trinitarian) *self-differentiation within God* without abandoning the doctrine
of the *one* God. The task, namely, to grasp and articulate at once both the
unity *and* difference between Jesus Christ's divinity and humanity, was
to be accomplished by what is known as the *doctrine of two natures*. We
can get a clearer picture of the problems this doctrine faced by examining Karl Barth's explication of the *Nicaeno-Constantinopolitanum*, and
Paul Tillich's critique of the doctrine of two natures, and with a consideration of some of the theological queries made on the classic formulations
that emerged from the Council of Chalcedon in what is known as the
Chalcedonian Definition.[7]

Self-Differentiation in God

Karl Barth's point of departure in his own explication to the *Nicaeno-
Constantinopolitanum* is that Christ's divinity cannot be understood as
an apotheosis, that is, as the deification of an individual human being,
even a great human being. Nor can it be interpreted either individualisti-
cally or collectively, as if referring to the personification of a great idea
or universal truth.[8] Barth relentlessly emphasizes how human beings
are incapable of attaining knowledge of God on their own initiative; because we are God's adversaries, because we stand in opposition to God,
God must enable us *from within this very situation* to recognize that
Jesus Christ is God's Son and our Lord. It is nothing less than a miracle
that takes place in and with regard to the fallen world in this sense, for
nothing less than a miracle is required to bring about this knowledge of
Christ. Barth trenchantly expresses this in stating that just as creation
is *creation ex nihilo*, so also is reconciliation an act of an awaking of the
dead. Just as we owe life to God the Creator, so also do we owe eternal
life to God the Reconciler.

Grasping this requires first that we understand that it is not revela-

7. In the year 451; *The Ecumenical Documents of Faith*, ed. T. Herbert Bindley (London: Methuen &Co., 1899), 292–94; Denzinger, 70f (see part 5.2, note 1).

8. Cf. Barth, *CD I/1*, § 11, God the Son, 399ff (parenthetical pagination in the following discussion refers to this text). Concerning Barth's doctrinal understanding, see Walter
Kreck, *Grundentscheidungen in Karl Barths Dogmatik. Zur Diskussion seines Verständ-
nisses von Offenbarung und Erwählung*, Neukirchener Studienbücher 11 (Neukirchen-
Vluyn: Neukirchener, 1978), 82ff; though also Hans Urs von Balthasar, *The Theology of
Karl Barth: Exposition and Interpretation*, trans. Edward T. Oakes (San Francisco: Com-
munio Books, Ignatius Press, 1992), 107ff; Eberhard Jüngel, *Barth-Studien*, Ökumenische
Theologie 9 (Zürich/Köln, Gütersloh: Benziger, Gütersloher, 1982), 136ff.

tion and reconciliation that create Christ's divinity, but rather Christ's divinity that creates revelation and reconciliation (cf. 475f). Barth summarizes as follows: "He is the Son or the Word of God *for us*, because he was so previously *in himself*" (476). Barth is, of course, acutely aware that his emphasis of the expression "previously in himself" can be viewed and discredited as metaphysical speculation (cf. 476f). He cites Luther with considerable sympathy, who insists that the path to God must lead "from below upward," that is, from human nature up to knowledge of God's divinity. Barth, however, nonetheless considers his emphasis on "previously *in himself*" to be an important point lest the notion of *God-being for us* be taken as a *necessary* attribute of God.

Barth considers any notion that human beings are somehow indispensable for God to be dangerous, untheological speculation (cf. 420f). "Undoubtedly the dogma of Christ's deity snaps any correlation between the divine revelation and human faith" (422).[9]

Following these introductory considerations, Barth explicates the second article of the *Nicaeno-Constantinopolitanum*, which he considers to be the "most important record of the dogma of the deity of Christ" (423). He finds the notion of "being previously in himself" also brought to expression in the understanding of the mode of being of the "only begotten Son of God," in the assertion that Christ is in fact the one begotten by the Father before all time. "'Begotten of the Father before all time' means that He did not come into being in time as such, that He did not come into being in an event within the created world" (426). The assertion that Christ is "light of light, very God of very God, begotten, not made" means, on the one hand, that "in God's work and essence we have to *distinguish* light and light, God and God . . . Then we have to understand this distinction as a distinction in *God Himself*. We have not to understand it as though there were God on the one side and a creature on the other, but in such a way that the one God is found equally on both sides" (427; my emphasis). What we have to grasp here is a differentiated "being within itself," and in so doing, according to Barth, we are focusing on the "dialectic of revelation."

Barth repeatedly emphasizes that such references to begetting and

---

9. " . . . the illegitimate metaphysics in which the Reformers obviously did not indulge consists in absolutizing the correlation that we suppose we can attain and survey and understand, in regarding it as the reality in which God has as it were delivered Himself up to man and human thought and speech, instead of remembering that our being in the relation may always be pure illusion, and our thought within it and speech about it may always be pure ideology, if they are not grounded in God Himself and continually confirmed by God Himself. Because and to the extent that what the dogma states is true, that God's Word is the Word of God, for that reason and to that extent the correlation is also true" (422).

birth involve a "frail and contestable figure of speech" (431), and that because we are here approaching the limits of language any attempts to illustrate these concepts will necessarily be both problematical and dangerous. "We can speak of the truth only in untruth. We do not know what we are saying when we call God Father and Son" (433), and yet this assertion *does* clarify some things. "Begetting is *less* than creating inasmuch as the former denotes the bringing forth of creature from creature whereas the latter denotes the bringing forth of the creature by the Creator. Yet begetting is also *more* than creating inasmuch as—and here the closed circle of creature and creature as we see it in what we know as begetting is a figure—it denotes the bringing forth *of God* from God, whereas creating denotes only the bringing forth of the *creature* by God" (433; my emphasis).

This intensified notion—compared to creation in the normal sense—of *bringing forth from God within God* is intended to be understood with respect to God's revelation in Christ. Barth believes that the statement "Jesus Christ is the Word of God" similarly expresses this internal differentiation within God, notwithstanding it was not included in the *Nicaeno-Constantinopolitanum*.[10] Hence the differentiation and unity within God does indeed come to various expression in revelation, and yet precisely the inadequacy of any one figure of speech makes it "inadvisable to bring the concept of the deity of Christ" under any single denominator (cf. 437).

The statement that we believe Jesus Christ to be "*of one essence with the father*" (438) is directed against any understanding that may permit the internal distinctions within God to rigidify, so to speak, into two Gods, something the expression "of one essence" precludes. The expression "of one essence" similarly precludes the (Arian) misunderstanding that Jesus Christ was merely a "superman," or, as Barth puts it, a "demigod from below" (439), though equally the (subordinationist) misunderstanding of Jesus Christ as a "demi-god from above" subordinated to the first person of the Godhead. This powerful reference to Jesus as being *of one essence* with the Father thus simultaneously precludes several extremes of false doctrine.

The final turn of phrase Barth explicates in his discussion here reads as follows: "We believe in Jesus Christ '*by whom all things were made*'"

---

10. It does, Barth maintains, nonetheless state the same thing as does the metaphor of the Son of God. "One may perhaps say that the first term [Son of God] is more to the point when we understand God's action in Jesus Christ materially as reconciliation, and the second [Word of God] is more to the point when we understand the action formally as revelation" (434).

(441; my emphasis), which incorporates a literal citation from John 1:3.[11] Human understanding stands utterly helpless before this statement if, as is usually the case, it confuses *creation* with *nature* and *cosmos* or reduces the former to the latter. According to Barth, this expression directs us back to the event of revelation in the awaking; he emphasizes that Jesus Christ is the word through which God created the world out of nothing, and precisely as this word of the Father, it—in contrast to everything created through him—is equal to the Father—it is true God from eternity. Following Thomas Aquinas,[12] Barth risks asserting that God's word is not only the "precise image of the Father," but also "the original of the world" (443). In any case, for Barth the participation of the Son in God's creative work does make it clear that God, the Son, comes to "his own possession" through becoming human (John 1:11) (443).

Problems with the Doctrine of Two Natures

The doctrine of God's internal self-differentiation is but one step toward clarifying the unity and difference between Jesus Christ's divinity and humanity. Paul Tillich assessed the grand epistemological efforts undertaken by the early church that ultimately led to the creation of the christological dogma:

> The dogmatic work of the early church centers in the creation of the christological dogma. All other doctrinal statements—above all, those concerning God and man, the Spirit, and the Trinity—provide the presuppositions, or are the consequences, of the christological dogma. . . . The basic attacks on the Christian dogma are implicitly or explicitly on the Christological level.[13]

---

11. Similarly John 1:10; 1 Cor 8:6; Col 1:15f; Heb 1:2. Concerning the extremely difficult clarification of the connections between Christology, logos theology, and the doctrine of creation, cf. Winrich Löhr, "Logos," in *Reallexikon für Antike und Christentum*, vol. XXIII (2010), 406ff; Pannenberg, *Systematic Theology*, vol. 2, 22ff, 26ff (see part 2.2, note 1).

12. Thomas Aquinas, *Summa Theologica,* I qu. 34 art. 3; concerning the fruitful approach of the question concerning the "whether in Christ there is only one operation of the godhead and manhood," cf. III qu. 19 art. 1, and concerning the question of the "causality of the resurrection of Christ," cf. III qu. 56. Concerning the attempts of the Scholastics (following Aquinas) to distinguish a "threefold activity of Christ," cf. Karl Adam, *The Christ of Faith: The Christology of the Church*, trans. Joyce Crick (New York: Pantheon Books, 1957), 189ff; concerning the "crisis of the metaphysical idea of God" cf. Friedrich Mildenberger, *Biblische Dogmatik. Eine Biblische Theologie in dogmatischer Perspektive*, vol. 2: Ökonomie als Theologie (Stuttgart/Berlin/Köln: Kohlhammer, 1992), 12ff.

13. Tillich, *Systematic Theology*, II, 139 (see part 3.5, note 12) (parenthetical pagination in the following discussion refers to this work).

A dogma is a principle, a doctrinal statement, a binding statement of faith expressing a central content of faith such that it is capable of illuminating the interrelation between all insights of faith. Tillich quite rightly emphasizes that dogmas are created not out of any delight in religious speculation, but rather as "protective doctrines" meant to protect "the Christian message against distortions from outside or inside the church" (139–40). What Tillich laments is that the christological dogma—one so central to the church—was developed with such inadequate conceptual tools. In this context, he criticizes especially the doctrine of the "two natures," that is, the doctrine of the divine and human natures in Jesus Christ as classically formulated at the synod of Chalcedon:

> We confess one and the same Christ, Son, Lord, Only-begotten, to be acknowledged in two natures, inconfusedly, unchangeably, indivisibly, inseparably; the distinction of natures being by no means taken away by the union, but rather the property of each nature being preserved, and concurring in one Person and one hypostasis.[14]

Tillich does not simply lament that concepts were drawn here from conceptual and linguistic contexts essentially alien to the biblical traditions themselves. "Theology must be free from and for the concepts it uses" (142); although it *must* use universal concepts to express its message, it must at the same time constantly subject those concepts to critical examination (141). Tillich's fundamental objection is that the "doctrine of the two natures in the Christ raises the right question but uses wrong conceptual tools. The basic inadequacy lies in the term 'nature.' When applied to man, it is ambiguous; when applied to God, it is wrong" (142).

What, however, was the task with which the development of the christological dogma found itself confronted? According to Tillich, the dogma had to counter two potential misunderstandings: first, the denial of the character of *Christ* in Jesus as the Christ, and, second, the denial of the character of *Jesus* in Jesus as the Christ. A denial of the character of Christ in Jesus as the Christ obscures Christ's divinity.[15] Denying the character of Jesus in Jesus as the Christ risks falling into docetic Christology unable to express the true humanity of Christ and otherwise

---

14. *The Ecumenical Documents of Faith*, 297 (see part 5.2, note 7). Concerning the difficult concept of hypostasis, see Peter Lampe, "Hypostasis as a Component of New Testament Christology (Hebrews 1:3)," in *Who is Jesus Christ for Us Today?* 63–71 (see part 0.1, note 7).

15. This position risks falling into what is known as "Ebionite Christology," a doctrine Irenaeus attributed to certain Jewish-Christian circles that emphasized Jesus's mere humanity, notwithstanding Jesus did then receive particular distinction through his baptism.

inclined to assert that Christ's entire suffering and dying as well as the presence of the Resurrected were all merely "apparent."

This rather problematical terrain of balancing out the understanding of Christ's divinity and humanity drew the early church into a complicated dispute with heresies that in its own turn generated an extremely complex world of theological concepts. Tillich throws these problems into sharp relief by, among other things, juxtaposing the Arian and Athanasian positions. In Tillich's view, Athanasius rightly maintained that

> [o]nly the God who is really God can create the New Being, not a half-god. It was the term *homo-ousios*, "of equal essence," which was supposed to express this idea. But in that case, the semi-Arians asked, how could a difference exist between the Father and the Son, and does not the picture of the Jesus of history become completely ununderstandable? It was hard for Athanasius and his most intimate followers . . . to answer such questions. (143)

Although dialectical attempts at mediation between "true divinity" and "true humanity" did generate a variety of tensions, false prioritization, and perspectival distortion, they did also result in fruitful dogmatic reflections that prevented, as Tillich put it, the Jesus-character of the Christ from being completely lost and the Christ-character of Jesus denied (145).

Nor does this task involve a merely theoretically interesting concern for the church, but rather an existentially necessary one insofar as it involves the ability to answer the question of salvation itself. Emphasizing only the divine nature generates the paradox of a supernatural miracle. "And salvation can be derived only from him who fully participated in man's existential predicament, not from a God walking on earth, 'unequal to us in all respects'" (146–47). Tillich, picking up on Luther's lead, accordingly emphasizes that Christology must begin with Christ's humanity, with his cross and with his suffering. Only a "low Christology," as he put it, "is the truly high Christology" (147).

Yet how can one then avoid resorting to the kind of Ebionite Christology that either prevents any insight into salvation or, certainly, certainty of salvation from being attained in the first place, or destroys such by emphasizing solely Jesus's humanity? Tillich's view is that such cannot happen when Christ's divine nature is emphasized because the concept of *nature* is itself ambiguous and misleading.

> The assertion that Jesus as the Christ is the personal unity of a divine and a human nature must be replaced by the assertion *that in Jesus as the Christ the eternal unity of God and man has become historical reality*. In his

being, the New Being is real, and the New Being is the re-established unity between God and man. We replace the inadequate concept "divine nature" by the concepts "eternal God-man-unity" or "Eternal God-Manhood." . . . by eliminating the concept of "two natures," which lie beside each other like blocks and whose unity cannot be understood at all, we are open to relational concepts which make understandable the dynamic picture of Jesus as the Christ. (148; my emphasis)

Bonhoeffer on the Problems of the Doctrine of Two Natures

In his Berlin lectures on Christology during the summer of 1933,[16] Dietrich Bonhoeffer, picking up on the Chalcedonian formula, developed several constructive proposals for addressing the problems attaching to the doctrine of two natures; the *Chalcedonense* reads: "We confess one and the same Christ, Son, Lord, Only-begotten, to be acknowledged in two natures, *inconfusedly, unchangeably, indivisibly, inseparably.*"[17]

Bonhoeffer uses these four definitions as his point of departure, emphasizing that they were originally directed against the so-called *Monophysites* (e.g., Appolinaris of Laodicea, Eutyches), who taught that both human and divine natures were united into a *single* nature, the divine nature, in Christ.[18] As Bonhoeffer puts it, according to this teaching, Christ was "not an individual person; instead, he put on human nature like a garment." The Monophysites introduced docetic forms that threaten to destroy Christology. "For if God's nature had not been revealed within our human nature, how then could our nature have been made divine, been redeemed and healed?" (340). By contrast, the Nestorians understood Jesus's unity with God as a unity of will, of attitude, a position rejected by the Council of Chalcedon as *dyophysitism*, as a sundering of the two natures. Bonhoeffer contrasts monophysitism and dyophysitism as follows:

The Monophysites taught the mystery of the unity of divine and human nature; the Nestorians made a plain distinction between them, emphasizing the rationality of two entities over against the mystery of their unity. With the former, the mystery of the deification of the human; with the latter,

16. Dietrich Bonhoeffer, "Lectures on Christology (Student Notes)," DBWE 12:299–360 (see part 4.5, note 12); parenthetical pagination in the following discussion refers to this edition.

17. *The Ecumenical Documents of Faith,* 297 (see part 5.2, note 7).

18. Concerning the difficulties attaching to the attribution of this statement of challenge, see Adolf Martin Ritter, "Monophysites/Monophysitism," in *Religion Past and Present,* vol. 8, 515-16.

> the ethos of the servant's will gradually raising itself toward God, yielding itself to the will of God. In the one, the brighter glow of passion, the greater fervor, the more tenacious insistence; in the other, greater clarity and sobriety of thinking. (341)

Monophysitism is heretical because in it, Christ's human nature is devoured by the divine nature; dyophysitism is heretical because in it, humanity and divinity are sundered such that the unity of the person of Christ can no longer be conceived. By contrast, the *Chalcedonense* emphasizes one Christ, one person, one hypostasis—but two natures, divine and human, in this one person. With considerable acumen, Bonhoeffer observes that this emphasis comes at the price of a whole array of defensive measures ("inconfusedly, unchangeably, indivisibly, inseparably") all of which together make it clear that one cannot speak about human and divine natures in Jesus Christ the same way as one can about things or facts. In their own turn, however, precisely these defensive measures—these negative formulations—introduced movement into theological reflection, movement that picks up these concepts of nature (or two natures) and then immediately bursts them. "The Chalcedonian formula is an objective, living assertion about Christ that goes beyond all conceptual forms. Everything is encompassed in its very clear yet paradoxical agility" (343). There is but a single Christ in two natures, natures which, however, are to be conceived as being without confusion, without change, without distinction, and without separation (cf. 342); this position eliminates any conceptual forms that try to comprehend the two natures within the circumstantial parameters of things or facts.

How is such unity, however, to be conceived and understood? The result of systematic theological thinking over the centuries was that it is to be conceived as *unio hypostatica*, as a unity of person that preserves the integrity of both natures—that of God in its divinity, essentiality, and unchangeableness, and that of the human being in its finitude and changeability. The two natures combine in Christ within a *unitio*, a unification, in a *unio personalis* and a *communio naturarum*, to be conceived as a unity of person and community of natures. Bonhoeffer clarifies this notion by remarking that though one can indeed say that God is the human being, one cannot say that divinity is humanity (cf. 344). The tradition of dogma has referred to this situation with the technical expression *communicatio idiomatum*, that is, a mutual communication of characteristics between the two natures, a notion it developed or explicated in various forms, the most important being the *genus majestaticum*. "This asserts that the attributes of the divine nature can and must be expressed by the human nature" (345). Bonhoeffer, however, quite clearly sees that if such is done, for example, through such problematic statements as "Jesus is all-powerful" or "Jesus is ever-present," the doctrine risks falling into monophysitism, the transformation of the human nature into the divine nature—a situation calling into question the qualifications "inconfusedly, unchangeably" of the *Chalcedonense*.[19]

The high point in the development of this doctrine of the two natures within the history of dogma was what is known as the *kenosis* dispute during the seventeenth century between theologians at the universities in Tübingen and Giessen. More precisely, the dispute was between the so-called *kenotics* and *cryptics* (347). The *kenotics*, in Giessen, emphasized that the unity of the two natures was to be conceived such that in becoming human, Christ *renounced* any concrete use of the divine attributes, while the *cryptics*, in Tübingen, taught that rather than Christ renouncing use of these divine attributes, they were instead *veiled* after he became human.

Bonhoeffer comments that the cryptics, by insisting "on the identity of the one who became human . . . with the God-human," thereby tend toward a docetic Christology. By contrast, the kenotics follow Philippians 2 in emphasizing that the humiliation was real, that "Christ really died" (347–48). Unfortunately, this notion, too, is only inadequately expressed by *kenosis*, since if "Christ is said to have been continually suppressing in himself the exercise of his divine attributes," (333) then the reality of his renunciation is lost. In 1624 the kenotics and cryptics came to an agreement through the Salomonic (or, as Bonhoeffer puts it, the "inelegant") formulation that the "humiliated Christ made use of his godly attributes when he wanted to and did not use them when he did not want to" (348; altered translation). Bonhoeffer believed that by including its negative restrictions, the theology of the *Chalcedonense* represents a superior position precisely by tenaciously holding at bay such speculations concerning unity and difference. For Bonhoeffer, the *Chalcedonense* represents the exemplary attempt to focus on the reality of Jesus Christ by

19. Reformed theology countered with the assertion *finitum incapax infiniti*, namely, that the finite is incapable of taking on (or taking up) the infinite, a position that in its own turn generated difficulties by emphasizing that the *logos* is everywhere even though the God-human was at a specific locale, the famous *extra calvinisticum*, Calvin's doctrine that the *logos* remained outside human nature even after uniting with it. Lutherans countered with the assertion that though the finite was indeed not of itself capable of taking on the infinite, it was capable of such through the infinite itself: *finitum capax infiniti non per se sed per infinitum*. They then tried to grasp this interrelation between the two natures by developing the doctrine of Christ's two states, the *status exinanitionis* (state of humiliation) and the *status exaltationis* (state of exaltation), which facilitates conceiving the dynamic of the incarnational and becoming human as a process (concerning the complex problems attaching to creation theology and pneumatology in Bonhoeffer, cf. 345ff).

"letting the fact of the God-human stand as the presupposition" (352); it is precisely this decision to let that fact stand that was the result of the Christology of the *Chalcedonense*.

Any and all attempts to construe a God-human are rejected, including, on the one hand, an unequivocally positive statement concerning Jesus Christ allowing us to speak about Christ in an undifferentiated fashion, as well as, on the other hand, a conception that construes, juxtaposes, or interrelates the two natures after the fashion of two "things." Any reflection on the "how"-question is similarly rejected, namely, "how" divinity and humanity may or may not be distinct or related. The consistent focus here is, as Bonhoeffer says, a "positive Christology" that while incorporating once again the auxiliary constructs of the "two natures" simultaneously leaves them behind.

Bonhoeffer summarizes:

> Who is this God? He is the God who became human as we became human. He is completely human. Nothing human is foreign to him. The human being that I am is what Jesus Christ was also. We say of this human being, Jesus Christ, that he is God. . . . This person's being God is not something added onto the being human of Jesus Christ. (353)

Yet how are we to conceive or understand this "being God" with respect to human beings? It is

> *God's judgment about this human being!* It is God's Word, which takes this human being Jesus Christ and qualifies him as God. But the essential difference [between him and all other human beings] is that the Word of God that comes from above is at the same time right here in Jesus Christ himself. Because Jesus is himself God's judgment about him, he points both to himself and God. (354; altered translation)

God commits himself in Jesus Christ. God passes judgment on this human being that is at once also God's judgment on himself, that is, God's self-commitment. Thus does Bonhoeffer try to understand God's revelation in Jesus Christ. God considers it his honor to be there in human form. God considers it his honor to reveal himself as Creator in the creature. It is *this event*, as revealed in Christ, that must serve as our point of departure, not some idea of God or of human beings, nor some abstractly conceived divine nature or abstractly conceived human nature—but rather this particular event as revealed in the resurrection. God commits himself by qualifying the human being Jesus Christ as God. The defensive formulations of the *Chalcedonense* urge us to accept this reality and not look beyond it. They urge us to begin with the human being Jesus Christ, to discern and confess the deity in him, to discern therein as well our own involvement in his life and by doing so to acquire certainty concerning our own purpose in participating in God's life. Understanding and developing this insight further is the task of Christology.

What Does *Chalcedon* Accomplish?

Sarah Coakley has examined the capacity and influence of classic-dogmatic findings and statements in general and of the *Chalcendonense* in particular in a subtle and insightful investigation.[20] She first discusses Richard Norris's proposal that *Chalcedon* originally intended to offer merely a linguistic regulation (146).[21] Although she concurs with his observation that it does not really offer any clear definitions for "nature" and "hypostasis," she nonetheless thinks it inappropriate to think of "second-order guidelines" in the sense suggested by George Lindbeck, or to play these off against "first-order affirmations about the inner being of God or of Jesus Christ" (cf. 150). Polemic guided by a modern zeitgeist against "reification" fail to recognize that even linguistic regulations are not without ontological commitment[22] (cf. 152).

As early as 1985, Janet Soskice, warning against naïve theological realism capable of assuming both religious and anti-religious forms, advocated dealing quite carefully with the boundaries of what descriptive language is actually able to accomplish, yet also demonstrated how metaphorical language both in the (natural) sciences and in religious contexts can indeed be employed with meaningful results.[23] Addressing John Hicks's objection that orthodoxy and *Chalcedon* were unable to provide any real content to the doctrine of the two natures,[24] and that references

---

20. Sarah Coakley, "What Does Chalcedon Solve and What Does It Not? Some Reflections on the Status and Meaning of the Chalcedonian 'Definition,'" in *The Incarnation: An Interdisciplinary Symposium on the Incarnation of the Son of God*, ed. Stephen T. Davis, Daniel Kendall, and Gerald O'Collins (Oxford: Oxford University Press, 2002), 143–63 (parenthetical pagination in the following discussion refers to this edition). Cf. also Gerald O'Collins, "The Incarnation: The Critical Issues," in ibid., 1ff; Rowan Williams, "Jesus Christus, II. Alte Kirche," TRE 16 (1988), 726–45.

21. Cf. Richard Norris, "Chalcedon Revisited: A Historical and Theological Reflection," in *New Perspectives on Historical Theology*, ed. Bradley Nassif (Grand Rapids: Eerdmans, 1996), 140–58.

22. Complete explications can be found in Coakley's section I, "Chalcedon as 'Linguistic Regulation.'"

23. Cf. Janet Martin Soskice, *Metaphor and Religious Language* (Oxford: Clarendon, repr. 1988), esp. 142ff, 151ff; concerning the anthropological and ethical significance of these insights, see idem, *The Kindness of God: Metaphor, Gender, and Religious Language* (Oxford: Oxford University Press, 2007), esp. 7ff, 157f.

24. John Hick, "Jesus and the World Religions," in idem, ed., *The Myth of God Incarnate* (London: SCM Press, 1977), 167–85, 178.

to the incarnation were to be understood merely metaphorically,[25] Coakley in her own turn warns against believing that metaphorical speech puts us at a remove from reality rather than engaging it (cf. 154). Pointing out how references to paradox—in the sense of "contrary to expectation"—is frequently negatively assessed as being incoherent or self-contradictory, she describes how the *positive* meaning would by contrast emphasize the promissory character of a given reality, that is, that particular element in the reality that does indeed surprise us—and it is in this sense, so Coakley, that *Chalcedon* uses metaphorical language.

Coakley also throws considerable light on the multifaceted wealth of so-called literal or actual language, language often critically juxtaposed over against "merely" metaphorical language insofar as such "literal" language is accompanied by considerable expectations of reliability (156ff). Coakley argues that the confessional formulations of *Chalcedon* (and of Nicaea) look back at a salvific event on whose ontological reality they steadfastly insist. The confession's interest in regulative and metaphorical language, Coakley maintains, by no means implies any lack of ontological commitment (cf. 160). Although the confession's language does indeed establish a *horizon*, a framework and boundaries, it at once also respects the boundaries and limits of language about God, guided not by speculative enthusiasm for the concealed, indiscernible nature of God, but by respect—oriented toward revelation—for God's special reality.[26]

This present study has quite consciously positioned these classic christological documents of dogmatic development within the perspectives of twentieth- and early twenty-first-century theology. Both the Nicene Creed and the *Chalcedonense* think emphatically in dualistic structures such as Father and Son, God from God, above and below, heaven and earth, divinity and humanity, and two natures—structures similarly followed by interpretations presented during our own age. The *Nicaeno-Constantinopolitanum*, by explicitly adding explications concerning the Holy Spirit, moves the discussion toward the sort of Trinitarian, ecclesiological, and eschatological thinking that can be expressed inadequately—if at all—in and with such dualistic structures.

---

25. John Hick, *The Metaphor of God Incarnate* (London: SCM Press, 1993), 104.

26. Cf. also Sarah Coakley, *Powers and Submissions: Spirituality, Philosophy and Gender* (Oxford, Malden: Blackwell, 2002), 40ff, 130ff, concerning "contemplation" and "spiritual senses" following the initiative of Dom John Chapman and Wittgenstein. David Brown, *The Divine Trinity* (La Salle: Open Court, 1985), 159ff, strongly advocates examining from the perspective of pneumatology and biblical theology the possibility of reacquiring early-church doctrinal materials.

This shortcoming can be addressed by theological reflection, oriented toward worship and sacrament, concerning Christ's priestly presence in the power of his spirit, and biblically oriented reflection concerning his prophetic presence in communities that seek truth and justice. Such a perspective can develop and enhance what these doctrines concerning God's differentiated unity and two natures in one person tried to express succinctly and to the point, namely, that God revealed himself in Jesus Christ, and that through him, who became human, was resurrected and exalted, God reveals himself.

5.3 Christ's Priestly Presence with His Own and the Liberating Power of Faith: Worship and Baptism as Change of Lordship

Christ's royal ministry and his reign's royal gestalt are multidimensional and possess enormous charismatic power not only in churches and religions, in education, assistance, and diaconal organizations and institutions, and in morality and law. Christ's priestly office and the priestly gestalt of his reign similarly exhibit pronounced influential power, though rather less expansive charisma (see part 4.4).

The powerful voice of the letter to the Hebrews has often prompted the *priestly dimension* of the lordship of Jesus Christ and his reign to focus on the rather difficult theme of "high priest and sacrificial cult."[1] Jesus Christ is the eternal[2] high priest, chosen by God himself, who presents offerings not in the earthly temple, but in heaven, "that he might be a merciful and faithful high priest in the service of God, to make a sacrifice of atonement for the sins of the people" (Heb 2:17).[3] Here the letter to the Hebrews establishes a broad connection between the heavenly high priest chosen by God, who sits at the right hand of God (Heb 1:3; 8:1), to the misery and suffering of the "shepherd of the sheep" (Heb 2:5–18; 13:20) who goes to his death.[4] Although this consideration does indeed address one of the central areas of ministry of the exalted Christ, it does not encompass the entire breadth of participation he grants in his life through the power of his spirit, and similarly encompasses only part of his priestly ministry.

Over against this constriction of the *munus sacerdotale*,[5] Jesus

1. Heb 2:17; 3:1; 4:14f; 5:1ff; 6:20; 7:26ff; 8:1ff; 9:7ff, 24ff; 10:1ff.10ff; 13:11ff; cf. Romano Guardini, *The Lord* (Chicago: Henry Regnery, 1954; renewed 1982), 543ff.

2. " . . . according to the order of Melchizedek," Heb 5:6,10; 6:20; 7:1, 10, 11, 15, 17, picking up on an obscure figure in Ps 110:4 and Gen 14:1–24 that combines the office of king and priest. Cf. Erich Grässer, *An die Hebräer (Hebr 1–6)*, EKK XVII/1 and *(Hebr 7,1–10,18)*, EKK XVII/2 (Zürich/Braunschweig, Neukirchen-Vluyn: Benziger and Neukirchener, 1990 and 1993), vol. 1:288ff; vol. 2:9f. Grässer describes Melchizedek, following Hermann Gunkel, historically as a "Canaanite city-king with a sacral function, as the prototype of the Jebusite priest king" (ibid., vol. 2:13).

3. Concerning sacrificial theology in the letter to the Hebrews, see Brandt, *Opfer als Gedächtnis*, 174–204 (see part 3.5, note 23).

4. Cf. John Macquarrie, *Jesus Christ in Modern Thought* (London: SCM Press, 1990), 128ff; Samuel Vollenweider, "Christozentrisch oder theozentrisch? Christologie im Neuen Testament," in *Marburger Jahrbuch Theologie XXIII: Christologie*, 28f (concerning the *Jahrbuch*, see part 3.3, note 35).

5. The attendant difficulties seem to have prompted Karl Barth, in his discussion of the doctrine of Christ's threefold office, to replace explications concerning Christ the high

Christ's priestly ministry must first be discerned within the breadth and multidimensionality of the worship event as such. As previously mentioned, Francis Fiorenza has drawn attention to how the appearances of the resurrected Christ with the greeting of peace, breaking of bread, disclosure of scripture, baptismal directive, and missionary commissioning of the disciples already outline the fundamental forms of the life of worship in the (early) church and its charismatic power.[6] Greeting of peace, Holy Communion, baptism, exposition of scripture, sending—a polyphony of worship existence is associated with this priestly office, an office in which the "universal priesthood of all believers" also is granted participation and which comes to concrete expression in the priestly gestalt of God's reign.

"According to Luther's famous Torgau formula, worship is nothing other than that 'our dear Lord himself may speak to us through his holy word and we respond to him through prayer and praise.'"[7] Christoph Schwöbel provides an exemplary characterization of the entire breadth of this worship dialogue between Christ and the congregation:

> All the various ways Christ is mentioned in worship—in the Gospel narratives, kerygmatic assurances, instruction, liturgical formulas, and explanatory discourses in the epistolary literature—the focus is always on the gospel, on God's speaking with us in his word, a word that—also as law—has its center in the gospel, in the assurance of God's merciful love that mediates communion with God to us as creatures alienated from God. From the other side, our own speaking to Christ—or through Christ to God the Father—in prayer salutations as thanksgiving, petition, lament, and praise focuses on our neediness to be granted communion with God, and in doxological discourse it focuses on participation in God's glory in Christ through the Spirit.[8]

Schwöbel emphasizes that it is in this rich tapestry of communication that Christ's "personal presence" comes about[9] through which not

---

priest by Christ the judge judged in our place (*CD IV/2*, 259ff; cf. in this regard part 4.1, note 18).

6. Cf. once more Fiorenza, "The Resurrection of Jesus," 213–48, 238ff (see part 2.5, note 10); cf. also Welker, "Die Wirklichkeit der Auferstehung," esp. 318ff (see part 2.5, note 9).

7. Christoph Schwöbel, "'Wer sagt denn ihr, dass ich sei?' (Mt 16,15). Eine systematisch-theologische Skizze zur Lehre von der Person Christi," in *Marburger Jahrbuch Theologie XXIII: Christologie*, 47 (concerning the *Jahrbuch*, see part 3.3, note 35); concerning the Luther quote, see WA 49, 588, 16–18. Cf. idem, *Gott in Beziehung. Studien zur Dogmatik* (Tübingen: Mohr Siebeck, 2002), 301ff.

8. Schwöbel, "'Wer sagt denn ihr, dass ich sei?'" 47.

9. Dietrich Ritschl similarly tried to answer the question concerning *Christus praesens* by adducing the interaction between Christ and his church: "The Church not only

only the exalted Christ turns to us and discloses his identity, but which also discloses the appropriate access to God the Creator and the Holy Spirit.[10]

Correctly understood and correctly celebrated worship serves to disclose, secure, and deepen our knowledge of God, knowledge of God that is always also knowledge of salvation. The correctly celebrated worship service discloses thereby not simply an optimized concept or idea of God or an optimized sense of religious feeling, it also places us into an interrelational event in which the exalted Christ, as the Son of God, reveals

---

knows of the *Christus praesens* and his work, she is also *being dealt* with by him. The Church can, therefore, *address* him in doxological language, although she is incapable of defining the peculiar mode of his existence" (Dietrich Ritschl, *Memory and Hope: An Inquiry Concerning the Presence of Christ* [New York, London: Macmillan, 1967], 220f. See also idem, *Concerning Christ: Thinking of Our Past, Present and Future With Him* [Richmond, 1980], 14ff). Ritschl relates the doxological existence of the church and its diaconal mission with the Benedictine motto *ora et labora* (cf. *Memory and Hope*, 225ff). In later writings, he focused the diaconate on ministries of assistance and viewed a life focused fundamentally on assistance and doxology as an interpretation of the double commandment of love in Matt 22:37–40 (Ritschl, *The Logic of Theology: A Brief Account of the Relationship Between Basic Concepts in Theology* [Philadelphia: Fortress Press, 1987], 286; [see part 4.3, note 26]). – Ritschl's students pursued this line of thought further with reflections on a potential spirit-Christology and wisdom-Christology. Ulrike Link-Wieczorek, in a study of English-speaking incarnation-Christologies and spirit-Christologies (*Inkarnation oder Inspiration? Christologische Grundfragen in der Diskussion mit britischer anglikanischer Theologie*, FSÖTh 84 [Göttingen: Vandenhoeck, 1998]), examined the themes of God's opening for those who participate in the revelation, and the participation of witnesses in the life of the Resurrected. According to Link-Wieczorek, spirit-Christology is the point of departure for speaking appropriately about the incarnation, the Word becoming flesh. The incarnation as such becomes discernible when it becomes clear that even in Jesus's pre-Easter life, "the fullness of the deity dwells bodily" and the powers of eternal, worthy life are already at work, *even though* precisely these powers—prior to the cross and resurrection—yet remain subject to human incomprehension, misunderstanding, contempt, and resistance. The cross and resurrection reveal that the proclamation of the coming reign by Jesus of Nazareth is *already* announcing God's presence among human beings, a presence that then acquires earthly form through the life of the Resurrected in the Spirit with his witnesses" (ibid., 240ff). – Michael Press has reconstructed a broad spectrum of "Trinitarian influenced" spirit-Christologies in biblical traditions and more recent theological outlines. His own outline is heavily influenced by Boris Bobrinskoy, *Mystery of the Trinity*, trans. Anthony P. Gythiel (Crestwood, N.Y.: St. Vladimir's Seminary, 1999): "Bobrinskoy's Christology picks up on the best orthodox traditions: the roots of theological reflection in liturgical praxis, multiperspectival Trinitarian thought, and the equal value of the Spirit and Christ. What it lacks, however, is a fully explicated Christology" (Michael Press, *Jesus und der Geist. Grundlagen einer Geist-Christologie* [Neukirchen-Vluyn: Neukirchener, 2001], 31). Press seems to envision a Christology shaped by prayer and proclamation that prompts reflection on a Trinitarian-focused "regulative and doxological understanding of God's eschatological completion in his communion with human beings" (ibid., 293).

10. Schwöbel, "'Wer sagt denn ihr, dass ich sei?'" 50ff (see part 5.3, note 7).

the glory of the triune God and the breadth of God's creative activity. That said, one cannot expect this revelatory event to be accompanied by spiritually, emotionally, and intellectually enhanced experiences, though such can certainly come about in worship. God's person and God's life seek to become—and remain—interesting, familiar, and moving. God and God's life seek to benefit human beings—and it is in this complex modesty of divine self-disclosure that the experiential and cognitive flow of the worship event frequently takes place in many churches and congregations around the world.[11]

It is through unity with Jesus Christ that the Creator becomes discernible as a benevolent God and Father, and through unity with Jesus Christ that the Holy Spirit similarly can be experienced as the Spirit that lovingly saves and elevates human beings and grants them participation in the life of the Resurrected and Exalted. Luther provides a classic formulation of these insights in his interpretation of the third article of faith: "We could never recognize the Father's grace and mercy were it not for our Lord Christ, who is a mirror of his Father's heart. Without him we could see naught but an angry and terrible judge; and of Christ we could know nothing were he not revealed to us by the Holy Spirit."[12]

"Knowledge of Christ" does not come about through merely collecting arid information about him. Quite the contrary, the revelation of Jesus Christ through the Holy Spirit touches, seizes, and even transforms those who see and understand themselves as having been accepted as "his own." Through proclamation and the worship event, they encounter Jesus Christ as truly God and truly human, as brother and friend, as someone who was one of them—and still is—and as the God and Lord who saves and elevates them. Christoph Schwöbel quite accurately remarks that

---

11. Christoph Dinkel, *Was nützt der Gottesdienst? Eine funktionale Theorie des evangelischen Gottesdienstes*, Praktische Theologie und Kultur 2 (Gütersloh: Kaiser, 2000), esp. 217ff., examines the considerable wealth inhering in this context. Isolde Karle, *Kirche im Reformstress* (Gütersloh: Gütersloher, 2010), advocates a new self-understanding and reorganization of the church oriented toward the charismatic power associated with congregational assembly, focus on worship, and substantive theological proclamation; see also the discussion in idem, ed., *Kirchenreform. Interdisziplinäre Perspektiven*, Arbeiten zur Praktischen Theologie 41 (Leipzig: Evangelische Verlagsanstalt, 2009); concerning the powerful charismatic influence exercised by the *Christus praesens* in worship on the diaconal and prophetic form of God's reign, see John B. Cobb, *Christ in a Pluralistic Age* (Philadelphia: Westminster, 1975), 177ff.

12. *Luther's Large Catechism*, trans. John Nicholas Lenker et al. (Minneapolis, Minn.: The Luther Press, 1908), 126.

> It is in the unity of his person, constituted through his relationship with God the Father and by the Spirit, that Christ, as the Son of God, lives genuine existence as God, and, as the human likeness of God, genuine human existence in the life of a real human being.[13]

As the human likeness of God, Jesus Christ presents to human beings not some unattainably "ideal" notion of human existence, but rather perfect divine and human love and goodness that veritably seizes his fellow human beings and creatures that he may grant to them participation in the communion of God and human beings. This event comes to particularly vivid, clear, and intense expression in the sacramental celebrations of baptism and Holy Communion, which the church celebrates according to the directive of Jesus Christ (Matt 28:19f) and after his example. Whenever the church examines anew whether the sacraments are being celebrated commensurate with the directive of Jesus Christ and the biblical traditions, it is guided by the priestly influence and ministry of Jesus Christ.

In baptism, a change of lordship comes about for those who are baptized.[14] As "natural beings," they are part of what God has declared to be a "good" (Hebrew *tov*, i.e., beneficial to life) creation, a creation that, however, is clearly distinct from any divine or paradisiacal circumstances.[15] Creaturely life, human life is always life at risk, is life in danger, threatened by illness, distress, and mortality. Quite beyond such endangerment, however, it is also constantly threatened by self-incurred or otherwise sustained indifference, violence, and cruelty—and not merely such as is caused by individuals, but also such that is collectively planned and organized. Creaturely life is accompanied and surrounded by suffering and death, distress and the power of sin. Celebrating merely the "gift of the newborn child" and the "salutary gift of a new earthly life" in baptism fails to grasp fully what actually happens in baptism.

In baptism, the creative and saving God brings the baptized person into a life community, doing so publicly and through a symbolic experience accessible to witnesses. This new life community creatively pen-

---

13. Schwöbel, "'Wer sagt denn ihr, dass ich sei?'" 54 (see part 5.3, note 7); this vitality of Christ's presence constantly puts references to the "metaphysical Christ" on the defensive; cf. John Macquarrie, *Christology Revisited* (London: SCM Press, 1998), 98ff, esp. 99; Edward Farley, *Divine Empathy: A Theology of God* (Minneapolis: Fortress, 1996), 278ff.

14. The following discussion was incorporated in part into *Die Taufe. Eine Orientierungshilfe zu Verständnis und Praxis der Taufe in der evangelischen Kirche*, ed. EKD (Gütersloh: Gütersloh, 2008), 30ff.

15. Gen 1:4, 10, 12, 18, 21, 25, 31; cf. Michael Welker, "Was ist Schöpfung? Zur Subtilität antiken Weltordnungsdenkens," in *Jahrbuch der Heidelberger Akademie der Wissenschaften für 2006* (Heidelberg: Universitätsverlag Winter, 2007), 84–88.

etrates through and ultimately, in a saving act, surpasses or transcends earthly life that is not only infirm, transient, and finite, but also variously threatened by the powers of evil and sin. Günter Thomas remarks that "what happens in baptism" is that a life deemed worthy by God is turned about and claimed for God's reign.[16] In baptism, those baptized —and with them the entire church of Jesus Christ—celebrate the divine pledge and promise of life communion with God, communion that sustains their earthly life, elevates it to special dignity, and saves and preserves it even beyond its earthly course. For this reason, Christian baptism is destined to remain associated with the use and clarification of what are difficult and for many people offensive statements:

- liberation from the powers of sin and death;
- preservation for eternal life;
- communion with Christ and the living God;
- the gift of the strength and powers of the Spirit.

It is in faith itself that these dimensions and gifts of "new life" are gratefully accepted and disclosed, and it is in baptism that the gift of the fullness of faith itself comes about, which is much more than merely that a person somehow says "yes" to God.[17] Here God turns in goodness and grace to the baptized person, simultaneously making that person capable of a profound and rich relationship of trust with and also grounded by God.[18]

16. Günter Thomas, *Was geschieht in der Taufe? Das Taufgeschehen – zwischen Schöpfungsdank und Inanspruchnahme für das Reich Gottes* (Neukirchen-Vluyn: Neukirchener, 2011), 43; cf. also Miroslav Volf, *After Our Likeness: The Church as the Image of the Trinity*, trans. Douglas W. Stott, *Sacra Doctrina* (Grand Rapids and Cambridge, UK: Eerdmans, 1998), 152ff.

17. Concerning the double objectivity of faith that both sustains and extends beyond subjective concurrence and personal confession, see part 0.5.

18. This personal relationship of trust comes to strongest expression in prayer, concerning which Luther composed a moving introduction for his friend, the barber and surgeon Peter Beskendorf, *A Simple Way to Pray, for a Good Friend*, in which he describes the difficulties attaching to prayer and its blessing. He shows how prayer before God — taking its orientation from the Lord's Prayer, psalms, the confession of faith, and the Ten Commandments — can be accompanied by reflection on oneself and one's fellow human beings. In prayer, we should (1) seek instruction, reflect on God and ourselves, see what God both gives and expects from us, (2) give thanks to God, (3) confess to God, (4) ask for God's help. Luther speaks about a "garland of four strands" in prayer that he binds each day (Martin Luther, *A Simple Way to Pray* [Louisville, Ky.: Westminster John Knox Press, 2000]). See also Wolf Krötke, *Beten heute*, Evangelium konkret (München: Kösel, 1987), 11ff; Rudolf Bohren, *Das Gebet 1*, ed. Manfred Josuttis, edition bohren 2 (Waltrop: Spenner, 2003), 49ff; concerning the distinction between petition and lament, praise and thanksgiving, see Eva Harasta, *Lob und Bitte. Eine systematisch-theologische Untersuchung über das Gebet*

Christian baptism is based on the baptism of Jesus,[19] just as the celebration of Holy Communion is based on Jesus of Nazareth's own institution of the meal. Yet the full significance of these two sacraments is grasped only if the "liberation from the power of sin" they promise is taken seriously. Human beings are freed from the anxiety, care, and paralysis caused by both internal and external powers that drive them to turn away—either consciously or unconsciously, and with all the attendant, disastrous consequences—from both God and their fellow human beings.[20] The more profound dimension of this liberation emerges when we ask how Jesus understood *his own baptism*.

The account of Jesus's baptism is an account of the commencement of his appointed activity and influence on the plane of world history, or, more precisely: creation history, and eschatology. It recounts how the baptized Jesus enjoys a unique relationship with the Creator, whom he reveals as a beneficent Father, and with the divine powers "on high," powers of which he partakes and to which he himself grants participation. The biblical texts evoke this situation through the image in which the heavens open up above the baptized Jesus and the spirit of God descends on him.[21] For the biblical traditions, the "opening of the heavens" is by no means only a natural phenomenon. Though light and water, warmth and cold, do indeed come from heaven, and though life on earth is decisively influenced and shaped by natural forces "from on high," the

---

(Neukirchen-Vluyn: Neukirchener, 2005), esp. 37ff, 233ff; Rudolf Bohren, *Das Gebet 2*, ed. Manfred Josuttis, edition bohren 4 (Waltrop: Spenner, 2005), 99ff, 251ff; concerning prayer as the key to the doctrine of God, see Gerhard Ebeling, *Dogmatik des christlichen Glaubens*, vol. 1: *Prolegomena, Erster Teil: Der Glaube an Gott den Schöpfer der Welt* (Tübingen: Mohr Siebeck, 1979), 192–240; concerning the breadth of the treatment of prayer in the Bible, especially in the Old Testament, see the impressive work of Patrick D. Miller, *They Cried to the Lord: The Form and Theology of Biblical Prayer* (Minneapolis: Fortress, 1994). Miller also discloses various promising approaches to a praxis of prayer that spans religions; concerning the potential and difficulties of such praxis, see Hermann Barth, "Im Namen Jesu Christi beten. Beobachtungen und Folgerungen zur Frage des gemeinsamen Gebets von Christen und Angehörigen anderer Religionen," in *Gegenwart des lebendigen Christus*, 391–405 (see part 1.5, note 5).

19. Matt 3:13ff; Mark 1:9ff; Luke 3:21ff.

20. It should be kept in mind that Holy Communion was instituted during the "night of betrayal," and in order to free human beings ever anew from imprisonment by the powers of this world, and to guide them instead to God's peace (see in this regard part 5.4). Christian baptism similarly serves as a path into God's lordship and as an abiding entry into God's peace.

21. The comparison found in all the Gospels according to which the spirit of God descended "like a dove" and alighted on Jesus (Matt 3:16; Mark 1:10; Luke 3:22; John 1:32) might (cf. 1 Pet 2:20f) be picking up on the story of Noah's dove with its message of rescue after the Flood (Gen 8:8ff); cf. Thomas, *Was geschieht in der Taufe?*, 47 (see part 5.3, note 16).

"heavens" are for the biblical traditions *also* the locus of cultural and spiritual powers and forces that remain utterly unavailable to us human beings. Indeed, these same forces overcome us and direct and guide life on earth in ways we can hardly or not at all influence.[22] When Jesus has himself baptized, it is precisely this realm of power that opens above him, and it is the unequivocally good, creative, saving power of God, a power wholly beneficial to life, that descends on him, namely, the Holy Spirit. But after its descent and alighting on him, Jesus, rather than keeping this spirit of God solely for himself, instead grants participation in this Spirit, in this power of God to those who are baptized in his name or in the name of the triune God.[23]

With his request to be baptized, Jesus explicitly enters the circle of those who acknowledge their in part helpless, in part culpable entanglement in earthly institutions and powers and thereby also their imprisonment by the power of sin. He enters into the circle of those who submit to the lordship of God and seek to live in God's faithful communion. Baptism is not just a matter—or even primarily so—of a purification from personal guilt and transgressions, but rather of a redirection of a person's life toward a new Lord, toward God himself and God's reign. Ultimately it is neither a world power—at Jesus's own time the Romans, in ours perhaps unfettered capitalism—nor even this or that religion or ideology that rules over us; our Lord is rather God himself, or the Messiah of God, who brings with him God's justice and love. It is this interrelationship that is confessed and acknowledged in baptism and then accepted in faith, which is why baptism perpetually remains a revolutionary act and a radical change of lordship.

Those who are baptized are not just "subordinated" through baptism

---

22. See Welker, *Universalität Gottes und Relativität der Welt. Theologische Kosmologie im Dialog mit dem amerikanischen Prozeßdenken nach Whitehead*, 2nd ed. (Neukirchen-Vluyn: Neukirchener, 1988), 203ff; Barth, *CD III/1*, 99ff and *III/3*, 421ff; Welker, *Creation and Reality*, 33ff (see part 0.5, note 13); picking up on this position, see Moltmann, *God in Creation: A New Theology of Creation and the Spirit of God*, trans. Margaret Kohl (London: SCM Press, 1985), 164ff; Isolde Karle, "'Erzählen Sie mir was vom Jenseits.' Die Bedeutung des Himmels für die religiöse Kommunikation," *EvTh* 65 (2005), 334–49; Günter Thomas, "Hoffen auf einen 'Neuen Himmel.' Erwägungen zu einer Welt ohne die Macht der Nacht," in ibid., 382–97; idem, *Neue Schöpfung. Systematisch-theologische Untersuchungen zur Hoffnung auf das "Leben in der zukünftigen Welt"* (Neukirchen-Vluyn: Neukirchener, 2009); Michael Welker, "Schöpfung des Himmels und der Erde, des Sichtbaren und des Unsichtbaren," in *Jahrbuch für Biblische Theologie*, vol. 20 (2005): *Der Himmel* (Neukirchen-Vluyn: Neukirchener, 2006), 313–23. A multiperspectival examination of the connection between Jesus's heavenly existence and "unity with the Father" can be found in Robert W. Jenson, *Systematic Theology*, vol. 1: *The Triune God* (New York, Oxford: Oxford University Press, 1997), 90ff, 194ff.

23. Cf. part 4.2.

to the lordship of Christ and the triune God, they also come to *partici-pate* in that lordship. Through baptism, they acquire a portion in Jesus's royal, priestly, and prophetic office. In the biblical accounts of Jesus's baptism by John, this radical change of hierarchical social forms becomes discernible especially with respect to the priestly aristocracy. Through baptism as a purification ritual, John provokes the priestly hierarchy in Jerusalem as well as the temple cult itself, and the baptism of Jesus specifically intensified this provocation essentially to the breaking point. But why?

The cult and sacrificial rituals in the Jerusalem Temple, which John's baptism provocatively replaces, culminated on Yom Kippur, the great annual Day of Atonement (cf. Leviticus 16). It was on this day alone that God's name was pronounced, and on this day alone that the high priest stepped behind the curtain into the Holy of Holies to atone, through blood ritual, for himself, for the sanctuary, and for all Israel. And it was on this day alone that the high priest stepped before the Ark of the Covenant, the locus of encounter between heaven and earth, God and world. Leviticus 16:4 describes how the high priest prepared for this day when he would directly encounter God: "He shall put on the holy linen tunic ... *He shall bathe his body in water*" (my emphasis).

The story of Jesus's baptism, of the transparency between heaven and earth and of the direct encounter with God, is apparently alluding to this great Day of Atonement. In this case, however, it is no longer the high priest, nor the temple, nor even Yom Kippur itself, nor the cultic offering that provide the functionary, space, time, and medium of encounter. In this case, Jesus's direct encounter with God takes place at the Jordan River after Jesus has bathed his entire body in the water.[24] The accompanying theophany and Jesus's authorization by God's word and the Holy Spirit single him out as God's chosen representative, for it is from *heaven itself* that Jesus is directly authorized as God's Son. The Synoptics all mention a voice that tells Jesus, "You are my Son, my beloved Son; with you I am well pleased" (Mark 1:11; Luke 3:22; Matt 3:17: This is my Son, the Beloved [or: my beloved Son]) or even portray the surrounding spectators as witnesses

---

24. The second New Testament story involving an authentication of Jesus from heaven above, namely, what is known as the transfiguration, is apparently also alluding to the rite of purification on the great Day of Atonement, for we read there that Jesus's clothes became "dazzling white" (Matt 17:2; Mark 9:3; Luke 9:29). A purification bath, a sacred white garment—both stories are likely alluding to the high priest on the Day of Atonement. Concerning the story of the transfiguration as an anticipation of the resurrection in Orthodox and Protestant theology, see Vasile Cristescu, *Die Anthropologie und ihre christologische Begründung bei Wolfhart Pannenberg und Dumitru Staniloae*, Internationale Theologie 9 (Frankfurt: Peter Lang, 2003), 234ff.

to this authorization. Those baptized in Jesus's name or in the name of the triune God acquire participation in God's direct authorization of Jesus, an authorization which—like the change in lordship as well—is recognized, grasped, and accepted in faith.

Paul describes the dramatic nature of this event, of this change in lordship, as follows:

> Therefore we have been buried with him [Christ] by baptism into death, so that, just as Christ was raised from the dead by the glory of the Father, so we too might walk in newness of life. For if we have been united with him in a death like his, we will certainly be united with him in a resurrection like his. We know that our old self was crucified with him so that the body of sin might be destroyed, and we might no longer be enslaved to sin. (Rom 6:4–6)

Not only does our modern sensibility encounter great difficulties in appropriating such statements, they invariably also seem profoundly at odds with the widespread practice of infant baptism, for how can newborn children be associated with sin and the cross in any conceivable way? Or be called "our old self" that—even if but metaphorically—is to pass through death? While we can certainly countenance a child's acceptance as a child of God in infant baptism, any association with baptism unto Jesus's own death evokes a rather gloomy sort of theology wholly out-of-touch with the world we know, a theology we would clearly prefer to leave behind. But what Paul is thinking of here is that the bonds of this world—including those of our fleshly-bodily existence—can become bonds that enslave us and subject us to the power of sin that in its own turn separates us not only from God, but from the life God has destined for us.

Paul and other New Testament traditions thus understand baptism as an act that grants us "newness of life," a life in which we are freed from these powers. God's will is to grant us participation in divine life, and it is in baptism that we thus pass symbolically through death in preparation for resurrection with Christ and for the sake of receiving—already here and now—participation in God's eternal life.[25]

Baptism is an act of renewal in which a person not only becomes a child of God but is simultaneously symbolically extracted or indeed snatched away from the powers of this world. It is also an act that can

---

25. Cf. in this regard Edmund Schlink, *The Doctrine of Baptism*, trans. Herbert J. A. Bouman (Saint Louis: Concordia Pub. House, 1972), esp. 47ff; though also John Behr, *The Mystery of Christ: Life in Death* (Crestwood: St. Vladimir's Seminary Press, 2006), 96f, 117f.

take place at *any stage in a person's life,* and thus certainly also at the beginning. For even at its commencement, a person's earthly and temporal life can be incorporated symbolically into eternal life, that is, into life with and from God.[26] At the same time, this entry into new life with God is accompanied by a separation from the powers and forces of this world *so* radical in nature that the sheer singularity of this change in lordship can be grasped only through a reference to death, indeed to death on the cross,[27] for it is on the cross that this situation of the utter and complete helplessness and hopelessness of the world under the power of sin becomes an event—a situation that can be overcome solely by a new creation out of chaos.

Baptism in the name of Jesus, baptism in the name of the triune God, attests such a radical turn in human life, for it is through baptism that human beings allow themselves to be filled with God's saving power that creates new life from death and chaos.[28] Baptism presupposes this change to the lordship of Jesus Christ, which at once also includes fellowship and friendship; it derives from him and gratefully accepts his life communion.

Jesus's baptism by John also reveals the salvific significance of Jesus Christ: "and all flesh shall see the salvation of God" (Luke 3:6); John 1:29ff explicitly stresses precisely this significance:

> The next day he saw Jesus coming toward him and declared, "Here is the Lamb of God who takes away the sin of the world! This is he of whom I said, 'After me comes a man who ranks ahead of me because he was before me.' I myself did not know him; but I came baptizing with water for this reason, that he might be revealed to Israel."

This Jesus onto whom the Spirit descends and who is identified as God's Son does not himself baptize with water, but rather with the *Holy Spirit,*

---

26. For a circumspect discussion of the problems associated with infant baptism, see Wolfram Kerner, *Gläubigentaufe und Säuglingstaufe. Studien zur Taufe und gegenseitigen Taufanerkennung in der neueren evangelischen Theologie* (Heidelberg: W. Kerner, 2004); concerning the radical rejection of infant baptism, see Barth, *CD IV/4,* 164ff; for comments on this position, cf. again Kerner, *Gläubigentaufe,* 115f.

27. Cf. parts 3.1 and 3.4.

28. Early-church baptismal formulas—though also such in Old and Middle High German as well as Orthodox versions—recall this radical turn when they repeatedly mention a renunciation of the devil or Satan when emphasizing this change of lord and lordship that takes place in baptism. Such emphasis, however, does in any case beg the question of whether human beings are indeed able to "renounce" evil effectively on their own power. Even without the darker contrasts, one can demonstrate that Christian baptism constitutes not a turnabout into uncertainty and openness, but rather baptism *in the name of Jesus Christ.*

whose power counters sin and the powers of this world by freeing up not only faith, but also love and hope and a whole array of spiritual gifts in a person.

Baptism with the Holy Spirit and the bestowed power of the Spirit are not some sort of *numinosum*, and certainly in no way a matter of magic. It is shaped instead by Jesus's own person and life, by his proclamation and ministry. In their own turn, baptized persons are shaped by Jesus's identity, by his person and life, and by his death and resurrection (cf. Col 2:12), which, of course, is why they call themselves Christians, relating the name of Jesus Christ to themselves and their own identity. This appropriation, too, is accepted in faith. Yet even though the identity is, strictly speaking, received and bequeathed to them as a gift, it does not issue in a fundamentally passive disposition. To the contrary, these persons, baptized as they are not only with water, but also with the spirit of Christ, are given a share in Christ's power and lordship, becoming similarly capable of glorifying God in both word and deed and of functioning as witnesses within a mission existence.

This mission existence comes to expression in acts of assistance in the larger sense, in festive life together,[29] and in proclamation, instruction, and collective worship that includes baptizing others. This constant relating of missionary existence back to Jesus's identity and cross in both baptism and instruction is important lest it become indistinguishable from imperial and colonialist forms of so-called "integration into Christianity" of the sort that have enjoyed ascendancy in the church over the course of its history and unfortunately continue to do so. Through baptism and instruction, witnesses remind both their fellow human beings and themselves that religion and even one's own faith constantly risk falling under the power of sin. Because baptism in the name of Jesus and of the triune God together with a strict orientation toward Jesus and his life, ministry, and guidance counter precisely this danger, it also requires resolute and focused engagement in education, beginning with the spiritual education of the very young and moving up through the various stages of childhood and youth.

"As many of you as were baptized into Christ have clothed yourselves with Christ" (Gal 3:27). Christ as a garment, and the baptized as being clothed with Christ—Paul associates this protection, this fixing of a person's public identity, and this personal sheltering with a revolutionary view of the baptized as persons of equal status: "There is no longer Jew or Greek, there is no longer slave or free, there is no longer male and female for all of you are one in Christ Jesus" (Gal 3:28). First Corinthians 12:13

---

29. Concerning participation in the royal office, see part 4.4.

similarly asserts that "For in the one Spirit we were all baptized into one body—Jews or Greeks, slaves or free—and we were all made to drink of one Spirit."

Baptism creates and spreads freedom and equality among people of the sort characterizing the properly understood royal lordship of Christ.[30] Putting on Christ as a garment, however, does not render all baptized persons uniform or, as it were, "standardized"; instead, each acquires different gifts and powers of the Spirit through which they then attest God and disclose God's will both together and for one another, becoming different, individual members of the one body of Christ. The hierarchical circumstances of lordship, authority, or dominion otherwise attaching to political, biological, and other differences are "suspended," relativized, and preserved in a free and equal community and in a unity that promotes the development of the creative distinctions of *all* these various gifts of the Spirit.

Clearly defined and demarcated political, military, and other hierarchies in no way correspond to the community of those baptized in Christ. The problems generated by the human (and all-too-human) formation of special-interest groups, groups focused or even fixated on certain agendas and leadership personalities must constantly be addressed and relativized within the realm of Christ's lordship. In 1 Cor 1:13, Paul, reacting to the quarrels among those who, in turn, count themselves as belonging to Paul or Apollos or Cephas or Christ, critically asks, "were you baptized in the name of Paul?" That is, Christians are not baptized in the name of Paul, or Martin Luther or the pope or even the church or a specific denomination, but rather in the name of Jesus Christ and that of the triune God. Acceptance of Christ's identity connects the baptized with the God of Israel and the Creator of the world as well as with the spirit of God, "who with the Father and the Son together is worshiped and glorified."[31]

---

30. Cf. part 4.4.

31. Cf. part 5.2. Because this acceptance of Christ's identity and the commitment (or self-commitment) to the triune God is of such elementary importance for Christian baptism, so also does baptism offer a bond for promoting ecumenical peace. Cf. Friederike Nüssel and Dorothea Sattler, *Einführung in die ökumenische Theologie* (Darmstadt: Wissenschaftliche Buchgesellschaft, 2008), 73f, 148f, and the declaration of mutual recognition of baptism in the Magdeburg cathedral on April 29, 2007 (Konvergenzerklärungen der Kommission für Glauben und Kirchenverfasung des Ökumenischen Rates der Kirchen [Faith and Order], *Taufe*, Nr. 6).

5.4 Holy Communion / the Eucharist: The cultic presence of the exalted Christ and the triune God. Ecumenical Tasks

Almost all world churches agree that Holy Communion is the source and high point of church life. Intensive dialogue between the larger churches on a world level beginning in the 1960s yielded documents of "Growth in Agreement" concerning the purpose, meaning, and correct celebration of Holy Communion.[1] Because churches are unanimous in their conviction that they celebrate this sacrament at the directive of Jesus Christ, the specific biblical passages concerning the instituting of Holy Communion are of central significance for any fundamental orientation and for coming to an understanding in the case of open questions or, in any given instance, conflicts.[2]

For the Remembrance of Jesus Christ

According to the momentous tradition of Paul, though also of Luke,[3] Holy Communion is to be celebrated in remembrance of Jesus Christ:

---

1. These "texts of consensus" have been published in three large collections: *Growth in Agreement I: Reports and Agreed Statements of Ecumenical Conversations on a World Level*, ed. Harding Meyer and Lukas Vischer, Faith and Order Paper, no. 108 (New York: Paulist Press; Geneva: World Council of Churches, 1984); *Growth in Agreement II: Reports and Agreed Statements of Ecumenical Conversations on a World Level, 1982-1998*, ed. Jeffrey Gros, Harding Meyer, and William G. Rusch (Grand Rapids, MI: William B. Eerdmans; Geneva: WCC Publications, 2000); *Growth in Agreement III: International Dialogue Texts and Agreed Statements, 1998-2005*, ed. Jeffrey Gros, Thomas F. Best, and Lorelei F. Fuchs (Grand Rapids, MI: William B. Eerdmans; Geneva: WCC Publications, 2007); in the following discussion, these volumes are cited as *Growth in Agreement* with the volume number. The results of these dialogues have been assessed by André Birmelé, *Le Salut en Jésus Christ dans les dialogues oecuméniques* ([Paris:] Éditions du Cerf; [Geneva:] Labor et Fides, 1986), 131ff; Eckhard Lessing, *Abendmahl*, Bensheimer Ökumenische Studienhefte 1 (Göttingen: Vandenhoeck, 1993) (cited as Lessing, *Abendmahl*); Michael Welker, *What Happens in Holy Communion?* trans. John F. Hoffmeyer (Grand Rapids, Mich.: W.B. Eerdmans Pub.; London: SPCK, 2000) (cited as Welker, *Holy Communion*).

2. I have proposed speaking about a "preservation of Eucharistic succession through faithfulness to Scripture" and then using this as a basis for ecumenical dialogue that is trustworthy and truth-oriented, albeit a basis that at once must also serve Protestant self-criticism. Concerning this issue, see Lidija Matošević, *Lieber katholisch als neuprotestantisch. Karl Barths Rezeption der katholischen Theologie 1921-1930* (Neukirchen-Vluyn: Neukirchener, 2005), esp. 75ff. Concerning the following discussion cf. the more detailed discussions in Lessing, *Abendmahl*; Welker, *Holy Communion*. Cf. also Isolde Karle, "Eucharistie oder Abendmahl? Zur sakramentalen Präsenz Jesu Christi," in *Gegenwart des lebendigen Christus*, 299–318 (concerning this volume, see part 1.5, note 5).

3. Luke 22:19: "Do this in remembrance of me!"

> For I received from the Lord what I also handed on to you, that the Lord Jesus on the night when he was betrayed took a loaf of bread, and when he had given thanks, he broke it and said, "This is my body that is for you. Do this in remembrance of me." In the same way he took the cup also, after supper, saying, "This cup is the new covenant in my blood. Do this, as often as you drink it, in remembrance of me." For as often as you eat this bread and drink the cup, you proclaim the Lord's death until he comes. (1 Cor 11:23–26)

Asserting that the celebrating of Holy Communion institutes a remembrance of Jesus Christ implies far more than a mere act of intellectual remembrance of a "past event." Such remembrance is instead a reenactment.[4] It is not just that Jesus Christ's life, death, and resurrection are individually and collectively "internalized," they are also publically proclaimed and acquire a living monument, for this recollection of Jesus Christ is transmitted further, disseminated, his memory renewed, stimulated, and intensified. The entirety of God's act of reconciliation is contemporized in this concentration on Christ's person.[5] But how does such proper remembrance come about? What is really Jesus's directive to his disciples "on the night when he was betrayed"? Does he direct them to consecrate bread and wine so that this bread and wine be transformed thereby into the body and blood of Christ (transubstantiation)? Does he direct them to prepare a meal through this act, be it actually celebrated or not? Or does he direct them to celebrate the meal at least symbolically, just as he himself does with them?

Silent Mass or Communion?

Considerable differences unfortunately emerged on this issue between the Roman Catholic position, on the one side, and Orthodox and Protestant positions, on the other. In its thirteenth session in 1551, the Counter-Reformational Council of Trent had clearly stated: "For the apostles had not as yet received the Eucharist from the hand of the

---

4. Denver Report 1971, in *Growth in Agreement* I, 325, 326 (see part 5.4, note 1); cf. in this regard Jan Assmann, *Cultural Memory and Early Civilization: Writing, Remembrance, and Political Imagination* (Cambridge; New York: Cambridge University Press, 2011), esp. 111ff; idem, "Communicative and Cultural Memory," in *Cultural Memories: The Geographical Point of View*, ed. Peter Meusburger, Michael Heffernan, and Edgar Wunder, Knowledge and Space 4 (Heidelberg: Springer, 2011), 15ff; Michael Welker, "Kommunikatives, kollektives, kulturelles und kanonisches Gedächtnis," in *Jahrbuch für Biblische Theologie*, vol. 22: *Die Macht der Erinnerung* (Neukirchen-Vluyn: Neukirchener, 2008), 321–31.

5. Canterbury Declaration 1973, in *Growth in Agreement* I, 82.

Lord, who, nevertheless, Himself truly affirmed that to be His own body which He presented."[6] Eleven years later, in its twenty-second session in 1562, the council, in its statement on the "Institution of the most holy Sacrifice of the Mass," issued the anathema that "if any one shall say that masses in which the priest alone communicates sacramentally are unlawful and therefore to be abrogated, let him be anathema."[7]

This understanding is not supported by biblical traditions, least of all Paul (cf. in addition to 1 Cor 11:23–26 also 1 Cor 10:16b: "The bread that we break, is it not a sharing in the body of Christ?").

Mark 14:22 expressly positions the statement "this is my body" *after* the breaking of the bread and the directive to take it. It is only *after* explicitly *all* of them have drunk from the cup that the statement follows: "This is my blood of the covenant, which is poured out for many" (Mark 14:24).

According to Matt 26:26–28 as well, the breaking and distribution of the bread, the passing of the cup, as well as the directive "Take, eat" and "Drink from it, all of you" *precede* the identification of bread and wine as the body and blood of Christ. Luke 22:19–20 is no less clear.

Hence it was not without good reason that during the twentieth century the Roman Catholic Church cautiously formulated its own position more in line with that of the Orthodox and Protestant churches.[8] The conviction became increasingly accepted—including in ecumenical discussion on a world level authorized by Rome— that the "Lord's Supper is an act of divine worship that takes place when the congregation is assembled in the name of Jesus."[9] The results of ecumenical discussions essentially corresponded to statements published in the collective declaration of Europe's Reformation churches in 1973 (Leuenberg Concord), which clearly states the following in thesis 19: "We cannot separate the communion with Jesus Christ in his body and blood from the act of eating and drinking. An interest in the manner of the presence of Christ in Holy Communion which disregards this action is in danger of obscuring the meaning of the action of Holy Communion."[10] The liturgical reform

6. *The Canons and Decrees of the Council of Trent*, trans. Theodore Alois Buckley (London: George Routledge, 1851), 73.

7. Ibid., 146.

8. See in this regard Welker, *Holy Communion*, 37ff (see part 5.4, note 1).

9. The "Arnoldshain Theses" of 1957 and the "explanations" concerning the theses of 1962," in *Das Mahl des Herrn. 25 Jahre nach Arnoldshain. Ein Votum des theologischen Ausschusses der Arnoldshainer Konferenz* (Neukirchen-Vluyn: Neukirchener, 1982), thesis 3.

10. Rudolf Mau, *Evangelische Bekenntnisse. Bekenntnisschriften der Reformation*

initiated by the Second Vatican Council also explicitly affirmed the unity of priestly and congregational communion: "It is highly desirable that the believers, like the priest himself, receive the body of the Lord from the hosts consecrated in the same mass."[11] Gregor Etzelmüller summarizes the status of the question of Holy Communion between churches at that time:

> In taking its point of orientation from the Last Supper of Jesus, the most recent liturgical reform has succeeded in renewing the celebratory form of the Roman mass such that it is now recognizable as a mimetic imitation of Jesus's last meal with his disciples. By entering into the original situation of all Christian celebratory meals, namely, Jesus's last supper, the congregation receives what the disciples themselves received when Jesus said to them, "Take, eat; this is my body. . . . Drink from it, all of you; for this is my blood of the covenant, which is poured out for many for the forgiveness of sins" (Matt 26:26f).[12]

The encyclical *Ecclesia de eucharistia* (2003) of John Paul II, by explicitly promoting anew the worship of the elements bread and wine in the tabernacle even apart from the celebration of Holy Communion and sanctioning the celebration of the Eucharist in the absence of the congregation, falls woefully behind the level of knowledge attained through so many years of ecumenical discussions on the world level and in the work of the commissions of the council.[13]

Joseph Ratzinger / Benedict XVI dismisses this shared celebration even more radically in the second volume of his study of Jesus of Nazareth, asking, "What exactly did the Lord instruct them to repeat?"[14] Arguing that it was "certainly not the Passover meal (if that is what Jesus' Last Supper was)," nor a normal meal ("even if . . . Jesus' last meal on earth"), and in view of the "unworthy" abuse of the celebration in Corinth addressed by Paul,[15] the symbolic meal is also explicitly rejected:

---

und neuere Theologische Erklärungen, vol. 2 (Bielefeld: Luther, 1997), 293. Cf. Welker, *Holy Communion*, 36ff (see part 5.4, note 1). Translation from "The Leuenberg Concord," trans. John Drickamer, *The Springfielder*, vol. xxv, no. 4 (March 1972), 246.

11. *Missale Romanum. Editio Typica Tertia. Grundordnung des Römischen Messbuchs. Vorabpublikation zum Deutschen Messbuch*, 3rd ed. (Bonn, 2007), 85.

12. Etzelmüller, . . . *zu schauen die schönen Gottesdienste*, 131 (see part 4.4, note 6).

13. Cf. *Ecclesia de Eucharistia*, sections 25 and 31.

14. Ratzinger – Benedict XVI, *Jesus of Nazareth*, vol. 2, 139 (see part 1.3, note 20). The following quote ibid.

15. 1 Cor 11:20ff, 27. Cf. in this regard Otfried Hofius, "Herrenmahl und Herrenmahlsparadosis. Erwägungen zu 1Kor 11, 23b–25," in idem, *Paulusstudien*, WUNT 51, 2nd ed. (Tübingen: Mohr Siebeck, 1994), 203–40; Welker, *Holy Communion*, 69ff (see part 5.4, note 1).

> The instruction to repeat refers simply to what was new in Jesus' actions that evening: the breaking of bread, the prayer of blessing and thanksgiving accompanied by the words of consecration of bread and wine. We might say: through these words our "now" is taken up into the hour of Jesus.[16]

This position represses the momentous, clear, and unequivocal biblical message about the breaking, giving, and taking ("as often as you eat this bread and drink the cup"). The disdained congregation, disgracefully excluded thus from communion, is to be comforted—or rather: put off—by a nebulous turn of phrase of the sort one might expect from the school of Rudolf Bultmann, namely, "We might say: through these words our 'now' is taken up into the hour of Jesus."[17]

One must clearly acknowledge that this is an ecumenically extremely unfortunate conflict that the heads of the Roman Catholic clergy are renewing to the considerable detriment of their own church.[18] They will be unable, in the long run, to maintain their position in this ecumenical conflict —also with Orthodox theologians—against the biblical sources and the theological truth, and they must ask themselves whether the accusation they themselves raise against non-Roman Catholic churches, namely, that they "are not Churches in the proper sense" because they "have not preserved . . . the genuine and integral substance of the Eucharistic mystery,"[19] will not fall back on themselves despite their long tradition and quantitatively considered size.

This dilemma should in any case not cause us to overlook the *fruitful differences* and *common problems* attaching to the Roman Catholic and Protestant positions concerning Holy Communion. It is especially important to keep sight of the enormous shared future potential for a priestly orientation toward the celebration of Holy Communion, since it is nothing less than the cultic presence of the exalted Christ and triune God that can be disclosed through this particular sacramental celebration.

16. Ratzinger – Benedict XVI, *Jesus of Nazareth*, vol. 2, 139 (see part 1.3, note 20).

17. See in this regard the equally cautious and yet justified critique of Joachim Ringleben, "Lutherische Anfragen an Joseph Ratzingers Darstellung der Passion Jesu," in *Tod und Auferstehung Jesu*, 130ff (see part 1.3, note 23).

18. The conflict between Paul and Peter in Galatians 2, concerning Peter's failure to live up to his own earlier recognition of truth and freedom, is highly instructive in this context; cf. in this regard Michael Welker, *Kirche ohne Kurs? Aus Anlaß der EKD-Studie 'Christsein gestalten'* (Neukirchen-Vluyn: Neukirchener, 1987), 60f.

19. *Congregation for the Doctrine of the Faith: Declaration "Dominus Iesus" on the Unicity and Salvific Universality of Jesus Christ and the Church*, point 17.

Fruitful Ecumenical Differences

The symbolic acts of breaking, giving, and taking, of eating and drinking bread and wine in the celebration of Holy Communion, provide a profound and intensive sense of certainty as well as an extraordinarily concrete sense of community. Reformed traditions have been especially keen on emphasizing this sense of certainty, pointing out that Christ promised that "His body was offered, and broken on the cross for me, and His blood shed for me, as certainly as I see with my eyes the bread of the Lord broken for me, and the cup communicated to me." He promised, moreover, that, "with His crucified body and shed blood, He Himself feeds and nourishes my soul to everlasting life, as certainly as I receive from the hand of the minister, and taste with my mouth, the bread and cup of the Lord." And finally, we are told that

> Christ speaks thus . . . by this visible sign and pledge to assure us, that we are as really partakers of His true body and blood, through the working of the Holy Ghost, as we receive by the mouth of the body these holy tokens in remembrance of Him; and that all His sufferings and obedience are as certainly our own, as if we had ourselves suffered and done all in our own persons.[20]

This elementary sense of certainty is joined by an incomparably *concrete* experience of Christ's sacramental presence and an extremely intensive sense of community. During the celebration of Holy Communion, the congregation is not only interactive, but also coactive, experiencing an elementary sense of the equality of all and of mutual acceptance.[21]

Over against the significantly more commonly and consistently shared features and experience associated with the celebration of Holy Communion, the institution of the sermon, the proclamation of the word, is implemented in quite varied ways, its effect being dependent on the skill and talent, intelligence and language skills, and many other characteristics of those who proclaim as well as of their audience.[22] Its

20. *Heidelberg Catechism: Text of Tercentenary Edition* (Cleveland, Ohio: Publishing House of the Reformed Church, 1877), answers to questions 75 and 79; see also Brian A. Gerrish, *Grace and Gratitude: The Eucharistic Theology of John Calvin* (Minneapolis: Fortress, 1993), 1ff, 157ff.

21. Geiko Müller-Fahrenholz and Reiner Strunk have quite justifiably pointed out that my book, *What Happens in Holy Communion?* trans. John F. Hoffmeyer (Grand Rapids, Mich.: W.B. Eerdmans Pub.; London: SPCK, 2000), does not sufficiently assess and acknowledge the important *diaconal charisma* radiated by Holy Communion. Recognizing and cultivating this charisma is also important for understanding the connection between the priestly and royal offices. Cf. part 4.5.

22. When some time after transferring to a new congregation in Philadelphia the pow-

resonance and effectiveness depends on the time and circumstances, and on the experiential and educational background of those to whom such proclamation is being directed. The celebration of Holy Communion counters the inherent dangers attaching to such widely differing receptive capacity and contextual dependence. In hardly any other life situation, and in hardly any other situation within the church community itself does it become clear in so elementary a fashion that all human beings are equal before God. The contribution this fundamental sacramental situation makes toward the development of a culture of humanity, equality, justice, and egalitarian morality can hardly be overestimated.

Although the concrete sense of certainty inhering in the words "given for me and for us," here and now, in this concrete community, is both powerful and salutary, it can also foster a subjective sense of being in the right on the part of both individuals and small groups who cut themselves off and isolate themselves from the outside, or who develop group-centered or niche-ideologies. Such deceptive moral and religious self-confidence is particularly dangerous insofar as it is in precisely such situations that one's "fellow human beings," that is, those immediately present in that same context, are generally more than willing to support and even strengthen that self-confidence. Protestant and Orthodox believers have justifiably emphasized how extraordinarily important and indeed indispensable is the praxis of the assembled congregation in the celebration of Holy Communion. That said, the biblical traditions also confront us with the tension between the statements "given for you" and "given (or poured out) for many."[23]

Although this tension does not suspend the necessity of emphasizing the indispensable concrete presence of the assembled congregation for the celebration of Holy Communion, that same concrete presence of the assembled congregation is positioned within the larger context of the church of *all* ages and *all* regions of the world. That is, the presence of the resurrected Christ unites the concretely assembled congregation with an incalculable number of congregations celebrating Holy Communion in the Christian church of the past, present, and future, amid, moreover, a wealth of different denominations, theologies, and ecclesiastical organizational forms. It is interesting to note that the theologies of the Ortho-

---

erful preacher Cindy Jarvis was told by a member of the congregation that her preaching had become increasingly comprehensible, she suggested to the member in response, "Perhaps at the same time you also have learned to do a better job paying attention!"

23. Mark 14:23f; Matt 26:27; cf. Mark 10:45 and Matt 20:28. See also the circumspect reflections on this tension in Otto Weber, *Foundations of Dogmatics*, trans. Darrell L. Guder (Grand Rapids, Mich.: Eerdmans, 1983), vol. 2, 639ff; and Ratzinger – Benedict XVI, *Jesus of Nazareth*, vol. 2, 134ff (see part 1.3, note 20).

dox churches and of the Roman Catholic Church have often perceived and otherwise done justice to this breadth better than have Reformation positions that were more strongly oriented toward congregational theologies.[24] Hence they have also repeatedly and justifiably expressed their concern with the appropriate liturgy and celebration of Holy Communion and with maintaining an accompanying, serious presiding position in this context. For Holy Communion does *not* represent a field of "experimentation" in which capricious religious tastes of various congregations can simply be arbitrarily indulged.[25] In this context, then, differences among various ecumenical perspectives on Holy Communion provide both fruitful stimulus and orientation. Together, the various denominational positions can counter problematical developments such as celebration of Holy Communion apart from the concretely assembled congregation or arbitrary implementation or structuring of the celebration on the part of a given congregation.

The Night of Betrayal

An examination of discussions between the great churches on the world level led to the discovery of a "blind spot" that was equally astonishing and horrifying. The perspectives so clearly emphasized in liturgies through reference to the "night of betrayal" and the "announcement of Christ's death" are hardly—indeed, usually not at all—addressed in most documents, despite the fact that they can clarify and articulate an important distinction between Holy Communion and the Passover meal, and despite the fact that they illuminate a topic of perennial importance especially to Protestants, namely, liberation from the power of sin.

---

24. See, e. g., Dumitru Staniloae, *The Experience of God, Orthodox Dogmatic Theology* (vol. 5: *The Sanctifying Mysteries*) (Brookline, Mass.: Holy Cross Orthodox Press, 2012), 73ff; Johannes Betz, "Eucharistie als zentrales Mysterium," in *Mysterium Salutis*, 4,2: *Das Heilsgeschehen in der Gemeinde*, ed. Johannes Feiner and Magnus Löhrer (Einsiedeln/ Zürich/Köln: Benziger, 1973), 265ff; for an assessment of this breadth of perception from the Moravian and Mennonite perspective, see Peter Zimmerling, *Nikolaus Ludwig Graf von Zinzendorf und die Herrnhuter Brüdergemeinde. Geschichte, Spiritualität und Theologie* (Holzgerlingen: Hänssler, 1999), esp. 153ff, 171ff; and A. James Reimer, *Mennonites and Classical Theology: Dogmatic Foundations for Christian Ethics*, Anabaptist and Mennonite Studies 1 (Kitchener, Ontario, Scottdale, Pennsylvania: Pandora and Herald, 2001); Fernando Enns, *Ökumene und Frieden. Theologische Anstöße aus der Friedenskirche*, Theologische Anstöße 4 (Neukirchen-Vluyn: Neukirchener, 2012).

25. Concerning how to address this legitimate concern, see Welker, *Holy Communion*, 140ff (see part 5.4, note 1); and *Das Abendmahl. Eine Orientierungshilfe zu Verständnis und Praxis des Abendmahls in der evangelischen Kirche, vorgelegt von der EKD* (Gütersloh: Gütersloher, 2003), 53ff.

Whereas the Passover celebrates the departure initiative of a sworn community in the midst of *external* threats, Holy Communion focuses as well on *internal* threats (and self-threats) to the community. The celebration of Holy Communion contemporizes and stresses the danger that threatens community with Jesus from the inside. Jesus celebrates Holy Communion with the very disciples who will abandon and flee him,[26] with Peter, who will deny him three times,[27] nor is even Judas excluded, notwithstanding the cry of woe is spoken over him.[28] Such emphasis on how Christians, in celebrating Holy Communion, are at once also announcing the death of Jesus Christ also draws attention to how this celebration similarly evokes anew the sense of hopelessness and abandonment on the cross, which means, however, that precisely through such recollection and through the institution of such remembrance the Holy Communion also renews the larger sense of helplessness of the part of human beings, congregations, and an entire relative world as such in the face of the demonic entanglement the cross itself reveals.[29] The cross of Christ makes it unequivocally clear—and does so in a profoundly horrific fashion—how we human beings ourselves are capable of using and indeed *abusing* law, morality, politics, and public opinion to destroy our relationship with God and our life circumstances at large. Through announcing Christ's death in the celebration of Holy Communion, the congregation contemporizes for itself—invokes ever anew, as it were—the situation of the cross. It renews both for itself and for outsiders its sense of belonging to human beings at large, to congregations, indeed to an entire world that, by cutting itself off from God through helplessness, stupidity, indifference, and malice, endangers and even destroys itself. It renews the consciousness of being part of humankind that repeatedly, and with all possible means, tries to obscure and distort God's presence and the salvation and well-being for the world.

That these biblical perspectives on Holy Communion were so widely ignored in ecumenical documents and texts of consensus left wholly unaddressed a broad issue that still leaves considerable room for polemical conflict in attempts at ecumenical understanding. This thematic field is characterized by two phrases capable of generating conflict and tension: "liberation from the power of sin" and "saving for eternal life." Matthew 26:28 explicitly refers to how Holy Communion effects a liberation from

26. Matt 26:56; cf. 26:31; Mark 14:50, cf. also John 16:32.

27. Matt 26:57f, 69–75; Mark 14:53f, 66–72; Luke 22:54–62; John 18:12–18, 25–27.

28. Matt 26:24f ; cf. Ulrich Luz, *Matthew: A Commentary*, Hermeneia, 3 vols. (Minneapolis: Augsburg, 1989–2005; vol. 1 rev. 2007), vol. 3, *Matt 21–28*, trans. James E. Crouch, 358, cf. ibid., 359ff; cf. Mark 14:21; Luke 22:21f.

29. Cf. part 3.4.

sin: "For this is my blood of the covenant, which is poured out for many for the forgiveness of sins." References to being saved or preserved for eternal life occur especially in Johannine texts, an exemplary passage being John 6:51: "I am the living bread that came down from heaven. Whoever eats of this bread will live forever; and the bread that I will give for the life of the world is my flesh." John explicitly emphasizes that *even* the disciples found this reference extremely offensive and difficult (John 6:60f). Indeed, the notion that this "living bread" that descended from heaven was in fact the flesh of the Son of Man and was to be eaten by human beings met with almost universal opposition and rejection.

Documents of ecumenical consensus show that Reformation churches, and among them especially Lutherans, are the ones most keen on introducing into these discussions an emphasis on the forgiveness of sins and thereby also on the otherwise indisposable turn that God's acts bring about in a person's existence. On the other hand, it is especially Orthodox positions, though also Roman Catholic theology, that emphasize preservation on the path to participation in the divine glory, the "preservation" of the church "for eternal life."[30] On balance these ecumenical documents clearly demonstrate that emphasis on the forgiveness of sins is increasingly rigidifying into a merely empty phrase, while in a very concrete sense the "theology of preservation" seems to be asserting its dominance throughout the ecumene. In such circumstances, however, the recollection of Christ's cross threatens to fade and, along with it, the endangerment of the communion human beings have with God and among one another, as well as their radical dependence on a wholly inaccessible turn of their fate in times of extreme distress and self-endangerment.[31]

This rather indistinct understanding of sin and its forgiveness goes hand in hand with a disturbing *underestimation* of how radically God himself accepts sinners in Holy Communion. Simultaneously, the capacity of human and even ecclesiastical power is unfortunately severely *overestimated* as such concerns denying, for legal or moral reasons, participation or even admission to Holy Communion for certain persons.

The church, of course, has repeatedly invoked this "power of the keys" bestowed upon it, power which according to Matthew was granted to Peter, according to John to the disciples.[32] It must ask itself, however, whether God's radical acceptance of sinners in Holy Communion does

30. Cf. Welker, *Holy Communion*, 149ff (see part 5.4, part note 1).

31. Cf. also part 5.5.

32. Matt 16:19; John 20:23; see also Philipp Melanchthon, *Heubtartikel Christlicher Lere. Melanchthons deutsche Fassung seiner Loci Theologici* (1553), ed. Ralf Jenett and Johannes Schilling, 2nd ed. (Leipzig: Evangelische Verlagsanstalt, 2010), 370ff; Dietrich Pirson, "Power of the Keys," in *Religion Past and Present*, vol. 10, 270-71.

not set boundaries for the church in precisely this context, for the per-petual possibility that the entire church itself may become trapped by the power of sin must be taken quite seriously in light of Holy Communion. Here the specific context of the "night of betrayal" as the setting in which Holy Communion is in fact instituted must be recognized and acknowl-edged in its entire depth. Paul commensurately makes it quite clear that no person can be excluded from Holy Communion for moral reasons. That is, human beings are unequivocally *not* at liberty—neither through individual nor collective judgment—to exclude other persons directly from Holy Communion. Because Christ alone judges, the only exclusion from the celebration of Holy Communion that might come into question is self-exclusion,[33] something that can admittedly be suggested through submission to a person's own judgment through both teaching and proc-lamation. That is, this reservation does not suspend church discipline. Although exclusion from the church community includes the request for self-exclusion from Holy Communion, the use of such exclusion as a re-striction of a person's full membership in the body of Christ, that is, as a special measure of religious and moral reprimand (the "minor ban"), disregards the profound depth of God's love this sacrament reveals. In light of Holy Communion, the church must, on the one hand, recognize and take seriously its own endangerment and self-endangerment under the power of sin, and, on the other, recognize that it is not permitted to use Holy Communion for targeted legal, moral, or other normative mea-sures, and that it is precisely here that boundaries have indeed been set.

Surrounded and Permeated by the Exalted Christ

During celebration of Holy Communion, Christ's church is essentially surrounded by the presence of the resurrected and exalted Christ. For here it commemorates his pre-Easter life up to his death on the cross, re-calls the night of betrayal and proclaims his death on the cross, proclaims this death as a salvific sacrifice of both body and blood on behalf of hu-man beings who distance themselves from God, put themselves at risk in multifarious ways, and then even try to disguise that same situation. The church proclaims the presence of the resurrected and exalted Christ and petitions the coming of his reign in the Lord's Prayer. And finally, it focuses on Christ's Parousia by announcing his death "until he comes."

Martin Luther made the rather steep allegation that the entire gospel was contained in the words of Jesus Christ, "This is my body—given for you!" "Christ says . . . Take this, it is to be *yours*. [He wants] for us to

33. 1 Cor 11:28; 28ff; cf. Welker, *Holy Communion*, 74ff (see part 5.4, note 1).

make use of him." It is necessary, Luther says, for "you, too, to believe that *your* death, *your* sin, and *your* hell are here overcome and extirpated, and [that you] are thus saved."[34] In Holy Communion, we seize "life and all that is good, including God himself."[35] The sacrament is allegedly nothing less than a bridge, a ship, a stretcher to eternal life.[36] "Thus do you have all the power God himself has, i.e., that we become kneaded into a single cake with our Lord Christ, that we enter into the community of his goods and he into the community of our misfortune. . . . *You have everything and more that your heart desires, and now sit in paradise.*" Christ's "devotion and richness [devour] my sin and wretchedness such that I after have nothing but righteousness."[37]

Surrounded by God's Trinitarian Activity

During the celebration of Holy Communion, however, the church is not surrounded merely by the resurrected and exalted Christ; it also gratefully and joyfully celebrates the presence of the triune God. Holy Communion as *Eucharist* is a celebration of thanksgiving even if the element of the Eucharist does not entirely encompass adequately what happens. A Eucharist, or thanksgiving, is already intimated by

34. Cited in Karl Barth, "Ansatz und Absicht in Luthers Abendmahlslehre," in idem, *Vorträge und kleinere Arbeiten, 1922-1925*, ed. Holger Finze, *Gesamtausgabe* III (Zürich: Theologischer Verlag, 1990), 268; concerning the development of Luther's understanding of the sacrament, see Hans Joachim Iwand, *Nachgelassene Werke*, vol. 5: *Luthers Theologie*, ed. Johann Haar (München: Kaiser, 1974), 255ff; concerning the risk that this doctrine may overemphasize the word, see Eeva Martikainen, *Evangelium als Mitte. Das Verhältnis von Wort und Lehre in der ökumenischen Methode Hans Joachim Iwands,* Arbeiten zur Geschichte und Theologie des Luthertums, N. F. 9 (Hannover: Lutherisches Verlagshaus, 1989), 127ff.

35. Cited in Barth, "Ansatz und Absicht," 288; concerning the close connection between love of God and love of neighbor according to Luther, see Tuomo Mannermaa, *Der im Glauben gegenwärtige Christus. Rechtfertigung und Vergottung. Zum ökumenischen Dialog*, Arbeiten zur Geschichte und Theologie des Luthertums, N. F. 8 (Hannover: Lutherisches Verlagshaus, 1989), 95ff, 114ff, 165ff; Eeva Martikainen, *Doctrina. Studien zu Luthers Begriff der Lehre*, Schriften der Luther-Agricola-Gesellschaft 26 (Helsinki, 1992), 83ff; concerning the deeper grounding of love of neighbor in the love of God to human beings, see Anders Nygren, *Agape and Eros. The Christian Idea of Love*, trans. Philip S. Watson (Chicago: University of Chicago Press, 1982), part I: *A Study of the Christian Idea of Love*, 105ff, 211ff; H. R. Niebuhr, *Christ and Culture*, 15ff (see part 4.4, note 20).

36. Cf. Luther as cited in Barth, "Ansatz und Absicht," 276.

37. Cited in Barth, "Ansatz und Absicht," 281f. Barth remarks, ibid., 284: "No forgiveness of sins, nothing of God's compassion, no saving communion with Christ that does not constantly bring about forgiveness, compassion, and communion with Christ for a person. But also no morality, no obligation, no relationship with a person that is anything other than a constant reorganization of one's relationship with God through justification."

the presence of the gifts of bread and wine. A "eucharist" is made to God the Creator as thanks for the creation gifts bread and wine. These gifts of creation, however, are considerably more than merely "gifts of nature."[38] Although natural growth and formative human cultural activity must come together to produce bread and wine from grain and grapes, biblical traditions hold that such is utterly inconceivable without God's own creative activity, without the contribution of the creative Spirit. Nor, moreover, is it at all self-evident that in all ages and all regions people *are* genuinely able to come together to share both bread and wine with one another both concretely and symbolically. To wit, a simple reference to famine, ecological devastation, dangerous infectious disease, animosity, and unkindness between human beings makes it clear enough that this interplay of creaturely activity does not always succeed as a simple given. That bread and wine are present and accessible at all, that people are able to gather together for a common meal celebration who are relatively healthy and living in peaceful circumstances is certainly reason enough to give thanks to God the Creator and to rejoice in his creative activity.

The thanksgiving and praise of God that comes about within the actual cultic celebration of Holy Communion, however, move decidedly beyond this straightforward thanksgiving for the gifts of creation and the accompanying preservation and protection of human beings. That is, simple gratitude for the gifts of creation, and the joy at finding oneself in a peaceful community in which cordial communication flows freely, does not yet constitute a celebration of Holy Communion. Holy Communion is instead shaped by *anamnesis*, a recollection of the night of betrayal, of the suffering and dying of Jesus Christ. It is shaped by the announcement of his death and focuses on a remembrance of Christ's sacrifice, of his suffering and dying on the cross. As such, however, in Holy Communion a remembrance is similarly instituted to the injustice, quarrelsomeness, and distance from God on the part of human beings under the cross, to the "sin of the world." Here human injustice, quarrelsomeness, and remoteness from God are all vividly evoked in their most extreme forms. The distressful plight of and this extreme threat to God's good creation under the power of sin are present in this anamnesis, in this recollection of the suffering and death of Jesus Christ.

Finally, Holy Communion also celebrates the descending of the Holy Spirit and the saving and elevation of human beings, for whom these creation gifts of bread and wine now become "bread and wine from heaven,"

---

38. Polkinghorne/Welker, *Faith in the Living God: A Dialogue*, 66f (see introduction, note 4).

the body and blood of Christ, that bring them into the most intimate and steadfast community with the Resurrected.

It was especially the Lima Declaration[39] that awakened a consciousness for the disclosure of *God's Trinitarian activity in Holy Communion*.[40]

Hence in Holy Communion, thanksgiving is offered for far more than the preservation of creation, and for far more than the preservation of the church. God is also praised for *new creation*. For this reason, what is known as "thanksgiving" is in many texts—and justifiably so—more specifically referred to as "glorification." In this glorification, in doxology, human beings point beyond themselves, beyond any notions of what constitutes "normal," "good," or "successful" life, and instead praise God, who fills them with the power of his spirit, builds them into the body of Christ, and makes them bearers of his life. Bread and wine, the gifts of creation, become the gifts of new creation. Bread and wine become the body and blood of Christ that connects them corporeally with him and turns them into members of the new creation.

In addition to celebrating the preservation of creation as such, Holy Communion similarly celebrates the power of the new creation and liberation from the power of sin. This event of new creation derives from the activity of the Holy Spirit and of the triune God. In the power of the Spirit, bread and wine become gifts of the new creation, that is, bread and wine from heaven,[41] gifts that not only nourish creatures symbolically but also build up the body of Christ. It is through this new creation that human beings come closest to God, becoming bearers of God's creative power and, as members of the body of Christ, also bearers of his glorified earthly existence.

---

39. *Growth in Agreement* I, 466ff, esp. 475ff (see part 5.4, note 1).

40. A pioneering moment for the Trinitarian understanding of Holy Communion came from the discussion circle in France known as the "Dombes Group," a group composed of Catholic, Lutheran, and Reformed theologians that has existed since 1937, albeit without official status; in 1972 it published the text "Towards a Common Eucharistic Faith?" and exchanged views with the Faith and Order Commission in the World Council of Churches, which in 1971 published the study *Die Eucharistie im ökumenischen Denken* (cf. Lessing, *Abendmahl*, 44; cf. 44f [see part 5.4, note 1]). As Lessing quite accurately remarks, the two texts essentially offer a Trinitarian theological structure by examining Holy Communion from three perspectives, viz. that of *thanksgiving to the Father, remembrance (anamnesis/memorial) of Christ, and the gift of the Holy Spirit*, presenting thus a model for many later studies, including the important 1978 Lutheran and Roman Catholic text *The Eucharist* and esp. the Lima text itself (see Lessing, *Abendmahl*, 45).

41. Welker, *Holy Communion*, 169ff (see part 5.4, note 1).

5.5 The Prophetic Presence of Christ with His Own and the Liberating Power of Hope: Christologically and Biblically Oriented Proclamation in Truth- and Justice-Seeking Communities

Among all the offices of Jesus Christ, many people find the prophetic office to be the most offensive.[1] In his prophetic proclamation, Jesus Christ combines an announcement of salvation with that of judgment, that is, future, present, and eternity-oriented eschatology.[2] He repeatedly predicts his own sufferings[3] and anticipates his resurrection—something neither his own disciples nor the people around him understand. He also anticipates that Peter will deny him.[4] He predicts the fulfillment of the divine will, something which—as is evident from the prayer in Gethsemane[5]—can also fill him with anxiety and grief in his human existence: ". . . if you are willing, remove this cup from me; yet, not my will but yours be done." The prophetic power of prediction, then, does not necessarily exclude the possibility of temptation.[6] What we find demonstrated in these texts is how strong the conflicts are that accompany such prophetic existence.

Which conflicts, however, are experienced by those seeking to par-

---

1. This situation does not, however, become immediately clear from the New Testament texts that explicitly associate Jesus with the title "prophet" (e.g., Mark 6:4, 15; 8:28; Luke 7:16; 13:31ff; John 6:14; Acts 3:22; 7:37); a considerably more pronounced charisma is associated with the royal title in connection with the crucifixion and with the priestly title in the letter to the Hebrews.

2. See Theissen/Merz, *The Historical Jesus: A Comprehensive Guide*, 272, 240ff (see part 1.1, note 5).

3. Matt 16:21–23; 17:22f; 20:17–19; Mark 8:31–33; 9:30–32; 10:32–34; Luke 9:22, 43b–45; 18:31–34 – with intensification and increasing clarity concerning details of his fate: the Son of Man is handed over to the religious elite in Jerusalem – is handed over to "the people" – also "to the Gentiles to be mocked." Concerning the "violent fate" and the suffering of the biblical prophets in general, see Odil Hannes Steck, *Israel und das gewaltsame Geschick der Propheten. Untersuchungen zur Überlieferung des deuteronomistischen Geschichtsbildes im Alten Testament, Spätjudentum und Urchristentum*, WMANT 23 (Neukirchen-Vluyn: Neukirchener, 1967), esp. 317ff; Norbert Lohfink, "Charisma. Von der Last der Propheten," in idem, *Unsere großen Wörter. Das Alte Testament zu Themen dieser Jahre*, 2nd ed. (Freiburg/Basel/Wien: Herder, 1979), 241ff.

4. Matt 26:57f, 69–75; Mark 14:53f, 66–72; Luke 22:31–34, 54–62; John 18:12–18, 25–27.

5. Matt 26:36–46; Mark, 14:32–42; Luke 22:39–46.

6. Cf. in this regard Carl Heinz Ratschow, *Der angefochtene Glaube. Anfangs- und Grundprobleme der Dogmatik* (Gütersloh: Bertelsmann, 1957); see also Christoph Schwöbel, *Christlicher Glaube im Pluralismus. Studien zu einer Theologie der Kultur* (Tübingen: Mohr Siebeck, 2003), 157ff.

ticipate actively in Jesus Christ's prophetic presence? Such people are, of course, quite naturally always also confronted by the moral, social, cultural, societal, and political crises and conflicts occurring in their own immediate, concrete surroundings. Such are then joined by conflicts which human beings in global contexts participate—usually passively—concerning economics, the media, science, and politics. Numerous contexts emerge sorely in need of prophetic insight and prophetic voices, contexts in which we, too, want to emphasize our own warnings and admonitions, protests and encouragement, our yes and our no. Focusing solely on this truly overwhelming sea of problems, however, can drive us into resignation and cynicism. Although addressing this plethora of problems would essentially require a completely new outpouring of the Holy Spirit and whole hosts of prophets and prophetesses—such a view still does not even come close to grasping the true meaning of the prophetic directive in discipleship to Jesus Christ.

Prophetic discourse in discipleship to Jesus Christ is first and foremost discourse that serves God, discourse that allows God himself to speak and exert efficacious influence. "Long ago God spoke to our ancestors in many and various ways by the prophets, but in these last days he has spoken to us by a Son . . . the reflection of God's glory and the exact imprint of God's very being" (Heb 1:1–3). Because prophetic discourse in the presence of Christ *seeks his guidance and indications of God's will in conflicts of the present*, it is dependent on self-critical examination.[7] According to the biblical traditions, it is only false prophets, "prophets of lies," who are so eager and quick to bring their voices to bear—and preferably in the chorus of the politically supported moral majority.[8] True prophecy seeks truth and the realization of justice in concrete situations—in light of God's word. True prophecy examines its own position carefully to determine whether it is representing its own opinion or merely the currently regnant public opinion, or whether it is delivering a message genuinely oriented toward God's word. In this sense, prophetic service and priestly service that proclaims God's word are closely allied in discipleship to Christ and are, moreover, often accompanied by difficult self-examination and even temptation.[9]

---

7. Cf. Karl Barth, "The Word of God as the Task of Theology," in idem, *The Word of God and Theology*, 171ff (concerning this book, see part 3.4, note 3); concerning the attendant, lofty challenges on any "theology of culture," see Sung Hyun Oh, *Karl Barth und Friedrich Schleiermacher 1909-1930* (Neukirchen-Vluyn: Neukirchener, 2005), esp. 220ff, 285ff.

8. Concerning the problem of mendacious spirits and prophets, see Welker, *God the Spirit*, 84ff (see part 0.6, note 16).

9. A moving testimony of such circumstances is recounted in David J. Garrow, *Bear-*

Nor can the prophetic word be isolated from the diaconal service of the royal office. In discipleship to Christ, prophecy resolutely and rigorously serves love and protection of the weak, and never promotes the spread of hatred and violence. In discipleship to Christ, prophecy rigorously keeps "his own" on his path. "But as the common office of the prophets was to hold the Church in suspense, and at the same time support it until the advent of the Mediator; we read, that the faithful, during the dispersion, complained that they were deprived of that ordinary privilege."[10] True prophecy, then, overlaps, on the one hand, the concrete service of the diaconate and of love (the royal office), while, on the other hand, seeking to follow the larger overall trajectory of worship in recognizing the true and just God and his paths (the priestly office). Precisely in this alliance of offices, prophecy in discipleship to Jesus Christ takes the long, deep breath of eschatological hope: Not my will but yours be done!

Quite along the same lines, the two other offices and forms of God's reign exhibit more or less clearly a prophetic charisma of their own. Although participation in Jesus Christ's royal presence may occasionally well be inclined to make do with a modest, quiet life dedicated to the praxis and experience of love of neighbor, nonetheless active engagement on behalf of the weak, the poor, the oppressed, and the disadvantaged comes to exhibit prophetic charisma even when not *explicitly* associated with public criticism of circumstances causing poverty and discrimination. Under certain circumstances, quiet diaconal service both inside and outside the church may well provide a more powerful tremor of provocation through its persistent, steadfast example than perhaps many more boisterous moral-political stances. That notwithstanding, it is quite dis-

---

ing the Cross: Martin Luther King, Jr. and the Southern Christian Leadership Conference (New York: Viking Penguin, 1986), 58, cited in Thomas G. Long, *Hebrews*, Interpretation (Louisville: John Knox, 1997), 9. In the midst of the bus strike in Montgomery, Martin Luther King's first-hand experiences of persecution, hatred, threats, and suffering reached a low point. Over forty phone calls had threatened physical violence to both him and his family: "Late one night, King returned home from a meeting only to receive yet another call warning him to leave town soon if he wanted to stay alive. Unable to sleep after this disturbing threat, he sat at the kitchen table and worried. In the midst of his anxiety something told him that he could no longer call on anyone for help but God. So he prayed, confessing his weakness and his loss of courage. 'At that moment,' he said later, 'I could hear an inner voice saying to me "Martin Luther, stand up for righteousness. Stand up for justice. Stand up for truth. And lo, I will be with you, even until the end of the world."' It was, realized King, the voice of Jesus speaking a word of promise, a word of reassurance, a timely word of comfort and strength."

10. Calvin, *Institutes of the Christian Religion*, 3 vols., trans. Henry Beveridge (Edinburgh: Calvin Translation Society, 1845–46), 2:37 (II, 15,1).

tinct from prophetic ministry and activity, focusing on concrete alleviation of distress and need and on emergent developments of the "work of God's reign" (cf. part 4.3).

By contrast, by engaging in open critique and self-criticism,[11] prophetic testimony generates tension and conflicts in congregations, churches, and societies, tension and conflicts that can become especially vehement when priestly and prophetic ministries are at odds: "We want edifying worship services—not religio-political intrigues!" "Faith and church doctrine—not critical social agitation!" Most world churches have virtually from the outset explicitly sought and approved a close alliance between priestly and prophetic service, and that quite *without* forfeiting or questioning the blessing of quiet, joyous, edifying worship services.[12] These two forms of discipleship in God's reign can indeed be connected in an organized fashion through vigorous and contemporary worship proclamation in both preaching and education, on the one hand, and critical scholarly training of its office bearers, on the other. At the same time, churches must ensure that prophecy does not isolate itself as independent moral criticism—free of theology and no longer bound to God's word—of social, societal, political, and economic circumstances. That notwithstanding, in this context their worries about religious routines that merely strengthen inchoate "feel-good" sentiments or even generate insincere and vaguely obscuring versions of those same sentiments are generally less pronounced than the anxious fear of a religiously generated "moral battle of all against all."

It is especially in view of the cross of Christ that the *prophetic office*, the prophetic gestalt of God's reign, acquires particularly clear contours.

---

11. See in this regard Walter Rauschenbusch, *A Theology for the Social Gospel (1917)*, Library of Theological Ethics (Louisville: Westminster John Knox, 2010), esp. 118ff, 131ff; Reinhold Niebuhr, *The Nature and Destiny of Man*, vol. II: *Human Destiny (1943)*, Gifford Lectures (New York: Charles Scribner's, 1964), esp. 23–34, 244ff; cf. in this regard Milenko Andjelic, *Christlicher Glaube als prophetische Religion. Walter Rauschenbusch und Reinhold Niebuhr*, Internationale Theologie 3 (Frankfurt: Peter Lang, 1998), 55ff, 136ff, 183ff; Johann Baptist Metz, *The Emergent Church: The Future of Christianity in a Postbourgeois World*, trans. Peter Mann (New York: Crossroad, 1981), esp. 48ff, 67ff; Bedford-Strohm, *Vorrang für die Armen*, esp. 150ff (see part 4.3, note 8); Moltmann, "Politische Theologie in ökumenischen Kontexten," 1ff (see part 4.5, note 4); in connection with concrete diaconal challenges, see Rudolf Weth, "Diakonie in der Wende vom Sozialstaat zum Sozialmarkt," in idem (ed.), *Totaler Markt und Menschenwürde. Herausforderungen und Aufgaben christlicher Anthropologie heute* (Neukirchen-Vluyn: Neukirchener, 1996), 111–18; Cornel West, "Prophetic Religion and the Future of Capitalist Civilization," in *The Power of Religion in the Public Sphere*, 92–100 (concerning this book see part 4.4, note 24); and Judith Butler and Cornel West, "Dialogue," in ibid., 101ff.

12. Gillespie, *The First Theologians* (see part 2.5, note 1), emphasizes the dimension of proclamation and doxology that comes to expression in New Testament prophecy.

Discerning these contours, however, requires that we *not* reduce the message of the cross solely to the revelation of the suffering and co-suffering God, to the way God deals with death in this conflict, or to similar guiding notions (cf. in this regard parts 3.4 and 3.5). God's nearness in the poverty, weakness, and impotence of the Crucified, God's suffering from the sin of the world must *not* obscure how God's deals with the powers and authorities of this world in the cross and resurrection. To recognize how God goes about these dealings, we must grasp the weave of Jesus's own concrete conflicts as recounted in the story of his crucifixion. The Jesus Christ who brought to human beings the message of the coming reign of God, who mediated to them the powers of healing, of loving concern for children, for the weak, outcast, ill, and suffering—this same Jesus Christ is not just condemned by religion, law, politics, and public morality and opinion, he is even condemned by them from a position of complex unanimity.[13]

That is, it is not just malicious individuals, but rather the "powers and authorities" as such—all of whom are so quick to profile themselves as "good powers" that "wondrously shelter" us—who at the cross, together, oppose Jesus of Nazareth and the presence of God in Jesus Christ. The cross reveals the world "under the power of sin"; it reveals the "night of abandonment by God," not just for Jesus himself—but also as a constant, perpetual threat to this world. And it reveals that all the powerful public protective mechanisms—such as law, politics, religion, morality, public opinion—can fail or indeed even become *traps* in their obligation to us human beings and our societies.

It is against precisely this background that the great challenge and lofty significance of the prophetic office becomes pointedly clear. Or more precisely: the lofty significance of the Christian proclamation as such, of theological instruction, of the indispensable tasks of communities that seek truth and justice alongside concrete diaconal engagement and even beyond—all this acquires trenchant contours within the dimension of the prophetic office. The first thing that becomes clear is why the prophetic proclamation must absolutely take the form of *scripturally bound proclamation*. "God spoke to us by the prophets, and in these last days by Jesus Christ."[14] In the New Testament witnesses, the biblical canon focuses on the "word of God in the figure and message of Jesus Christ." Many different forms within the Old Testament

---

13. Cf. part 3.4.

14. Cf. Heb 1:1–2; cf. Barth's doctrine, similarly developed under the pressure of the devastating false doctrine of the German Christians: "The Word of God in its Threefold Form" as revelation – scripture – proclamation (*CD I/1*, 88ff).

witnesses—a canon that accrued during more than a millennium—point toward or anticipate Jesus's royal, priestly, and prophetic ministry. Like those in the New Testament, their prophetic voices, too, stand under the pressure of the regnant world power, be it Egypt, Assyria, Babylon, the Persians, the Greeks, or, finally, the Romans. That is, the biblical prophets develop their messages under the pressure of a world power. At the same time, however, they are similarly involved in various conflicts with the political and religious traditions and institutions of their own age and of their own countries, and in that context issue urgent warnings against the temptations of oversimplified religio-political-ideological solutions with respect to social, political, and religious conflicts.

By frequently emphasizing the qualification "according to scripture," "that scripture might be fulfilled," "according to the law and prophets," Jesus's proclamation and the New Testament writings themselves underscore this indispensable tie with their comprehensive source of inspiration and spiritually illuminating prophecy.[15]

Just as in the case of the royal office and royal gestalt of God's reign, so also does the activity and influence of the prophetic office extend far beyond merely the realm of churches in the narrower sense. In fact, this

---

15. Exegetical, systematic, and practical theologians from around the world have long engaged in an intensified interdisciplinary and ecumenical project together under the programmatic formula "biblical theology," a project seeking to reassess methodically, and by focusing on central themes, the orientational power of the biblical canon as such affects academic theology and Christian proclamation and life praxis, and in so doing to counter the increasing isolation among the various disciplines. Cf. *Jahrbuch für Biblische Theologie*, vol. 1: *Einheit und Vielfalt Biblischer Theologie*, ed. Bernd Janowski and Michael Welker (Neukirchen-Vluyn: Neukirchener, 1986; 3rd ed. 1991); Bernd Oberdorfer, "Biblisch-realistische Theologie. Methodologische Überlegungen zu einem dogmatischen Programm," in *Resonanzen. Theologische Beiträge, FS Michael Welker*, ed. Sigrid Brandt and Bernd Oberdorfer (Wuppertal: Foedus, 1997), 63–83; *Jahrbuch für Biblische Theologie*, vol. 12: *Biblische Hermeneutik*, ed. Bernd Janowski and Michael Welker (Neukirchen-Vluyn: Neukirchener, 1998); Michael Welker, "The Tasks of Biblical Theology and the Authority of Scripture," in *Theology in the Service of the Church, FS Thomas W. Gillespie*, ed. Wallace Alston (Grand Rapids: Eerdmans, 2000), 232–41; in the volume *Reconsidering the Boundaries Between Theological Disciplines. Zur Neubestimmung der Grenzen zwischen den theologischen Disziplinen, Theologie*, Forschung und Wissenschaft 8, ed. Michael Welker and Friedrich Schweitzer (Münster: Lit, 2005), cf. esp. the contributions by Patrick D. Miller, "Theology from Below: The Theological Interpretation of Scripture," 3–13; Don Juel, "The Project of a 'Biblical Theology' as a Reshaping of the Boundaries Between Systematic and Exegetical Theology. Response to Michael Welker," 31–34; Ellen F. Davies, "Salvific Surprise: The Shared and Complementary Tasks of Exegetical and Critical or Constructive Theologians," 35–44; cf. further *Biblische Theologie*, Altes Testament und Moderne 14, ed. Paul Hanson, Bernd Janowski, and Michael Welker (Münster: Lit, 2005); Leo G. Perdue, Robert Morgan, and Benjamin D. Sommer, *Biblical Theology: Introducing the Conversation*, Library of Biblical Theology (Nashville: Abingdon, 2009).

office can even turn against an overbearing, self-righteous, or ideologically blinded church and ecclesiastical religiosity. The increasing willingness of many churches to have their theologians trained in seminaries and universities in self-critical dialogue with secular scholarly disciplines and under their critical observation attests this will to engage in self-criticism in "truth-seeking communities."[16] Similarly, the mutual cooperation between theology and the legal sciences, which can already look back on an extremely fruitful shared tradition,[17] should once more engage in more intensive work extending beyond merely historical research, work on church law, and cooperation in issues of administrative church leadership.[18]

Hence within the context of proclamation, prophetic service not only needs to orient itself ever anew toward both Christology and scripture, it must also constantly be trained and cultivated anew through engagement in intensive interdisciplinary cooperation that focuses specifically on themes that serve to connect and otherwise bring various disciplines together within communities that seek truth and justice.[19] An adequate assessment and cultivation of the "prophetic gestalt of God's reign" also requires, finally, that one thoroughly reassess and rework, from a self-critical perspective, the normative history of influence of biblical traditions—both with and against churches—in the development of freedom-based societies[20] and

16. Cf. Polkinghorne/Welker, *Faith in the Living God: A Dialogue*, ch. 9 (see introduction, note 4); Wolfhart Pannenberg, *Theology and the Philosophy of Science*, trans. Francis McDonag (Philadelphia: Westminster Press, 1976), esp. 297ff; Härle, *Dogmatik*, 14ff (see part 4.4, note 17).

17. Cf. in this regard Christoph Strohm, *Calvinismus und Recht. Weltanschaulich-konfessionelle Aspekte im Werk reformierter Juristen in der Frühen Neuzeit* (Tübingen: Mohr Siebeck, 2008); John Witte, Jr., *The Reformation of Rights: Law, Religion, and Human Rights in Early Modern Calvinism* (Cambridge: Cambridge University Press, 2007; repr. 2010); idem, *Law and Protestantism: The Legal Teachings of the Lutheran Reformation* (Cambridge: Cambridge University Press, 2002); *Christianity and Law: An Introduction*, ed. John Witte, Jr. and Frank S. Alexander (Cambridge: Cambridge University Press, 2008).

18. Cf. Huber, *Gerechtigkeit und Recht*, 17ff, 197ff (see part 4.3, note 4); Welker, "Theologie und Recht" (see part 3.5, note 18).

19. John Polkinghorne, *The Faith of a Physicist: Reflections of a Bottom-Up Thinker, The Gifford Lectures for 1993-4* (Princeton: Princeton University Press, 1994), demonstrates how thinking schooled and experienced in this dialogue between theology and the natural sciences can also relate constructively to questions of Christology, eschatology, and pneumatology; cf. idem, *Science and Religion in Quest of Truth* (see introduction, note 4); see also *The End of the World and the Ends of God: Science and Theology on Eschatology*, ed. John Polkinghorne and Michael Welker, 2nd ed. (Harrisburg: Trinity, 2000); *Resurrection: Theological and Scientific Assessments*, ed. Ted Peters, Robert John Russell, and Michael Welker (Grand Rapids: Eerdmans, 2002).

20. At the turn of the millennium, *Freedom House 1999: Freedom in the World. The*

modern human rights. "The idea of legally establishing inalienable, inherent and sacred rights of the individual is not of political but religious origin. What has been held to be a work of the Revolution was in reality a fruit of the Reformation and its struggles."[21] This thesis has certainly not gone unchallenged. Hans Joas has proposed a "new genealogy of human rights" which aims at eclipsing and indeed outdoing the contentious discussion concerning whether the notion of human rights had a Judeo-Christian or Enlightenment origin by focusing instead on the overall guiding notion of the "sacredness of the person."[22]

An examination of this thesis needs first to establish the extent to which the concrete charismatic power of this guiding notion derives from a multifaceted ritual life praxis that in fact is common to many religions. This conviction concerning the "sacredness of the person" is intensively inculturated through what is usually a religiously grounded, ongoing practical-cultic cultivation of the dignity of the person—from infant baptism and analogous rites to rites of passage and ceremonial burial. This religiously shaped life praxis then influences theoretical and doctrinal thinking, which without this background, one wholly disposed to generate loyalty, would degenerate into mere propaganda.

Another point needing clarification is whether the dynamic biblical normativity in the tension between legal evolution, on the one hand, and

---

Annual Survey of Political Rights & Civil Liberties 1998-1999 (New York) classified eighty-eight countries around the world as "free," among which seventy-nine were majority Christian, and three others – South Korea, Taiwan, and Mauritius – also included influential Christian groups among their populations.

21. Georg Jellinek, *The Declaration of the Rights of Man and of Citizens: A Contribution to Modern Constitutional History*, trans. Max Farrand (New York: H. Holt, 1901; repr. Westport, Conn.: Hyperion Press, 1979), 77; cf. *Christianity and Human Rights: An Introduction*, ed. John Witte Jr. and Frank S. Alexander (Cambridge: Cambridge University Press, 2010); *Religious Human Rights in Global Perspective*, ed. John Witte Jr. and Johan D. van der Vyver, vol. 1: *Religious Perspectives*, vol. 2: *Legal Perspectives* (The Hague, Boston, London: Martinus Nijhoff, 1996). The normative religious foundations and motivation presented in numerous other anthologies and studies are unfortunately often only sketchy or thinly worked out if not entirely ignored. For example, Micheline R. Ishay, *The Human Rights Reader: Major Political Essays, Speeches, and Documents from Ancient Times to the Present*, 2nd ed. (New York, London: Routledge, 2007), allows far less space to the (moreover, poorly chosen) biblical traditions than to texts of Karl Marx, cf. 31–35, 50–52, 64f, 86–89 with 218–33, 255ff, 263–72; see also Thomas Pogge, *World Poverty and Human Rights: Cosmopolitan Responsibilities and Reforms* (Cambridge; Malden, MA: Polity, 2002). Ulrich Duchrow, *Alternatives to Global Capitalism: Drawn from Biblical History, Design for Political Action*, trans. Elizabeth Hicks et al. (Utrecht: International Books, 1995), tries to combine a biblical orientation with a political position critically focused on economic issues.

22. Hans Joas, *The Sacredness of the Person: A New Genealogy of Human Rights*, trans. Alex Skinner (Washington, D.C.: Georgetown University Press, 2013), 5ff, 173f.

a culture of mercy, on the other, has not functioned as a kind of ongoing stimulus for this guiding notion and also as an immune system against theoretical and practical challenges to the sacralization of the person. How, moreover, have the secularizing and universalizing tendencies of Enlightenment thought and their effects on educational systems and political culture stimulated the driving forces of religious development and yet *simultaneously* created a climate against them in which precisely this idea of the sacredness of the person might commend itself? Hans Joas concludes with the vague perspective that "[i]n the long term, human rights and the sacralization of the person will have a chance only . . . if human rights are supported by institutions and civil society, defended through argument, and incarnated in the practices of everyday life."[23] If this hope is not to remain merely a pious wish, one will have to examine critically how complex societal and social formative forces in the form of more complex religious rationalities and ritual praxis are being, if not wholly ignored, then at least severely downplayed or obscured. And finally, one must with Joas also critically examine how the ongoing but fruitful formative conflict between religious and secular orientational claims and accomplishments is similarly downplayed or obscured.

The discussion concerning the potential for biblically grounding the notion of human rights has by no means been concluded.[24] The cooperation between "symbolically dense," biblically and theologically inspired, on the one hand, and Enlightenment traditions that may be critical of theology, on the other[25]—cooperation that has often been staged more as conflict despite its fruitful results for both church and cultural history—remains an extremely promising and fruitful field of future inquiry. Their shared influence on the educational and political programs in

---

23. Joas, *Sacredness of the Person*, 190f.

24. See *Jahrbuch für Biblische Theologie*, vol. 15: *Würde des Menschen*, ed. Berndt Hamm and Michael Welker (Neukirchen-Vluyn: Neukirchener, 2001); Peter Lampe, "Menschliche Würde in frühchristlicher Perspektive," in *Menschenbild und Menschenwürde*, Veröffentlichungen der Wissenschaftlichen Gesellschaft für Theologie 17, ed. Eilert Herms (Gütersloh: Kaiser, 2001), 288ff; Wilfried Härle, "Der Mensch Gottes. Die öffentliche Orientierungsleistung des christlichen Menschenverständnisses," in ibid., 529ff; *Menschenwürde in der säkularen Verfassungsordnung. Rechtswissenschaftliche und theologische Perspektiven*, Religion und Aufklärung 12, ed. Petra Bahr and Hans Michael Heinig (Tübingen: Mohr Siebeck, 2006); Stephan Schaede, "Würde – Eine ideengeschichtliche Annäherung aus theologischer Perspektive," in ibid., 7ff; a theologically rather disillusioning approach is taken by Christopher McCrudden, "Human Dignity and Judicial Interpretation of Human Rights," *European Journal of International Law* 19 (2008), 655–724.

25. Klaus Tanner, "Stabilisierung durch Dauerreflexion," in idem, *Christentumstheorie. Geschichtsschreibung und Kulturdeutung*, Theologie – Kultur – Hermeneutik 9 (Leipzig: Evangelische Verlagsanstalt, 2008), 231–37.

building up democratic societies are considerable and indeed continue to be extremely important.[26] "The twenty-first century could become even more a century of democracy than was the second half of the twentieth century—a century of in part good, in part mediocre, and in part miserably functioning democracies in the midst of an imposing host of states constituted as either authoritarian or totalitarian."[27]

Most contributions to the thematic complex "civil society, human rights, and human dignity" from the perspective of sociology and political science contain only extremely sparse research approaches to the sociology of religion that are informed by any rigorous theological underpinnings, not to speak of approaches to more substantive theological issues. Because the "vast majority" of democratic societies are simultaneously shaped by what are usually tenaciously abiding Christian traditions *and* processes of secularization,[28] the question must also be raised concerning exactly how the tense interplay between prophetic theological and religious motivational forces as well as the critical debate with them influences or otherwise affects the development of active and radical-democratic civil societies.[29] The focus on the prophetic office of Jesus Christ and the prophetic gestalt of God's reign remains a central theological task—including for the sake of a constructive, theologically oriented debate with the various complex systemic distortions that arise in the interplay between religion, politics, law, morality, and education.

26. For a balanced assessment of the advantages and disadvantages of the current (at most: thirty-six) democracies and concerning the criteria necessary for their optimization, see Manfred G. Schmidt, *Demokratietheorien. Eine Einführung*, 5th ed. (Wiesbaden: Verlag für Sozialwissenschaften, 2010), 453ff.

27. Schmidt, *Demokratietheorien*, 503.

28. Schmidt, *Demokratietheorien*, 422.

29. See in this regard Heinrich Bedford-Strohm, *Gemeinschaft aus kommunikativer Freiheit. Sozialer Zusammenhalt in der modernen Gesellschaft. Ein theologischer Beitrag* (Gütersloh: Kaiser, 1999); David Fergusson, *Church, State and Civil Society* (Cambridge, UK: Cambridge University Press, 2004); Ralph Fischer, *Kirche und Zivilgesellschaft. Probleme und Potentiale* (Stuttgart: Kohlhammer, 2008).

5.6 New Creation, Saving, Elevation, and Redemption in Christ: Anticipation of his Parousia for Judgment and Eternal Life

"The view beyond is barred immutably:
A fool, who there his blinking eyes directeth,
And o'er his clouds of peers a place expecteth!"
(Goethe, *Faust*, Part 2, "Midnight"; 1832)[1]

"What is thy only comfort in life and in death?
That I, with body and soul, both in life and in death, am not my own, but belong to my faithful Saviour Jesus Christ, who . . . by His Holy Spirit . . . also assures me of eternal life, and makes me heartily willing and ready henceforth to live unto Him."
(*Heidelberg Catechism of 1563*)[2]

The doctrine of the threefold gestalt of Christ's reign unfolds before us a rich and vivid picture of God's revelation in Jesus Christ. In both continuity and discontinuity with his pre-Easter life, Jesus Christ reveals himself as the Resurrected and the Exalted. He reveals the strength and power of the Holy Spirit to bring "his own" into his royal-diaconal, priestly, and prophetic life. He reveals God's creative and re-creative presence with its saving, elevating, and redemptive powers. This revelation of the triune God has been the consistent and sure guide for the ecumenical church during every age and in every region of the world because it makes it possible both to understand and to appreciate fully all the varying profiles of belief and piety found throughout the Christian denominations, confessions, and lifestyles with all their differences, commonalities, and potential for mutual reinforcement. Even potentially conflict-laden self-profiling can be replaced by a cultivated interest in examining fruitful contrasts and engaging creative forms of cooperation.

The realization that the royal and prophetic powers of God's reign can also enter into critical and constructive debate and conflict with various forms of church life itself facilitates dialogue as well as cooperation with other religions and with secular engagement in shaping more effective ways of living together. Despite this breadth and wealth of possibilities, any fully developed understanding of revelation must deal with christophobic attitudes and positions both inside and outside

---

1. Johann Wolfgang von Goethe, *Faust: A Tragedy*, trans. Bayard Taylor, 2 vols. in 1 (Boston, New York: Houghton Mifflin Company, 1870), part 2 (vol. 2), act 5, 289.
2. *Heidelberg Catechism: Text of Tercentenary Edition* (Cleveland, Ohio: Publishing House of the Reformed Church, 1877), 3 (first question and answer).

the church. People will invariably seek and indeed recommend other images and ideas of God, and will always take offense in one fashion or the other at Christian theologies and forms of Christian life. Both the internal tension of life lived in light of revelation (tension, e.g., in the assessment of which of the three forms of God's reign is to be given priority and how their hierarchy is to be understood) as well as various external critical queries and differing or even alien religious certainties and competing truth claims will all prevent the search for a more perfect understanding of God and salvation from ever coming to rest. Metaphysical, transcendental-philosophical, existentialist, and other conceptual approaches and forms of examining human experience will repeatedly recommend themselves in this context—as clearer, more profound offerings that take us beyond otherwise familiar forms of religious orientation. Again and again, our unfathomable yearning for more perfect or complete love, for more profound comfort and consolation, for more just forms of life, for a clearer understanding of God and more elevating and uplifting religious experiences will seek and, as it were, insist on intensifying and finding the crowning conclusion to our understanding of revelation.

Can these needs be satisfied by the doctrine of the Parousia of Jesus Christ, by the "efficacious presence of Christ to establish the universal kingdom of God through the judgment, redemption, and consummation of the world"?[3] Can that doctrine provide a concluding perspective on revelation and information concerning the *final* gestalt of God's reign?

Although church creeds and theology have repeatedly spoken about a "return" of Jesus Christ to complete or perfect his reign, this reference is misleading because of its potential association with the absurd notion that the *pre-Easter* Jesus would return or that the *post-Easter* resurrection appearances would in some way be repeated. By contrast, the biblical traditions themselves state quite clearly and soberly that the Parousia of Christ will *not* be an event that takes place within the natural parameters of time and space. Anyone who alleges that the Messiah, the Son of Man, will be appearing "here or there" for his final and ultimate revelation is a false prophet and is in no way to be trusted.[4] Matthew and Luke use the image of lightning in referring to the Parousia: "For as the lightning comes from the east [rising] and flashes as far as the west [set-

3. Chr. Auffahrt, "Parousia; III. Dogmatics," in *Religion Past and Present*, vol. 9, 556f; see also Hans-Joachim Kraus, *Systematische Theologie im Kontext biblischer Geschichte und Eschatologie* (Neukirchen-Vluyn: Neukirchener, 1983), 553ff; Hans Schwarz, *Christology* (Grand Rapids, Cambridge, UK: Eerdmans, 1998), 324ff.

4. Cf. Mark 13:21–23; Matt 24:23–26; Luke 21:25–28; 17:20–22; cf. part 4.5, note 16.

ting], so will be the Parousia of the Son of Man."[5] Yet even this image is still too naturalistic and, as it were, earthbound. Mark 13:27 mentions how the Son of Man will send out angels and gather his elect "from the ends of the earth to the ends of heaven."

The Son of Man will not be coming to only a single place or at only a specific time. The content of this visionary view is his coming *into all times and into all the regions of the world*. Commensurate with this content, these views also envision a *passing away* of this earthly world. That is, not just individual human life is finite and mortal, "heaven and earth" themselves will also "pass away," will flee "from his [God's] presence."[6] The comforting message amid such visions, however, is the message of the resurrection. Heaven and earth do not simply "pass away" into nothingness or into dark transcendence, but rather into the "new creation."

One of the most important results of multi-year discourses and cooperation between theologians and natural scientists concerning the difficult questions of eschatology was the discovery that the eschatological symbols found in the biblical traditions speak about the *continuity and discontinuity* between the passing and coming eschatological reality. "Flesh and blood cannot inherit the kingdom of God, nor does the perishable inherit the imperishable" (1 Cor 15:50)—a rather harsh message of discontinuity that, however, is countered by the attestation of the resurrection, in which fleshly existence is "sublated" or suspended into the bodily, and bodily existence into spiritual existence, and then—transformed—is preserved within it.[7] References to *new* creation, *new* heaven, and *new* earth emphasize the element of discontinuity; references to *creation, heaven*, and *earth* emphasize the element of continuity.[8]

This eschatological transformation is at once both comforting and

5. Matt 24:27; Luke 17:24; cf. Ulrich Luz, *Matthew: A Commentary*, 199ff (see part 5.4, note 28).

6. Matt 5:18; 24:35; Mark 13:31; Luke 21:33; 2 Pet 3:10, 13; Rev 20:11; cf. the presentation of end-time scenarios in Polkinghorne/Welker, *The End of the World* (see part 5.5, note 19), esp. William R. Stoeger, "Scientific Accounts of Ultimate Catastrophes in Our Life-Bearing Universe," 19ff; and for biblical reference part III: "Themes of the End-Time," 141ff.

7. Cf. parts 2.4 and 2.5; cf. Polkinghorne/Welker, *The End of the World*, introduction, 1–13; also Peters/Russell/Welker, *Resurrection* (see part 5.5, note 19), esp. the contributions of Robert John Russell, "Bodily Resurrection, Eschatology, and Scientific Cosmology: The Mutual Interaction of Christian Theology and Science," 3–30; Michael Welker, "Theological Realism and Eschatological Symbol Systems," 31–42; John Polkinghorne, "Eschatological Credibility: Emergent and Teleological Processes," 43–55; Nancey Murphy, "The Resurrection Body and Personal Identity: Possibilities and Limits of Eschatological Knowledge," 202–18; Andreas Schüle, "Transformed into the Image of Christ: Identity, Personality, and Resurrection," 219–35.

8. See, e.g., 2 Cor 5:17; Gal 6:15; Rev 21:1; even passages as early as Isa 65:17; 66:22.

oppressive. On the one hand, there will be no more suffering and death; on the other, there will also be no more fleshly existence and hence no sensory earthly consciousness. On the one hand, joyous metaphors of a heavenly banquet and wedding celebration[9] emphasize that "eternal life" is not only genuinely alive, but also *joyously* alive and blessed; on the other hand, we in our own turn can hardly conceive vitality and life of this sort utterly void of sensory perception. Additionally, this promise of joyous eternal life is also associated with the notion of *judgment* by Christ, who will carry out a separation and purification.[10] The discontinuity between creation and new creation is accompanied by breaks and breakoffs.

One comforting aspect of this eschatological judgment has repeatedly been adduced, namely, that it is to be carried out by the kind and loving Jesus Christ himself, who will accept and comfort beforehand *even* those who will abandon, flee, and betray him.[11] He is the divine "fellow-sufferer who understands."[12] The divine judgment, however, will also be carried out by the Crucified, who not only suffered the aggressive brutality of the world on his own body, but also defined solidarity with the "least of these who are members of my family" as the touchstone of his true presence,[13] and by the partisan of the poor, who "ignored all those who are high and mighty and wealthy in the world in favour of the weak and meek and lowly."[14] And it is carried out by the divine prophet who discloses and reveals the excessive normative demands and normative expectational conflicts among human beings in light of God's coming reign.[15]

9. Matt 22:2ff; 26:29; Mark 14:25; Rev 19:7; 21:2; cf. Moltmann, *The Coming of God*, 336ff (see part 4.2, note 12); concerning further imagery associated with joy in God's reign, see Catherine Keller, "Forces of Love: The Christopoetics of Desire," in Schuele/Thomas, *Who is Jesus Christ for Us Today?* 115–33 (concerning this volume, see part 0.1, note 7).

10. Matt 25:33; John 5:22ff; 16:8ff; cf. Gregor Etzelmüller, . . . *zu richten die Lebendigen und die Toten. Zur Rede vom Jüngsten Gericht im Anschluß an Karl Barth* (Neukirchen-Vluyn: Neukirchener, 2001), 243ff; Jürgen Moltmann, "Is there Life after Death?" in Polkinghorne/Welker, *The End of the World*, 238–55, concerning purgatory, see ibid., 247f (concerning this book, see part 5.5, note 19).

11. Cf. part 5.4; Welker, *Holy Communion*, 43ff, 149ff (see part 5.4, note 1).

12. Whitehead, *Process and Reality*, 532 (see part 2.4, note 6).

13. Cf. Matt 25:31–46; Hoffmeyer, *Christology and Diakonia*, 152ff (see part 4.4, note 23); see also part 4.4.

14. Barth, *CD IV/2*, 168, cf. 163ff.

15. Cf. Michael Welker, "'Richten und Retten.' Systematische Überlegungen zu einer unverzichtbaren Funktion der Religion," in *Gerechtigkeit. Richten und Retten in der abendländischen Tradition und ihren altorientalischen Ursprüngen*, ed. Jan Assmann, Bernd Janowski, and Michael Welker (München: Fink, 1998), 28–35; Etzelmüller, . . . *zu richten die Lebendigen und die Toten*, 321ff (see part 5.6, note 10).

The point of the double promise of both judgment and joy is not some reestablishment of a "blessed state of nature," but rather transformation into a *new* creation "where righteousness is at home" (2 Pet 3:13) and where God's glory shines among human beings.[16] What status, however, can really be attributed to all these visions of Christ's Parousia if, after all, it will *not* be taking place during *our* present age and in *our* present world? The breakthrough insight of eternity-eschatology emerges from the statements concerning the resurrection and coming reign of God. The grand message of consolation and comfort is precisely that the Parousia *will* not only take place, but has *already*—and *always*—taken place, and takes place *even now*, that judgment and salvation, elevation and redemption, are always coming about in this, our relative, real world and, moreover, in a fashion going beyond it.[17] All yearning or longing for the new creation, for salvation, elevation, and redemption, is thus consistently referred back to the reign of God that has *already* come and is *yet* coming, a reign that permeates and overarches the lives that human beings live and complete on this earth. Royal-diaconal, priestly, and prophetic life are anticipatory forms that make it possible for God's creation to live in that tension articulated by Paul:

- "I consider that the sufferings of this present time are not worth comparing with the glory about to be revealed to us" (Rom 8:18).
- "And all of us, with unveiled faces, seeing the glory of the Lord as though reflected in a mirror, are being transformed into the same image from one degree of glory to another; for this comes from the Lord, the Spirit" (2 Cor 3:18).

God's revelation in Jesus Christ discloses access to eternal life already in *this present* life and in *this present* time. In this context, this life is to be understood strictly as perpetually *coming*, and is to be contemporized in prayer and hope and contra any inclinations toward religious or moral

16. Etzelmüller, . . . *zu richten die Lebendigen und die Toten*, 321ff, offers a subtle description of the process of the healing of even the memories of victims and perpetrators; Günter Thomas, *Neue Schöpfung*, 471ff, 499ff (see part 5.3, note 22), focusing on the vision of the "descent of the heavenly Jerusalem," finds one characteristic of the new creation in the opening up of a new community space and spectrum of possibilities brought about by the radiant presence of God's *doxa*.

17. Cf. Gerhard Sauter, "Eschatologische Rationalität," in idem, *In der Freiheit des Geistes. Theologische Studien* (Göttingen: Vandenhoeck, 1988), 166ff; idem, "Our Reasons for Hope," in Polkinghorne/Welker, *The End of the World*, 209–21 (concerning this book, see part 5.5, note 19); see ibid., also Kathryn Tanner, "Eschatology without a Future?" 222–37; and Miroslav Volf, "Enter into Joy! Sin, Death, and the Life of the World to Come," 256–78.

self-righteousness or any form of corresponding triumphalism.[18] Revelation casts a harsh light on the anxiety and impotence of earthly life, on its resignation and despair in the face of creaturely coldness, brutality, and what seems to be ultimate futility. On the other hand, it illuminates all the more brightly life's destiny to be sheltered in the depths of God the Creator, in the living vitality of the Spirit, and through participation in the resurrection. It encourages us to trust—even now, even in this limited span of life—in the power of love, justice, and truth. In so doing, it awakens and fortifies our living hope for participation in the life of the exalted Christ,[19] in divine life, in a life of perfect freedom, perfect peace, and perfect blessedness.

18. Concerning analogies between Old and New Testament perspectives, see Andreas Schuele, "'On earth as it is in heaven': Eschatology and the Ethics of Forgiveness," in Schuele/Thomas, *Who is Jesus Christ for Us Today?* 185–202 (concerning this book, see part 0.1, note 7).

19. Pannenberg, *Systematic Theology*, vol. 3, 646 (see part 3.5, note 39), speaks about an "incursion of the eternal future of God to the salvation of creatures" until the salvific eschatological consummation; Pheme Perkins, *Resurrection: New Testament Witness and Contemporary Reflection* (Garden City: Doubleday, 1984), 309ff, shows how in various biblical traditions the "language of the resurrection" connects these two dimensions of eschatology, something similarly accomplished in references to the "corporate Christ," cf. John Polkinghorne, "The Corporate Christ," in Schuele/Thomas, *Who is Jesus Christ for Us Today?* 103–11 (concerning this book see part 0.1, note 7).

Afterword

This book is the considerably expanded version of the six *Gunning Lectures* I delivered in 2004 at New College in Edinburgh. I would like to thank my Scottish colleagues, especially David Fergusson, Larry Hurtado, and the late Alistair Kee for the invitation to deliver these lectures, for their hospitality, and for fruitful theological conversations. I previously presented key ideas of this Christology in the *Horace De Y. Lentz Memorial Lecture* in 2001/02 in connection with a guest professorship at the Harvard Divinity School.[1] I would like to thank Sarah Coakley and Elisabeth and Francis Schüssler Fiorenza for having provided helpful theological stimulation even beyond this period. In 2008 I had the opportunity to discuss intensively ten lectures on Christology with colleagues and post-doctoral students from Hong Kong and the People's Republic of China, for which I am most grateful to Hong Kong Baptist University and especially my colleague Phee Seng Kang.

I am particularly grateful to the Center of Theological Inquiry, Princeton (CTI), and its directors, Wallace Alston and William Storrar. The invitations to attend the Center as a Senior Consultant Scholar and as a Scheide Fellow gave me the time to work on questions of Christology and eschatology, and also the opportunity for dialogue with the Scholars in Residence from all over the world and with Princeton colleagues. This book profited greatly from my interdisciplinary work over many years with Heidelberg colleagues in the department of theology, in the postgraduate program "Religion and Normativity," and in the discussion circles "Cultural Analysis" and "The Natural Sciences and the Humanities" in the International Science Forum (IWH) of Heidelberg University and in the Heidelberg Academy of Sciences and Humanities. Key insights emerged from international and interdisciplinary dialogues over several years between theology and the natural sciences on questions of escha-

---

1. "Who is Jesus Christ for us Today?" *Harvard Theological Review* 95 (2002), 129–46.

tology[2] and anthropology.[3] I acknowledge with great gratitude that many of the international and interdisciplinary exchanges over the years were supported by the Center of Theological Inquiry, Princeton, the Center of Science and Religion, Berkeley, the Internationales Wissenschaftsforum Heidelberg, the John Templeton Foundation, the Protestant Church in the Rhineland, the German Research Foundation, the Fritz Thyssen Foundation, and the Volkswagen Foundation.

Many of the insights in this book were presented for discussion in presentations and lectures both in Germany and abroad, and not merely in the context of universities, but also at church conferences, pastoral retreats, and ecclesiastical administrative board meetings. Lengthier contributions to our understanding of baptism and the Holy Communion have been incorporated into ecclesial "orientational aids."[4] This book has profited equally from the discussions conducted in church contexts and from the theological engagement of students in the department of theology at the University of Heidelberg and the Harvard Divinity School. I am particularly grateful to my circle of doctoral candidates and post-doctoral students as well as the Heidelberg students who attended my lecture course on Christology during the summer semester 2009.

My earlier academic assistants and current colleagues Günter Thomas (Bochum, Germany) and Andreas Schüle (Leipzig, Germany) both surprised and delighted me with their publication of a German and American *Festschrift* focused on themes associated with Christology.[5]

For critical reading and commentary on parts of this book I am indebted to my academic assistants Dr. Gregor Etzelmüller, Dr. Alexander Maßmann, Dr. Nina-Dorothee Mützlitz, Hanna Reichel, and Dr. Heike Springhart. Let me also thank Candace Kohli, Chicago, for initial help with the translation initiative, and my student assistants Hajo Kenkel, Mareike Meiß-Schleifenbaum, Maren Ossenberg-Engels, and Charlotte Reda for help with the footnote apparatus and indexes. I would like to thank Dr. Douglas W. Stott for the excellent translation and for our con-

---

2. Cf. Polkinghorne/Welker, *The End of the World* (see part 5.5, note 19); Peters/Russell/Welker, *Resurrection* (see part 5.5, note 19).

3. Cf. *God and Human Dignity*, ed. E. K. Soulen and L. Woodhead (Grand Rapids: Eerdmans, 2006); Welker, *The Depth of the Human Person* (see part 2.4, note 9).

4. *Das Abendmahl. Eine Orientierungshilfe zu Verständnis und Praxis des Abendmahls in der evangelischen Kirche* (Gütersloh: Gütersloher, 2003); *Die Taufe. Eine Orientierungshilfe zu Verständnis und Praxis der Taufe in der evangelischen Kirche* (Gütersloh: Gütersloher, 2008).

5. Thomas/Schüle, *Gegenwart des lebendigen Christus* (see part 1.5, note 5); Schuele/Thomas, *Who is Jesus Christ for Us Today?* (see part 0.1, note 7).

sistently gratifying and pleasant work together. I am obliged to William B. Eerdmans for his spontaneous willingness to publish this book, and to Hajo Kenkel for the layout and to the publishing staff at Eerdmans for their excellent cooperation.

Finally, I would like to extend particular thanks to my wife, Ulrike Welker, who for forty years has encouraged and supported my theological reflection through daily conversation and critical reading of my drafts and manuscripts, and who in quite the same spirit closely accompanied my work on this present book. As an expression of the joyous companionship we have experienced traveling life's path together, this book is dedicated to her.

Heidelberg, Spring 2013
M.W.

INDEXES

Scripture Index

Author Index

Boldface numbers indicate that the cited name
appears in a footnote on that page.

Subject Index